CHINESE POLITICS AND CHRISTIAN MISSIONS

THE ANTI-CHRISTIAN MOVEMENTS OF 1920-28

JESSIE GREGORY LUTZ
Rutgers University

Volume III
THE CHURCH AND THE WORLD

Cyriac K. Pullapilly, General Editor
George H. Williams, Consulting Editor

(Also Volume II, THE WEST AND THE WIDER WORLD)

CROSS CULTURAL PUBLICATIONS, INC.
CROSS ROADS BOOKS

BR
1288
.L88
1988

Published by **CROSS CULTURAL PUBLICATIONS,INC.**
CROSS ROADS BOOKS
P. O. Box 506
Notre Dame, Indiana 46556, U.S.A.
Phone: (219) 272-3321

© 1988 CROSS CULTURAL PUBLICATIONS, INC.
ALL RIGHTS RESERVED
ISBN: 0-940121-05-0
Library of Congress Catalog Number: 87-72480

NOTE FROM THE GENERAL EDITOR

It is with great pleasure that I present to the scholarly world this Volume III of THE CHURCH AND THE WORLD series. Two years have elapsed since the publication of Volume II, and in these two years nearly one hundred manuscripts crossed our desks. The consulting editor, Professor George H. Williams of Harvard University, and the twelve or so scholarly consultants of the series helped select just a few books out the many we considered for the series using the usual criteria for the selection of scholarly books plus a special consideration, that is, to establish firmly the profile of the series. Due to this consideration we were obliged to forego publication of some very good studies. The works we have selected conform to the announced goals and purposes of the series.

I am particularly happy about this study by Professor Jessie G. Lutz as it focuses on a phenomenon that occurred in many Asian and African nations in the first half of this century, that is, the interaction between Christian missionary enterprises and rising forces of nationalism. In many cases the inspiration for nationalism came from Western missionary sources. This study does not show that, but it does show a later and peculiar twist in China where conflicting nationalist forces used the Christian missionary activities as a common enemy and a rallying point. In fact, much of the ideological validity of such diverse nationalist groups as the Kuomintang and the Chinese Communist Party, as well as the emotional energy that propelled them into political action came from their common antipathy toward the Christian influence on China--at least in the crucial two decades before the outbreak of the Second World War. While in the final analysis this may have been a development peculiar to China this story contains many parallels to the growth of nationalist movements in other countries of Asia and Africa.

One thing that Professor Lutz brings into clearer focus, through meticulous analysis of Chinese and

Western sources, is the pervasive influence of the Christian educational establishment in China, ironically enough, through her elaborate description of the Kuomintang and Communist efforts to dismantle it. In the long history of the love-hate relationship between China and the Christian West this episode stands out as a landmark.

Saint Mary's College, Notre Dame   Cyriac K. Pullapilly
March 3, 1988

THE CHURCH AND THE WORLD

SERIES

General Editor:

Cyriac K. Pullapilly
Saint Mary's College, Notre Dame

Consulting Editor:

George H. Williams
Harvard University

This series is dedicated to the scholarly investigation of Christianity's interaction with the non-Christian world. This includes the Church's initial encounters with the civilizations of the ancient world, its influence on various tribal nationalities of the medieval times and its missionary impact in more modern times. It also includes Christianity's ideological and institutional impacts on the secular worlds of science, technology, politics, economics and the arts. It is hoped that this series will encourage scholars to research and publish monographs on themes in some of these areas in which scholarship is particularly deficient.

Scholars who have works in progress that may be suitable for the series are encouraged to contact the general editor:

Cyriac K. Pullapilly
Saint Mary's College
Notre Dame, Indiana 46556
U.S.A.

FOR RAY

PREFACE

The origins of this study lie in a general history of the Protestant Christian Colleges in China that I wrote some years ago. At the time I was fascinated by the reciprocal relation between Chinese nationalism and the foreign presence. I was also struck by the emotional power that foreign intervention and humiliation could bring to nationalism. The anti-Christian movements of the 1920s offered a focus for examination of these issues. Though I was aware of the anti-Christian tradition in China and of Chinese nationalists' penchant for verbal hyperbole, there seemed a need for a clearer understanding of the anti-Christian movements of the 1920s and of their relationship with the rapid intellectual and political changes of these years.

At the start of my research, I viewed the campaigns as essentially student movements, largely initiated and executed by young intellectuals. Linkages with the Kuomintang and the Chinese Communist Party were known, while the inspiration of the May Fourth and the May Thirtieth Movements was obvious, but the nature and intricacy of the ties were obscure. The more research I did, the more significant appeared the interplay between the political parties and the anti-Christian movements. The contributions of the Kuomintang, the Chinese Communist Party, and the Young China Party were not only essential to the second of the anti-Christian movements, that is, the Movement to Restore Educational Rights, 1924-1928, but that movement was also important to the parties. As the movement unfolded, the parties were able to identify and to provide political experience for future cadres. The parties developed techniques for coopting multi-group organizations to their cause. In mobilizing students, therefore, the United Front of the Kuomintang and the Chinese Communist Party was simultaneously developing a vital component of their support base. The alliance between political parties and student movements remained, even so, an uneasy one, with intellectuals retaining a degree of autonomy. While the Anti-Christian Movement of 1920-1922 can be understood as one expression of the iconoclasm and scientism of the New Culture Movement, the subsequent Educational Rights Movement can be best understood as one facet of the anti-imperialism nationalism of May Thirtieth and the Northern Expedition. The anti-Christian movements were not only integral to the major historical events of the 1920s, but they contributed a personal dimension to the emotional fervor accompanying the search for ideological guidance and the drive for national union.

Because the Chinese sources for the 1920s are generally cataloged and referenced according to the Wade-Giles transliteration, I use this system; the glossary, however, provides pin yin equivalents along with the Chinese characters.

My thanks to John K. Fairbank and Knight Biggerstaff for reading the manuscript and offering helpful suggestions as well as encouragement. I have benefited from reading Ka-che Yip's, *Religion Nationalism, and Chinese Students,* particularly his insightful comments on student subculture during the 1920s. My thanks also to the numerous individuals who provided access to sources at libraries in the U.S. and Taiwan. Three individuals in particular should be mentioned: Li Yun-han of the Kuomintang Party History Commission, Carol Kinsey of the New Brunswick Seminary Library, and Nelson Chou of the East Asian Library, Rutgers University. With pleasure, I acknowledge support from the Rutgers University Research Council, the American Council of Learned Societies and Social Science Research Council, and the Douglass College Fellows' Opportunity Fund.

Some of my findings have been previously presented as articles or essays in edited works. I am grateful to the following for granting permission to incorporate materials from these publications in this monograph: to Cambridge University Press, which published Jessie G. Lutz, "Chinese Nationalism and the Anti-Christian Campaigns of the 1920s," *Modern Asian Studies*; to the Historical Commission of the Kuomintang, which published "Students and Political Parties in the Educational Rights Movement, 1924-1928," in *Symposium on the History of the Republic of China,* vol. III; and to the University Press of America, which published "Students and Politics, Revolution and Historical Continuity: The Chinese Anti-Christian Campaigns of the 1920s," in *Tradition and Modernity. The Role of Traditionalism in the Modernization Process,* edited by Jessie G. Lutz and Salah El-Shakhs.

My gratitude to Ray, who helped all along the way.

Jessie G. Lutz

Rutgers University
New Brunswick, NJ
January 1988

CONTENTS

Preface

Introduction 1

I. The Anti-Christian Tradition and the Beginnings of Modern Chinese Nationalism 11

II. The Anti-Christian Movement of 1920-1922: First Stage 27
 Chinese Reassessment
 Christian Missions in Transition

III. The 1922 Anti-Christian Campaign; Reactions 55
 Course of the 1922 Anti-Christian Campaign
 Responses to the Campaign

IV. Groundwork for the Educational Rights Movement 91
 Rising Tide of Anti-Imperialism and Anti-Westernism
 United Front Links
 Educators and Educational Rights
 The Young China Party and Educational Rights
 Targeting Christian Schools

V. The Move to Restore Educational Rights; First Stage 129
 Tactics and Themes
 Confrontations and Student Storms
 Schisms
 Christian Responses

VI. May 30, 1925 and the Educational Rights Movement 160
 The Nanking Road Massacre and Its Aftermath
 May Thirtieth, Anti-Christians and Christians
 The Politicization of the Educational Rights Movement
 Role of the Political Parties
 Campaign Strategy in Swatow, Canton, and Szechwan

VII. **The Educational Rights Movement Incorporated
into the Northern Expedition** 209
    KMT and CCP Policies toward Mass Movements
    Educational Rights Campaign in Fukien
    Educational Rights Campaign in Hunan and Hupei
    Nanking Incident of 1927
    Factionalism and Radicalism

VIII. **Demise** 257
    The Shanghai Coup and the Demise of the
    1920s Student Movement

Conclusion 279

Abbreviations 291

Notes 293

Bibliography 357

Glossary 373

Index 389

INTRODUCTION

Few scholars would deny the crucial importance of the 1917-1927 decade for the course of modern Chinese history. Nor would they deny the rapidity and complexity of change in its interplay with the residual dynamic of China's cultural heritage. The anti-Christian movements during this decade embrace both the *Fei Chi-tu-chiao yun-tung* (Anti-Christian Movement) of 1920-1922 and the *Shou-hui chiao-yü ch-üan yun-tung* (Movement to Restore Educational Rights) of 1924-1928. The transition from the first campaign accentuating intellectual and cultural concerns to the second campaign with primary emphasis on attaining national unity and sovereignty parallels the unfolding story of the 1920s. Analysis of these movements can, therefore, contribute to an understanding of several interdependent themes of the period: maturation of Chinese nationalism, relations between students and the emerging political parties, and iconoclastic condemnation of tradition leading to a search for new ideological guideposts. All of these trends were most pronounced in urban China, especially Peking and the treaty ports, where a Sino-Western hybrid culture was evolving. With young urban intellectuals prominent in the anti-Christian movements, in party and political activities, and also in cultural reassessments, the three became closely intertwined. Though the first anti-Christian campaign focused on Christian doctrines and church activities whereas the Educational Rights movement was more specifically directed at parochial schools, both censured missionaries in general and the broad spectrum of mission pursuits in China.

Consequent upon Roman Catholic efforts to bring Christianity to China in the 16th and 17th centuries, Christianity had been officially proscribed as heterodox in 1724 and evangelism declared illegal. During the early 19th century a half dozen or so Protestant missionaries tried, nevertheless, to spread the word along the coastal fringes of China and a larger number of Catholic priests worked underground in the interior. In the mid-19th century treaties, Westerners demanded and obtained both the right to proselytize in China and a guarantee of toleration for Chinese converts. After a slow start, the crusade to convert China captured the imagination of American Protestantism. The number of missionaries posted to China grew rapidly beginning in the last two decades of the 19th century and continuing into the first two decades of the 20th. Western Protestant evangelists increased from 1,296 in 1889 to 3,833 in 1906 to 6,636 in 1919. Roman Catholics listed 1,075 foreign priests in 1901 and 2,500-3,000 foreign priests and nuns in 1920. The number of Protestant communicants multiplied almost ten fold during these years from ca. 37,000 to ca. 346,000, while estimates for Catholic communicants were 721,000 in 1901 and 2,000,000 by 1920. Only 106 *hsien* (counties) out of 1,704 in China proper and Manchuria were without some Protestant evangelical activity.[1]

These missionary ventures met with considerable and increasing hostility. During the period between the 1860s and the 1880s, hundreds of separate and localized attacks on missions and Chinese converts erupted.[2] With the proliferation of missions came widespread protests, sometimes deliberately fomented and sometimes sparked by a single incident. Chinese aimed to protect their heritage from external contamination and to deny the foreigners power in China. Based among the peasantry but often backed by the gentry and/or government, endemic protests climaxed in the ill-fated Boxer attempt to rid China of all foreign influence in 1900.

The Anti-Christian Movement of 1920-1922, while reiterating many criticisms of the 19th century, originated with young intellectuals seeking to destroy, not salvage, old orthodoxies. Citing Western critiques of Christianity and courting world opinion, the anti-Christian nationalists were contending in an international arena. The campaign's derivations were urban rather than rural. As a spin-off of the May Fourth Movement, the 1920-1922 anti-Christian ferment and publicity helped to highlight the distinctiveness, the diversity, and the amorphism of the urban intellectual scene, 1917-1922.

The protests on May 4, 1919 against the Versailles

peace settlement allowing Japan to keep the German Shantung concessions marked for many urban intellectuals a new phase in national consciousness.[3] Apolitical youth like the early communist party member Ch'ü Ch'iu-pai were activated and radicalized by the experience of demonstrating in the streets and suffering arrest and imprisonment. Ch'ü recalled: "I believed that the world was to be saved through the practice of bodhisattvahood (*p'u-ha'-hsing*), and that everything was impermanent, including the social system. But such a philosophy could not hold for long when the May Fourth Movement sucked me in like a whirlpool. My solitude was finally broken."[4]

The term May Fourth Movement is, however, often used to embrace the whole period from 1917 to 1922 and to include the entire range of cultural and intellectual protests against tradition during these years. As such, it is interchangeable with the term New Culture Movement. As such, it was protean. It was as full of contradictions as of excitement. Students might use the vocabulary of populism but their alienation from village society and values was deep and pervasive. The New Youth operated in a heady atmosphere replete with paradoxes: hopes for China's future and iconoclastic despair regarding her tradition, anti-imperialist nationalism and intellectual cosmopolitanism, existential individualism and demands for a powerful unified state.[5] Even intellectuals moving toward Marxism viewed a revolution in ideas as crucial to the political and economic revolution, as indeed a precondition for a revolution in the substructure. They, as the "foreknowers," had a moral obligation to inform and lead the masses.

May Fourth expressed the nihilism and anarchism of many educated youth. It attested to the totalistic rejection of conventional authority permeating the intellectual environment. What began with attacks on Confucianism soon broadened to include condemnation of religion in general and Christianity in particular. The initial targets might be the purveyors of familistic ethics, but no one in authority was immune: teacher and school administrator, government official, the whole father generation. Strikes hit the mission schools as well as the national colleges and universities. Even while the critics employed science to demonstrate the errors of Christianity, though, they built on the long-standing anti-Christian tradition. The ideological approach to national problems continued despite rejection of both Eastern and Western orthodoxies.

For certain individual participants, May Fourth was an awakening bolt of lightning; they saw it as a watershed in Chinese history. For more than one future leader in the Kuomintang (KMT) and the Chinese Communist Party (CCP), it served as a *rite de passage* in personal maturation. In actuality, of course, continuities with both past and future can be traced for May Fourth in its broader definition. The same is true for the anti-Christian campaigns. Nationalist protests, even student-initiated demonstrations against imperialism, had occurred ever since the examination candidates' condemnation of the Sino-Japanese Treaty of 1895. Charlotte Furth locates the first modern student protest in the year 1903 when several hundred students in Tokyo, Shanghai, and Peking challenged Russia's delay in withdrawing troops from Manchuria.[6] Denunciations of U.S. immigration practices culminated in 1905 in an anti-American boycott initiated by merchants; students and other social strata in several treaty ports joined in the action. The boycott even penetrated mission schools, with students at Canton Christian College (later Lingnan University) refusing to purchase the American-manufactured shoes that were part of their school uniform.[7] These and other nationalist protests during the pre-1919 period were, says Furth, like May Fourth in that they were urban, populist, anti-imperialist, and opinion molding.

Other linkages with past and with future obtained. Reformers in the 19th century were already moving away from Confucian categories of analysis. Revolutionaries in the early 20th century condemned the monarchy and the theory that the mandate to rule came from Heaven, both at the heart of Confucian political concepts. Yet reliance on the personal leader retained its importance through much of the 20th century. In building constituencies outside the bureaucracy, pre-1911 advocates of change published journals in simplified literary style. Later populists seeking models created a run on Bibles translated by missionaries into easy Chinese. Even after *pai hua* (vernacular language) began to gain wide acceptance during the New Culture Movement, however, many writers found it difficult to put into practice. Its famous advocate, Hu Shih, employed an admixture of classical and vernacular Chinese plus foreign neologisms, not a style readily accessible to the semi-literate, whatever its populist goals.

Despite similarities and continuities, May Fourth and not earlier movements became a tradition. Even if its real substance was transcended by its role as myth, it was a national event. No earlier protest against tradition or against imperialism had set up such national resonances. The intersection of personal and career crises with social and political crises made May Fourth decisive, even if not unique.[8] During the 1925 movement against the unequal treaties, the CCP called for revival of the May Fourth spirit. Students self-consciously emulated the May Fourth generation in 1931 and in 1935-1936 when they resorted to direct confrontation tactics in protesting Japanese aggression and KMT appeasement. The Great Proletarian Cultural Revolution of the 1960s deliberately recalled May Fourth and the New Culture Movement.

May Fourth and its offspring, the Anti-Christian Movement of 1920-1922, involved something new as well as something old under the sun. Both were products of a strategically located and alienated student sub-culture. Both received guidance and inspiration from certain notable members of the father generation. Both were characterized by a highly developed, if theoretical, sense of social consciousness on the part of an elite. Both were attuned to the international scene, politically and also ideologically. Though "moral intellectuals" had been transformed into "action intellectuals" before, the political and intellectual progression in the 1920s seems to have greater coherence. The student Anti-Christian Movement of 1920-1922 emerged out of the May Fourth Movement. May Thirtieth succeeded the May Fourth and Anti-Christian Movements. The Movement to Restore Educational Rights evolved out of the Anti-Christian Movement and was energized by the May Thirtieth Movement.

The student sub-culture that was the essential context for all these movements had been germinating in Peking, in Tokyo, in Shanghai and other treaty ports since the turn of the century. Because modern-type university education existed in relatively few Chinese cities, gentry sons and daughters flowed from market towns and villages to the burgeoning academic communities in the eastern cities and along the Yangtze. Children of merchants, new industrialists, and professionals added to enrollments, especially after the abolition of the traditional civil service examinations in 1905. Though still a tiny elite of 0.1% of the total population, middle school and college students had increased in their concentration as well as their numbers by 1919. The premier institution, Peking National University (Peita) had grown from 818 students in 1912 to 2,413 in 1919. Institutions in the two cities of Peking and Shanghai accounted for over half of all college students in China.[9]

Divorced from family and traditional norms and behavior patterns, the New Youth participated in a hybrid culture. Their break with tradition, unlike that of their fathers, often extended to their life style as well as their world outlook and cultural values. Their sense of historical discontinuity was greater than that of their fathers and their awareness of international politics and intellectual trends more acute. Perhaps in response to this estrangement, the youth cohort which made up China's new studentry assumed some of the functions of surrogate family. The phenomenon so characteristic of the modernizing process evidenced itself: the peer group stepped into the vacuum created by the deauthoritization of the parent generation. Out of this experience there evolved what became known as the "New Youth". The term implies the emergence of a self-consciously modern youth cohort. Even though activitist students are always a minority, it was the New Youth which created fresh guidelines for its members and provided a sense of community. For many, generational loyalty took primacy over loyalty to family and home community.

The New Youth did not, however, view itself as an isolated student community. It was not only deliberately modern in outlook; it came to see itself as the agent of

China's modernization. It demanded nothing less than a historical shortcut to modernity, a utopian reconstruction of China. If faith in the commitment of the Manchu dynasty to the revitalization of China was dwindling during the first decade of the 20th century, respect for the power and good intentions of its successor, the Peking warlord regime, hit a new low in 1919. Student unions, publications, social clubs, and cause-oriented associations flourished after May Fourth. They were the core of the student sub-culture and they were also ready instruments for publicity and for direct action. But the New Culture Movement, like the Anti-Christian Movement, was weak in structure; formlessness and absence of a unified national leadership typified both movements. The New Culture and the Anti-Christian Movement characteristically lacked an attainable goal and a clear focus. Without these, neither fulfillment nor a clean terminus was possible.

Despite the fact that nationalism was a common denominator of the New Culture and Anti-Christian Movements, nationalism did not sweep all before it until the May Thirtieth Movement of 1925. The anti-imperialist upsurge in the wake of the shooting of Shanghai demonstrators by British police opened doors for the KMT and the CCP. The need for political power and military force had been demonstrated; the opportunity for the parties to build a mass base had been offered. Nationalism, politicized and heavily laced with anti-imperialism and anti-capitalism, would be the "cement of the revolutionary alliance and the engine of the revolutionary movement."[10] No longer did activists hope to create a new China via cultural transformation. Leadership by political parties with troops at their disposal was essential to oust the imperialists and the militarists, opponents of China's sovereignty and unity.

Urban elites in China as elsewhere in developing countries might sound the clarion for revolution and even provide its theoretical framework but they could not, by themselves, mount a revolution. As a miniscule part of the population, they had to mobilize the masses. Thus a Chinese citizenry had to be created, nationalized, and politicized. To accomplish this, education in a new Chinese orthodoxy appeared crucial. The diversity and openness of May Fourth was no longer acceptable. A campaign to recover educational rights, to gain for China monopolistic control over education, was almost a natural in combining the interest of the parties and young intellectuals. Here was an issue that could draw on the widespread hostility to Christian missions as well as on the popularity of the new crusade against imperialism. Here was a movement through which the parties could expand their base and locate future cadres and propagandists. The Rights Recovery Movement, having brought the student movement and the political parties together in a common enterprise, was after May Thirtieth coopted to the parties' cause. As Chinese abandoned the pluralism of May Fourth, autonomous mission schools came to be considered an aberration and an obstacle to the unity of the nation state. For Chinese Christians, the Movement to Restore Educational Rights presented conflicting claims of Chinese patriotism and Christianity. Desiring to reduce the incompatibility, they turned toward a Sinified Christianity; they endeavored to distinguish between a Chinese Christian church and Christian missions.

Nationalists targeted the parochial schools with good reason, if not always with good will. During the second half of the 19th century, Protestant missionaries had founded schools out of a variety of motivations.[11] Partly they were seeking a stable audience among a Chinese largely indifferent to the Gospel; partly they desired educational institutions where the children of converts could obtain literacy without being subjected to Confucian indoctrination; partly they hoped to train Chinese assistants, and partly they were building on a traditional tie between Protestantism and education, a tie derived from the concept of the Bible as the centerpiece of faith. At variance with Chinese schools in purpose, curriculum, and structure, they flouted the Chinese educational norm. They were immune to Chinese regulation and outside the purview of most Chinese. Their growth during the 19th century was relatively slow. By 1900 there were some 2,000 Protestant schools, mostly primary, with some forty to fifty middle schools, and six institutions claiming the status of college or university. Approximately 40,000 students attended these parochial schools, not an insignificant number, but only a tiny fraction of the total school population.

As reform and revolutionary movements gathered momentum at the turn of the century, parochial schools entered a new phase. For a brief time from the 1890s until the 1920s, they enjoyed a new-found popularity. Not only did they have more applicants than they could accept, but many of the students came from gentry and well-to-do merchant families. Their graduates were sought after as teachers and consultants.

With the abolition of the traditional civil service examinations in 1905, the government attempted to inaugurate a national school system incorporating a Western educational structure and curriculum. No longer was study of Confucian classics sufficient to open the door to government employment. Ambitious youths rushed to acquire modern learning at home and abroad; educators struggled to devise the national educational program. By this time, of course, Chinese were turning directly to the West and Japan for information, and the first educational blueprint followed the Japanese pattern. The parochial schools in China were, nevertheless, accessible models; their textbooks were in print, their teachers and graduates were available resources. They were used. For those who could not afford to study abroad, these schools offered the training sought, though students were required, additionally, to take religion courses and to participate in church services. For those seeking admission to schools in Britain and the U.S., the Protestant institutions offered some of the best English-language instruction in China. Many of those "returned students" who moved rapidly into responsible positions during the Republican period had gained the necessary English language facility in the mission schools.

As a result of their new-found favor, the Protestant institutions were able to expand and raise their standards. By 1920 schools ranging from primary through middle level enrolled approximately 200,000 pupils while the twenty colleges and medical schools then in existence had slightly over 2,000 students.[12] Roman Catholics also conducted schools and their enrollments actually surpassed those of the Protestants. But the Catholics, concentrating on catechismal and primary education, operated only one college and several seminaries of varying academic standards in 1920. Protestant schools, more nearly the competitors of the national institutions than the Catholic ones, became the focus of the Movement to Restore Educational Rights.

Between 1917 and 1927 China's foreign relations were deeply influenced by the Bolshevik Revolution and World War I, by the intensification of anti-imperialist nationalism, and by the beginnings of unification under the KMT-CCP United Front. Though the vociferous anti-Western and anti-capitalist propaganda of the mid-1920s moderated after Chiang Kai-shek's victory, China's views of foreign affairs continued to bear the marks of Leninist theories on imperialism. The fruits of World War I were mutliple. The new prominence of the U. S. and Japan, along with the waning strength of England and France, altered the international balance of power. Simultaneously, the horrors of modern warfare took the bloom off Western civilization for both Chinese and Westerner. Nationalistic Chinese became readier to challenge the unequal treaty system while the Western powers became more hesitant to defend its rectitude. As the Northern Expedition of 1926-1928 closed the decade, both China and the foreign powers were seeking a new basis for intercourse to replace the unequal treaty system. Christian missions, dubbed the cultural arm of Western capitalists and closely associated with the West's expansion, inevitably reflected these shifts in East-West relations.

Chapter I

The Anti-Christian Tradition
and the Beginnings of Modern Chinese Nationalism

The Anti-Christian Movement of 1920-1922 was part of China's reassessment of Western and Chinese traditions and one facet of her quest for intellectual direction. Pervading the search were the emotionalized nationalism and anti-imperialism of May Fourth. Young intellectuals intensified both their attack on the Confucian heritage and their search for alternative guides. With increasing knowledge of the West came a realization of its pluralism; Chinese selected and adapted their importations. Many, furthermore, were well enough acquainted with Western thought to add Western criticisms of Western civilization to the Chinese ones.

Such intellectual struggles were never far removed from politics despite the rejection of political activism by certain Chinese liberals during the early 1920s. No sooner did an "ism" gain favor than a society was established to foster its doctrines. No sooner did a philosophy lose favor than the students organized to attack it. And in every instance, the operative question was, "Will this doctrine contribute to the power and prosperity of China?" In 1919-1920, one of the future founders of the Chinese Community Party, Ch'en Tu-hsiu, had briefly examined Christianity and had found Christ's teachings one source of the West's dynamism.[1] Christian precepts, he wrote, were deserving of serious study. Such a favorable evaluation did not, of course, extend to the Christian church or to Christian missions, and Ch'en soon deserted Jesus' teachings for those of Marx, opting for the latter as having greater revolutionary and national relevance. The intellectual journeys of Ch'en would find parallels among many of the New Youth. Even though all did not embrace Marxism, few could find a role for Christianity in modernizing China; rather, they came to view Christian missions as a deterrent to national strength and unity.

When radicals and liberals joined in criticism of
Christianity and Christian missions during 1920-1922, the
campaign built on a long anti-Christian tradition.² The i-
conoclasm, rationalism, and individualism of the New
Culture Movement, however, distinguished the anti-Christianism of the early 1920s from that of the 19th century;
even so, the modern critics were well aware of the anti-
Christian legacy. They often argued that many of its
objections were still valid. Though their intellectual assumptions and political goals differed from those of the
Boxers and the scholar-bureaucrats, their literature reiterated many of the 19th-century condemnations. One
constant theme was the arrogance of the Westerner.
During the 19th century, most educated Chinese and
most evangelists functioned within their own cultural
context, acquiring little appreciation or comprehension
of the values of the other. Missionaries viewed themselves as bringing light and truth to a benighted people
and more often than not they judged Chinese society by
the values of their own heritage. Believing Christianity
central to the superiority of Western civilization, they
assumed that China would benefit from being made over
in the Western image; frequently, furthermore, they
equated Christianity with its West European incarnation.
Christianity, for most, included the denominational churches
as well as theology enriched by Greco-Roman concepts,
sectarian ritual as well as 19th century mores.

What has been called the law of cultural diffraction
operated in the meeting of Chinese and Westerner;each
was attuned to the views and values of his own nationals,
but much less sensitive to the reactions of the other
side.³ Seeing Chinese society through his own cultural
prism, a missionary might not be aware that his actions
offended, that his very presence could be interpreted as
an insult. Even when protests brought Chinese dissatisfac-
tion forcibly to his attention, he could find justification
in the sanctity of his mission to spread the gospel. No
matter that Chinese objected to the tall church steeples
that disturbed the spirits of wind and water;the sooner
Chinese abandoned such superstitions the better. Why
such concern that Christian school graduates rarely mas-
tered the Confucian classics? They had learned a higher
truth in their Bible study. Why could not a Chinese
stand on his own two feet like a Westerner and make his
own decision about baptism instead of eternally worrying

about the opinions of his father and mother or even his great uncle and second cousin? Under the circumstances, the possibilities for misunderstandings and hostile confrontations were almost limitless.

Nineteenth-century Protestant missionaries usually left Western shores with little to guide them except the call and whatever college or theological education they had. As for knowledge of Chinese language and culture, they were truly innocents abroad. Perhaps they had read accounts of China by missionary forerunners, but most of those from the 1830s and 1840s were not calculated to inspire any great respect for the Chinese heritage.

Many gradually became aware of the complexities of their venture, though this did not mean that they were willing to allow Chinese to evolve their own version of Christianity, much less incorporate Christian teachings into a Chinese religious amalgam. Missionaries, more than Western merchants or military personnel, came into daily contact with Chinese; of necessity, they had to attempt to acquire linguistic facility, which meant struggling with the Confucian classics. Reactions varied. For some, their experiences seemed to confirm the alliance of heathenism, dirt, and hypocrisy. A few, becoming students of Chinese history and literature, made significant scholarly contributions. Even missionaries who gained appreciation of aspects of Confucian ethics remained teachers of the true faith, with the Chinese as learners.[4] Timothy Richard, despite his empathy and tolerance, devoted his life to altering the very fundamentals of Chinese culture. Protected by the cocoon of extraterritoriality, all Westerners were constrained to embark upon less cultural questioning and less cultural adjustment than otherwise.[5] Individual friendships between Chinese and Westerners overcame the essential inequality of the relationship with difficulty.

The Chinese, for their part, interpreted the actions of the missionary within their cultural framework and certain features seemed inexplicable. Over and over again they sought the motive of the foreigner in abandoning homeland to preach to uninterested Chinese.[6] The Chinese had their own teachings; what need had they for an alien doctrine? The Chinese had not invited the missionary;

the reason for his coming must derive, therefore, from his needs and those of the West. Pearl Buck offers a popular explanation in an oft-quoted description of her father's itineration.[7] As her father's audience began to slip away during a lengthy sermon, an elderly woman admonished the remnant congregation: "Do not offend this good foreigner! He is making a pilgrimage in our country so that he may acquire merit in heaven. Let us help him to save his soul!" Other interpretations were less kindly. Chinese noted the substantial compounds of the missionary community, the servants, the demands regarding sanitation, nutrition, and medical care, the summer retreats; contrasting these with the living standard of most Chinese, they concluded that the comfortable easy life attracted evangelists to China.[8] Foreshadowing psychological interpretations of the 20th century, other Chinese surmised that missionaries found greater personal and financial reward in China than their talents would have brought them in the West.

Schools, orphanages, and hospitals were consistently regarded as bribes to secure converts and the missionaries themselves admitted that the institutions had been established partly to facilitate contact with the indifferent Chinese and that evangelism was an essential function. But while Westerners anticipated gratitude for the sacrifices made in promoting good works, Chinese were saying that the Westerners had had their reward. Why should China continue to serve the needs of the West to its own detriment?

Specific objections to Christian doctrines and to mission methodology thus had fertile soil in which to grow. Christian missions, as several scholars have demonstrated, disrupted the stability and harmony of Chinese society in numerous ways.[9] The scholar gentry, who felt especially threatened, emerged as the articulators of criticisms of the Christian missionary enterprise. As far as the Confucian mainstream was concerned, Christian teachings were foreign and heterodox; they brought the Confucian ethic into question. Literati considered such doctrines as the Trinity, the Virgin Birth, and the miracles of Christ superstitious; they found the ceremonies of the mass, confession, extreme unction, and immersion objectionable. The rituals were mysterious. They flaunted Chinese social customs and they appeared dangerously reminiscent of the secret rites of rebels and bandits. By assuming the role of teachers and ethical leaders, by interfering in court cases involving converts, by insisting on their extraterritorial privileges, by arrogating to themselves the prerogatives of the literati in dress, means of conveyance, and forms of address, missionaries undermined the status and authority of the gentry.

Just as Chinese questioned the motives of the evangelists, so they were skeptical of the motives of the converts. A favorite economic explanation identified converts as "rice Christians" who filled their bowls by accepting baptism and gaining employment with the missions. When referring to conversion, Chinese frequently used the phrase, "He has eaten the foreign teaching."

Other criticisms focused on the attempt of converts to escape from jurisdiction under the Chinese law. And indeed, Chinese did occasionally use the guarantee of tolerance for Christians as a cover for illegal activities or a means to obtain immunity from prosecution. One revealing and troublesome case at Haimen, Chekiang, in 1906 arose from a feud between pirate clans and robber chieftains claiming to be Christian converts. Fueled by sectarian enmity between Catholic and Protestant adherents, the contest escalated into armed violence with each side seeking missionary protection. A truce required the intervention of several Chinese administrators and military officers plus Protestant and Catholic missionaries and the British consul. Since Catholic and Protestant blamed each other's converts, the two versions of the incident were markedly different.[10] In other instances, sectarian religious groups sought to escape persecution by local authorities and gain protection from harrassment by converting to Christianity.[11]

Heterodox ideologies and their proponents had long been regarded as threats to political order and social harmony in China. The line between heterodoxy and legitimacy was not, however, sharp and clear. Confucianism obviously represented orthodoxy, though even in Confucianism variant strains existed. From the Confucian perspective, Buddhism and Taoism were not orthodox, but they, along with certain religious sects, could be tolerated, ignored, or embraced so long as they were not rivals to state power and ideology. Those teachings declared heterodox and illegal were ones that threatened to set up an alternative authority and undermine the state's maintenance of order and control.[12] Catholicism had been placed in the latter category in 1724 after the Papacy had overruled the Chinese emperor relative to the accommodation of Christianity to Chinese rituals and religious terminology. An imperial decree in 1784 had lamented that European propagators of Christianity were leading the people into error, "fatal to the manners and customs and to the human heart."[13] The ban on Christianity was reiterated and Chinese priests who had been "misled by the opportunity to earn money" were to be banished to the inner Asian frontier and given as slaves to local inhabitants. A dynastic decree of 1812 forbidding evangelism had stated: "Reflecting that the said religion [Christianity], neither holds spirits in veneration nor ancestors in reverence, clearly this is to walk contrary to sound doctrine; and the common people who follow and familiarize themselves with such delusions, in what respect do they differ from a rebel mob?"[14]

Protestant evangelism during the second half of the 19th century did little to disabuse Chinese leaders of the idea that Christianity and Christian missions were subversive. Christianity's exclusivism isolated converts from fellow villagers and they often became estranged elements in peasant society. Prohibitions concerning observance of the Sabbath, smoking and gambling, participation in village festivals, and ancestral rites set practicing Christians apart. Not only did the missionaries preach doctrines alien to Confucianism, but they appeared to attract marginal sectors of society as converts. Hakkas and other minorities, sectarian religious communities seemed particularly susceptible to conversion. Sectarian groups apparently found Christianity meaningful and attractive because of similarities in customs and beliefs: creator deity, savior intermediary, personal repentance, salvation in a future paradise, regular group worship, initiation rituals, and so forth.[15] Though such communities might not initially be anti-dynastic, they could readily be provoked into rebellion by government attempts at repression. For many Confucianists, the Taiping Rebellion, 1850-1864, with its own version of messianic Christianity was proof positive of the dangers of Christian teachings. Whatever the attitude of Western Christians toward this version of Protestantism, the near success of the Taipings in overthrowing the Ch'ing dynasty fed suspicions that Chinese Christians were not to be trusted.

These criticisms and objections, enunciated during the 19th century, still found expression in anti-Christian tracts and articles published in 1919 and 1920. The mood of this literature is outrage at the humiliation of China and the losses resulting from Christian missions. Smoldering anger expresses itself in biting sarcasm and scurrilous attacks on Christians and on Jesus himself. Their inflammatory accusations echo the tone of pamphlets issued by the gentry during the 19th century and their purpose is similar: to raise popular consciousness regarding offenses against the community. Chinese must be awakened to threats by foreigners and by their ideology to the cultural and political entity that is China.

To promote their cause, gentry in the 19th century sent some of their tracts to schools to be used by students and to be read aloud to popular audiences. Several of the Hunan brochures included an appendix with instructions on organizing activities to oust missionaries and eradicate converts.[16] With anti-foreignism and anti-Christianism providing a common ground for leaders and the masses, Christian missions inspired early organized opposition to Western culture and political intrusion. Both the gentry during the 19th century and the political parties in the 20th century occasionally used anti-Christian sentiment for internal political purposes.[17] It could help reduce the gap between the elite and followers. Populism, so essential to nationalism, drew on the anti-Christian tradition throughout the period.

One reason for the focus on Christian missions was the fact that, for many, the missionary concretized the foreign threat. Merchants ordinarily remained ensconced in the international settlements associating with their fellow nationals while diplomats had their legation quarters. Not only did missionaries itinerate from village to village, but they instituted a multitude of services that placed them in face-to-face contact with the populace: orphanages, schools, famine relief, hospitals, and so forth.

Good works they were, but missionaries often approached their labors with a battle mentality. The forces of evil had to be battered down. "The street chapel is the missionary's fort, where he throws hot shot and shell into the enemy's camp," according to one evangelist.[18]

Chinese opposition to Christian evangelism acquired a personal as well as a national dimension. Because the developing sense of national identity was derived from an unequal relationship, it also acquired deep emotional connotations for individuals. In the evolution of Chinese nationalism, it garnered that emotional strength which would make it superior to class consciousness as a means of mass mobilization.[19] That Chinese in the 20th century would commemorate humiliating international incidents as National Days tells much about the relationship between recollections of past sufferings and the nature of Chinese nationalism. That students during the May Thirtieth Movement against the unequal treaties should insist on the introduction of National Humiliation classes into school curricula reveals the linkage between Chinese nationalism and foreign privilege. A poignant little essay by the Tsing Hua University professor Chu Tzu-ch'ing portrays the identification of personal experience with the national experience. Chu tells about a tram ride in which he sat opposite an Occidental father and his small son. He found the child adorable, expressive of innocence, peace, and beauty. Until the very end of the journey, the child ignored his glance, but just as father and son stepped off the trolley, the beautiful young Occidental turned toward Chu and twisted his face into an expression of contempt and arrogance. The child, having achieved his triumph, quickly passed on, but Chu reflected: "My self-respect wounded, I experienced simultaneously feelings of despair and great anger. Then the idea of the nation intruded itself violently on me. . . . I was a Chinese, a Yellow, but the real world was always that of the Whites; they were arrogant and trampled us under their feet . . . on the child's face was inscribed all of Chinese diplomatic history." [20]

Even Chinese Marxists who accepted the Hobson-Leninist interpretation of imperialism were inclined to stress the intellectual and psychological harm. Chang Kuo-t'ao,

Anti-Christian Tradition and Beginnings of Modern Nationalism 19

writing in 1922, denied that the open door policy offered China any protection against imperialism. After all, he stated, the U. S. expends more than $30,000,000 annually on salaries for pastors, journalists, spies, advisers, and scholars in order to increase the power and impact of pro-American propaganda. He censured foreign missionaries for protecting bandits and riff-raff and for insulting the peasants. Threaded through his entire condemnation of imperialism were such phrases as "profound humiliation," "great suffering," "foreign insults," "our shame," "bowed head".[21]

A comparison of two incendiary anti-Christian tracts written over fifty years apart illustrates the intense emotionalism which the anti-Christian tradition could contribute to Chinese nationalism.[22] *Pi-hsieh chi-shih* (A Record of Facts to Ward off Heterodoxy) is a pamphlet issued by members of the Hunan gentry in 1861 and reprinted numerous times. "Yeh-su shih shen-ma tung-hsi?" (What is Jesus?) was written in 1919 by Chu Chih-hsin, supporter of Sun Yat-sen and a Marxian nationalist. First published in the "Jesus Issue" of *Ch'ien-she* (Reconstruction), organ of the KMT in Shanghai, the essay was frequently reproduced. Copies were distributed at an evangelistic meeting during the Christmas season, 1920, and members of Fei Chi-tu-chiao t'ung-meng (Anti-Christian Federation) used it during the campaigns of 1922 and 1924; the Propaganda Board of the KMT in Kiangsu added a 2,000 word preface and reissued it as part of the rights recovery movement.[23]

The authors of both tracts are well enough acquainted with Christian doctrines and practices to give their accusations a certain verisimilitude. While *Pi-hsieh chi-shih* concentrates on the activities and teachings of the evangelist within the Chinese context, Chu adds details on the role of the church in Western history and the textual criticisms of Western scholars. The nineteenth-century document denigrates Christianity with scatological accounts of church rituals, while the twentieth-century article scoffs at the validity of the Gospels and the virtue of Jesus. Both are the fulminations of angry men. One of the bolder accounts in *Pi-hsieh chi-shih* pictured the Sunday services as inducing a trance which climaxed in copulation among the congregation and sodomy with the castrated priest. Deliberate and frequent sexual allusions contributed much to the popularity of the various Hunan tracts. Chu used Gospel parables in depicting Jesus as a "hypocritical, selfish, narrow-minded, easily provoked man, with a strong desire for revenge." In condemning the barren fig tree, Jesus not only vented his anger at not being able to appease his hunger but he deprived others of the right to gather fruit from the tree simply because it had disappointed him. Chu then relates specific incidents in support of his argument that a similar vengeful selfishness characterized Paul, the Roman Catholic hierarchy, Luther, and Christian evangelists in China.

In *Pi-hsieh chi-shih* the teachings of the Chinese classics are counterpoised to such concepts as original sin, salvation by grace, and canonical truth to demonstrate the absurdity and anti-social morality of Christianity. Chu ridicules Christian mysticism, not as a traditionalist upholding Confucian orthodoxy, but as a Marxist and a nationalist condemning obstacles to China's sovereignty and progress. Chu quotes the hypothesis of the scientist Ernest Haeckel, that Jesus was the product of the free love of Mary and a Roman centurion and that the myth of the virgin birth was commonplace religious concoction. The new context of anti-Christianism of the 1920s illustrates the triumph of a political definition of China. China is no longer the Middle Kingdom, the magnet for all seeking civilization; China is now a nation-state, struggling to survive in a competitive international community. The continuities of the anti-Christian tradition, however, indicate that culturalism has been transmuted into nationalism, not replaced. Questions of ideological commitment, self-respect, and Chinese identity are at the heart of Chinese nationalism during the 1920s. Throughout this process the continuity in the tone of the attacks reveals the centrality of the anti-Christian tradition in the maturation of Chinese nationalism.

The role of the anti-Christian tradition in the delineation of China had its origins in the Chinese heritage as well as in mission methodology. For both Westerner and Chinese in the 19th century, no clear boundary line separated ideology and government. Though the definition of

China in the Great Tradition might be more cultural than political, the Confucian ethic was integral to political power. Chinese bureaucrats were exhorted to rely on moral suasion in the exercise of power and to alert Peking to the activities of heterdox societies.

The phrase, the Christian West, was more than common parlance, for England and other nations reckoned on the support of an established church. Despite anti-clericalism at home, the French government jealously guarded its role as protector of all Catholic missions and reacted hostilely to any proposal for direct relations between Peking and the Vatican. To distinguish Christianity from Western civilization was not a simple matter and many Westerners felt little need to do so since they viewed Christianity as one of the salient reasons for the West's power and wealth. Just as in Europe where identity formation had depended on group consciousness relative to other groups, so the Chinese sense of identity was heightened in counterpoint to the foreign challenge. The union of ideology and government on both sides made it difficult for Chinese to accept state to state relations without also acknowledging the existence and legitimacy of other civilizations. As one scholar has put it, the cosmic image was no longer a given, but one of many to be analyzed and compared.[24] The concept of *T'ien hsia,* the Emperor's mandate to rule all under heaven, ceased to be viable.

Christian evangelism helped bring a new political dimension to the Chinese concept of foreign relations and helped strengthen the sense of state and sovereignty. Since missionaries were among the few Westerners who attained competence in spoken Chinese during the 19th century, they often acted as government interpreters and secretaries in treaty negotiations and other official exchanges. Following the Opium War of 1839-1842, Karl Gützlaff assisted in negotiating the British treaty, Peter Parker and Elijah Bridgman did the same for the U. S., and J.M.Callery for the French; all had come to China as missionaries and three of them eventually accepted full-time government positions, though they often continued evangelistic activities on the side.[25] Caleb Cushing, appointed to China in order to conclude America's first treaty and knowing little of the Chinese political situation or language, wrote of Parker and Bridgman: "They were pre-eminently useful to the Legation, not only as interpreters and translators, but also as advisors, by reason of their long and exact knowledge of China."[26] Two other individuals who followed a similar route from evangelist to government servant, S. Wells Williams and W. A. P. Martin, were the American interpreters at treaty parleys in 1858. Missionary mediators used their influence to obtain clauses guaranteeing toleration of Christianity and promising protection to missionaries and converts. France demanded and obtained the restoration of property confiscated after the Rites Controversy of the 17th and 18th centuries; when the Vicar Apostolic reopened the South Church in Peking, he was accompanied by a French officer and a *Te Deum* of thanksgiving was sung in honor of Napoleon III and the French army.[27] Little wonder that Chinese failed to differentiate evangelist from political emissary.

Based on their experience with Catholic missionaries during the 17th and 18th centuries, the Chinese were wary of Christian evangelism, but even so, the full implications of the unequal treaties were not apparent at the time of negotiation at mid-century. Chinese had not, for example, objected strenuously to granting extraterritorial rights to Westerners, apparently considering such as an extension of their traditional practice of making foreign merchants responsible for policing themselves. The weakness of the Ch'ing dynasty combined with the aggressiveness of the Westerners, however, to make implementation of this privilege ever more of an infringement on Chinese sovereignty. As growing numbers of evangelists journeyed into the interior, far from any foreign consul supposedly having jurisdiction over them, magistrates were frustrated in attempts to settle property disputes and other issues that arose. Missionaries used the guarantee of religious toleration and the privilege of extraterritoriality to provide political and legal protection to converts. In one instance, a particularly combative missionary had interfered in lawsuits so freely that the acting magistrate first inquired whether or not an accused person was a Christian before ordering his apprehension.[28]

Though British and American governments might disavow any official commitment to missions, the right to evangelize had been obtained via Western diplomats and gunboats, and the governments continued to back up missionaries in their insistence on this right. The concern of Western officials over the multiplication of mission cases often verged on exasperation with the result that missionaries did not always receive the whole-hearted support sought. Sir Ernest Satow, British ambassador to China, became so disturbed by missionaries making direct representations to Chinese officials that he issued a public notice stating that missionaries were not the accredited agents of the British government for enforcement of treaties and that the treaties had not conferred on missionaries "any right of intervention on behalf of native Christians."[29] Even so, foreign consuls insisted on and defended the extraterritorial status of their nationals; they frequently displayed a readiness to accept the missionary version of a controversy rather than the Chinese. In preference to risking confrontation with political authorities and greater loss of prestige and authority, Chinese magistrates often acceded to the demands of evangelists.

As Chinese officials came to realize the serious implications of extraterritoriality for Chinese sovereignty, they began to use modern legal concepts to restrict the privilege. They argued that, since Christian converts were still Chinese citizens and under Chinese jurisdiction, missionaries had no right to invoke the guarantee of toleration to prevent the arrest and trial of an accused convert. In 1870 the Tsungli Yamen (foreign office) formally proposed that both missionaries and converts be made subject to Chinese law. This office requested an end to rights whereby missionaries were "like so many independent hostile states within another state" and they asked that converts be placed on an equal footing with ordinary Chinese, no longer able to rely on religion to evade government labor service, payment of taxes and rents, or submission to the local judicial system.[30] A growing appreciation of the concepts of sovereignty and citizenship along with a search for ways to regain political control are evident in this request. Needless to say, the Western powers rejected these proposals and Chinese continued to believe that the loyalty of converts followed their economic and political dependence. During the Sino-French conflict of 1883-85, Chinese Christians were accused of spying for the French. The accusation was not based on concrete evidence so much as the assumption that the converts had lost their Chinese identity when they accepted foreigners as mentors. Protestants as well as Catholics were suspect.

Indemnities, economic concessions, territorial losses, the stationing of foreign soldiers and police on Chinese soil, even warfare, resulted from incidents involving missionaries and converts. France found cause for entering the Arrow War, 1856-60, in the judicial torture and execution of a French missionary on grounds of subversion. The Tientsin Massacre of 1870 in which the French consul, ten nuns, and several other foreigners lost their lives, led to a massing of foreign warships and a collective note by foreign powers demanding justice. Despite the provocative actions of the French consul, the settlement required that 18 Chinese be executed, two officials be banished, Viceroy Tseng Kuo-fan be transferred, a mission of apology be sent to France, and an indemnity be paid.[31] In 1897-98 Germany used the murder of a missionary to obtain mining, railway and port rights in Shantung. To restore the balance of power, Britain, France, Japan and Russia followed hard upon the heels of Germany with demands.

All of these incidents seemed to confirm the Social Darwinist writings that had become available in translation. Struggle and competition, not compromise and harmony, ruled in international affairs. If China were not to be cut like a melon, she must resist further imperialist demands. Wealth and power were required; unity among the people and political reform became the goal of both bureaucratic and non-official reformers.

Parochial schools, hospitals, and the introduction of the modern medical and nursing professions also had implications for Chinese concepts of sovereignty, citizenship, and social structure. The training offered by missionaries as aids to evangelism differed markedly from traditional Chinese education, though more so at the higher levels than at the primary level.[32] Since the first years had to be devoted to acquiring literacy in classical Chinese, missionaries generally were dependent on traditional scholars as tutors in the primary grades. Attempts to alter the rote memorization approach to learning Chinese characters were largely unsuccessful during the 19th century, though graded texts with explication accompanying memorization came into increasing use during the 20th century. Fearful of "heathen indoctrination" by the tutor and the Confucian texts, the missionary educators took care to point out to their pupils the inadequacies of Confucianism and the superiority of Christianity. They even composed Christian versions of the basic text *San-tzu ching* (Trimetrical Classic). The instruction in the classics was, as a rule, inadequate preparation for the civil service examinations. Religion courses bulked large in the curriculum. As the pupil moved up through the grades in the parochial schools, the course of study reflected more and more closely Western models. Science and mathematics, Western history, geography, and philosophy, and above all English language training occupied the pupil. The clientele of the mission schools generally came from families which did not expect to place a son in the bureaucracy but hoped for mission or treaty port employment. For some non-gentry families, especially those of urban commercial background, and for Christians somewhat above the poverty level, mission schools provided an alternate means of social mobility.

As concern over national sovereignty intensified, the parochial schools came in for criticism on political as well as cultural grounds. The schools, according to Chinese nationalists, infringed on a nation's sovereign right to determine and to administer its own educational program. Collegiate-level institutions with their own walled campuses generally flew the foreign flag and were treated as islands of extraterritoriality. Not just Westerners, but Chinese students and teachers acquired immunity upon entering the compound. In times of disorder, the campuses were frequently inundated with refugees seeking protection from bandits or warlord armies. This heightened national sensitivity was revealed when several missionaries requested government recognition for their schools as Peking began to institute a national educational system in the early 20th century. The Chinese Board of Education refused recognition because it did not wish "to encourage foreign interference" in China's education and it did not wish to hinder the "attainment of extraterritorial abolition."[33]

Mission hospitals and medical schools attempted to

follow Western practices regarding the use of surgery, isolation of patients, medical training, the professional status of the physician, and doctor-patient relations. Missionaries often regarded traditional medical practitioners as charlatans and they set little store by Chinese medicines which they considered spurious. Despite misgivings, desperately ill Chinese patronized the Western mission doctors because of the efficacy of their medicine. Proselytizing, however, accompanied medical care.

The anti-Christian tradition, fed by xenophobia, by personal humiliations experienced in hundreds of mission cases, and by a desperate desire to keep China whole, exploded into the Boxer Rebellion of 1900. As the International Expedition sent to relieve the foreign legations approached Peking, the Ch'ing imperial leadership fled the city in disarray. The Chinese were saddled with an enormous indemnity in addition to the shame of having their capital occupied and looted. Exposed to public view was the weakness of Ch'ing as well as the weakness of China. And the Manchu dynasty became the scapegoat, blamed for past and for subsequent failures to protect and strengthen the state. Also exposed was a loss of legitimacy. Some of the leading provincial governors had simply ignored imperial edicts commending the Boxers and, instead of giving them support, had offered guarantees of protection to foreigners. Consensus was fast dissipating. Certain reformers turned revolutionary; others rejected violence, but demanded fundamental change. Ch'ing leaders see-sawed between conservatism and reformism but could not meet the escalating demands of nationalists.

During the gestation period of Chinese nationalism, territorial, financial, and political losses arising from mission cases had fostered a consciousness of China as a political entity and helped make Chinese aware of the nature and importance of state sovereignty. Evangelistic work, as it expanded into educational, medical, and social service activities, had necessitated recognition of other civilizations with competing ideologies and values. The dual role of many missionaries inextricably linked imperialism and missions in the minds of the Chinese. Anti-imperialism placed nationalism, not Christianity, on the side of the angels.

Chapter II

The Anti-Christian Movement of 1920-1922:
First Stage

The first Anti-Christian Movement of the 1920s can be divided into two phases: (1) a period of inquiry and criticism within the context of the New Culture Movement, followed by (2) a period of concerted attack led by anti-religious associations specifically organized for the purpose. Though the movement did not peak until the spring and early summer of 1922, the critical reappraisal of Christianity grew naturally out of the nationalism and iconoclasm of the New Culture Movement. Conservative attempts to gain recognition for Confucianism as the state religion had raised questions about the nature of religion, its significance for a sense of national identity, and its role in creating a new China. Even if the questions focused on Confucianism initially, advocates of modernization examining the Western experience could hardly avoid consideration of Christianity. Almost inevitably, it seems, the scrutiny would conclude on a negative note. In the background were the skeptical secularism historically popular among educated Chinese and the long-standing anti-Christian tradition. In the foreground were the highlighting of anti-imperialism by May Fourth and the burgeoning interest in Marxism. During 1920-22, furthermore, a major reassessment of national educational objectives focused attention on the separate and independent status of mission schools and their evangelistic goals.

CHINESE REASSESSMENTS

The initial thrust of the New Culture Movement stressed destruction. Even as New Youth, like earlier reformers, expressed faith in historical progress toward a utopian future, their attitude toward the past was one of radical negation. New Youth argued that the 1911 revolution failed because it had altered political forms without discarding the social and philosophical foundation, which was Confucianism. Accepting an instrumental, environmentalist approach to evolution, they postulated that social conditions, institutions, and ethics determined the political system. Traditional intellectual constraints and assumptions had to be demolished in order to achieve the cultural change that would in turn lay the basis for political change. Indicative of the centrality of Confucianism, they said, were attempts at revival by conservative intellectuals and military officials.

For centuries the Mandate of Heaven thesis had validated the political power of the dynasty while the dictum of leadership by the virtuous had sanctioned the authority of the scholar bureaucrat. That disillusionment with the republic and the search for legitimacy should persuade certain leaders to revert to the auspices of Confucianism hardly seems surprising. As a matter of fact, many of the pragmatists who grasped the reins of power in 1912 felt quite comfortable within the Confucian social and ethical system. Even among literate Chinese alienation was confined to a minority. Confucian rituals continued in many of the yamen and in 1913 the Ministry of Education ordered the celebration of Confucius' birthday in schools. Presidential mandates restored ancient titles and privileges to the descendants of Confucius and recommended repair of Confucian temples. Attributing the loss of a sense of political community to abandonment of monarchy, certain veterans of the 1898 reforms advocated a Confucian renaissance; a renewed Confucian ethic was required to fill the moral vacuum.[1]

Though some conservatives favored recognition of Confucianism as the established religion of China while others defined Confucianism as a moral philosophy, both employed utilitarian arguments. Immediately after the 1911 revolution, Yen Fu, Ch'en Huan-chang, and other venerable literati founded K'ung-chiao hui (Confucian Society) to champion Confucianism as the national doctrine of China. K'ang Yu-wei, who had proposed the establishment of a Confucian state religion during the 1898 reform era, enthusiastically supported the society in his magazine *Pu-jen tsa-chih* (Compassion). In cooperation with Liang Ch'i-ch'ao and members of Chin-pu tang (Progressive Party), K'ung-chiao hui lobbied for formal recognition of a national Confucianism in the constitution.[2]

1920-1922: First Stage

A petition presented to parliament stated that "morality is the foundation of a nation and the standard of morality depends on religion".[3] Confucianism embodied the Chinese national religion and had served as the state religion in practice if not in theory for thousands of years. Since republican government must be based on morality, the constitution should recognize the morality that is Chinese, Confucianism. K'ang and Ch'en reasoned that Confucianism expressed the national essence of China just as Christianity gave the West its distinctive identity. Western political leaders, aware of religion as a source of unifying loyalty, had utilized established churches. By acknowledging Confucianism as the state religion, the Chinese government would be expressing the will of the people and simultaneously consolidating the nation, they maintained. If in fact, Confucianism were abandoned, the uniqueness of China would evaporate and China would lose its raison d'être. Even as K'ang argued for a state Confucianism, however, his goal was a political and social ethic, not a transcendent theology; Confucianism should be interpreted so as to be compatible with science and industrialism.

Others, including Yuan Shih-k'ai, maintained that recognizing the special status of Confucianism did not infringe on religious freedom since Confucianism was not a religion and China permitted the propagation and practice of any religion. In several gestures, such as permitting G. Sherwood Eddy to hold evangelistic meetings in the Forbidden City in 1914, Peking officials demonstrated their tolerance. Presidential decrees, nevertheless, fostered a Confucian revival with the intent of reducing the moral chaos of the land and strengthening the national spirit bequeathed by the ancestors. Confucian principles were to provide the guidelines for the cultivation of character in the state schools. Hoping to enhance his position as the embodiment of national will, Yuan in 1914 performed the annual ritual at the Temple of Heaven dressed in robes designed in the style of the Chou dynasty.[4]

Opposition to the establishment of a Confucian state religion came from many quarters, but particularly from Christians and from Kuomintang members of Parliament. Chinese Protestants in Peking formed an Anti-State Religion Society, which attracted Roman Catholics as well as

Taoists, Muslims, and Buddhists. To offset the flow of petitions from Confucianists, they drew up a counter petition and secured signatures from denominational representatives throughout China. Ch'eng Ching-yi and other prominent Christians circulated protests and the Union for Catholic Action, along with Protestant organizations, expressed their disapproval in the religious and secular press. They contended that such a move would infringe on religious freedom and become a divisive force in China.[5]

With Yuan's rejection of the draft constitution, the tempest subsided. When Yuan prepared to inaugurate a new dynasty in 1916, however, he turned to Confucian societies and classical scholars for support and legitimation. Again, opposition came from many quarters: New Youth, republican reformers, and even military rivals, though not generally from Christian organizations this time.[6] Upon the death of Yuan and the renewal of attempts to write a constitution, the campaign for recognition of Confucianism as the state religion revived once again. Some nineteen generals supported such proposals with their own demands, and one of their number led a brief abortive attempt to restore the Manchu dynasty in July, 1917.

The controversy heated up. Ma Liang, a prominent Catholic and founder of both Chen-tan ta-hsueh (Aurora University) and a secessionist institution, Fu-tan ta-hsueh (New Aurora University), sponsored a United Catholic Congress to oppose the adoption of a Confucian state religion. Roman Catholics and Protestants presented to the Parliament petitions opposing a state religion. Public rallies culminated in the formation of an Association for Religious Freedom to lobby for a constitutional clause guaranteeing freedom of belief. President was Hsu Ch'ien, a legal expert and a republican who had accepted Christianity after his prayers for the death of Yuan Shih-k'ai came true.[7] Ma Liang represented the Catholics in the association while Ch'eng Ching-yi representd the Protestants. Muslims, Buddhists, and other religious groups pledged support and the society eventually gained over one hundred assemblymen as members. Telegrams, circular letters, and broadsides flowed from printing presses so that by the time the issue came up for debate, parliamentarians had received over 10,000 telegrams and quantities of other literature on the subject. They passed a religious liberty clause.

Despite the success of the lobbyists, iconoclastic intellectuals responded with outrage to this most recent evidence of the continuing force of Confucianism. Ch'en Tu-hsiu wrote that even though Yuan had died, there were still "numerous Yuan Shih-k'ai's thinking, talking, and acting in China"; they must be excised.[8] Between 1916 and 1918 he published frequent articles inveighing against Confucianism in *Hsin ch'ing-nien* ("La Jeunesse"). While the religious groups emphasized the issue of religious freedom, this was a minor theme for most of the intelligentsia. The latter condemned Confucianism as an obstacle to progress and an ethic of oppression. Wu Yü, long a critic of Confucianism, discovered a ready outlet for his sentiments in *Hsin ch'ing-nien* and some of the sharpest attacks were his essays in five successive issues from March to July, 1917.[9]

Wu's approach was not unlike that later employed in appraisals of Christianity. A doctrine, according to Wu, should be evaluated on the bases of its practical consequences for politics and society, not on the beauty of its ethical principles; Wu, furthermore, drew on both heterodox Chinese tradition and Western scholarship in his argumentation. The Confucian code of ritual propriety *(li)* assumed a hierarchical, unequal relationship, Wu wrote; thus, it sanctioned the patriarchal family with its oppression of youth and women and it sanctioned monarchism with its demand for meekness and obedience from the people. Itself the product of a feudal culture, Confucianism helped perpetuate a barbarous society of intellectual repression and political and social despotism.

Ch'en Tu-hsiu found Confucianism incompatible with modern society; by teaching obedience and harmony, it made the Chinese people too weak and passive to survive in the contemporary world of struggle and competition; by placing a premium on family loyalty, it undermined the development of independent individuals, essential to democracy and economic growth. The hopes of 1911 for a new society and a new state would remain elusive until Confucianism was abandoned.[10]

The most telling attack of all, perhaps, was "The Diary of a Madman" published by Chou Shu-jen (Lu Hsun) in *Hsin ch'ing-nien,* April, 1918. While Confucianism ostensibly preached "Benevolence, Righteousness, Morality," the madman discovered that it was actually a cloak for a cannibalistic society in which all existed through oppression of others. Only some children had possibly not yet become cannibals. "Save the children."[11] These writers condemned more than Confucian teachings; they struck at the entire ethical and institutional foundation of the Great Tradition. The ground had to be cleared for new doctrines to guide a new China. "Down with Confucius and Sons" became a popular slogan of the New Culture Movement.

In the midst of the polemics, Ch'ien Hsuan-t'ung, one of the editors of *Hsin ch'ing-nien,* planted a letter inquiring why the magazine concentrated its attacks on Confucianism and did not include Western religions. Another editor, Liu Fu, replied that the pervasiveness of Confucianism in China made it the greater evil. Simultaneously Liu declared, as did Ch'en Tu-hsiu, that any religion or ideology should be judged on the basis of social utility; did it injure or benefit China?[12]

Several of the leaders of the New Culture Movement did actually discuss in general terms the nature and role of religion in modern society. Yun Tai-ying, a frequent contributor to *Hsin ch'ing-nien* stated flatly that faith and knowledge were usually in conflict; to accept on faith despite knowledge to the contrary was stupid.[13] Those who possessed knowledge did not require supernatural explanations and with increasing understanding, society has no need to preserve religion. Ts'ai Yuan-p'ei, Chancellor of Peking National University, offered aesthetics as a substitute for religion.[14] A sense of beauty, he said, was universal and transcended human distinctions, whereas religions were exclusive and inspired enmity and division. Cultivation of the aesthetic sense would contribute to peace. According to Hu Shih, humankind should be able to dispense with religious mythology because social immortality could satisfy the human desire for eternity. Since every individual was the product of society and since all thoughts and actions lived on in society, no human being existed without a legacy.[15]

1920-1922: First Stage   33

Characterizing all these discussions were skepticism regarding the supernatural and acceptance of a social criterion of value. Such an approach, as old as Confucius, had been used in critiques of Buddhism and Christianity during centuries past. What had altered was the definition of the good society. Progress and change were esteemed rather than stability and tradition; secular scientism provided the criterion for the good society. On this note, some New Youth began to look specifically at Christianity. The role of Chinese Christians in the Anti-Confucian campaign had given them prominence and had inspired some to question whether Christians could speak for China.

Taking the lead in the inquiry was the Shao-nien Chung-kuo hsueh-hui (Young China Association). This society included some of the most prolific essayists of the New Culture Movement and published a magazine, *Shao-nien Chung-kuo,* which exercised great influence for a year or so. Though the organization was not in 1920-21 identified with a particular political ideology, its members were intensely nationalistic and shared a faith in science as a necessary instrument of China's salvation. Several of its leaders were well acquainted with the writings of European anarchists and continued to accord high priority to the destructive phase of China's modernization. Indicative of the importance of Western-educated scholars in the organization is the prominent role of those studying in France.

The decision to focus on the religious question originated with a recommendation from the Paris branch that persons of religious faith be barred from membership. After the executive committee passed the resolution in September, 1920, there were protests over its precipitate action and a request for investigation prior to imposing the ban. T'ien Han, a student in Tokyo who later became a prominent playwright, asked reconsideration on grounds that the Chinese constitution guaranteed religious freedom and that the teachings of Jesus and the Bible merited attention even if one did not accept Jesus as the divine son of God.[16] The Young China Association accordingly organized a series of lectures on "The Problem of Religion", sponsored translations of Biblical criticism by Westerners and in 1921 devoted three issues of its magazine to the question.[17] The Christian religion, rather than religion per se, was the focus and few of the findings were calculated to enhance the reputation of Christianity among New Youth; rather, the Young China Association served as harbinger of the 1922 Anti-Christian campaign.

Most of the basic criticisms of religion from the scientific viewpoint were enunciated in *Shao-nien Chung-kuo*, to be repeated frequently throughout the Anti-Christian Movement. The journal, according to its frontispiece, was dedicated to the "social services under the guidance of the scientific spirit in order to realize our ideal of creating a Young China." Underlying this statement was the assumption that there existed a natural law ordering human society similar to a natural law describing the physical universe. The scholarly investigation of natural law, furthermore, was purposive. New Youth were searching for ideological guidelines for a new national culture as well as for knowledge itself. Science, for many of the essayists, was more than a method for examining nature; it had become a belief in the general applicability of scientific principles; it had become scientism, a technique for rational decision making.[18] Because of the commonality of assumptions and goals, many of the criticisms of Christianity and religion in 1921 foreshadow the criticisms of metaphysics in the famous Debate on Science and the Philosophy of Life in 1923.

The February issue of *Shao-nien Chung-kuo* included (1) the letter of T'ien Han urging serious investigation of the religious issue, (2) a speech by Bertrand Russell, then on lecture tour in China, and (3) essays by a group of relatively young Chinese scholars who had studied abroad and as a consequence already held professorial positions at Peita and other universities. At least four of the contributors were subsequently to participate in the Anti-Christian campaigns: Wang Hsing-kung, Li Shih-tseng, Yun Tai-ying, and T'u Hsiao-shih. Wang, who had studied in England before becoming Professor of Chemistry at Peita, presented a simple and straight-forward argument from a scientist's viewpoint. Scientific discoveries, he stated, had provided explanations for many phenomena that primitive humans attributed to the supernatural. Though there were still unknowns, humans had no logical basis for resorting to the metaphysical since there was no proof of supernatural existence. Science would continue to bring mysteries into the realm of the known; science, rather than religious dogma, provided the better foundation for progress. Reliance on faith could lead to such tragedies as the Children's Crusade and the Boxer Rebellion. In an open letter to Shanghai journals during the spring of 1922, Wang would reiterate these arguments and add that man had as much right not to believe as to believe; it was religion with its aggressive evangelism that infringed on freedom of thought, not the Anti-Christian organizations.

Li Shih-Tseng, who was to become president of Fei tsung-chiao ta t'ung-meng (Great Anti-Religion Federation), had been an early Chinese advocate of anarchism and founder of Liu-Fa chien-hsueh hui (Society for Frugal Study in France). He was at the time of his *Shao-nien* essay, a member of the Peita faculty and an officer with Sino-French University near Peking. Li stated that he agreed to talk on religion and evangelism only because of their great injury to the Chinese people.[19] His opening questions revealed as much about his views as his answers. He asked: Is religion a science? Is it art? Is it necessary for morality? Is it necessary to explain the incomprehensible? After answering in the negative, Li asserted that the old schools of religion had become outdated because they had made no accommodation with modern scholarship while the new schools had followed the tide and become little more than applied sociology. Religion was like astrology before astronomy, alchemy before chemistry, and wizardry before medicine; it would eventually fade away. Meanwhile, China should take a lesson from France and insist on separation of religion and education.

Yun Tai-ying, a young Marxist, had already questioned the validity of faith in a 1917 article in *Hsin ch'ing-nien* and he would later support the anti-Christian campaigns in his roles as editor of *Chung-kuo ch'ing-nien* (Chinese Youth), instructor at Shanghai University, and leader in She-hui ch'ing-nien t'uan (Socialist Youth Corps).[20] Yun invoked the authority of a fascinating array of Western writers, some eminent, some largely forgotten today: Goethe, William R. Smith, Tolstoy, Kant, Darwin, William T. Kelvin, Francis Bacon, Samuel Laing, etc. Acknowledging that some of these accepted the existence of God, he stated that they could provide no scientific evidence for what they believed and that as far as he was concerned, man created God rather than vice versa. Humans turned to religion out of ignorance, poverty, and fear, but supernatural explanations of the mysteries of nature denied the findings of Darwin, Galileo and other scientists. The church, furthermore, neglected practical matters in its concentration on evangelism and the spiritual life. Religion, therefore, had no justification from the standpoint of science or of social usefulness and it could injure China as the "foreign slaves" nurtured by Christian missions obstructed China's unity.

The philosopher T'u Hsiao-shih adopted the Kantian postion that there is knowledge based on religious or emotional experience as well as knowledge based on scientific data. In both this lecture and one given to the Peking Philosophy Society in 1922, T'u declared that religious knowledge was not identical with superstition and might have a certain authenticity.[21] Even so, his discussions were no brief for religion. As with many Chinese literati, T'u indicated that religious knowledge was irrelevant and unimportant to him; he found it difficult, in fact, to stake out the province of non-scientific knowledge even after admitting the possibility of its existence. The bulk of his 1921 essay was devoted to cataloguing Christian doctrines that had been disproved by science: the earth as the center of the cosmos, God as regulator of the stars and planets, truth as absolute and independent of time and circumstance, etc. While granting that religion could inspire worthy ideals, he denied religious knowledge a monopoly over the realm of morality. T'u buttressed each criticism with references to Western scientists and philosophers, but his essays convey the impression that his agnosticism preceded rather than emanated from his scientific studies. Scientism served his own needs and those of a modernizing China and so he, like so many participants in the New Culture Movement, turned to science to disintegrate the old and validate the new.

During Bertrand Russell's visit to China in 1920-21, he offered a detailed critique of religion and his prestige and popularity encouraged Chinese to fortify their attacks on Christianity with the argments of this eminent philosopher from the West. *Shao-nien Chung-kuo* and other magazines reprinted translations of Russell's lectures, and students even organized a Russell Society and founded *Lo-su yueh-k'an* (The Russell Monthly) to propagate his doctrines.[22] Having delineated two categories of religion, institutional and individual, Russell found both detrimental. Institutional religion served society poorly, for it provoked strife, reinforced the status quo, and stultified creative thought. Religion at the individual level encouraged the substitution of emotions for reason and the acceptance of ideas without scientific foundation; consequently, it handicapped individual growth. Such assertions seemed almost tailor-made for the Young China Association critics and were to enjoy frequent repetition.

The May, 1921, issue of *Shao-nien Chung-kuo* contained essays by three Chinese who might have been expected to present some of the positive values of religion.[23] Interesting and revealing is their selectivity in singling out the beneficial aspects of Christianity. The social and ethical teachings of Jesus, not institutional religion or theology, merited praise. Chou Tso-jen, a writer associated with the literature departments of Peita and Yenching University, admitted that he had not studied Christianity in depth. He liked the Sermon on the Mount, however; certain individuals, he said, might find science or aesthetics sufficient, but the Chinese masses could benefit from Jesus' advocacy of love and charity. Another scholar, Liu Po-ming, also selected Christ's social ethic as admirable but stated that China needed none of the additives, i.e., the church and metaphysics. Such an elitist defense of Christianity on the basis of utilitarianism was little better than none. Nationalists would have little difficulty demonstrating that other institutions and organizations could serve China's social needs more effectively than the church. Even while acknowledging the good works of missions, many would argue that the harm outweighed the benefits. A religion deemed fit only for the masses could scarcely be acceptable to advocates of populism and democracy.

Much of this second issue on "The Problem of Religion" consists of translations from Western writers or summations of their religious views.[24] Some of those cited are relatively obscure: Hermann Gorter, a Dutch socialist and anarchist, and Harold Hoffding, a Danish positivist. Others need no identification; William James, Romain Rolland. The young scholars obviously had an insatiable appetite for all kinds of literature and in the open and intellectually charged atmosphere of the New Culture Movement, they read almost anything they could get their hands on. For the moment, the positivists and pragmatists spoke to the idealistic iconoclasts.

The Association's Paris branch, which had initially raised the religious question, solicited the views of French scholars for the third issue.[25] Their letters of inquiry, dated February 25, 1921, asked: (1) Is man a religious animal? (2) Have the old and new religions any chance of survival in modern life? (3) Will new China need a religion? The replies by novelist Henri Barbusse and by professors Marcel Granet and Celestin Bouglé suggested that Christianity had little to offer modernizing China. Their arguments reiterated the themes set forth by Chinese scholars in previous issues. Primitive man had been obliged to seek supernatural explanations for the many unknowns of his universe but now that modern man could find answers in science, religion was becoming less and less necessary. Morality, furthermore, was separable from religion and did not require religious sanctions. Ideological guidance should be sought elsewhere. In articles on "Religion and the Future of China," "Religion and the Theory of Evolution," "Sociology and Religion," Chinese added glosses and outlined criticisms which they would develop in the course of the anti-Christian campaigns.

The nature and role of religion proved to be a popular issue among New Youth and numerous periodicals followed the lead of *Shao-nien* with articles evaluating religion in general and Christianity in particular. Among those publishing on the subject were: *Hsin ch'ing-nien, Min-to* (People's tocsin), *Che-hsueh,* ("Philosophia"), *Hsueh heng* ("The Critical Review"), *Min-kuo jih-pao* (Republic Daily), *Hsing-ch'i p'ing-lun* (The Weekly Review), *Hsueh-i* ("Wissen und Wissenschaft"), *Hsin ch'ao* (New tide), *Chueh-wu* (Awakening). Other societies in Peking and branch organizations outside the capital sponsored lectures on the "problem of religion".

One attraction of the subject was that it combined

several major themes of the New Culture Movement: iconoclasm, nationalism, scientism, and individual freedom. Many May Fourth advocates of individualism appeared less concerned about civil rights and individual worth than about freedom from intellectual and cultural ccnstraints. In their view, religion in the West, like Confucianism in China, had informed the whole social and ethical system. Totalistic iconoclasm, therefore, was essential to create an environment where intellectual openness and cultural change could flourish. In the transformation of consciousness necessary to cultural revolution, science was to be the cutting instrument and Christianity even more than Confucianism appeared to fly in the face of science. Nationalism and the strengthening of the central government could be espoused by the proponents of individualism since it was not the state, but traditional teachings and communal groups like the family which were the offenders.

Attacks on Christianity could, therefore, serve a multiple purpose for the nationalistic iconoclasts of the New Culture Movement. What began for some as intellectual inquiry became in many instances an outpouring of anti-imperialist nationalism and in a few instances even pointed toward political action. Tai Chi-t'ao, a Marxist member of Sun Yat-sen's entourage, published in *Hsing-ch'i p'ing-lun* a poem, "Amen," calling for the abolition of both the Christian church and Christianity in China.[26] Another member of the Kuomintang, Chang Chi, informed Chinese studying in France that no believers would receive subsidies from *Liu Fa ch'in-kung chien hsueh hui* (Society for Frugal Study by Means of Manual Labor in France).[27] Both these individuals would later become leaders in the anti-religious federation.

Not until the spring of 1922. however, did the controversy over religion acquire the structure and focus of a campaign: specific anti-Christian organizations and publications, demonstrations, and concerted propaganda. In the immediate background of the transformation were changes within Christian missions and the growth of a radical nationalism characterized by intense anti-imperialism.

CHRISTIAN MISSIONS IN TRANSITION

The decade of the 1920s marked a divide for China missions as well as for the ongoing Chinese revolution; for both, the years of the New Culture Movement encompassed the transition. Following the hiatus of World War I, mission societies anticipated a renewed impetus in the Christianizing of the world; the return to peacetime concerns would bring money into church coffers and volunteers into the mission field. Expansive hopes seemed confirmed, initially, by statistics showing increases in the number of converts and mission activities.

Perhaps the optimistic reports delayed realization that the heyday of Western evangelism was passing. Perhaps they misled mission societies concerning the revolution that was occurring in China and the timetable for adjustment. At any rate missions devoted much energy between 1918 and 1925 to survey commissions, data-collecting committees, organs to coordinate denominational work, and conferences for self-examination. What was initiated with confident enthusiasm was often concluded with somber doubt. To adversities in the field were added trials on the home-front. Fund raising campaigns in the United States failed as the populace turned inward to national problems; recovery and reconstruction absorbed the attention and monies of Europeans.[28] Missions were asked to justify more than their methodology; their very existence was called into question.

One indication that the tide had turned was the fact that efforts to meet the challenges of the 1920s often exacerbated difficulties. When task forces gathered data for their appraisals, the growth statistics touched off cries of alarm by Chinese nationalists. The broadening definition of mission goals and functions placed missions more directly in conflict with national educational and social service institutions; Christians, it appeared, wanted to take over the task of social reform. On the other hand, critics and Chinese Christians also accused the church of failing to meet the needs of the nation. The caustic quarrels between religious liberals and conservatives over the essence of Christianity and the purpose of Christian missions were an embarrassment, particularly to the Chinese Christians. It was, in fact, a move to demonstrate the relevancy of Christianity for reformist China that actually sparked the founding of the Anti-Christian Federation and the launching of a concerted campaign in the spring of 1922.

Though Chinese did not always distinguish between Protestants and Roman Catholics, the Protestant churches experienced the greater difficulties. Protestant missionaries were more numerous and in some ways more visible to educated urban Chinese. China was the foremost mission field for Protestant churches and by 1920, 130 societies were sponsoring some 6,500 evangelists; over half the missionaries resided in the cities, with an especially heavy concentration in the treaty ports.[29] Duplication of effort by competing denominations was widespread. Roman Catholics supported approximately 3,000 Western priests, sisters and lay workers and while not escaping the competition of orders and national groups within the church, they benefited from coordination through the Papacy.[30] Partly because they were free of family demands, many of the priests worked in market towns and rural areas, away from the centers of nationalist movements.

Americans formed the largest component among Protestant missionaries whereas most of the Roman Catholic workers came from Europe. This difference in national origins was significant because the fundamentalist-liberal controversy was particularly sharp among Americans. Also, American missionaries devoted unusual attention to higher education; for them, as for most Protestants, evangelism was one major function of parochial education; both Christian and non-Christian students were therefore required to participate in religious activities. European Catholics, not regarding education as a significant means of proselytism, put most of their educational efforts into semnaries and elementary schools for children of the parish. In their limited number of institutions of higher education, Roman Catholics ordinarily did not expect non-Christians to attend church rites; in fact, the celebration of the sacraments was generally closed to non-Christians. The slender European suport for missions, especially after World War I, forced Catholics to rely increasingly on Chinese clergy, with the result that the proportion of Chinese clergy to Western clergy was higher among Catholics than among Protestants. As with the Protestants, however, ecclesiastical authority was usually held by Westerners rather than Chinese and relations were not always harmonious.[31]

Roman Catholic church membership was actually almost five times that of Protestants, but as late comers to the China mission field, the Protestant rate of growth was higher. In 1920 baptized Chinese Christians numbered about 350,000 Protestants and 2,000,000 Catholics.[32] Though Chinese Christians never comprised more than 1% of the total population and mission school students formed a small portion of enrolled students, about two-thirds of the Protestant communicants attended church schools and Protestants made up a somewhat larger segment among literate Chinese than their numbers might indicate. With 1900 as the base, the percentage increase of Protestants could appear quite impressive. Surveys published in 1922, for example, announced that the number of Protestant societies and missionaries had doubled during the past two decades and the number of Chinese communicants had trebled; the growth rate for students was even higher since the majority of schools had been founded since 1900.[33] Agnostics, religious critics, and nationalists expressed consternation at the expansion rate of the Christian establishment. If the current pace continued, might not Christians dominate the educational and intellectual life of China, they asked.

Such fears were aggravated by the approach of many mission societies to the China field, an approach typified by the volume, *The Christian Occupation of China*.[34] This historical survey of Protestant missions published in the spring of 1922 epitomized the ethnocentric presumption of the evangelistic crusade during the 19th and early 20th centuries. *The Christian Occupation of China* detailed the "claimed" areas of the country, that is, the districts containing a mission station. Maps illustrated the "occupied" sectors, the extent of "occupation" and the reservation of sectors for specific Protestant denominations in order to reduce duplication of effort. (No such common cause with their competitors, Roman Catholic missions, was acknowledged.) Over one hundred pages of tables, diagrams and charts quantified Protestant activity among students, ethnic minorities, rickshaw pullers, opium

1920-1922: First Stage

addicts, lepers, and so forth. There was even a "table of urgency" to guide in further occupation. Depiction of China as a territory to be conquered and Christianized outraged Chinese, who complained, further, that mission reports frequently concentrated on the failings of Chinese society in order to make a case for Christian evangelism.[35] Missionaries themselves were placed on their mettle as the editor stated that the purpose of the massive and expensive survey was the "speedier and more effective evangelization" of all China. To maintain the growth rate would not be easy in the light of increasing doubt and cynicism in the West and active opposition in China.

Equally troublesome was the fact that missions had already built an institutional structure beyond the ability of the small Chinese Christian community to staff or finance. At the same time, both Christian and non-Christian nationalists were demanding Chinese control of the institutions. By 1920 over 300 mission hospitals existed, many with fewer than fifty beds and no isolation ward, some without trained nurses. Female Catholic orders concentrated much of their energy on the maintenance of hundreds of orphanages, often understaffed and overcrowded. Protestants operated 7,000 schools enrolling ca. 213,000 students while Catholics sponsored 8,700 schools with 182,000 pupils, mostly at the primary level.[36] Catholic orders, however, decried the church's neglect of higher education and began to plan a major university in Peking.[37] Most existent institutions were seeking to expand and raise standards. Once China had abolished the traditional civil service examinations in 1905 and begun to construct a modern school system, the mission schools and the national schools had become alternatives, even competitors; the isolation and disparity between the two educational systems declined. Christian middle schools, colleges, and hospitals informed mission boards that they had to improve the quality of their equipment and staff if they were not to fall behind the government ones.

Mission boards faced difficult choices in their allocations of funds and personnel. Should they provide increasing aid to social service institutions whose contribution to evangelism was being questioned and whose control must pass to the Chinese? Should they emphasize support to

Westerners in specifically evangelistic activities despite the pleas of Chinese Christians that the church serve society? Both questions appeared to demand affirmative responses and in the optimism of the immediate post-war period the mission societies hoped that continued expansion would obviate the necessity for choice.

Certain Western Christians were, however, asking theological questions similar to those of the Young China Association.[38] Had recent scientific knowledge destroyed the validity of the Biblical chronicles? How could one reconcile humanitarianism with belief in original sin and the damnation of the heathen? Did not the crusade for individual conversion in a non-Christian society defy the findings of anthropology, sociology, and psychology? Since the questions were asked in a different context from that of the Young China Association, the answers of Christians differed. Nevertheless, serious cleavages were added to sectarian divisions.

A small group accepted the fundamental similarity of the essential doctrines of all major religions and said, in effect, to each his own. They found no justification for Christian evangelism in the homelands of such great teachings as Hinduism, Buddhism, and Confucianism. Some, often known as conservatives or fundamentalists, insisted on the uniqueness and exclusiveness of the Christian gospel and the literal truth of the Bible and the Christian creed. In China, evangelists of this persuasion founded the Bible Union of China in 1920 and requested that home boards refuse to appoint individuals as missionaries unless they accepted "the fundamental and saving truths revealed in the Bible, especially those now being assailed, such as the Deity of our Lord and Saviour Jesus Christ, His Virgin Birth, His Atoning Sacrifice for sin, . . . the miracles both of the Old and New Testaments. . ."[39]

The liberals, as they were often called, became advocates of the Social Gospel.[40] They presented the ethical teachings of Jesus as the core of Christianity and adopted a figurative interpretation of the Bible. Thus, they saw little conflict between modern science and Christianity and they argued that Chinese Christians should have the right to evolve their own version of church ritual, architecture, music, etc. Employing concepts from sociology and anthropology, they acknowledged the ostracizing effect of conversion in a non-Christian environment. The emphasis of missions, they stated, should not be the conversion of individuals so much as the Christianizing of the whole Chinese environment; thereby, they would demonstrate the relevance of Christianity for a modernizing China. They professed no uneasiness over the concentration of mission monies and personnel in social service activities whether or not they brought immediate returns in conversions. The number of new converts listed in the annual report should not be the only criteria of success, they said. While agreeing on the need for Sinification of Christianity, however, liberals diverged when it came to defining the essential doctrines to be retained, nor did they concur on a time schedule for Sinification.

The split between liberals and conservatives seems to have been especially deep and acrimonious in China and it did not help the mission cause. Existing divisions between rural and urban-based missionaries and between the preaching evangelists and those in educational and medical work widened. When Frank Rawlinson, liberal editor of the *China Mission Year Book,* requested a member of the conservative Bible Union to contribute an article on the organization, he met with rebuff.[41] On the other hand, Rawlinson, who also edited *The Chinese Recorder,* declared on one occasion that he would not print fundamentalist critiques of a survey advocating a new mission methodology for China. The Catholic church was not immune to the controversy even though differences were more pronounced among Protestants. The popular Catholic newspaper, *I-shih pao* (Social welfare newspaper), edited briefly by Hsu Ch'ien, was disavowed by church officials for its activist role. Chinese Christians could only view the quarrel with perplexed dismay, for such bitter debates over theological issues held little meaning for most of them. Mission critics, finding grist for their mills, were quick to proclaim the discrepancy between such acrimony and the doctrine of love preached by the foreigners.

Though fundamentalism remained influential among certain groups and denominations, the Social Gospel gained in favor among mission theorists at home and Christian spokesmen in China. Chinese workers, often combining the Social Gospel approach with attempts to Sinify Christianity, sought to demonstrate the continuing relevance of Christianity for a reformist China. Liu T'ing-fang (Timothy T'ing-fang Lew) of Yenching University's School of Theology argued that Christianity had long been fighting for goals similar to those of the New Culture Movement: the liberation of women, education of the poor, and suppression of opium, prostitution, and footbinding.[42] The cultural revolution thus gave indirect support to Christian work and provided an entree for expanded activity among youth, according to Liu. If the church abandoned those superstitions without scientific foundation and concentrated on preaching the Social Gospel of Jesus Christ, it could benefit from the new mood of China. Hsu Pao-ch'ien, a YMCA secretary, wrote that Christianity and the New Culture Movement supplemented each other because both stood for science and democracy and both encouraged youth to dedicate themselves to social service.[43] The change from indifference to critical examination of Christianity should be welcomed as an opportunity to demonstrate true Christianity; Hsu pointedly remarked that essential Christianity was not necessarily identical with the Christian church or the Christian nations but was the spirit of Christ actualized in society.

YMCA secretaries, leaders in independent Chinese churches, Western and Chinese Christian educators recommended greater attention to the student community. Work should be initiated in government universities, where there had been little proselytism, and work among youth in the Christian institutions should be reformed; all too many were abandoning their faith upon graduation. The message sent to the nation's elite should be youth's obligation to serve society.

Peking with 15,440 students in 40 institutions of higher learning, represented a special challenge. In September 1918 leaders from the YMCA and six Peking churches agreed upon a cooperative effort to provide youth with facilities for recreation and religious education.[44] They would propagandize in the name of the Chinese church rather than mission societies; they would include youth, both male and female, in the executive planning committees, and they would inculcate the social service ideal as the highest form of patriotism. Between 1917 and 1921 the number of YMCA secretaries assigned to student work in Peking rose from 3 to 21, with fifteen of them being Chinese.

Among the hundreds of associations founded in the aftermath of May Fourth were several Christian organizations designed to compete for the loyalty of youth: Sheng-ming she (Life Fellowship), a student branch of Chung-hua kuei-chu (China for Christ), Chen-li she (Truth Society), Pei-ching Chi-tu-chiao hsuen-chiao shih-yeh lien-ho (in English, Peking Christian Scholars United Association).[45] These organizations are indicative of the lessening isolation of parochial students and a few nationalistic Christian leaders. Perhaps not yet full participants in the student sub-culture, many students in urban mission schools, nevertheless, shared the New Culture scene and were influenced by its nationalism and readiness to challenge authority. The Life Fellowship drew up a Christian Social Creed of 38 goals combining the values of classical liberalism and American Protestantism with a smattering of socialism.[46] The desiderata ranged from sexual equality and freedom of marriage to cooperatives and restrictions on private property, from national sovereignty to international fraternity, from universal suffrage to abstention from gambling, alcohol, tobacco and concubinage. As in many May Fourth manifestoes, the Christian students were using the shotgun approach; their goals shared the diverse and utopian qualities of the New Culture Movement. Also in the May Fourth tradition, the associations generally published a house organ to propagate their views.

Two meetings scheduled for the spring of 1922 inspired a whole spate of articles advocating the Social Gospel and a national Christian church. One was the international conference of the World's Student Christian Federation held at Tsing Hua University, April 4-8. Peking had been chosen as the site for the Federation's first major postwar conference with the theme, "Reconstruction of the World according to the Christian Plan," in order to demonstrate the pertinence of the church's social message to the New Youth of China. The second gathering was a national Protestant Synod in Shanghai in May; its subject was a true Chinese Christian church and its representatives were to include for the first time as many Chinese delegates as missionaries. The China YMCA Monthly, *Ch'ing-*

nien chin-pu (Youth Progress, but generally known as "Association Progress"), *Chung-hua kuei-chu, Sheng-minq* and WSCF's *The Student World* all put out special issues on "Christ and the Reconstruction of the World." Practically all of the China Christian magazines carried articles expressing high hopes for a new era for Christianity, with Chinese assuming church leadership. Practically all expressed the desire for a modern, reformed China.[47]

Ironically, the publicity surrounding these attempts to demonstrate the relevance of Christianity for a new China sparked the founding of the Anti-Christian Students Federation in March, 1922.[48] Why? Such actions clearly were not the major source of the anti-Christian sentiment, for it had a broad base and a long history in China. But why did the critics seize upon a youth conference dedicated to social service as the occasion for launching an anti-Christian campaign? And why did attempts to Sinify Christian doctrine and structure activate rather than allay criticisms? The answers are related partly to the message proclaimed in the publicity. The timing of the campaign, however, is also a function of the rapidly changing intellectual and political scene in China during the early 1920s.

Essays hailing the World's Student Christian Federation conference reflect the idealism, openness and contradictions of the New Culture Movement and like the writings of New Youth they do not speak with one voice. Christ, the guide for the reconstruction of China, becomes all things for all humankind; he is presented as a democrat, a revolutionary who fought tradition and abuse of authority, an advocate of the masses, an idealistic reformer who actualized his doctrine of love and charity, a respecter of national interests but also a proponent of international humanitarianism. Citing incidents from the Gospels, *Sheng-ming* called on Christians to work for political reform and to give priority to communal economic needs rather than those of the capitalist or the holder of private property; the social and economic order should be Christianized so that production was for use instead of profit.[49] An essayist in *Chung-hua kuei-chu,* on the other hand, argued that political, economic, even creedal reforms could accomplish little without renovation of the whole people; spiritual renewal beginning with the individual and extend-

1920-1922: First Stage

ing outward through family, society, nation and world was the means to achieving a truly democratic China and a harmonious international community.[50] "Moral power" was basic to all other forms of power. Christianity must be pared down to its essentials and youth must acknowledge that to be a real Christian was to live for society, not for self.

The message, or messages, in such amorphous form might seem unexceptional. They reflected the revivalist approach of the Protestant ethic and they accorded as well with the assumptions of Confucianism and the New Culture Movement that inner sagehood must find expression in outer kingliness. But for many reformist intellectuals the pronouncements remained irrelevant. Where was the practical model for social change? What, they wondered, was specifically Christian about the social reforms advocated by groups such as the Life Fellowship? They found little reason to accept Christianity in order to achieve their primary goal: building a new and strong China. For those turning toward radical activism, the proposals were hypocritical and deceiving. Yun Tai-ying ridiculed the China for Christ Movement and interpreted all Christian educational and social service activities as bribes, harmful to the Chinese polity.[51]

For the majority, they were an offense against Chinese nationalism. Christians were still arguing that the power of the West rested on a Christian base; their premise was that morality was identical with Christian morality and that Christianity was the source of Western progress. China could not hope for regeneration except through the Christianization of her society; she must follow in the footsteps of the superior West. Chinese found such assumptions ethnocentric and readily pointed out that Christendom had no monopoly on social virtues. Christians were presenting Western society in terms of its goals and treating Christendom's evils and failings as exceptions; simultaneously they seized upon the inadequacies of non-Christian civilizations as proof that Christianity was essential to the good society. The Social Gospel did not alter the inequality of a relationship in which the West was the teacher and the source of truth.[52]

Chinese Christians themselves endeavored to resolve

the contradictions but with little success. When they presented Chinese impressions of Christianity to the World's Student Christian Federation conference, they pointed out the dichotomy between the actions and the precepts of the Christian nations: declarations of justice and national sovereignty betrayed at Versailles, invocation of toleration clauses to demand indemnities and territorial concessions, pretensions to brotherhood and equality belied in the double standard for Chinese and Western preachers and teachers.[53] While acknowledging that a nation could be expected to pursue its own interest, they concluded: "But from the standpoint of Chinese Christians, suppose they were asked, Can all this above-mentioned aggression, oppression, conservatism, and unreality exist in a Christian country? What can they answer? They may say, China has many weak points, and should not blame others more than herself. But as to the countries of the West, they are 'Christian' and 'advanced'; they should feel more responsibility to act according to Christian truth. For as Jesus says: 'To whomsoever much is given, of him shall much be required'."

Chinese reformers who believed religion unessential to and separate from industrialism, science, and nationhood were apt to be less tolerant and kindly in their criticism of Christian missions. *Sheng-ming* requested statements from leaders of the New Culture Movement in order to acquaint the World's Student Christian Federation representatives with their religious views; institutionalized Christianity found favor with none of the five respondents.[54] Even those who acknowledged the contribution of mission hospitals, schools, and famine relief were not convinced that the benefits outweighed the losses; to the contrary, the evangelistic motivation behind the social services conjured up images of bribery. Although some noted the attractiveness of Christ's moral teachings, they found no merit in theology or "superstitious" rituals and myths, as they called them. Interviews with women of variant backgrounds elicited similar responses.

A major theme of the World's Student Christian Federation publicity was world brotherhood; youth were urged to look beyond the nation and become world-minded so that peace might reign. Christ preached the equality of all races and love of all humankind, not the division of the world into competing nations. Hoping to harmonize national loyalties and internationalism, Chinese Christians embraced both. They followed up their praises for world brotherhood, however, with pleas to the representatives from the West to suit deed to word. Such cosmopolitanism struck no responsive chord among most young Chinese nationalists. It was all very well, they said, for the rich and powerful nations to advocate internationalism; the oppressed peoples of the world had first to achieve sovereign nationhood.[55] Anyway, it was hypocrisy for the imperialists to preach internationalism since they practiced it only when it was to their benefit; it was evidence of the denationalization of Chinese Christians that they joined in the chorus.

Radicals found the growth of Christian organizations preaching the Social Gospel a threat rather than an auxiliary. With some justice, they questioned the Christians' commitment to social revolution and political activism. Among conservative evangelists, personal salvation was the prime goal so that individual rebirth, not the external environment, was crucial. The majority of missionaries subscribed to the doctrine of separation of church and state and they argued further that their extraterritorial status made a political stance on internal matters inappropriate. Even when evangelists continued to use diplomatic pressure in mission cases, they differentiated between actions to ensure implementation of the "toleration" clauses and those to prompt government action in other realms. Certain Christians, such as members of the Peking Sheng-ming she or the YMCA, did favor direct action to influence government policy but this was ordinarily on an individual basis. Those few advocating a public role for religious institutions and organizations met with great resistance. Christian educators might condone temporary suspension of academic routine in a national crisis, but they did not consider their students makers of revolution and they had little patience with extended disruption or extra-legal activity.

Despite the fact that numerous Christian groups cooperated in the demonstrations and boycotts of the May Fourth Movement, these activities were accorded little recognition and many nationalists were highly critical of what they termed minimal participation. During May,

1919, students from certain Christian colleges and middle schools had marched in the streets and helped organize the boycott of Japanese and British goods. Students in several of the colleges had formed student unions which became affiliated with the municipal and National Student Union while a number of Christian eduators expressed satisfaction at the opportunity to join the academic community in support of Chinese nationalism.[56] The Peking Missionary Association sent telegrams to the United States and British governments expressing fear that the Versailles settlement would jeopardize peace in East Asia and Chinese respect for Christendom.

The YMCA, which had a higher proportion of Chinese leadership than most Christian organizations, offered support in a variety of ways. In Shanghai and Peking, they made their facilities available for meetings of the Student Union and other patriotic associations. In Canton, they provided counsel to workers seeking to unionize. Radicalized and politicized by participation in May Fourth, Ch'ü Ch'iu-pai and his friends in Peking founded *Hsin she-hui* (New Society) "to disclose the evils of the old society and to establish a democratic new society", "to rally all forces in the interest of social reconstruction". Financial support came from *She-hui shih-chin hui* (Association for the Advancement of Society), an affiliate of the YMCA.[57] After six months, Peking banned the magazine for propagating anarchism and socialism.

But the national YMCA and most church organizations maintained an official position of neutrality. Administrators in the Christian schools quickly lost their enthusiasm for political activism by students and each successive disruption of the educational process met with declining tolerance. Christian educators generally put pressure on their students to resume academic responsibilities after making their views known and they were soon reporting with pride that their students had not engaged in the "excesses" of many of the nationalistic youth.

Critics cited the sequence of events at St. John's University, one of the most prestigious Christian schools.[58] For ten days during June, 1919, St. John's students held lectures and protest meetings, sent propaganda teams to nearby villages, and devoted themselves to the patriotic campaign. When, however, the students requested suspension of classes for the remainder of the term so that they could give full time to political activities, college officials closed the school and asked the students to leave campus. They argued that as an institution with extraterritorial rights in China, they could not harbor individuals who were openly defying government officials and policies. Six months later the college refused to sanction a strike called by the Shanghai Student Union but took no punitive action against the majority of students who demonstrated in Shanghai for four days instead of attending classes. Then, the following April, the administration not only refused to authorize a strike summoned by the National Student Union, but they forbade demonstrations on campus and required participating students to leave the premises. For New Youth at Peita and other government schools this placing of studies before politics was selfish and unpatriotic; the action of the Westerners was proof of intent to denationalize their pupils.

Practical as well as theoretical considerations reduced the Christians' role in the continuing revolution. They lacked a nationwide, disciplined organization and they were without the power of coercion in an environment where political power originated in military force. That Christian institutions would develop the requisite instruments for a political role or that many would even consider it fitting to function in such a fashion was implausible. Hsu Ch'ien had in 1918 instigated the founding of Chi-tu-chiao chiu-kuo chu-yi (Christian National Salvation Association), but the society, under Hsu's directorship, remained a loose and ineffectual organization.[59] The call of the World's Student Christian Federation for renovation of Chinese society led them eventually back to the traditional technique of seeking individual conversion. Dedicated Christians would be models for Chinese citizens; through their lives and work, they would illustrate the validity and relevance of the Christian ethic and they would inspire others to follow the doctrine of love and charity. While talking of the regeneration of China and the world, Christians came back full circle to a campaign to cultivate individuals of strong Christian character. It almost seemed that Christians had accepted Confucius' faith in the power of example.

One segment of the social reformist wing turned to data gathering and self-help projects.⁶⁰ Since specific information about incomes, literacy rates, landholding arrangements, even the average family size was lacking, the compiling of detailed statistics seemed a logical first step toward change. Thus, John S. Burgess and Sidney Gamble of Princeton-in-Peking and the YMCA conducted pioneering surveys of the life of rickshaw pullers and of the status and living conditions of Peking workers. Daniel H. Kulp of Shanghai Baptist College published one of the first village studies based on field work in China. The YMCA, the Yangtzepoo Social Center of Shanghai Baptist College, and other Christian institutions provided recreational facilities for factory workers and their children, organized literacy classes, set up day care centers, and ran Bible courses and lecture series on health, sanitation, and the evils of gambling, smoking and drinking. Such measures were palliatives which might aid individuals but could have little real influence on the lives of the masses. In the long run they served to accentuate the complexity of reform and its revolutionary implications. That the YMCA slogans for the 1920s were *"jen-ko ch'iu kuo"* (individual character to save China), "Christianize industry," and "Character-China's Hope" is understandable. The slogans were simultaneously an indication that Christian institutions were peripheral to the power struggle accompanying China's political and economic transformation.⁶¹

Chapter III

The 1922 Anti-Christian Compaign: Reactions

Essential to the Anti-Christian Campaign of 1922 were a renewed interest in political activism among intellectuals and accentuation of the anti-imperialist component in Chinese nationalism. The young radicals who telegraphed a protest against the WSCF meeting at Tsing Hua University were not seeking a review of the utility of religion. They announced the formation of Fei Chi-tu-chiao hsueh-sheng t'ung-meng (Anti-Christian Student Federation) and they exhorted all patriots to unite in a drive against the missionaries and their lackeys. Democracy, science, and religious freedom were not the bases for their opposition; for them, the enemy was capitalism. They denounced the church as the head of the plutocrats' assault column against China and they condemned the YMCA for creating "running dogs" of the capitalist class.

Though the composers of the initial declarations of the Anti-Christian Student Federation are unknown, the Shanghai branch of the Socialist Youth Corps (SYC), apparently was a participant and may well have taken the initiative. Chang Kuo-t'ao, *The Rise of the Chinese Communist Party, 1921-1927* and *Wu-ssu shih-ch'i ch'i-k'an chieh-shao* (Introduction to the Periodicals of the May Fourth Period) both credit the SYC with launching the movement, while two contemporary sources also make this claim. The language of the founding manifesto lends credence to this contention; Marxism-Leninism provided their vocabulary and the ideological framework.

"We know that in the world today, it is Capitalism that rules. Society is organized so that there are the class of property-holders who eat without working and the class of proletarians who work without obtaining the means to eat. In other words, on one side robbers and oppressors, on the other side the robbed and oppressed. Christianity and the Christian church are the evil demons who aid the capitalists in robbing the proletarians, who encourage those who possess, to oppress those who have nothing.

"We are convinced that capitalist society today, tyrannical and cruel, unreasonable and inhumane, ought to be destroyed without mercy. Consequently we declare that Christianity and the Christian church today, evil demons which aid the merchants in doing wrong are our enemies. We must battle against them in a war to the death. . . .

"The capitalists of every country . . . invade China in order to cut her to pieces and exploit her economically and the Christian church is the head of their assault column."²

Socialist organizations were among the first to respond to the March 9 declarations. *Hsien-ch'ü* (Pioneer), organ of the Socialist Youth Corps, issued a special Anti-Christian number six days after the founding of the Anti-Christian Federation. In addition to the constitution, telegram, and manifesto of the federation, the number included criticisms of Christianity by Ch'en Tu-hsiu, Tai Chi-t'ao, and Lo Ch'i-yuan, all prominent in the Socialist Youth Corps at the time.³ Other articles by Ch'ih Kuang (pseud. for Shih Ts'un-t'ung?), "Chi-tu-chiao yü shih-chieh kai-tsao" (Christianity and World Reform) and Lu Shu, "Chi-tu-chiao yü tzu-pen chu-i" (Christianity and Capitalism), condemned Christianity as a narcotic used by captialists and as a source of conflict and of intellectual oppression. On March 11, only two days after the Shanghai manifesto, Peking students announced the founding of an anti-religious federation; interested supporters were urged to contact Chin Chia-feng, a Peita student who had been active in socialist and anarchist groups in Shanghai and Peking.⁴ The rapidity of the responses suggests organizational ties possibly through branches of the Socialist Youth Corps.

Even though radical socialism did not characterize most young students in 1922, anti-imperialist nationalism according to the Hobson-Leninist thesis was fast becoming part of the vocabularly of New Youth. For over a quarter of a century nationalism had been a political force among urbanized intellectuals. Appreciation of the concept of national sovereignty had grown steadily, and since the examination candidates' condemnation of the Treaty of Shimonoseki in 1895, protests by scholars against infringements on Chinese sovereignty had punctuated her politics. During the 1920s Chinese nationalism acquired greater ideological coherence and force along with an increasing emphasis on anti-imperialism and populism. Historical events plus Marxist-Leninst theory underscored the anti-Western connotations.

The image of progressive Western Christendom, already blemished by World War I, was further eroded by the Versailles settlement. Despite talk of national self-determination and sovereignty, the capitalist democracies accepted compromises enhancing their power at the expense of lesser states. Japan's Twenty-One Demands, the Shantung agreement, and the Allied Expedition into Siberia all proved to Chinese that imperialism remained very much alive. It seemed furthermore, that Japan and the Western nations were only too willing to support the quarreling warlord factions of China in return for economic reward. As foreign manufactured goods and capital investment resumed their flow into the treaty ports, the portrait of capitalism in Shanghai and Canton was not pretty.

Little wonder that translations of anarchist and socialist writings met with a favorable response. Little wonder that the anti-capitalist, anti-imperialist explication of China's troubles spoke to Chinese of varying political persuasion. As several scholars have pointed out, Leninist nationalism displaced Social Darwinist nationalism. The source of China's weakness and disunity was not within, was no longer primarily the Manchus or the Han Chinese; the enemy came from without. This perspective "permitted a release from the bitterness of silent humiliation" before the Western reform model; external evils became responsible for many of China's problems. Capitalism, in this view, was not so much a Marxist stage of historical development as an aggressive force that found expression in imperialism.[5] The capitalists who dominated the governments in Washington, London, and Tokyo could not afford to abandon their imperialist privileges, according to the argument. In their desperate competition, they had to use every available avenue of influence, including the Chinese militarists and religious institutions. Chinese nationalists should accept no compromise with the capitalists and their minions. Within the nationalism of the 1920s, anti-imperialism and anti-capitalism had become interwoven with anti-militarism. For many, it was also interwoven with anti-Christianism and anti-Westernism.

Even the populism on which the New Culture Movement was based acquired new meaning. A major justification for the cultural revolution had been the need to build a popular base for the democracy supposedly established by the 1911 revolution. If the Chinese people were the true source of sovereignty, they must be prepared for the exercise of their political power; consequently, the Confucian value system which emphasized hierarchy, status, family, age, etc. must be destroyed. While idealizing the Chinese peasantry as carrier of Chinese nationhood, most activist intellectuals were actually urban dwellers. The down-trodden masses whom they saw were less apt to be tradition-bound villagers than proletarians in the treaty ports; here the economy and culture were Sino-Western hybrids and the plight of the worker derived from imperialism together with Confucianism.

Just as the revolutionaries considered the defects of Chinese society and culture causally related to Confucianism, so they assumed an inter-relationship between Christianity and imperialism. The presumption of a bonded ideology, polity, and culture held for revolutionaries as well as for reformers and conservatives. Populism and nationalism required a fight against cultural aggression as well as economic and political incursions. The Anti-Christian campaign was for its radical founders in Shanghai one aspect of the struggle against the capitalists, enemy of all Chinese nationalists, oppressor of the revolutionary proletariat.

For most radical intellectuals, however, the year 1922 was still a time of transition; few had made the shift from idealistic iconoclast to professional revolutionary. In the May Fourth tradition, the students assumed that they could and must speak for the nation. As the elite, they were responsible for making the truth known; as populists, they had faith that the people would provide support once awakened. The masses were considered objects to be revolutionized more than participants in the revolution and only after attaining understanding could they provide the popular sanction required for legitimacy. Transforming consciousness became a prerequisite to political action. The Shanghai telegram of March 9 opens with the students stating that they are resolved to protect the well-being of humanity; they are publishing the anti-Christian declaration so that "the public will recognize" what they know: Christianity and the Christian church have throughout history committed many crimes against humanity; they continue to do so in China.[6]

Practical as well as theoretical considerations dictated the emphasis on the written and spoken word. Regularized avenues of political action in the republic were underdeveloped; political parties were in their infancy, and the bureaucracy was not the maker of policy. Though a few politicized radicals had lost faith in the techniques of the New Culture Movement and were turning to party building, even Ch'en Tu-hsiu and Ch'ü Ch'iu-pai were at this time more interested in Marxism-Leninism as a new intellectual framework than as a guide to political action. Much work would be necessary before the revolutionary parties could become effective political instruments. The campaign weapons in 1922 were demonstrations and petitions, telegrams and manifestoes, essays and pamphlets. The Student Union, the Socialist Youth Corps, the Young China Association, and other May Fourth organizations provided the principal communication links. Despite change in the intellectual climate since 1919, the May Fourth tradition dominated the anti-Christian campaign in that publicity was the major technique and New Youth the major audience.

COURSE OF THE 1922 ANTI-CHRISTIAN CAMPAIGN

The Shanghai radicals, having founded the Anti-Christian Student Federation, ended their March 9 declaration by summoning students, youth and workers to rise up and join the battle against capitalism.

Students! Youth! Workers! Who of you can ignore the misdeeds of capitalism? Who of you can ignore that capitalists are cruel and heartless beings? How can we fail to rise against them when we see with our own eyes their spies holding a conference for our loss? Rise up! Rise up! Rise up! [7]

Two days later Peking responded with the formation of Fei tsung-chiao ta t'ung-meng. The change in name from anti-Christian to anti-religion federation is significant. Though Christianity was still the primary focus of attack, the change indicated that religion would be condemned in the name of science, progress, and intellectual freedom as well as national sovereignty. The campaign would cross generational and political lines and build on the potent anti-Christian tradition. Peita radicals may have been the initiators of the drive in the north but a circular telegram issued on March 21 welcomed adherents of any race, age or sex and included the signatures of such intellectual leaders as Li Ta-chao and Li Shih-tseng.[8] The president of the federation was Hsiao Tzu-sheng, a former associate of Mao Tse-tung in Hsin min hsueh hui (New Peoples' Study Society) and Hua-Fa chiao-yü hui (Franco-Chinese Education Society). Hsiao was, however, an apologist for anarchism and socialism rather than communism and he would eventually join the KMT. Activists included two Peking students: Chin Chia-feng, who was secretary, and Miao Po-ying, one of the founders of the Peking Socialist Youth Corps.

The differing emphasis of the Peking and Shanghai telegrams reflected the ambiance of each originating city.[9] Though political activism was on the rise, Peking was still the proud center of the New Culture Movement and the criticisms of religion were those of intelligentsia seeking to destroy tradition and to discover new intellectual foundations for China. A Peking declaration on March 21 attacked all religions; instead of mentioning imperialism, capitalism, or class struggle, it reiterated many arguments from the pages of *Shao nien:* the contradiction between religious superstition and human progress through science, the missions' use of bribery to indoctrinate immature youth, and so forth. Shanghai, which exemplified capitalist imperialism in China and which was a haven for radical activists, indicated the turn of many nationalists toward revolutionary politics. For them, the anti-Christian campaign was one aspect of the drive to restore Chinese unity and sovereignty by ousting the militarists and imperialists; it was an initial step in a revolution against capitalism, with Christianity being targeted first as the weakest link. But Shanghai was also the prototype of the hybrid culture developing in China; it was condemned for its "comprador" culture even as it was becoming a national center for the printing industry, the Chinese press, literateurs, and party builders. The locus of political dynamism and intellectual ferment in China was shifting south.

Common to the declarations of both were the acrimony and indignation characteristic of the anti-Christian tradition. Peking fulminated against the virulent religious vermin infecting a China that had formerly been clean, i.e., irreligious. Shanghai prodded all virile youth to rise up against those who sucked the blood of the Chinese people. Both were aware of recent Christian publicity and activism and declared that such expansionism had created a crisis situation. Both included Western scholarship in their battle gear.

The anti-Christian declarations swiftly provoked a paper war. During March and April numerous groups proclaimed their support in manifestoes and telegrams; Peking *Ch'en pao* (Morning Post), for example, published formal statements of adherence by some thirty partisans.[10] Taking the lead were students in government institutions such as Peita, Peking Higher Normal University, National Southeastern University at Nanking, the provincial normal colleges of Chihli and Shansi, etc. Also prominent were youth organizations such as the several different Shanghai youth leagues that issued public pronouncements. A number of the pieces linked the Washington Conference, the rising power of capitalist America, and the growing threat of Christian missions. A manifesto by the Socialist Youth Corps of Peking, for instance, stated that at the Washington Conference, the missions had decided on a plan to exploit the entire world.[11] Earlier, a student had criticized the Chinese delegation at Washington as not representative of Chinese nationalist sentiment; all three delegates, he pointed out, were returned students from America and two of the three were products of mission institutions run by Americans; the intellectual subservience of the delegates was only too characteristic of parochial students, he concluded.[12]

Perhaps a couple of dozen branches of the Anti-Christian Federation or the Anti-Religion Federation were organized in urban centers having a high concentration of educational and mission institutions. Typical was the Nanking anti-religion committee, which announced its formation in a proclamation including 120 signatures and shortly thereafter issued a manifesto accusing Christians of producing divisions in China and of using bribery to attract converts.[13]

Party journals such as *Min-kuo jih-pao, Hsien-ch'ü* and *Chueh-wu* opened their pages to the campaign. The April 7 issue of *Chueh-wu,* for example, printed criticisms of Christianity and Christian missions by Wang Ching-wei, Ch'en Tu-hsiu, and Shen Yen-ping (Mao Tun); it also published many of the proclamations of support and reproduced the speeches of the April 9 rally protesting the World's Student Christian Federation meeting. Following its airing of the March 9 Manifesto of the Shanghai Anti-Christian Student Federation, *Min-kuo jih-pao* published critiques of religion and of Christian evangelism by Chinese of varying persuasion: Wang Hsing-kung, Li Shih-tseng, Ts'ai Yuan-p'ei, and Wang Ching-wei among others. In the highly respected *Tung-fang tsa-chih* ("Eastern Miscellany"), Liang Ch'i-ch'ao welcomed the Anti-Christian Federation as a sign of national vitality, though he favored open debate on the merits of religion rather than an aggressive campaign by either the pro-religionists or the anti-religionists.[14] Many of the New Culture magazines, *Shao-nien, Hsin ch'ing-nien, Hsueh-sheng tsa-chih* (Students' Magazine), *Che-hsueh,* took up the issue and even such opponents of the new literature as *Hsueh heng* entered the fray.[15] A major publicity outlet was the Japanese-owned *Shun-t'ien shih-pao* (Shun-t'ien Times), which added criticisms of Christian missions from the Japanese viewpoint.[16]

Canton, rapidly becoming a focal point for both KMT and CCP radicals, voiced support. One of the most prominent advocates was Wang Ching-wei, close associate of Sun Yat-sen and chair of the Kwangtung Educational Association. In a telegram to the Canton Educational Association, he commended the work of sweeping out the "poison of religion" and in an article on the errors of Christianity he referred to an evangelistic poster in illustrating its narrow exclusiveness.[17]   According to a placard in Canton First Public Park, "Believers in Jesus will enjoy life in paradise; non-believers will suffer in hell." Wang argued that such a belief was typical of the intolerance that had led to disasters like the Crusades, persecution of the Jews, and Christian colonizing throughout the world; autocratic, bigoted Christianity contradicted Chinese educational principles and was the enemy of science and democracy.

Ch-ün-pao (The Masses), edited by three young communists, T'an Chih-t'ang, Ch'en Kung-po and T'an P'ing-shan, was the source of much of the anti-Christian publicity in Canton.[18]   The Higher Normal School and the Law College in Canton where the T'ans held posts were important centers. In May, 1922 the Socialist Youth Corps held its first national congress in Canton and passed resolutions supporting the anti-Christian and anti-religious organizations and attacking the YMCA.[19]

Though left-wing groups instigated the attacks in several cities and furnished much of the copy, they were not alone. Indicative of the widespread appeal of the anti-Christian campaign was the commendation by *Chiao-yü tsa-chih* (Educational Review).[20] The editorial support was restrained, for the *Review* had recently expressed concern over the frequency of student storms and the triviality of some of the confrontations; nevertheless, this voice of the educational establishment and the older generation endorsed the movement as an example of positive student activism. Why? The justification was very much within the culturalist and elitist outlook of the New Culture movement. The campaign, according to the editorial, indicated an awareness of the need to change many aspects of Chinese society, not just politics; religion could not save China; it only deflected energy from the real problems; China needed science. The commentator concluded with the hope that the movement would expand to include all students and intellectuals. It should, however, be restricted to the educated class because if it should spread to the rural masses, their anger over religious oppression might lead to another Boxer tragedy. The author thus expressed the ambivalence of many Chinese reformers toward the West; he offered assurances that opposition to religion was not an expression of anti-Westernism; he acknowledged simultaneously the prevalent antagonism toward Christian missions and the urgency of avoiding violence that might lead to foreign reprisal and further national losses.

Through the spring the battle of words continued. Handbills and leaflets poured from the presses for distribution at anti-Christian rallies, religious assemblies, and demonstrations on national days, such as May 4. The Anti-Christian Federation reprinted articles from the *Shao-nien* issues on religion and from *Hsien-chü* in a booklet entitled *Wo-men wei shen-ma fan tui shih-chieh Chi-tu-chiao hsueh-sheng t'ung-meng?* (Why Do We Oppose the WSCF?). In June the Peking Anti-Religion Federation put out a larger collection of some three hundred pages, thereby making available many of the proclamations and essays published during the height of the campaign. It also reproduced a map showing the location and extent of Protestant mission work in China; the map, reprinted from *The Christian Occupation in China* and designed to demonstrate the rapid expansion of Christianity in China since 1900, carried the caption, "The Spreading Infection of Religious Poison".[21] In Paris Chou En-lai reviewed the anti-Christian pamphlet for the European organ of the Socialist Youth Corps.[22] The April, 1922 issue of *Shao-nien* published an article entitled "Wo-men pu kai fan-tui Yeh-chiao yü chi yun-tung ma?" (Shouldn't We Oppose Christianity and Its Works?) by Ch'en Ch'i-t'ien, a prominent member of the Young China Association and one of those liberal and anarchist teachers recruited to Hunan First Normal College in 1920. Criticisms of Christianity, Ch'en said, did not arise out of xenophobia but as a consequence of Christian missions' infringement on freedom of belief in their schools and denial of scientific findings in their teachings. Another article in the July issue of *Shao-nien* found the anti-Christian campaign necessitated by the aggressiveness of Christian propagandists.[23]

A minor controversy erupted when on March 31, 1922

five Peita professors and New Culture leaders issued a statement criticizing activists of the Anti-Religion Federation for infringing on religious freedom.²⁴ Ch'en Tu-hsiu, Shen Yen-ping, Li Shih-tseng, and Ts'ai Yuan-p'ei promptly defended the right of non-believers to organize and propagandize in response to the zealous proselytizing of Christian missions; the latter with their dogmatism and required religious activities in parochial schools were the real transgressors against freedom.

A few examples of direct action can be cited. In Canton about fifty representatives of the Anti-Christian Federation invaded a YMCA meeting and repeatedly interrupted the speaker with demands for immediate answers to their accusations. After heated debate, the anti-Christians opposed an attempt to adjourn before their viewpoint had an adequate hearing; the meeting broke up in disorder as the intruders threw anti-Christian pamphlets and leaflets in the air. Similar tactics were used to terminate a YMCA meeting in Shanghai and a small group attacked a Canton street chapel, prompting the female missionary in charge to request a proclamation of protection for the chapel.²⁵ Chinese Christian students in France protested that their subsidies had been cut because the Society for Frugal Study had decided against aid to believers. In Peking the Student Anti-Religion Federation protested to Tsing Hua University students over the use of government facilities for religious purposes and asked for support in preserving the purity of the national education of youth and the separation of church and state. As the WSCF conference concluded on April 9, the Peking Anti-Religion Federation held a rally at Peita; approximately three thousand students and young intellectuals were reported to have cheered speeches by Hsiao Tzu-sheng, Ts'ai Yuan-pei, and Li Shih-tseng emphasizing the uselessness of religion in the modern world.²⁶

The Anti-Religion Federation, however, made no effort to prevent or disrupt the WSCF meetings; nor did it seek direct confrontations with government officials. Most churches and parochial schools continued their activities with little or no interruption. Upon occasion, local administrators restricted student activities; for example, in Wuhu, Anhwei, the civil governor and the police chief accused the anti-Christians of fomenting dissension; they demanded tranquility lest a second Boxer Rebellion occur. Certain periodicals, especially the English language ones, criticized the discourtesy toward foreign guests and the juvenile quality of the protestations, while some attributed the activities to the influence of a few Bolsheviks.[27] An article in the *China Weekly Review* by a St. John's graduate specifically denied the denationalizing influence of mission schools and stated that on the contrary some of China's leading patriots were Christians. If authorities simply ignored the Anti-Christian Movement, it would die, for the fickle students would soon move on to other "anti" movements, editorialized the *China Weekly Review*.[28] Perhaps out of concern for world opinion, the Peking government accorded the WSCF conference members a conspicuous welcome: special transportation rates for sightseeing in China, a reception by President Hsu Shih-ch'ang, and a luncheon tendered by former President Li Yuan-hung and the Tientsin Chamber of Commerce.[29]

The campaign itself showed little progress or development and activities by anti-Christian and anti-religion associations tapered off sharply as students dispersed for summer holidays. The students seem to have spent themselves in the propaganda techniques of May Fourth: staging parades and public assemblies to arouse and educate the populace, issuing pronouncements, manifestoes, and open letters for distribution as handbills and for publication in newspapers, periodicals, and pamphlets, founding associations to publicize the cause, securing statements from and providing a forum for speeches by intellectuals popular with youth. The major activity recorded for the Peking Anti-Religion Federation in August was participation, along with thirteen other societies, in a reception organized by Li Ta-chao to welcome A. A. Joffe, Soviet envoy to Peking. Joffe presented the thesis that the U.S. had now become the great imperialist power and since China needed a social revolution like that of the U.S.S.R., he hoped to work for improved Sino-Soviet relations.[30] Even after students returned from the summer break, however, most branch associations of the anti-Christian and anti-religion federations remained dormant.

One explanation for the brevity and looseness of the anti-Christian campaign of 1922 was the gap between radicalized intellectuals moving toward political activism and liberals continuing the New Culture emphasis on educational and intellectual reform. For both groups nationalism was a primary value so that a specific incident perceived as a threat to the life of the nation could temporarily paste over differences. The May Fourth and May Thirtieth Movements were such occasions. The meeting of the WSCF at Tsing Hua was, however, not in the same category as the Versailles decision on the Shantung concessions or the shooting of student demonstrators on May 30th. Though concern over the ambitions of Social Gospel Christianity and over recent church growth was real, the conference created no sense of national crisis. No specific event galvanized national emotions to override political and intellectual differences; no specific goal inspired New Youth to carry the cause to the urban populace.

The campaign, furthermore, lacked a carrier movement to provide continuity and structure, while the Anti-Christian Federation itself never developed the discipline or strategy to give direction to branch associations. By 1922 the National Student Union was in decline, with most students concentrating on careerist concerns and the radical minority dominating its executive committees. Neither the Kuomintang nor the Chinese Communist Party was yet ready to offer guidance and organization. No cultural brokers linked the campaign to the masses. Even though the leaders believed themselves spokesmen for the nation, the Anti-Christian Movement of 1920-1922 remained an in-group, elitist affair. Under these circumstances, differences among intellectuals had free play and divergencies in methodology and goals were endemic.

As indicated above, documentary evidence points to the vital role of the Socialist Youth Corps and other radical groups, especially during the early stages of the campaign. The movement was for them part of a long-range struggle to revolutionize all of Chinese society. The transformation of politics, economics, and culture was integral to the holistic struggle. Contributing to the strength of the left was the Marxist historical framework that provided broad categories for defining good and evil while also assuring eventual victory. Marxists argued that the real enemy was capitalism, but since the Christian church was the tool of the capitalists and Christian missions the vanguard of imperialism, one could not be anti-capitalist without also being anti-Christian.[31] Marxian references to religion as an opiate employed by the ruling class had special poignancy in China and references to the Opium Wars of the mid-19th century clinched many an argument. Within this context, criticism by radicals concentrated on the church and missions rather than Christian doctrine.

The campaign coincided with a turning away from the West on the part of revolutionary nationalists and some of the literature assumed a specifically anti-American tinge. It was logical, radicals asserted, that the leading capitalist nation, i.e., the U.S., should also be the major supporter of missions. When Marxists fused disappointment over the failure of the 1922 Washington Conference to return Shantung concessions with resentment toward the WSCF meetings, they touched a raw nerve. Delineating good and bad along class lines, they interpreted both events as instruments used by the capitalists for their own imperial purposes. A circular by Chungking students criticized the naivete of Chinese who looked to the U.S. for help against Japan; in both countries, the government and the military forces were in the hands of the capitalists; why shouldn't the two nations back each other in their plunders?[32] In designating the enemy, Marxists frequently distinguished between the people and the capitalists, but they, nevertheless, condemned numerous organizations as pawns of the capitalists. The Boy Scouts, it was said, had been used by Western and Chinese merchants during a recent Hong Kong seamen's strike; the YMCA, financially dependent on the American and Chinese business communities, could advocate only palliatives, not the drastic alteration of the power structure required in China.[33]

Students even more than their elders, viewed the struggle in puristic terms and painted the foe in broad strokes. Even as they assured public authorities that they had no intention of using violence and that fears of another Boxer Rebellion were groundless, New Youth proclaimed that they would sacrifice their lives to the campaign, if necessary, that they stood ready to shed their blood to rid China of the Christian vermin. If in 1922 such language proved to be hyperbole, it had not always been so and the ever-present possibility of direct action lent reality to the emotional appeals to martyrdom. Hopefully, the polemics would inspire the kind of commitment incompatible with reasoned, balanced discussion.

Though the socialists' criticisms of the church carried conviction for many Chinese, their approach had certain weaknesses in the China of 1922. They were not able to control the movement or to expand it into a mass compaign. They might write in theoretical class terms, but they were children of the elite and their actual contact with the masses was minimal; in fact, they made little effort to incorporate the proletariat. Most Chinese, whether workers or bourgeoisie, had not attained the class consciousness that would make meaningful an appeal based on class struggle. In mid-April a workers' congress declared its adherence to the anti-religious movement and uged all laborers to accept the guidance of the students in resisting the blandishments of evangelists; twenty-seven workers in Canton were reported to have joined the campaign.[34] These, however, are almost isolated incidents.

The activities and outlook of the campaigners, like those of most radical party leaders in 1922, were those of moral foreknowers, rather than those of professional revolutionaries and organizers. Essentially the radical intellectuals were talking to themselves and to other educated youth. To hope to oust the Christian church from China via dialogue was hardly realistic. To be effective the attacks would have to be directed toward a more limited and attainable objective, one within the province of intellectuals. The campaign would need political and military backing and this in turn was dependent upon party expansion and coordination. Though the Socialist Youth Corps outnumbered the Chinese Communist Party in the spring of 1922, it could only claim approximately 15 branches and 2000 members. Finally, the campaign would require an environment in which anti-imperialist nationalism overrode all other considerations.

Among the anti-Christians of the generation born in

the late 19th century, many were educators who had studied abroad. A sizable contingent were anarchists or former anarchists; some were liberals, a few were communists. Anarchism was actually losing favor among intellectuals by 1922, for the pull of nationalism was too strong and the need for organized power too great. Because, however, many anarchists had not yet found a political and ideological home, iconoclasm continued to influence their outlook. Participation in the Anti-Christian Movement, therefore, was consonant with their predilections. After all, Chinese anarchist magazines of the first two decades of the 20th century had included religion among their targets; the Japanese mentor for many young Chinese radicals, Kotoku Shusui, had been outspokenly anti-Christian, and a core of those opposing religion had been members of the Paris branch of the Young China Association that originally proposed banning membership to all believers.[35]

With the exception of the communist members of this generation, their brief against Christianity in particular and religion in general shows some interesting similarities. They perceived the campaign in a more restricted framework than the Marxists. For them, the battle against religion was more a continuation of the New Culture Movement than a historical stage in revolution. Though some concurred with the communists in condemning capitalism and visualizing a classless, stateless communalism, they saw as their immediate task the destruction of all deterrents to the triumph of science. Members of this generation frequently had embarked on a classical Chinese education but had switched to a Western curriculum while still young, often gaining part of their training abroad. The necessity of obliterating a segment of their personal experience contributed to their emphasis on nihilism. As Ch'en Ch'i-t'ien put it, "We have just been struggling to break the hold of Confucian tradition, why should we permit another outmoded ideology, Christianity, to spread its influence in China?"[36]

The anarchists and former anarchists, like the liberals, therefore, placed a high value on freedom. In accord with the New Culture outlook, freeing the individual from outmoded social bonds, values, and beliefs still held priority over disciplining him for political action.

Religious faith, they said, restricted the ability to criticize and inhibited acceptance of new concepts. Religious ritual and mythology, in the words of Yü Chia-chü, denigrated man as a rational being. Their opposition, therefore, extended beyond religion as a doctrine to religion as an institution.[37] It was the church, especially the Christian church, which aggressively insisted on its monopoly of truth.

These counter-culture intellectuals turned their ire particularly against parochial schools. Compulsory Bible courses and religious activities infringed on individual freedom and indoctrinated youth before they reached the age of discrimination. Thus, they pinpointed the future object of attack in the Movement to Restore Educational Rights and formulated some of its arguments.

There was, nonetheless, a difference. In 1922 the dominant theme was intellectual freedom and the right to question. Ts'ai Yuan-p'ei spoke for many when he called for an education independent of both religion and politics; subsequently, Peking educators founded Ch'üan-kuo chiao-yü tu-li yun-tung hui (National Association for Educational Independence) to defend educational autonomy.[38] According to the president of the Anti-Religion Federation, his organization followed the dictates of neither nationalism, nor socialism, nor any political party, only those of science and liberty.[39] When Chung-hua chiao-yü kai-chin she (National Association for the Advancement of Education) met in July, Hu Shih, T'ao Meng-ho (L.K.Tao), and Ting Wen-chiang (V.K. Ting) proposed a resolution forbidding all religious instruction and ritual in elementary schools.[40]

Educators in 1922 inveighed against indoctrination in any dogma but they also saw threats to freedom in the traditional association of politics and culture and in the fiscal needs of warlords. Having been educated abroad and having accepted much from Western culture, they insisted that anti-Christianism was separable from anti-Westernism just as Christianity was separable from Western civilization. Though resentful of foreign aggression, they had not joined the radicals in rejecting the Western reform model after World War I, Versailles, and the Bolshevik Revolution. They were opposed to all who infringed on the liberty of the individual and of the educational system, whether they were government officials appointing political hacks as university administrators, or warlords depleting educational budgets for their own purposes, or parochial educators presiding over autonomous schools that championed a specific religion.

The older generation, even more than the students, hoped to accomplish their goals through the written or spoken word. They not only did not seek mass support or confrontation tactics, but they indicated that they would not welcome them. They used their professional associations as lobbies to influence the Ministry of Education but essentially they, like radical youth, relied on a war of telegrams, manifestoes, essays, and letters to the editors. Such weapons were ineffective against militarists, imperialists, or evangelists.

The movement, nevertheless, was not without significance. It laid the groundwork both intellectually and organizationally for the Educational Rights Movement of 1924-1928. It pointed up the expanding role of the mission schools and their use for Christian indoctrination. Christianity was increasingly viewed as unessential to Western power and wealth; thus it appeared less necessary to tolerate the privileges of foreign evangelists.

For Christian missions in China the 1920-1922 movement was a turning point, a fact that only gradually became apparent as a result of reactions by the home churches and by Chinese associated with Christian institutions. The campaign, furthermore, marked a transitional stage between the New Culture Movement and united front politics. It demonstrated the continuing and broad appeal of the anti-Christian tradition and the decisive role of anti-imperialism in China's revolution. Party builders would not ignore the lesson. When education became tied to revolutionary nationalism and the student movement after May Thirtieth, the Christian schools were considered an intolerable infringement on Chinese sovereignty.

RESPONSES TO THE CAMPAIGN

The Anti-Christian Movement stimulated relatively little dialogue between the separate circles of Christian and non-Christian intellectuals. Yü Chia-chü of the Young China Association remarked in the summer of 1922 on the failure of Christians to reply to the attacks and attributed the silence to ignorance; most Chinese Christians, he said, lacked real understanding of their faith since they had accepted Christianity either to fill their rice bowls or to show filial respect for their Christian parents.[41] Wang Chih-hsin in his *Chung-kuo Chi-tu-chiao shih kang* (Outline History of Christianity in China) noted the minimal response of Christians.[42] Though the reverberations were surprisingly few and minor, the reaction in Christian circles was more significant than most Chinese realized. The reasons for the limited number of rebuttals and for the fact that even these rarely came to the attention of Chinese intellectuals are indicative of the problems of the Christian church. Underlined once again were the isolation of the adult Christian community, and with it, potential for misunderstanding and misjudgment on both sides.

Many Western Christians were deceived by the brevity and the urban elitist character of the campaign. Missionaries working in interior towns and villages had been only indirectly affected by the New Culture Movement; they were scarcely touched by the Anti-Christian Movement; little response could be expected from them. Even in the metropolitan centers, missionaries often found their clientele among the lower middle class and the poor, not among the academic elite, who were the source of the anti-Christian literature. Neither the missionaries nor most of their converts habitually read such periodicals as *Shao-nien, Chueh-wu,* or *Hsin ch'ing-nien*; most criticisms reaching them were apt to be in the toned-down versions of Christian magazines or the disparaging reports of newspapers like the *North China Herald*. Quite understandably, the attacks struck many as one more expression of the long-lived anti-Christian tradition rather than a new threat. Amid the political disorder and intellectual ferment of China during the 1920s, sorting out the dominant trends was not easy.[43] More than one missionary found consolation in the thought that persecution had ever been the lot of Christians; they had only to retain faith in the eventual triumph of truth and to work even harder to clear up misconceptions; the mote was in the eye of the critics, not of the harbingers of the Gospel.

Those Westerners most likely to have their work affected were educators and YMCA secretaries. Even their awareness of the campaign was dulled by their preoccupation with day-to-day responsibilities, limited facility in Chinese, and the turmoil of the Chinese environment.⁴⁴ The Anti-Christian Movement, furthermore, was centered in the government universities with which they had limited contact; in 1923, for example, youth leader Wu Yao-tsung stated that only a dozen of the 180 YMCA branches were in national institutions.⁴⁵

Some information in English was, however, available. To acquaint readers with the debate over religion in 1920-1921, *The Chinese Recorder* had run a series entitled "What the Chinese are thinking about Christianity."⁴⁶ Most of the essays were by Chinese Christians, who prefaced their criticisms of methodology with acknowledgment of the necessity of faith and appreciation of the good works of missionaries. Supplementing these, however, were occasion translations or summaries of articles from *Shao nien* and *Hsing ch'ing-nien*. *Shengming* put out an English language edition in March 1922 on the occasion of the WSCF conference; included were comments on Christianity by several agnostic New Culture proponents and a translation of the Shanghai Manifesto by the Anti-Christian Federation. Remarking on the manifesto, the editors found it propagandistic and immature, but written in a forcible, appealing vernacular; "the tone of the circular is too partisan, too unbalanced to deserve any discussion, but it gives us Christians and the delegates to the Federation Conference tiely food for thought and basis for searching self-examination."⁴⁷

The May 1922 edition of *Shang-hai kuang-tung Chunghua Chi-tu-chiao hui yueh-pao* inserted an English language editorial on "The Non-Christian Student Federation." Expressing relief that the WSCF conference had not been marred by the anti-religion protestors, the editor viewed attacks on religion as part of a world-wide phenomenon in which "every sanction is questioned, and every authority is doubted. . . . In the long run this movement is not likely to injure Christianity which thrives best under persecution."[48] John Mott, president of the conference, observed that if the anti-Christian agitators could do more for humanity than the Christians, then believers should imitate them; but, if not, the world would soon learn to expect no benefit from those opposing religion; in the latter case, Christians could afford to ignore the attacks.

Except for brief comments in the April 1922 issue of the (Christian) *Educational Review* and the May issue of the *Chinese Recorder,* however, specific and detailed response to the Anti-Christian Campaign in English language publications was belated. In December, 1922, the *Recorder* printed an article by Chao Tzu-ch'en entitled, "Christians and Non-Christians Reply to the Anti-Religion Movement".[49] All of the respondents mentioned were Chinese publishing in Chinese language periodicals. In addition to the five professors who had protested that anti-Christian activists were threatening religious freedom, Chao quoted Liang Ch'i-ch'ao at some length; he pointed out that though Liang courteously saluted the anti-religion movement as a sign of serious intellectual consideration of the important question of religion, Liang devoted most of his speech to differentiating between science, which is the product of reason, and faith, which is the product of emotion; both reason and emotion were integral to human nature. Liang, furthermore, stated that the anti-religionists might be well advised to direct their ire at superstitious folk cults rather than at Christianity, which had brought benefits to China. Also included in the December issue of *Chinese Recorder* was Chao's translation of an essay from the June edition of *Hsueh heng*. Liu Po-ming (K.S. Liu), a Christian and a professor of philosophy at Southeastern University (later National Central University), criticized students for blindly joining in a general attack on religion instead of undertaking a scholarly investigation of the content and nature of Christianity.[50] Most of the Christian dogmas and ecclesiastical regulations to which they were objecting, were unessential to Christianity, he concluded.

At the request of the Peking Missionaries' Association, three leaders of the city YMCA, Chang Ch'in-shih, Wu Yao-tsung, and Hu Hsueh-ch'eng, offered a symposium on the Anti-Christian Movement in December 1922.[51] In 1923 the *China Mission Year Book* commissioned essays exploring the relationship between Chinese students and the Christian church while the *Chinese Recorder* in August 1923 provided several Chinese Christian responses under the heading, "The Intellectual Awakening of Young China."[52]

By the time these materials appeared, the campaign was quiescent and it was easy to dismiss it as a Roman candle sent up by a small group of extremists. *The Chinese Recorder* editorialized in November, 1922: "We are all interested in watching that fluctuating thermometer, the Chinese Student Mind....The present Chinese student mind is good soil for revolutionary influences. This socialistic tendency of the student mind is also seen in the formation by the weakening anti-religious movement of a 'Socialist Young Men's Association.'...Moreover, the whole tale is told when we recognize that the Chinese Student Mind is strongly motivated by the joy of protesting!"[53] In listing the four outstanding events of Chinese Christianity in 1922, a professor at the University of Nanking included the WSCF conference, but not the Anti-Christian Campaign.[54]

The acrimonious criticisms, nevertheless, shocked some well-informed missionaries into a realization of the need for review. Simultaneously, the brevity of the paper war persuaded them that such reassessment could be undertaken with all due deliberation and that Christians would retain control of the process; the churches would be able to dictate the nature as well as the timing of the readjustments. Thus, Frank Rawlinson of the *Recorder* admonished Christians to study the basis for linking Christianity with capitalism and imperialism and to consider what might be altered.[55] The nationalistic agnostics, he said, identified old Chinese superstitions with Christianity and failing to distinguish between the actions of Christians and the ideals of Christianity; now was the chance to clear up misconceptions. Some evangelists assumed the determinedly optimistic view that the new interest of Chinese students in religion presented an unparalleled opportunity; since iconoclasts were a small minority, proselytism among the great majority without prejudice should be intensified.

One missionary boldly recommended in the July 1923 issue of the (Christian) *Educational Review* that Christians re-examine the issue of compulsory religious activities in parochial schools; he personally could see some merit in a monitored voluntary system that would challenge teachers of religion to raise the quality of their work. Another missionary responded that Chinese hostility toward religious requirements was just a school-boy grouse, not a deep-seated antipathy; the issue would "come to a head soon if we wish it to, and not otherwise." [56] According to a visitor to China in late August, 1922, most missionaries, if queried, would agree that "Orientals" would eventually be capable of conducting their own schools, hospitals, and industries, "but only after years and years of teaching by Christian (i.e., Western) nations. Pressed for an estimate of the period of tutelage, the missionaries answer vaguely indicating a long, long time." [57] Calls for re-examination frequently expressed the hope that the trials would deepen the commitment of Christians, for individual re-dedication was the best answer to criticisms.

A small but energetic cluster of Chinese Christians in Peking, Shanghai, and Canton offered rebuttals, many of which differed from those of Westerners in that they were prompt and they urged drastic and rapid change. Since the authors lacked access to the leading journals of the New Culture Movement, they generally published in Christian journals: the YMCA's *Ch'ing-nien chin-pu, Sheng-ming* in Peking, *Chen kuang tsa-chih* (True Light Review), a Baptist publication, and *Shang-hai kuang-tung Chung-hua Chi-tu-chiao hui yueh-pao*. On May 7, 1922, a Christian in Changsha, Hsu Ch'ing-yü published at his own expense a booklet entitled "The Anti-Religion Federation and a Church Revolution." [58] These were in-house organs serving tight little Christian circles, for the days when Chinese looked to Christian periodicals for information about the West were long since gone. The essays, directed to Christian audiences, could and did go unnoticed by most Chinese intellectuals and students, thus creating the impression of lack of response.⁵⁹

Many of the respondents shared characteristics which set them apart from the general church membership. Quite a few belonged to independent churches administered by Chinese instead of missionaries, for example, the Mi-Shih Chinese Christian Church in Peking and the Union Baptist Church for Cantonese in Shanghai. They included pastors, educators, and secretaries of the YMCA, an institution that had consistently fostered indigenization. They were well educated, frequently enjoying the status of returned students with graduate degrees in addition to their Christian college diplomas. As nationalists, they believed in their ability and authority to interpret Christianity for Chinese and were already deeply involved in the Sinification of Christian institutions. Several had participated in the organization of such activist societies as Chung-hua kuei-chu, Sheng-ming she, and the YMCA. Radical changes in Christianity created few problems of identity for them; they would not experience the sense of personal loss that a product of Western Christendom might. The Westerners, taking Christianity as a given, were cognizant of the sectarian differences; the Chinese, contrasting Christianity with the Chinese religious heritage, saw the commonalities.

In contrast to the Westerners, not all the Chinese apologists belonged to the liberal wing of Christianity. The majority certainly emphasized the Social Gospel, but some of the most articulate and prolific defenders were conservatives like Chang I-ching and Liang Chün-mo. In two special issues of *Chen kuang,* Chang, Liang, and their colleagues offered point by point refutations of the accusations by Ch'en Tu-hsiu, Wang Ching-wei, and the essayists in *Hsien-ch'ü*.⁶⁰ Among the liberal spokesmen were Chien Yu-wen (Timothy Jen), Hsu Pao-ch'ien, Hu I-ku (Y.K. Woo), and Wu Yao-tsung. The May issue of the *Cantonese Union Church Bulletin* answered the charges of the March 9 Manifesto with an English-language editorial as well as signed declarations and articles in Chinese.⁶¹ Chien Yu-wen, editor of the *Bulletin* and pastor of the Church of Christ for Cantonese in Shanghai, also defended religion in two books published by the YMCA press: *Tsung-chiao yü k'o-hsueh* (Religion and Science) and *Hsin tsung-chiao kuan* (The New Religious

View). At a Student Training Conference sponsored by the YMCA during the summer of 1922, the delegates drew up declarations advocating an autonomous Chinese church free of superstition and exhorting youth to unite the responsibilities of citizenship and church membership. Other rejoiners came from such prominent members of the Christian community as Chao Tzu-ch'en, Lu Chih-wei, Yu Jih-chang (David Z.T. Yui), Fan Tzu-mei (T.M. Van), Wu Lei-ch'uan, Ch'eng Ching-yi, and Chang Ch'in-shih.[62]

Common to these responses was the assumption that it would serve no useful purpose to ignore, scorn, or scold the critics, as many seemed to think. They, along with the Chinese delegates to the WSCF conference, readily admitted the factual basis for certain criticisms even while they argued that the accusations were exaggerated. Though youth might go on to other campaigns, the movement should be taken seriously. The attitude that produced the movement would not change until the Christian church changed and Christianity would have a future in China only if it reverted to essentials.

Conservative and liberal alike turned to a Christocentric religion. The greatness of Jesus for Chang I-ching and Liang Chün-mo was his divinity, his saving grace, which offered assurance of salvation in the next life. For liberals, Jesus was the perfection of humanity offering guidance for the achievement of the Kingdom of God on this earth. For both, Jesus was Christianity stripped to its fundamentals. Unessential accretions, rituals, sectarianism, even much of the dogma, could be abandoned. As products of foreign cultures, these addenda held little meaning for Christian nationalists and their deletion obviated the necessity of defending the historical blunders of the church and the undesirable behavior of its members. Chinese Christians did not dispute the linkage between missionary incidents and China's losses; nor did they condone the imperialism of the "so-called" Christian nations. They heartily agreed that Christianity in China had remained a foreign religion under foreign control; Chien Yu-wen, for example, portrayed the churches as tributaries of the foreigners in violation of Christ's assertions of the equality and brotherhood of all. Their contention was that the un-Christian actions of Westerners did not represent true Christianity;

rather they attested to the need for a Chinese church.⁶³ Hsu Ch'ing-yü stated that the church was not Christianity; much had been added by Westerners to Christ's basic teachings of freedom, equality, love, and sacrifice. Not only should Christians abolish all useless ceremony and form but they should abandon decadent and old creeds; they should return to a simplified, essential Christianity.

The defenders denied that science and Christianity were incompatible. Conservatives, along with some liberals, maintained that each offered truth in its own realm and that humankind required both science and religion to satisfy intellectual and emotional needs. The critics, according to Hsu Pao-ch'ien, Chien Yu-wen and others, were not employing scientific methodology when they took facts out of historical context, condemned Christianity on the basis of misconceptions rather than research, and vilified through public confrontation instead of engaging in academic debate. ⁶⁴ Such tactics were a denial of intellectual freedom as well as of rational scholarship. Ma Liang, in an essay for the fiftieth anniversary issue of Shanghai *Shen pao* (Daily News), April, 1922, asserted that religion and science were not mutually exclusive.

More radical theologians dealt with the contradiction between scientific findings and Biblical writings by advocating that Christian teachings contrary to science be abandoned.⁶⁵ Christianity, they said, must continue to evolve as it had in the past, adjusting to the changing environment; unscientific myths such as the virgin birth, the creation story, and the miracles of Christ must be discarded; a medieval morality stressing original sin and heavenly reward for earthly suffering was irrelevant to China's social needs.

Applying the technique of selectivity to Christianity, the Social Gospel advocates portrayed Jesus preaching democracy and social service, both essential to the renovation of China. In so far as individuals were transformed internally by Christ and followed his teachings in their personal lives, they were Christians. The YMCA designated the week of May 4-10, "Good Citizenship Week"; in commemoration of the student movement tradition, members should rededicate themselves to social service and should "substitute for a narrow, negative, destructive patriotism a liberal positive and constructive spirit." Later the YMCA formed a Ch'ing-nien chin-pu hsueh hui (Young Progressive Student Society) of those members working for China's reconstruction.[66]

Envisioning a kind of cooperative communalism, a few Christians termed socialism a literal application of Christ's teachings; witness the structure of the early church. Wu Lei-ch'uan deemed social reform the ultimate goal of Jesus and he stated, furthermore, that the abolition of private property, which was essential to reforming society, was implicit in Jesus' teachings.[67] Even some conservatives freely condemned capitalism as unchristian, though individual revival rather than Christian activism was central to their creed.

Another aspect of the response was acceleration of the Chinese crusade for an independent national church. Already scheduled for May, 1922, was a nation-wide conference of Protestants, a conference in which Chinese delegates would form the majority and would have important leadership positions. Many looked to the National Christian Conference as simply an opportunity to exchange information and to devise an instrument for coordinating denominational work, but a small corps had set their sights far higher. They aspired to a unified church that was self-governing, self-supporting, and self-propagating; several of the most outspoken apologists for Christianity were the principals in this drive. Only as Christianity was assimilated into Chinese culture could it have real impact on Chinese society, they wrote; only as missionaries accepted the role of aides instead of authoritarian directors would the image of Christianity as a denationalizing foreign religion disappear; the time had come for the churches, not the missions, to be the source of authority.[68]

By creating a sense of urgency in the Sinification of Christianity, the Anti-Christian Movement appeared to some to create the opportunity for a break-through to Chinese control.[69] Chien Yu-wen asked that the National Christian Conference face up to "the great modern princple of nationalism. Chinese Christians, the hour is solemn! This time the church will become what we wish it to become. For the power is in our hands. . . .henceforth the church of China ought to be a Chinese church, our church racially and nationally. The time of denominationalism is past. . . Among us, as others, all is being reconstructed, called into question, declared in need of radical reform: government, administration, public education, philosophy, morality, and the rest. Then how can religion alone escape this general movement? It is impossible. . . To our independent people belongs the right of self-government, self-determination, self-consciousness *(tzu-chih, tzu-chüeh, tzu-chüeh)*. This being so in all things, how could religion be the sole exception?" [70]

For certain Chinese Christians, Sinification took the form of demonstrating the compatibility of Christianity with aspects of the Chinese heritage. They tried to answer the charges of denationalization by denying that converts should be required to break with traditional customs and beliefs. Commemoration of the ancestors, for example, should be "purified" and even highlighted by a special memorial day observed by the churches. Such action would be a move toward indigenization and would also remove a great obstacle to conversion. In a series of articles between 1918 and 1928, Chao Tzu-ch'en tried to demonstrated the essential oneness of the teachings of Jesus, Confucius, Buddha, and Mohammed. Desiring to meet the demands for social activism, he called for a practical Christianity, but he also protested against the destruction of the Chinese "ethical" spirit by the New Culture Movement. Christianity, he said, should fulfill the best in Confucian culture, not destroy it.[71]

The rebuttals to the Anti-Christian Movement were, on the whole, ineffectual. Partly it was that their audience rarely included the critics. Partly, it was that discussions of theology per se or of church organization held little interest for New Youth; certainly they were unimpressed by attempts to illustrate the harmony of Confucianism and Christianity. Equally important, the response of Westerners seemed inadequate to many Chinese Christians. Attempts to answer the nationalist argument were undercut when progress toward Chinese leadership and control proved excruciatingly slow. Though the number of ordained Chinese ministers came to exceed that of Westerners and the proportion of Chinese in church administration and on school faculties increased, their authority was not commensurate with their numbers. Most of the income for churches, schools, and social service activities came from Western mission societies and was channeled through mission boards, not the Chinese churches. With the ability to finance usually went the power to decide policy.

The China for Christ Movement, launched in 1919 to cultivate a more active and well informed church membership was defunct by 1923, a victim of denominationalism, understaffing, and inadequate communication facilities. In 1922 representatives from the Congregational and Presbyterian denominations drew up guidelines for union; when Western delegates proposed the name Chung-hua Chi-tu-chiao lien-hui ("Federal Council of Christian Churches in China"), the Chinese signified their aspirations by insisting on Chung-hua Chi-tu-chiao hui (Chinese Christian Church).[72] Chinese opposed such words as union or federation in the title on the grounds that they were founding a new Chinese church, not uniting Western denominations. The English rendition, Church of Christ in China, was, nevertheless, subtly different from a literal translation. Despite the fact that member churches were permitted to retain their own ritual and dogma, the process of ratifying the constitution by the numerous synods, councils, etc., was still in process two years, even four years later. Not until 1927 was the First General Assembly of the Church of Christ in China held and the constitution ratified. Compared with Ch'eng Ching-yi's summons of 1922, his plea in 1928 was both more cautious and less sanguine: "the time has come for missions and churches at least to begin to look forward to the day when the work will be truly church-centric rather than mission-centric."

The National Christian Council, organized at the May 1922 conference, included such eminent Chinese Christians as Ch'eng Ching-yi, Yü Jih-chang, K.T. Chung, and Fan Yu-jung among its executives. They, nevertheless, met with resistance whenever they tried to make it more than an information gathering operation or a coordinating agency for non-controversial activities such as religious retreats or anti-opium and anti-footbinding campaigns. Suggestive of their sense of frustration is a 1927 history reiterating more timidly the goals of 1922: "China. . . needs a Christ who speaks to her in her own language, who appreciates her deepest aspirations. . . and who will enable her to realize them. Not speaking with discordant voices, not with pride of race or overbearing manner, not tied to alien civilizations or outworn dogmas, must the messengers of Christ come if they are to bring Him to the mind and heart of this people."[73] To characterize liberal and nationalist leaders of the church as discouraged would be an understatement; some were already abandoning institutionalized Christianity for their own personal faith.

Christian and anti-Christian nationalists were impatient with the numerous explanations offered for the lack of progress toward independence and Sinification. Though Chinese liberals might argue that sectarianism was a Western heritage meaningless to Chinese, most missionaries and mission boards did not agree. Denominationalism and institutional loyalties remained strong. Not only did emotional ties exist, but denominational structures and loyalties were crucial in fund drives and missionary recruitment.[74] Some Chinese as well as Westerners saw their status and employment closely linked to the existing institutions. A crusade to save the heathen from damnation brought more nickels and dimes into collection plates and more volunteers to the mission field than the gospel of social reconstruction. Only a minority could strip Christian theology as bare as Ch'ao Tzu-ch'en, Hsu Ch'ing-yü, or Wu Lei-ch'uan did. Some feared that the distinctiveness and the essence of Christianity would be lost in universal humanitarianism, while others believed that a social ethic was an inadequate substitute for creedal religion. The cherished Biblical stories, whether interpreted figuratively or literally, were not easily discarded.

Missionaries, therefore, anticipated eventual devolution, but for the present the obstacles loomed large: a shortage of trained and experienced personnel, a Chinese laity without the income to support the schools, hospitals, churches, etc. built by the missions, the proprietary concern of the home mission boards. When protection from the exactions of bandits or warlords was required, the authority that accompanied extraterritorial rights continued to prove valuable. The brief 1922 campaign prompted a readiness to work toward overcoming some of these obstacles but it aroused little appreciation of the urgency of Sinification.

To iconoclasts, the willingness of Christians to attack Confucianism and folk religion while hedging on Christian dogma appeared hypocritical. To revolutionaries, the hope of peaceful, evolutionary change was illusory. Fan Wan-hui of the YMCA entreated the Christian elite to help workers raise their social and economic level but he also rebuked anarchists, who, he said, believed in the forced leveling of classes.[75] In Shanghai cooperation between employers and Protestant organizations led to evening adult literacy courses, a workers' hospital and the Yantzepoo Social Center, which housed recreation facilities and a school for some two hundred laborers' children. Perceiving the inadequacy of a self-help approach based on literacy, morality and hard work, the YMCA and the YWCA initiated studies of industrial conditions to obtain the knowledge necessary for reform recommendations. They hoped, in the spirit of New Youth elitism and populism, to use this information to help "create the public opinion that must precede legislation". Both the YMCA and the National Christian Council appointed special secretaries for industrial work.

Lacking political power, however, YMCA leaders and the National Christian Council were forced to rely on persuasion vis à vis the business community. The key phrases for them were gradualism, cooperation, the Christianizing of industry, not struggle or coercion. To alleviate the distressing working conditions in Shanghai factories, for example, the council drew up a list of modest guidelines which included a weekly day of rest, no employment of children under twelve, and improvement of safety and sanitary conditions. Hours and months of conferences with businessmen came to naught when the factory owners, including the Chinese industrialists without special privileges and capital margins, decided that they would not be able to survive in the fiercely competitive economy of the International Settlement.[76] Partially as a result of publicity by missionaries, the

International Labor Office recommended to the Peking government a number of limited reforms for Chinese labor and Peking responded in 1923 by issuing the Provisional Factory Regulations.⁷⁷ Enforcement, though, remained problematic, especially in the foreign concessions not subject to Chinese control. Radicals were more than ever convinced that real change would require nationwide organization and political force. And indeed the YWCA would eventually conclude: "Activities in which the YWCA formerly took the lead have become the programme of the Government and the party. They are able to pursue these upon such an extensive scale that the Association has had to seek other emphases."⁷⁸

Even the Mass Campaign launched in Changsha in 1922 became grist for the radicals' mills. During World War I, James Y.C. Yen, moving force behind the campaign, had been recruited by the YMCA to organize a recreational program among the Chinese workers in France. Yen was so impressed by the abilities of these trench diggers and coolies that he began to construct a scheme to impart basic literacy. Upon returning to China, Yen secured YMCA support for a pilot project to teach laborers a thousand characters and Changsha was chosen as the site partly because of its reputation as an anti-Christian center. The Hunan P'ing-min chiao-yü she (Mass Education Association) had been founded and plans were on the drawing board by early fall, 1922. A Sinicized YMCA was seeking innovative ways to implement the Social Gospel by educating China's citizenry.

As far as the radicals in Hunan were concerned, however, "imperialist money" had become available for the organization of workers. Mao Tse-tung instructed "Party members of some social standing who were active in the leadership of the mass education movement" to use it to help the party set up night schools for workers.⁷⁹ In some of these schools leftists displaced the original textbook with one that condemned the injustices of capitalism and taught that the workers were the true creators of wealth. Why, then, did they not have nice clothes to wear, enough to eat, and a decent place to live? In 1922 CCP member Li Li-san used the Mass Education Movement as a cover when he went to Anyuan to organize miners and railroad workers. Before leaving

Changsha, Li secured credentials from the Mass Education Association and an official letter of approval for a night school from the magistrate. He built up a core group among the worker students, organized an Anyuan Miners and Railway Workers' Club which was registered with the district official, and subsequently transformed the club into a union which struck the Hanyang Ironworks in July, 1922. According to L. Shaffer, nine strikes had been called and twelve unions founded before the YMCA secretary realized that the Mass Education Association was serving as a front for radical organization and for strike activity.

Finally, most Chinese found their image of Christianity inseparable from the actions of Western nations and individuals. A 1924 resolution of interracial good will, passed by a YMCA conference in the U.S., was later presented at a mass meeting of Shanghai students. At the conclusion of the meeting, it was discovered that the Chinese character for hypocrisy had been scrawled across every copy of the resolution posted around the room.[80] The contention that Christianity should not be blamed for the past and present sins of Christians carried little weight, especially since the Western governments continued to resist abrogation of the unequal treaties with their toleration clauses. France refused to relinquish her role as protector of Roman Catholic missions and in 1918 when the Chinese government proposed to establish direct relations with the Vatican, she protested so vigorously that implementation had to be postponed.[81] Flying the foreign flag to protect property was common practice among missions; even small chapels ran up the flag when threatened by soldiers or bandits. Such conduct spoke louder than demurrers concerning the interdependence of missions and imperialism.

Other repercussions of the 1920-1922 movement gradually became apparent. Interest in the Christian message and willingness to make a public commitment declined. Only two of seven Bible study classes at Peita survived and when Dr. Sherwood Eddy conducted an evangelistic campaign following the WSCF conference, only 12 of the 350 students registering for Bible study came from Peita. In a later nationwide crusade, less than half as many government school students signed pledge cards as in the previous revival.[82] Even for students in parochial schools, the ostensible contradictions between Christianity and science and between Christianity and Chinese nationalism raised the social cost of conversion. The proportion of Christian to non-Christian students attending mission colleges declined as did the percentage of conversions and of decisions to enter the ministry. Equally distressing to Christian leaders was the fact that a large portion of those converted dropped formal ties with the church after graduation. Perhaps the failure to maintain church membership was related to the tendency to identify Christianity with Jesus's teachings rather than with doctrines or institutions, but the net effect was to weaken the church and to make it even less attractive to intellectuals. Stung by the criticisms of the Anti-Christian Movement, parochial students increasingly felt the need to demonstrate their patriotism, to manifest their independence of foreign dictation.

Disenchantment over the pace of devolution contributed to estrangment between missionaries and Chinese Christians. Though resentment was ordinarily restrained by Chinese courtesy and by a conscious effort to practice Christian charity, it surfaced on occasion. Wu Lei-ch'uan of Yenching University launched Chen-li she in 1923; modeled on Sheng-ming she, it was open only to Chinese and published its own periodical, where the need for an independent Chinese church was a frequent theme.[83] In 1924 Chien Yu-wen left the ministry for a teaching post at Yenching and a few years later he deserted his role as advocate of a Sinified Christianity for political office and historical research.[84] The slow pace of change meant that the church had not improved its position or its image when confronted with the much more serious challenge of 1924-1928. For most Chinese, Christianity remained an alien doctrine propagated by foreigners under the protection of the unequal treaties.

On the home front the 1922 campaign was one impetus, albeit a minor one, to a review of the whole conccept of missions. Amid the disillusionment and isolationism following World War I, Westerners became less certain of their duty to save the world. The criticisms of the Anti-Christian Movement, even though heard only in muted form, complicated an already troublesome issue. In reporting on the movement or explaining the reduction in student inquirers, evangelists asserted that the church would emerge strengthened because the fair-weather Christians had departed and the true Christians had been forced to reexamine their faith. To what extent this amounted to whistling in the dark is hard to judge; whether it satisfied those already asking for a review of missions is questionable.

Serious challenges in the U.S. to the Christian crusade would come only after the nationalist outburst of May 30, 1925 and the Northern Campaign of 1926-1928. But the missionary's halo was already dimming and America's love-hate relationship with China appeared ready for another flip-flop. *Rain,* Somerset Maugham's play lampooning missionaries, opened on Broadway in 1922. Two years later delegates to the Student Volunteer Convention heard that they should be concerned about wrongs in the U.S. and Canada, not just those overseas; in both areas of the world life and living conditions were "essentially pagan".[85] British, French and American diplomats in China were sufficiently disturbed by the Anti-Christian Campaign of 1922 to send a joint communique to the Chinese Commissioner of Foreign Affairs demanding protection for all persons professing or teaching Christianity. In mid-May, however, a query to treaty port consuls about an increase in anti-foreignism elicited generally negative replies. "Old China hands," who considered turmoil the norm in the Orient, were unimpressed by the small ripple created by the protesters. The American minister's report, nevertheless, was not wholly inaccurate: "there is no indication in Peking of anti-foreign sentiment except for an anti-Christian agitation which is regarded less as an anti-foreign outbreak than as a reassertion of Chinese civilization as opposed to occidental civilization. . . ."[86] *Asia* magazine commissioned a series of articles on the "Christian missionary problem" in response to the anti-Christian movement in China and the fundamentalist-modernist controversy. The first echoed the theme of the American minister's report; the outburst had been not so much an anti-Christian movement as "a declaration of equality, a throwing off of the inferiority complex by people who had long accepted unprotestingly the role of the taught."[87] The author, a specialist in international relations, then rebuked missionaries for their superior, patronizing, and even contemptuous attitude toward Chinese people and their culture, for religious dogmatism and sectarianism.

Many Chinese, for their part, saw little need to distinguish between nationalism, anti-imperialism, and anti-Christianism, between the doctrines of Christianity and the actions of evangelists, between resentment of missionaries and the struggle for equality and independence.

Chapter IV

Groundwork for the Educational Rights Movement

In late March, 1924, students at Holy Trinity College, an Anglican middle school in Carton, began to organize a student union preparatory to instituting student government. Though the principal was incensed at the pupils' organizing without his permission and vetoed the idea of student government, the students insisted on their right to assemble and to form associations. The upshot was an angry exchange at which the principal allegedly stated: "This is an English school controlled by the English consul in Canton. We cannot accede to your desires nor let you Chinese do as you please." When the students refused to apologize or cease organizational activities, the principal closed the school, ordered all students off the premises by April 9, and expelled the student leaders. The students thereupon drew up a "Declaration against Slavish Education" which they sent to the local newspapers in order to rally public support. All who opposed cultural imperialism should join the fight against slave education and for restoration of educational rights, concluded the manifesto.[1] The Trinity College incident signaled a new phase in anti-Christian activities just as the March Manifesto had sparked the Anti-Christian Campaign of 1922. The repercussions in 1924, however, differed from those of 1922; they also differed from previous responses to "student storms" in parochial schools.

Though mission schools had a reputation for maintaining discipline, strikes and dissension had not been unknown to them. In 1905 student storms had occurred at Chentan ta-hsueh (Aurora University), a Jesuit school in Shanghai, and at Canton Christian College, a non-denominational Protestant institution later called Lingnan University.[2] At issue at Aurora were relations between Western teachers and Chinese staff, especially the Chinese benefactor and principal, Ma Liang. Questions of authority became entangled with differences over religious emphasis and as was often the case, divergent social mores compounded the misunderstanding. The result was that Ma, numerous Chinese faculty members, along with many students, withdrew to found Fu-tan ta-hsueh (New Aurora); Aurora closed temporarily for reorganization. To protest anti-Chinese riots in California and the mistreatment of Chinese students and merchants by U.S. immigration officials, Cantonese had in mid-1905 started a boycott of American goods. Some students decided not to return to the American-run Canton Christian College for the fall semester; others refused to buy the prescribed American textbooks and the American-manufactured shoes that were part of their uniform. After President Theodore Roosevelt promised courteous treatment of Chinese entering the U.S. legitimately, the boycott faded.

A recurrent source of contention was the religious requirement. During this same period two Muslim students at the University of Nanking objected to the compulsory Christian services and gained widespread sympathy and support among the student body, some even threatening to leave. When the Muslims were given the option of compliance or departure, however, they withdrew and the furor subsided.[3] These and other student storms remained isolated episodes, though the points in question--religious emphasis, patriotic activism, and personal relations between Chinese and Westerners--were typical of many confrontations.

With the growth of self-conscious nationalism after the May Fourth Movement and the challenge to all authority by the New Culture Movement, the frequency of student storms escalated. Missionaries in Fukien, for example, reported the following incidents during 1923: (1) the entire student body of a primary school went on strike for the remainder of the term after several pupils were punished for objecting to required religious services; (2) students at another primary school struck when they could not join a second school in a united anti-Japanese demonstration and both schools closed for the term; (3) a fracas at a benefit entertainment by a YMCA middle school forced a two-week closing; after several students were expelled, the school principal received threatening letters and three teachers were beaten; (4) the Student Union at Foochow middle school, having called a strike over the expulsion of a rebellious student, distributed handbills justifying its action to parents and to the public.⁴

Obviously the student subculture fostered by the modern educational system and the New Culture Movement had begun to invade the parochial schools. Critical of their fathers' ineffectiveness in reconstructing China, New Youth had founded their own associations and journals to realize change. They were looking to models other than the sage-scholar for guidance: Dewey, Kropotkin, Marx, etc. They showed an increasing readiness to resort to political organization and direct action to alter Chinese state and society. They were unwilling to be passive recipients of an educational program that they found irrelevant.

Not until the Trinity storm in 1924, however, was there a domino reaction in other mission schools. Not until mid-summer, 1924, did there arise a concerted and continuing drive to alter the status of the foreign institutions. Even educators of the period recognized substantial differences in the revived campaign. Liu Chan-en (Herman Liu), Educational Secretary for the YMCA, contrasted the outbursts of 1922 and 1924 and noted that (1) the target in 1924 was Christian education as an instrument of imperialism rather than religion in general; (2) a nation-wide organization with regular publications had replaced the loosely associated societies with their sporadic manifestoes, articles, etc.; (3) mission school students participated along with those in government and private schools; and (4) there was close cooperation with left-wing political factions, the Student Union, and other associations.⁵

Many of these differences of 1924 were not unique to the Educational Rights and Anti-Christian Movements but indeed were typical of China during the 1920s. Study of the campaigns can, therefore, advance our understanding of the broader shifts in the political and intellectual scene. As emphasis on cultural change was fading before the demand for political effectiveness, the developing strength of the KMT and the CCP inspired the hopes of idealistic youth. The Anti-Christian Movement, like other rights recovery activities, was transformed by the creation of the United Front. The contest between politicians and professional educators for control of the educational system, the curriculum, and the students was accentuated, while the anti-Western and Leninist overtones of urban nationalism grew stronger.

RISING TIDE OF ANTI-IMPERIALISM AND ANTI-WESTERNISM

In March, 1922, the Anti-Christian Manifesto with its Marxian vocabulary and hypothesis had expressed the views of a radical minority. Before 1924, Sun Yat-sen, KMT leaders, and May Fourth nationalists condemned the aggression of the great powers *(ch'iang ch'uan)*, but imperialism was a concept rarely employed.[6] Rejection of inequality among nations was accompanied by expressions of shame over China's weakness and exhortations to build a new China from within. Calls for abrogation of the unequal treaty system as the major evil coincided with the acceptance of the United Front as policy in 1923. Nationalism faced increasingly outward.

One could argue that with the formation of the United Front, the Chinese nationalist movement entered the third stage as defined by Miroslav Hroch.[7] In the first stage, according to Hroch, small groups of intellectuals elaborate the category of the nation; then in the second stage, wider networks of patriots spread the word through concerted agitation; finally, serious popular mobilization is embarked upon. In China, the three stages obviously were not discrete, but overlapping. If the 1898 reformers began the process of defining the nation, the search continued during the 1920s. Though revolutionaries and nationalists worked to spread the "national idea" during the pre-1911 decade, May Fourth marked a significant leap forward in building networks of patriots. With the United Front, however, came the institutional structure for concerted and penetrating mobilization of the masses that would extend beyond the cities and into the countryside. The process, though short-circuited in 1927, would be renewed during the second United Front a decade later.

Since the entry of the masses was essential to transform ethnicity or culturalism into nationalism, nationalist movements were inevitably populist. But in China as elsewhere in Asia and Africa, the growth of nationalist sentiment outran the development of political institutions.[8] The 1911 revolutionaries were fatally weakened by underdevelopment in the area of popular mobilization. Despite the fact that May Fourth acquired force and legitimacy as a result of incorporation of the urban masses, its unity was brief and limited. Not until the founding of the CCP, the restructuring of the KMT, and the formation of the United Front did the third stage of the nationalist movement become a possibility. The institutional mechanisms for guiding and structuring political participation were being constructed. They included numerous collateral associations and ladder organizations leading toward membership in the parties.

The significance of the United Front was further enhanced by the fact that it signaled the fusion of nationalism with left-wing revolutionism. Theories linking the Chinese revolution, anti-imperialism, and nationalism acquired a new coherence and potency. By 1924, many Chinese intellectuals, whether pro-Communist or not, were viewing imperialism within the Leninist framework.[9] For them, it provided insights into the multiple forms of imperialist expansion and it incorporated the struggle against imperialism into the course of world history and of the Chinese national revolution. It built on a rising anti-Western tide among Chinese revolutionaries. Though Lenin argued that imperialism originated in the economic needs of the capitalists, the Marxian doctrine of economic determinism dictated a necessary relationship between the economic foundations and the political, social, and cultural superstructure. Society was an integral whole and imperialism did not take the exclusive form of colonial conquest; it insinuated itself into China in many ways, including cultural aggression.

The relevance of the cultural emphasis for the Educational Rights Movement was, of course, the designation of foreign educational activities as a form of imperialism; furthermore, the U.S., as the major supporter of mission schools and Boxer indemnity scholarships, became a prime offender. Ts'ai Ho-sen, CCP official and editor of the CCP journal *Hsiang-tao chou-pao* (Guide Weekly), claimed that the U.S., having become the leading capitalist and Christian nation as a result of World War I, was seeking to expand throughout the world. Because England, France, and Japan had already established spheres of influence in China, the U.S. was using evangelism, mission education and social service activities to extend its power in China.[10] Since cultural oppression seemed more value laden than economic or political aggression, educational rights issues set up powerful emotional reverberations. Stuart Schram relates an incident at a soccer game between Hunan First Normal College and Yale-in-China, when Mao Tse-tung rose in the audience and shouted: "Beat the slaves of the foreigners!", that is, defeat those who submitted to the authority of the Yale missionary educators and thereby became denationalized lackeys.[11]

During the early 1920s proposals for educational use of Boxer funds came from Britain, France, Japan, and USSR, and though educators for the most part anticipated considerable benefit to Chinese schools, they were less than enthusiastic about the possibility that some funds might be channeled to parochial institutions. An article in *Hsiang-tao chou-pao* expressed the attitude of many radicals toward the negotiations; the author depicted all imperialists as fluttering about trying to follow the "demonical example" of America in using Boxer funds to educate hirelings. Chinese were mistaken, he said, if they criticized only those who directly invaded Chinese territory; education was becoming a prime form of aggression.[12]

The strong anti-Western accents were evoked by repeated disappointments with U.S. and European policies and Sun Yat-sen spoke for many nationalists when he told a YMCA audience in December, 1923: "We no longer look to the Western Powers. Our faces are turned toward Russia."[13] Though those who blamed the "Bolsheviks" for the outbursts of anti-foreignism were clearly mistaken, the USSR and the Comintern stood to gain from the growth of anti-Westernism and they cultivated it. Their role was not the creation of antagonism; rather they trained the focus on the U.S. in particular. The stridency of anti-Americanism quickened as Soviet influence expanded, but numerous Western moves supplied abundant material for radical propagandists.

Dismay over the Versailles Treaty was compounded by the failure of the Washington Conference in 1921 to assure reversion of the Shantung concessions or to abrogate the unequal treaties. Assurances of respect for China's sovereignty and promises of future negotiation regarding the Shantung concessions, extraterritoriality, and the treaty tariff fell far short of Chinese hopes and expectations. The Soviet Union, excluded from the Washington Conference, convened the Congress of Toilers of the Far East as counterpoint and invited Kuomintang and Chinese Communist representatives. A Congress manifesto contrasting the two assemblies gained the affirmation of the Chinese delegates: "The oppressors ...have met lately in the halls of the American Exchange in Washington, in order to come to an understanding on how to plunder anew the countries of the Far East....The principle of equal rights of robbery in China has been set up, leaving the leading role in this base affair to American capital....We have met in the Red capitals of the Soviet republic--Moscow and Petrograd--in order to raise our voices from this world tribune against the world executioners and against the Washington union of the four bloodsuckers...."[14] At A.A. Joffe's first interview with Peking journalists on August 17, 1922, the Soviet envoy stated that the U.S. had become the great imperialist power since World War I and both he and his successor, Leo M. Krakhan, frequently contrasted the Soviet Union and its renunciation of special privileges with the Washington Conference, which simply appointed a committee to investigate the question. In Changsha, radicals organized a mass demonstration against the conference and "the continued imperialist aggression in China," while *Lao-tung chou-pao* (Labor Weekly), an anarchist paper, denounced the imperialists at Washington and their hirelings, the militarists.[15]

Hard upon the heels of the Washington Conference came a series of British and American moves further antagonizing the Canton government and the revolutionary parties: negotiations between the powers and the Peking government for loans and railway concessions while the West was rejecting Sun Yat-sen's requests for assistance; threats of an international expedition over the kidnapping of foreign railway passengers (Lin Cheng Affair, May, 1923); a naval demonstration by the U.S. and others in response to Canton's attempt to collect port customs, December, 1923; postponement of the meeting of the Commission on Extraterritoriality in 1923; British support of the Canton Merchants' Association in a lengthy dispute which led in October, 1924, to a skirmish between the merchants' militia and the troops backing the Kuomintang.

As incident piled upon incident, nationalists saw imperialism at the root of all China's troubles. Settlement of specific grievances would not suffice; overthrow of the whole power structure, internal and external, was required. *Hsiang-tao,* for example, was critical of Christian youths who demonstrated against Japan in the spring of 1923; why didn't parochial students stop acting as the tools of the American imperialists and wake up to the fact that all imperialists were the enemy? asked the author; the great weakness of the May Fourth Movement had been its pro-American spirit.[16] Hsin hsueh-sheng hui (New Student Society), sponsored by the KMT and CCP, issued a vehement condemnation of the Canton naval demonstration and urged the whole nation to unite in a battle for restoration of tariff autonomy and all other sovereign rights. *Hsiang-tao* published a Kwangtung manifesto asking the peasants and workers of America, England, Italy, and Japan to join in the struggle against gunboat diplomacy.[17] Among the resolutions of the first general congress of the Kuomintang in January, 1924, was a demand for the end of the unequal treaties and all forms of encroachment.

UNITED FRONT LINKS

Of particular significance for the rights recovery drive was the concept of a nationalist united front against the foreign capitalists and Chinese militarists. Since imperialist expansion was essential to the health of capitalism, Lenin argued, a struggle by a nationalist coalition to rid China of colonialism constituted a first stage in the downfall of capitalism. The battle versus Chinese warlords, furthermore, was integral to the process, for the militarists were able to retain power only with aid from Japan and the Western powers. The beauty of this thesis was twofold: first, China gained a role in the world revolution and in doing so, joined the tide of history; second, all nationalists could participate in this stage: those seeking to overthrow the northern militarists and unify China, those desiring social revolution, and those working to restore national sovereignty; the petty bourgeoisie along with the peasantry and the proletariate. The fight was one.[18]

One of the vanguard in becoming acquainted with this theory was CCP founder, Chang Kuo-t'ao; he expressed his reaction at the Congress of Toilers of the Far East in 1922:

"[M]ost of us delegates were filled with indignation at the various lawless acts of the Powers in China. But we had also been among those who welcomed Western civilization, and some of us looked upon missionary activities and certain charitable cultural enterprises operated by foreign nationals in China as having played an active role in the dissemination of Western culture. After this fresh examination . . . to deny that they also affected China harmfully seemed pointless... As a result of our discussions, we unanimously agreed that the reactionary forces within China were merely the tools of foreign imperialism and that opposition to imperialism must be the starting point of the Chinese revolutionary movement if it were to succeed." [19]

The CCP, Chang wrote, had hitherto considered social revolution its main task and had regarded opposition to imperialism as a subsidiary patriotic movement. Though Chinese political organizations had previously formed temporary alliances to promote a specific cause, the idea of an anti-imperialist united front was outlined at the Congress. Chang concludes with some exaggeration:

"In those days the Chinese people did not know what was meant by imperialism. But within a short time, as a result of CCP propaganda, and of the various presentations of the subject by the many delegates to the Moscow Congress, the term 'anti-imperialism' represented for everybody a new and immutable goal." [20]

As indicated above, Chang claims too much credit for

the communists. The Western powers made their own contribution toward intensifying anti-imperialist sentiment; furthermore, the various student strikes and demonstrations gave Sun Yat-sen and the Kuomintang a heightened estimation of the popularity and usefulness of anti-imperialist nationalism. Though the anti-Western and anti-capitalist emphases of China's new nationalism provided the intellectual rationale for a united front of the KMT and the CCP, the proposal met with stiff opposition in both parties. Only the threat of Comintern discipline and the force of Sun's personality made the consummation possible. For the proponents, the United Front was grounded in expectations of concrete kinds of aid, Sun looking for military materials and fiscal assistance, organizational know-how, and avenues to influence among the urban populace; the CCP expecting to benefit from the greater respectability of the KMT, the attraction of Sun's revolutionary image, and the extensive network of KMT branches. Chang is, nevertheless, correct in citing the popularity of the integral aproach to revolution; it explained China's disunity and impotence in other than humiliating terms and its logic linked internal and external enemies in their opposition to the goals of unification, national sovereignty, and cultural change.

Documentary evidence points to the decisive role of party members in initiating and guiding the Educational Rights Movement. With good reason, historians have scrutinized the parties' nurturing of labor unions and peasant associations. The parties also frequently classified the students (or scholars) as a separate group to be incorporated into the revolution. Ch'en Tu-hsiu, for example, employed the four Confucian class categories in a 1923 article encouraging political activism: scholar, farmer, worker (artisan), merchant.[21] Early in his career as reformer, Ch'en had come to believe that educated youth had a unique role to play in the creation of a new China and, even after he accepted Marxism and the necessity of class struggle, he continued to stress the importance of attracting revolutionary youth to the KMT-CCP United Front. He used traditional student-teacher relationships to build a vanguard who would be both knowers and moral leaders.[22] But Ch'en was not alone in his recruitment tactics or in his estimation of New Youth. He was joined by the Young China Party and by segments of the KMT. Throughout the nationalist campaigns of the 1920s, manifestoes identified students and teachers as a social class, a distinct category to be wooed and organized. The proclamation of the Third National Congress of the CCP in June, 1923, appealed to the workers, peasants, students, and the "peaceful and moderate merchants". The First National Congress of the KMT, 1924, stated that in the fight to emancipate the Chinese people, KMT members "rely on the intelligentsia, on the farmers, and on the merchants for defense and support." "Laborers, Farmers, Students, Merchants, and all who are oppressed!" were addressed in a handbill issued by the Changsha Anti-Christian Federation in January, 1924.[23]

In organizations and government bodies, KMT and CCP leaders frequently designated separate representation for intellectuals and/or students. When Li Li-san and other CCP officials set up a Shanghai coordinating body after May 30, 1925, it was the Kung-shang-hsueh lien-ho-hui (United Society of Workers, Merchants, and Students). Sun Yat-sen's proposals to Chief Executive Tuan Ch'i-jui for a national reunification conference suggested representation for student unions, educational associations, and universities as well as representation for workers, merchants, and peasants. One indication of the conscious and continuing competition for the loyalty of students was a statement by Karl Radek, president of Sun Yat-sen University in Moscow.[24] This institution to train Chinese communist cadres would, according to Radek, enable the Soviet Union at last to counteract the bourgeois educational propaganda of the American mission schools in China. Another professor at the university stated: Our goal "is twofold: first to offset the pro-Western cultural propaganda of foreign mission schools in China by giving Chinese students a taste of Soviet culture; second, to teach the Chinese the lessons of our revolution. . . ." For the parties, the intellectuals served more than one purpose: the adherence of New Youth provided cadre leadership and broadened support, while the prestige of scholars helped legitimize the revolutionary cause. The CCP leadership, concerned with ideological orthodoxy, termed the "educational propagandists" the "central elements in the Party cells" and also the instrument for politicizing elements outside the party.[25]

To assert purposefulness by the parties in fostering the Educational Rights Movement is to deny neither the prevalence of anti-Christian sentiment nor the magnetism of rights recovery slogans. It says rather that political leaders recognized both and so promoted the Educational Rights Movement as part of their construction of a national network through mass movements. Themselves urban and elitist in orientation, they appreciated and sought to utilize the influence of the educated in articulating nationalist sentiments and in conveying the impression of popular support.

Within the educated urban community, the parties employed a variety of organizations for purposes similar to those of the labor unions and peasant associations. In addition to the educational rights and anti-Christian associations, for example, there were Wai-chiao hou-yuan wei-yuan hui (Committee for Diplomatic Support), the New Student Society and the Socialist Youth Corps. Mao Tse-tung employed his very considerable genius for organization to extend his personal influence and to politicize and radicalize youth. Whether founding new societies or making use of existent associations, Mao quite naturally turned to educational colleagues and institutions, as the titles of the organizations indicate: Chien hsueh hui (Strengthen Learning Society), Hsin min hsueh hui (New People's Study Society), Wen hua shu she (Cultural Book Society), Wang Fu-chih Study Society, Tzu-hsiu ta-hsueh (Self Study University), Ma-k'o-ssu chu-i yen-chiu hui (Society for the Study of Marxism), not to mention the Mass Education Association, the Hunan Student Union, the Hunan Socialist Youth Corps, and the Hunan Provincial Educational Association, in all of which Mao was active. Though Mao was more energetic than most party builders, he was not atypical in his reliance on multiple organizations constructed through academic networking. Not only did the membership overlap, but the linkages were employed in the correlative causes of: anti-imperialism, rights recovery, anti-warlordism, and anti-Christianism. The youth department of the Kuomintang organized party branches in colleges and middle schools while the National Student Union, which had languished, was revitalized with subsidies and personnel from the KMT and the Socialist Youth Corps. In July, 1924, many of these associations were brought together in an umbrella organization known as Fan ti-kuo-chu-i ta t'ung-meng (Great Anti-Imperialist League).

Shanghai University supplemented the Peasant Movement Training Institute and the Whampoa Military Academy in providing leadership for the United Front's drive to power. Founded in 1923 to recruit and train KMT cadres, it quickly came under CCP control and served as a locus for radicals in the city. In December, 1924, British police invaded the premises of Shanghai University and seized a large number of books and magazines. Despite student protests, the Municipal Court subsequently ordered confiscation of these materials as revolutionary works, published in violation of the press law; it also charged the administration with being a menace to the peace and order of the settlement.[26]

That Shanghai University was a major center for the educational rights and anti-Christian campaigns was no coincidence. Among the Shanghai staff and short-term lecturers were: Shih Ts'un-t'ung, a member of the Executive Committee of the Anti-Christian Federation and speaker at an anti-Christian rally held at Shanghai University on December 25, 1924; Tung I-hsiang, another speaker at the December 25th rally and author of an early anti-Christian article in *Fei Chi-tu-chiao t'e-k'an;* Tai Chi-t'ao, a prominent supporter of the 1922 Anti-Christian Campaign; Ts'ai Ho-sen, author of an article "Chin-tai Chi-tu-chiao" (Modern Christianity), which was reprinted in a pamphlet issued by the Shanghai Anti-Christian Association and *Chung-kuo ch'ing-nien;* K'o Po-nien (Li Ch'un-fan), another member of the Anti-Christian Executive Committee, who solicited anti-Christian articles for *Chueh-wu* and contributed several himself; his speech at the inaugural meeting of the Anti-Christian Association was also reprinted in the anti-Christian pamphlet; Hsiao Ch'u-nü, who published condemnations of cultural aggression in *Chung-kuo ch'ing-nien;* and Yün Tai-ying, editor and contributor of anti-Christian articles for *Chung-kuo ch'ing-nien.* Wang Chia-hsiang, a leader in a 1924 student protest against religious requirements at St. James Senior High School in Wuhu, Anhwei, enrolled at Shanghai University shortly after the protest incident. A third Shanghai University instructor who was a member of the Anti-Christian Executive Committee was Kao Erh-po, secretary of the political bureau of the Shanghai KMT branch. Complementing Shanghai University and sharing its staff was Shang-hai p'ing-min nü hsiao (Shanghai Girls' School for the Masses), which recruited and trained female cadres for the CCP.[27]

The political parties opened the pages of their newspapers to student contributors and reprinted their manifestoes and circular telegrams; literary supplements, special editions, and regular columns were tailored to the interests of New Youth. Leaders of party youth bureaus and propaganda departments offered guidance, often serving on the executive committees of the Anti-Christian Federation, the Educational Rights Federation, and other societies. Indicative of the significant role of the parties is the fact that the focal points of the Educational Rights Movement were the cities where the revolutionary activists were concentrated. In major radical centers such as Changsha, Canton, and Shanghai, the Educational Rights Movement was generally a stage ahead of the campaign elsewhere. Peking, the proud carrier of the May Fourth tradition but also the seat of the warlord government, played a satellite role.[28]

Three themes relevant to the Educational Rights Movement were the subject of frequent articles in party publications before the summer of 1924. One was the artificiality of trying to divorce education from government or students from politics. Early in 1923 Ch'en Tu-hsiu wrote a series of articles and editorials urging political activism by students and intellectuals.[29] Was it realistic, he asked, for educators to shun politics when the very functioning of the educational system depended on government financing? Students must not confine their protests to foreign affairs but must realize that internal revolution was intrinsic to the destruction of China's enemies; he listed as escapist and impractical "moral regeneration to save the country" (YMCA slogan), "Christianity to save the country," humanitarian mutual assistance, etc. He tried to shame patriotic students into action against the Japanese who destroyed China physically and Americans who destroyed China culturally.

Later in the year, left-wing periodicals such as *Chung-kuo ch'ing-nien* and radical groups such as the Hunan

Student Union reiterated that the times demanded a social morality, not an individual morality; China had no place for romantic egotists or subservient church school students.[30] From Hunan came a Student Union manifesto published in *Min-kuo jih-pao* (August 23, 1923) and protesting against an education independent of politics; recommendations that students concentrate on education to the exclusion of politics, it said, were designed to narcotize and stupefy them. In addressing the Fifth Congress of the National Student Union, Sun Yat-sen urged students to discharge their role in the revolution, though he warned against violence or precipitate action.[31] Some months later, Shao Li-tzu, editor of *Min-kuo jih-pao* spoke out in favor of students joining the KMT in order to foster revolution, while *Chueh-wu* invoked action, not talk.[32]

The other two themes had been stated during the 1920-1922 Anti-Christian Movement but gained a new prominence shortly before the rights recovery drive: one was the importance of education as a form of imperialism; closely related was the second, the argument that England and America represented a more serious threat to Chinese integrity than Japan. Both were, of course, facets of the anti-Western and anti-imperialist connotations of Chinese nationalism. The first and second issues of *Ch'ien-feng yueh-k'an* (Vanguard Monthly) founded in July, 1923 and edited by Ch'ü Ch'iu-pai, were devoted to "*Ti-kuo-chu-i ch'in lueh Chung-kuo chih ko-chung fang-shih*" (All Methods of Imperialist Encroachment against China) and "*Chung-kuo chiao-yü wen-t'i*" (The Chinese Educational Question). The theme of the subtle but dangerous forms of British and American aggression also appeared in articles by Chen Yü and Mao Tse-tung in *Hsiang tao* and in early issues of *Hsin hsueh-sheng*.[33]

Manifestoes and formal declarations by political societies signaled their concern with recovery of national rights and their concept of educational autonomy as essential to sovereignty. The political platform passed by the Third Congress of the CCP, June, 1923, demanded nullification of the unequal treaties and cancellation of foreign privilege, including that of establishing schools; it also opposed all religious instruction in schools. Two months later, the Second Congress of the Socialist Youth Corps followed suit with resolutions condemning parochial schools and recommending the formation of anti-Christian cells in the mission institutions.[34] KMT leaders, who had called for treaty revision in 1923, pledged in 1924 to abolish the treaties, including infringements on national educational rights. With radicals in control of the Executive Committee, the National Student Union sent a letter to the KMT Youth Bureau in March, 1924 insisting upon the importance of fostering anti-Christian propaganda, especially in Shanghai and Canton, where mission schools were numerous. According to the union, students needed to be made conscious of the national threat represented by foreign-controlled education.[35]

At this time a move by Turkey against mission education served as a stimulus and a guide. Ch'en Tu-hsiu and other revolutionary nationalists hailed the attempt of the newly-established Turkish republic to oust missionaries and close all alien schools. Equating China and Turkey as the two great old sick men of the East, Ch'en stated that Turkey was recovering her national rights with the aid of the Soviet Union. Why, he asked, did China continue to kowtow before the armies of the Great Powers and submit to religious aggression? A communique from Moscow to Peking praising Turkey's action was widely publicized under the lead line: "The Turkish government closes foreign schools; the U.S., Italy, and France protest but world opinion is with the Turks."[36]

EDUCATORS AND EDUCATIONAL RIGHTS

The Educational Rights Movement was not, however, simply the creation of the revolutionary parties.[37] Though students had reason to believe that party backing would be forthcoming, they were not merely pawns of left-wing organizations. Support for the cause was broad and deep; it included educators of the older generation and even some Chinese Christians, who found themselves in accord with certain proposals for changes in the mission schools. A small group of nationalists who belonged to neither the KMT nor the CCP made rights recovery a central issue in their bid for political power. Advocates of the Educational Rights Movement, though, differed in their specific goals and tactics so that the patronage and guidance of the KMT, the CCP, and their affiliates were crucial to the blossoming of the protests into a full-fledged movement.

Among educated Chinese, social generations were short in the twentieth century; mounting domestic and foreign pressures during the nineteenth century and shifts in *weltanschauung* had cleared the way for change at an accelerating rate after 1900. Fathers and sons often shared the quest for intellectual guidelines in strengthening China and radical sons frequently sprang from radical fathers. Change, however, was so rapid that radical sons of formerly radical fathers might have quite different experiences and perspectives. As indicated above, Marxist economics and Leninist theories on imperialism gained a new relevancy after the Bolshevik Revolution and began to displace anarchism as an intellectual referent. Fathers generally lagged behind sons in abandonment of traditional guidelines in social relations. Many a business man or government administrator shed his business suit upon returning from the office and slipped into the security of the patriarchal family. The life style of university and middle school youth was much more deeply enmeshed in the hybrid culture emerging in China's commercial and administrative cities. Congregated in the eastern metropolises, they lived in an environment influenced by a monetary economy, foreign imports and the imperialist presence. Intellectuals spoke with many voices.

All members of the educated elite, however, shared the need to redefine the role of literati in China. Not only had the abolition of the examination system in 1905 and the end of dynastic government in 1911 cut the tie between scholar and official but the disintegration of the Confucian universe had given rise to new political competitors. Scholars might still have enormous prestige and the ideal of state service might still be strong, but the route to power and wealth was no longer clearly demarcated. Lacking the political capital of either soldiers or gold, reformist intellectuals had few desirable outlets. They might enter government employ, where they would probably function as professional technicians or as members of a faction dominated by a warlord. They might seek fortune and glory by building a local empire, autonomous except for providing tax receipts and draftees to the regional militarist. They might become intelligentsia, that is, critics of society and culture, and hope that by transforming the culture, they could determine China's future political form. Or, trading on their prestige, they could attempt to influence government policy by extra-legal and confrontational tactics. Finally, they could join the politically ambitious in creating alternative instruments of power in order to challenge the incumbents in Peking. As China's politics deteriorated, the latter strategy gained popularity.

For many educated patriots, the period between the May Fourth Movement of 1919 and the May Thirtieth Movement of 1925 was a time of narrowing options. The New Culture Movement had arisen out of disillusionment with the weakness and corruption of the young republic; scholars turned to building a foundation for effective democracy by revolutionizing society and culture. This approach with its abstention from political activism was, however, quickly called into question. Only a few months after the May Fourth incident, Hu Shih and Li Ta-chao engaged in a public debate over tactics, Hu Shih arguing that transformation must proceed by tackling individual problems, by inches and drops. Li argued that an "ism" was essential as a baseline for perceiving problems and as a guide for solving inter-related problems; already Li was abandoning the evolutionary path via cultural transformation. By December 1920 Hu Shih and Ch'en Tu-hsiu had come to an open break over Ch'en's inclusion of political articles in *Hsin ch'ing-nien* and his advocacy of political activism.[38]

Hu, Chiang Meng-lin, Ts'ai Yuan-pei, Kuo Ping-wen and a few other liberals continued, nevertheless, to abjure politics and to give priority to cultural reform; for them, education was the principal instrument of regeneration.[39] Education, they believed, must foster individual development and social progress while eradicating the Confucian veneration of hierarchy, tradition, and ritual; education must help define and preserve *kuo ts'ui* (national essence). A reassessment of the function and content of education was required.

In imperial China education had been the means of

transmitting the *kuo* (cultural community, polity, nation). It trained the leadership, both the literati who attained civil service positions and those who operated at the level of informal governance. Within the Confucian concept of a leadership based on virtue and created by study and self-cultivation, the function of education was dual; its goal was inculcation and internalization of the social ethic along with mastery of the literary and political heritage. In a very real sense, education had conveyed the national essence as perceived by the elite. Education and power were linked in the scholar-official, who held temporal authority and who also cultivated and perpetuated social and aesthetic norms.

As the cultural definition of China gave way to a national definition, however, the mission and content of education altered. A reconstructionist education began to replace a reflective education. If the people were China, then they must be raised to the level of national consciousness; they must be sensitized to a shared body of values and forms. Education had to create the *kuo* rather than transmit the *kuo;* it should train the citizenry as well as the leadership. It must, if a new China were to arise, cultivate specialized talents to build an industrial economy. Through a centralized and unified educational system, access to schooling would be made more widespread. Still unanswered, however, were such questions as: What was the nature of the national soul if one deleted the Confucian political structure and social morality? Could one use education as an instrument of nationalization and yet separate political affairs from ideology? Where were the resources for such an ambitious educational program and who would control their allocation?

Reformist educators wanted the school system under their stewardship and briefly during the early 1920s, prospects for professional, rather than political, control seemed bright. Many of the academic leaders, having studied abroad, benefited from the aura of power and progress associated with all that was considered modern. Concentration of the intellectual elite at universities located in a few urban centers facilitated communication and also the growth of a sense of community.

Taking advantage of the limited power of the central government, educators created their own vehicles for publicizing their views and concerting their influence. In January, 1919, Hsin chiao-yu kung-chin she (Society for the Promotion of New Education) was founded to provide leadership for five progressive educational bodies. Through its annual conferences and its magazine, *Hsin chiao-yü* (New Education), it became an energetic advocate for teachers and administrators. Ch'üan-kuo chiao-yü hui lien-ho-hui (National Federation of Educational Associations) served as the coordinating body for the provincial educational associations and it too lobbied through its yearly convention and its organs, *Chiao-yü tsa-chih* (Educational Review and *Chung-hua chiao-yü chieh* (Chinese Educational Circles). Numerous other organizations emerged to promote particular objectives: Chiao-yü tu-li yun-tung (Educational Autonomy Movement), Chung-hua chih-yeh chiao-yü she (Chinese Vocational Educational Association), P'ing-min chiao-yü she (Mass Education Society), and so forth. Because of political chaos at the national level and the near bankrupt state of the Ministry of Education's finances, these associations were able temporarily to take the lead in reconstructing the national educational system. The central administration, in fact, encouraged professional organizations to assume responsibility for self regulation and to perform other quasi-governmental functions with the result that they came to be considered legitimate public bodies.[40]

In the fall of 1922, the Peking Ministry of Education promulgated a School Reform Decree establishing a new school system. The program, modeled on that of the U.S., was actually the work of various professional associations and reflected the influence of John Dewey and Paul Monroe of Columbia University, alma mater of several of the authors. Its objectives were to promote the spirit of democratic education and to relate the training of the individual to existing social needs. Since most educational leaders assumed that this meant a secular program designed to cultivate a national citizenry, they advocated the elimination or restriction of religious activities in all schools and they urged that all schools be brought under the supervision of the national educational administration.

Insistence on the secularization of education was strengthened by a well-publicized debate on science and philosophy of life in 1923. Chang Chün-mai (Carsun Chang) of Tsing Hua University opened the year-long exchange with a lecture in which he questioned the ability of science to solve all problems. A philosophy of life was subjective, intuitive, synthetic, and individual, he argued, and in this realm science had no contribution to make; furthermore, materialistic Western civilization based on science had amply demonstrated its failings. Chinese should treasure the ethical and philosophical achievements of their own spiritual civilization.

Rebuttals came quickly, in quantity, and with wit and style. Leading lights of the New Culture Movement condemned the "Ghost Metaphysics" of Chang and affirmed China's need for *k'o-hsueh shen* (the science spirit or the deity, science). For them, the only knowledge was that which could be critically and logically studied; nothing, therefore, was beyond the ken of science. Science was deemed the most effective weapon against tradition and the best hope for progress; it was an ideological entity not to be lightly challenged. Despite a context different from that of 1920-1921, the debate served to publicize many of the arguments against religion propounded earlier in *Shao-nien*. With some injustice to Chang Chün-mai, religion along with metaphysics, conservatism, and parochial schools were lumped together as impediments to a modern China. The cost of public commitment to religion had been raised another notch.

Though the eminence of the liberal educators enabled them to dominate the professional associations during the early 1920s, their position contained contradictions that could be called into question. Liberals advocated education for individual development but the primary goal was service to society rather than personal satisfaction. They upheld freedom of intellectual inquiry and condemned inculcation of any orthodoxy but they would use education to create a Chinese polity. They desired popular participation in government, partially at least, as a means of forging a sense of identity between the masses and the central government and thereby enhancing state power. While acknowledging the contributions of mission education, they objected to one of its intrinsic aims, Christianization of Chinese society and culture.

Not all non-Communist intellectuals agreed with Hu Shih that they should abstain from politics for twenty years; for them the issue of national unity and sovereignty became the overriding consideration and appeared to require a political solution. In numerous cities, the headquarters of the provincial educational association served as the locus for rallies of students and multi-class protesters, as administrative center for workers' clubs and anti-imperialist societies, and as an outlet for rights recovery publicity. The educational association in Changsha, for example, had taken the initiative in calling a meeting to organize a boycott of Japanese goods during the May Fourth Movement while its offices were used in negotiating strike settlements in 1922. One explanation for the broad range of activities is the fact that many party cadres were educators, earning a living as teachers, and they had access to the facilities. But it is also true that the line between politics, ideology, and education was not easily drawn.

Indicative of the cruel choices facing idealistic nationalists in the China of the 1920s was the demise of the Young China Association in 1924. The society's ban on political activity by members became so controversial after the May Fourth incident that frequent articles and conferences debated the deletion of the regulation and the adoption of doctrinal guidelines. Though some leaders had already accepted Marxism and were moving toward founding a Communist party, others could not accept the concept of class struggle, the international goals of Marxism or the democratic centralism of Leninist party structure. Yet they agreed that political clout was essential to overthrow the militarists and the imperialists.

The First Chihli-Fengtien War between warlord cliques during the spring of 1922 and the ousting of Sun Yat-sen by Canton militarists accentuated China's political disarray; such conflicts also diverted educational funds. At the whim of the military governors, cabinets rose and fell, ministers were appointed or arrested. Salaries of teachers were often in arrears so that one professor remarked that he was lucky to receive wages five months out of the year and strikes by unpaid teachers were not uncommon. Particularly disillusioning for many intellectuals was the short life of the 1922 "able men cabinet". This cabinet, composed of some of China's most distinguished and highly educated public servants, elicited widespread support and high hopes; it lasted just 71 days and ended with the summary arrest and incarceration of the Minister of Finance. In 1923 Peking students went on strike and the heads of four institutions of higher education resigned in protest over the imprisonment of one cabinet member and the forced resignation of another. Eight colleges threatened to close because of insufficient funds while provincial middle schools in northeast and southeast China operated on a hand-to-mouth basis. Imperialist pressures showed little sign of diminishing; rather, the militarists helped finance their wars by loans secured on concessions to the powers.

In October 1923, the Young China Association held a last conference and agreed on certain anti-imperialist, anti-militarist goals but not on ideological guidelines or the proper role for literati. Worth noting is the fact that the conference did unite behind a resolution opposing church education and advocating a national education to promote national consciousness and a patriotic spirit. This stance cut across political divisions. After the split of the association, one faction emerged as officers in the CCP; another formed Chung-kuo kuo-chia-chu-i ch'ing-nien tuan (Chinese Nationalist Youth Corps), and a few either remained aloof from politics or joined the Kuomintang.

THE YOUNG CHINA PARTY AND EDUCATIONAL RIGHTS

The Nationalist Youth Corps, later known as Chung-kuo ch'ing-nien tang (Young China Party) became one of the most vociferous supporters of the educational rights and anti-Christian movements.[41] Many of the leaders were former anarchists for whom Chinese nationalism had become the overriding concern and they had earlier been outspoken critics of religion, especially Christianity. Modeled on Giuseppe Mazzini's Young Italy and Kemal Ataturk's Young Turkey, the association stood for national unity and sovereignty. Spokesmen opposed the CCP because of its ties with the U.S.S.R. and its doctrines of class struggle and international revolution. They believed that the CCP was trying to subvert the KMT for its own purposes and therefore condemned the United Front. Though many Young China leaders would later be identified as conservatives, the organization was during the 1920s essentially a one-issue party, i.e., anti-imperialist nationalism.

Founded primarily by educators, the Young China Party recruited through universities and middle schools; like the CCP and the KMT, it formed an adjunct society for juveniles, most of whom were students.[42] Its membership of students, educators, and other professionals made it natural to emphasize the issue of sovereign control over education as it enlisted new members and attempted to develop an identity separable from that of the CCP and the KMT. From late 1924 to early 1928 Young China members published *Hsing-shih chou-pao* (Awakening Lion Weekly), whose pages were peppered with articles on the importance of nationalistic education and the injury wrought by foreign-controlled schools.[43] Its slogan was "eliminate domestic traitors and resist foreign authoritarian forces". In the first category were militarists, political parties collaborating with foreign powers (CCP), compradors, and Chinese Christians who oppressed fellow countrymen. Authoritarian forces included all forms of foreign influence but particularly Christian evangelism and schools under foreign control. After mid-1924 members of Young China organized branch units of the Anti-Christian Federation and the Movement for Restoration of Educational Rights; they also founded *Hsing-shih she* (Awakening Lion Society) to combat all forms of imperialist aggression and all deterrents to national unity.

The writings of Ch'en Ch'i-t'ien, a former anarchist, Young China Party leader, and editor of *Chung-hua chiao-yü chieh*, illustrate the new approach in arguments against parochial education. In 1922 Ch'en had stated that just as Chinese had demolished Confucius in the name of freedom of thought, so they must demolish Jesus for the same reasons. Less than two years later Ch'en recommended using education to instill national ideals and to provide for national needs, a task for which foreigners were not qualified.[44] Another leader of the Youth Corps and chief editor of the Chung-hua Book Co., Tso Shun-sheng, castigated educators for believing that they could remain apolitical and concentrate on educational reform.⁴⁵ Those "snobbish nincompoops," he said, dreamed of a completely intellectual and absolutely independent education; he would speak, not to them but to youth. Youth could understand that the problems were political, not pedagogical, and they were willing to risk working for a revolution against the reactionary military government. The new China that youth helped create should be a well-organized closed system, one that stressed civic education and eliminated foreign institutions. Yet another member, Yü Chia-chü of Wuchang Normal University (later National Wuhan University) delivered a series of lectures in central China on the cultural aggression of Christian institutions and the need for restoration of Chinese control over all education.⁴⁶

Traditional Chinese assumptions about socialization through education appeared substantiated by the theories of John Dewey and Paul Monroe. China should learn from the example of America, where public education had been essential to the effectiveness of the melting pot. Nationalists became alarmed, however, when Monroe applied his theories to mission education. *Hsin chiao-yü* translated an article in which Monroe defined the goals of parochial schools in relation to national identity. The basis of an effective nationality, Monroe wrote, was a common culture. In the manufacture of that common culture, education was the primary instrument, as many national governments were beginning to realize. If a nation were to be Christianized, therefore, it was not sufficient to provide religious education; rather, Christian education must modify every phase of culture. In particular, it must seek to train the future political and social leaders. Since missions could afford to educate only a small fraction of Chinese youth, Monroe recommended that they concentrate on a few strong institutions to serve as models to the Chinese and to attract the best talent. They should devote special attention to normal schools, for here they could shape "the character of those who are to teach and control the government schools." Ch'en Ch'i-t'ien quoted Monroe in a renewed attack on mission education.⁴⁷ Following up Monroe's thesis on the utility of education in nation building, Ch'en concluded that China must assume exclusive responsibility for schools; instead of preserving and inculcating China's distinctive national spirit, church schools were destroying the national essence.

At the annual meeting of the National Association for the Advancement of Education in July, 1924, Yü Chia-chü, Ch'en Ch'i-t'ien, Wu Shih-ch'ung, Hsieh Hsun-ch'u, Sun En-yuan, and other nationalistic educators sparked a move to restrict parochial schools.[48] Their resolutions ranged from demands for closure or take-over of all foreign schools, to strict enforcement of registration requirements, to government supervision of private institutions. After vigorous debate, liberals were able to moderate the broader demands so that the government was simply enjoined to determine and apply registration regulations and to restrain those foreigners using schools as a means of aggression. A motion to deny full recognition to kindergarten, primary and middle schools providing religious instruction was tabled.

By mid-1924 professional educators generally acknowledged that education was central to the building of a new China; they agreed that Chinese, not foreigners, should specify the overall structure and standards of the school system, and they found the current status of parochial schools unsatisfactory. They were not in accord on the concrete meaning of the phrase, "Restore Educational Rights," nor on the strategy for implementation. Not until the May Thirtieth Movement of 1925 would the policies of the Young China Party gain general acceptance and by then political rather than educational considerations were decisive.

The weakness of professionals operating without institutionalized political support was demonstrated in a brief flurry over Japanese educational activities in Fengtien before the Educational Rights Movement was formally launched. Early in the 20th century Japan had begun to establish schools emphasizing Japanese language and culture in the Liaotung peninsula and she had, since World War I, expanded her activities there and also along the South Manchurian Railway concession. By the 1920s educational institutions under Japanese control numbered some 450 schools ranging from kindergarten through the university level; they included normal colleges, technical institutes, eighteen centers for popular education, and over one hundred circulating libraries. Financial support came primarily from the Japanese concession areas while staffing and curriculum reflected Japanese colonial interests.[49]

Hsieh Yin-chang, Director of the Mukden Educational Bureau, had in 1923 expressed concern over Japan's expanding educational activities and had urged that all secondary and lower level schools and all teacher training institutes be staffed solely by Chinese citizens. Early in 1924 he helped organize an "Association to Promote the Restoration of Educational Rights in Fengtien." Party organs such as *Min-kuo jih pao, Hsiang-tao* and *Cheng-chih chou-pao* (Political Weekly) picked up the issue with warnings that Japanese cultural aggression was even more insidious and destructive of national sovereignty than her military and economic infringements. By April Fengtien educators were planning a three-fold campaign: publicity to awaken world opinion and the Chinese educational community, committees to investigate all aspects of Japanese cultural invasion, and representations to Japanese and government officials. Recommending a boycott of Japanese schools, the South Manchurian Educational Association called on the provincial government to protest to the Japanese and to establish substitute Chinese schools.[50]

The drive undertaken by teachers and educational administrators never got off the ground. Responding promptly and in no uncertain terms, the Japanese indicated that they would tolerate no interference with their educational activities and would hold provincial authorities responsible for "unfriendly acts". They interrogated Chinese educational and government leaders and they put such pressure on the *Feng-tien tung pao* (Fengtien Eastern Press) for publicizing educational rights issues that it temporarily ceased publication. Though Ch'en Tu-hsiu pointedly welcomed the paper's reappearance on April 20, Fengtien was far from the major centers of party influence so that party aid was largely verbal. Local provincial authorities blunted the drive by asking a halt to educational rights protests while they discussed the matter with the Japanese.[51] The instigators apparently decided that the risks of defying the Japanese were too high, for after May, 1924, only occasional protests against Japanese schools were heard: a brief article in August, 1925 on usurpation of educational rights by foreigners in Changchun, Chilin, and a condemnation of Japanese administrators for closing Tung Wen College to prevent patriotic demonstrations during the May Thirtieth Movement.[52] Direct action was exceedingly rare.

TARGETING CHRISTIAN SCHOOLS

The Christian schools became the primary targets, though Japan's hard line toward protests was only one of the reasons. Several essays in 1923 had pointed out that the Western educational effort was much more extensive than the Japanese and that Chinese must cease to consider mission schools charitable supplements to national education; they must see the schools for what they were: instruments of cultural aggression. In May 1923, Ch'en Tu-hsiu protested the lack of concern and publicity regarding foreign influence over students. After brief mention of the Japanese, Ch'en quoted an American missionary educator, who reportedly informed his students that they should abandon national loyalties when they entered church schools for study; how, Ch'en wondered, could such students still consider themselves Chinese?[53] Yun Tai-ying, as editor of *Chung-kuo ch'ing nien*, ironically asked how Christians could talk of saving China when they were the ones primarily responsible for destroying China's dignity and welfare; China would be saved when China's youth realized the hypocrisy of Christians, delivered her from foreign tyranny, and developed her national industry.[54]

Not only did Christian schools occupy an anomalous position in China, but recent actions on their part had drawn attention to their irregular status. Most schools, from their founding in the 19th century, had been entirely separate from the regular Chinese program.[55] Since the Westerners had generally used their own educational experience as a model for middle and higher level schools while Chinese had concentrated on mastering the Confucian corpus in preparation for the civil service examinations, the institutions differed in purpose, curriculum, clientele and organization. Christian colleges, for example, secured rights of incorporation from Western governments and offered Western degrees. Following the pattern of the church-related liberal arts college, the missionary educators attempted to develop self-contained academic communities with their own extra-curricular recreational activities, housing for both faculty and students, dining hall, and a chapel, all on a campus set apart from its environs. Westerners held the senior teaching and administrative positions while monies from mission societies provided the basic income. In Protestant institutions, especially, religion courses and worship services held pride of place, with participation required of Christian and non-Christian alike; revival meetings, religious emphasis weeks, and sectarian societies reinforced the proselytizing effort. Despite the fact that many schools originated as pet projects of individual missionaries, mission societies were by 1900 supporting Christian institutions extending all the way from nurseries for orphans through colleges, medical schools and seminaries.

The ability of the Christian colleges to offer a large portion of their graduates employment in mission institutions held out promise of economic security. English language training provided entree to new occupations in the treaty ports. In order to attract pupils, many of the mission schools during the 19th century charged little or no tuition. The schools thus served as a means of mobility for sons and daughters of non-gentry families; they did so as an alternative to, not as a competitor of, traditional education. So long as the examination system existed, classical training was the preferred and prestigious route for those who could afford it. In the 20th century, however, when the Chinese government began to construct a national educational system with modern curriculum and graded programs, the differences between mission and Chinese schools lessened so that the two came more directly into competition. Spurred by the challenge and also by institutional pride, Christian educators endeavored to raise standards. They paid greater attention to quality of teacher preparation, to laboratory and library facilities, entrance requirements, and so forth. Such emphasis on educational goals, however, often came into conflict with evangelistic goals and a satisfactory balance was difficult to maintain.

Well into the 20th century the parochial schools continued to have no formal relation with the Chinese government. Neither regulated by nor recognized by Peking, they cherished their autonomy. They were in many ways islands of extraterritoriality outside the mainstream of Chinese intellectual life.[56] An alumnus who returned to teach at a Christian middle school in Shenchow, Hunan, expressed unhappiness over the lack of interchange with the government school next door.[57] Not only were the two sets of teachers from diametrically opposite backgrounds, said he, but they differed in religion, in ideals, and in philosophy. "[E]ach group despised the other. They never met for friendly discussions on methods of teaching or on school administration in general."

Concern arose briefly in 1905 when the government ruled that graduation from a registered school was a prerequisite for the right to vote and to stand for election, for government scholarships to study abroad, and for examinations leading to bureaucratic office and diplomatic service. Several missionaries, therefore, requested the U.S. ambassador to inquire about the possibility of registering their schools so as to secure citizenship rights for their graduates. The Chinese government refused on the grounds that it did not wish to encourage external interference in China's education. Regarding the mission schools as foreign institutions protected by unequal treaties, the government would not include Christian schools in the same category with other private Chinese institutions. Since it did not feel powerful enough to control the parochial establishments, it chose to ignore them.[58] Here the matter rested until the 1920s.

Between 1911 and 1921 the republican government issued several sets of regulations for official registration of private schools. Requirements common to most of them were: Chinese participation in the school administration; equal treatment of Chinese and Western faculty members; voluntary religious activities and courses, no requirements; educational rather than evangelistic goals. Though non-registered schools and their graduates were theoretically subject to penalties, the Ministry of Education did not enforce the regulations and did not ordinarily restrict the citizenship rights of mission school graduates or deny them government scholarships and jobs. Some Chinese Christians were uncomfortable with their ill-defined status and stressed the urgency of clarifying the position of their alma maters but the Chinese government and the missionaries seemed little inclined to pursue the matter.⁵⁹

When rising nationalism questioned the status of the Christian schools during the early 1920s, mission societies were already reassessing the role of parochial education.⁶⁰ The Social Gospel, along with a sense of concern over the disruptive effect of missions, had provided church schools with a new legitimacy so that the educational branch of Protestant work was expanding rapidly. Spurred by a sense of competition with Protestants, Roman Catholics were also undertaking new initiatives in higher education. Western mission societies, on the other hand, were increasingly apprehensive about the haphazard proliferation of schools, which strained budgets, led to duplication of effort, and impeded the raising of standards. When the American Presbyterians (North) found themselves supporting nine institutions of higher education and the Methodists (North, U.S.A.), found themselves supporting seven, each struggling to become a college in fact as well as name, reconsideration became urgent. A committee of church leaders and educators was commissioned to undertake an overall survey of Protestant education in China. The resulting report, *Christian Education in China,* was published in 1922 in both Chinese and English versions and was widely circulated.⁶¹

Theme of the report was "Missionary education must be more efficient, more Christian, and more Chinese." To accomplish this, the survey commission recommended amalgamation of several institutions and coordination of curricula and standards by a revitalized China Christian Educational Association. The teaching of religion courses should receive greater attention in order to improve their quality and appeal, but above all the spirit of Christianity should pervade every aspect of the educational program. Christian nationalists such as Wu Lei-ch'uan and Wu Yao-tsung picked up the refrain and called for an end to the separatism of mission schools and students.⁶² For China to be Christianized, they said, Christian students must assume leadership; they must recognize their responsibilities to society and take an active part in patriotic movements. Mission education, furthermore, must be reorganized so that it would mesh with the Ministry of Education's School Reform Decree of 1922;

the Social Gospel should be carried to students in government schools.

The new directions proposed for Christian education were well publicized by those Chinese educators who were alarmed by the ambitions of the missions. *Hsin chiao-yü* printed an interview with the head of the Christian Educational Commission, Ernest Burton, and also a summary of the recommendations.⁶³ Yü Chia-chü protested that China was not "an uncivilized place", nor a "nation without men of learning" that foreigners should come to propagate religion and foster education.⁶⁴ The Westerners came for their own evangelistic and imperialistic purposes, not out of a desire to serve China and he quoted from *Christian Education in China* to document his contention that mission schools were a threat to the very existence of the Chinese nation: '"Now is the hour of opportunity so to strengthen the Christian schools of China that from them shall come the men and women who will make China a Christian nation"' (p. 15). '"It is not yet settled whether Christian education is to be the determining force or a relatively insignificant and diminishing factor in Chinese life. On the answer to this question will largely hang the decision whether China will become a Christian nation, perhaps the stronghold of Christianity in future centuries."' (p. 6) Chou T'ai-hsuan of the Young China Party stated that the missions' proposal to organize a nationwide coordinated hierarchy of Christian schools infringed on a national monopoly; education should be of the people, by the people, and for the people; it should be supervised and controlled by the people it serves, not by politicians or foreigners.⁶⁵

When, therefore, the strike at Holy Trinity set off a chain reaction of student storms and anti-Christian literature, the mission schools were vulnerable. The support base for a rights recovery campaign was wide and varied, ranging from Chinese Christians desiring Sinification of Christianity to Marxists espousing materialism and atheism. Even so, an analysis of the protests initiating the movement points to students in the cities of central and south China and to publicists and youth leaders of the United Front. Most of the "storms" occurred in the Christian middle schools rather than colleges, which were to be the scene of many later strikes, and the locale ranged from Shanghai to Canton and from Hsuchow in Kiangsu to Changsha in Hunan. The major periodicals providing publicity were organs of the political parties: *Chueh-wu* and *Fu-nü chou pao* (Women's Weekly) which were supplements to the *Min-kuo jih-pao;* *Hsiang tao* and *Chung-kuo ch'ing-nien* under CCP auspices, *Hsin Hsueh-sheng,* sponsored by the United Front, and *Hsing-shih chou-pao,* published by Young China Party leaders.

Several magazine editors and some of the frequent contributors had had direct experience with Christian education or were associated with Fu Tan University, founded by dissidents from Aurora.[66] Tseng Ch'i, Li Huang and Tso Shun-sheng of the Young China Party, had all been at Aurora together. Yeh Ch'u-t'sang and Shao Li-tzu, editors of *Min-kuo jih-pao* and *Chueh-wu,* both had taught at Fu Tan and Shao had earlier been one of those students withdrawing from Aurora to establish Fu Tan. As director of the department of youth and women in the KMT's Shanghai headquarters, Yeh was responsible for propaganda among students and almost every issue of *Chueh-wu* during May carried material on the student strikes and educational rights. At Fu Tan in 1924 were Yang Yu-chiung and Liu K'ang-hou, who contributed articles and letters to *Chueh-wu* and *Chung-kuo ch'ing-nien*. K'o Po-nien (pseud. Li Ch'un-fan), whose essays in *Chueh-wu* were reprinted in anti-Christian publications, had apparently attended one of the Protestant colleges. Some publicists, Ts'ai Ho-sen, Ch'en Tu-hsiu, and Wu Chih-hui for instance, had studied in France, where parochial education, anti-clericalism, and Biblical criticisms were controversial issues. Though exaggeration commonly characterized patriotic protests, the anguish and animosity of the denunciations are striking and appear in many instances to be the outgrowth of personal experience.

Ch'en, Wu, Hu Han-min, and others rejected the concept of the school as a house of study and admonished youth to accept the responsibility of political activism. They, along with most writers, reiterated the familiar criticisms of Christianity and Christian education, but a new specificity reinforced their impact. To illustrate the denationalization of Christian school graduates, K'o

Po-nien described a Chinese language class in a mission school: "Some students are eating peanuts, some reading a novel, some studying English, some reading newspapers, some sleeping, some having private talks with their friends. No one is really learning Chinese."[67] The result, he said, was that none could write a decent paragraph in Chinese. K'o also used his knowledge of world history to illustrate his contention that Christian missions were deliberately employed as forerunners of imperialism. After providing examples of Spanish, Portuguese, French, and English solicitude for the heathen, he listed mission cases which had led to loss of Chinese territory and sovereign rights. To deny that Christianity was an opening wedge for Western imperialism was, he concluded, to contradict the facts of history. Shao Li-tzu protested that pupils in foreign schools knew more about Washington, Napoleon, and Western culture than about Duke Wen of Chin, Duke Huan of Ch'i, and Chinese culture; what was worse, they learned no contemporary Chinese history and were unaware of the shame and impoverishment of China by the imperialists.[68] Instead of becoming patriots, they became lackeys of the foreigner in the customs, diplomatic, and railway services, aiding and abetting his aggression.

The Holy Trinity declaration spoke of pitiful oppression and of treatment like a colonial people; are we not citizens of an independent nation rather than subjects of foreign masters, they asked. Yang Yu-chiung announced that the imperialists had practically taken control of Chinese education and were using it for their own purposes; it was imperialism in its most nefarious guise.[69] In response to Yang's letters, an anonymous student wrote: "If I detest the poison of the churches, it is because I have known it well. I have been for three years a student in a Christian school. I have breathed to satiety the slavish atmosphere there. I have had to murmur prayers. . . . Those schools of servility are fatal to our country. . . . It is necessary to close them as the Turks have done. . . ." One of the students at P'ei-hsin Middle School in Hsuchow solicited aid in ending the "servile and outdated" education of the Christian schools, where students had to endure the tyranny and effrontery of foreign administrators, where missionaries used their Bible and their prayers as weapons "to kill our souls" and extinguish the life of youth.[70]

The incident touching off the "student storm" at P'ei-hsin Middle School in Hsuchow gives some insight into the nature of relations that could generate animosities not amenable to rational compromise. According to Chu Wu-p'ing's account in *Hsiang-tao,* he and other students were eating lunch on May 11 when the principal entered the dining room and stood watching them; suddenly the missionary blurted out: ' "You Chinese are bandits [*t'u-fei*], beasts [*tsou-shou*]; you revile the Japanese as no good; you are not as good as the Japanese; you are worth even less!' More than two hundred people remained silent as if suffering death. . . ." Later at vespers the principal scolded the teachers for not fulfilling their responsibilities and for not participating in worship. The student body thereupon drew up demands for self-government, control of dining hall matters, dismissal of three teachers, and a prohibition on public reprimands by the principal. In rejecting the demands, the Westerners told the student representatives that they would have to make a choice: study in a church school in preparation for serving China later or transfer to a public school where they were free to engage in patriotic activities.[71]

The language of the principal displayed unusual insensitivity on his part; labelling the students uncivilized and barbarous was bad enough; adding insult to injury was his ranking them lower than the Japanese. After all, the Japanese were assumed to have derived their culture from China and they had saddled the Chinese with the "Twenty-one Demands" and numerous concessions in Shantung and the Northeastern provinces. On the other hand, authoritarianism was not uncommon in either Chinese or parochial schools and the principal was quite typical of mission educators in his desire to keep his institution apolitical. The novel ingredient was the readiness of New Youth to question authority. A Kuomintang youth assembly in Shanghai proclaimed students the soul of the revolution; they could not, therefore, devote themselves exclusively to study and leave politics to their elders; rather they must persuade all students of the primacy of their duty to the nation. A Hunanese student manifesto declared that an education independent of the state would lack vitality. Though critics dubbed parochial students denationalized and submissive while the students themselves spoke of the foreign, servile environment, the flurry of student storms during the spring of 1924 clearly indicated that the isolation of the mission schools was eroding. In addition to the conflicts clustered around the Holy Trinity strike, storms arose at parochial schools in Canton and Nanking over the observance of Humiliation Day in May, 1924.

Two aspects of Chu's narrative of the P'ei-hsin storm are worth noting. The half-dozen or so strikes in mission schools during May had become common knowledge among students by mid-June, for Chu repeated statements attributed to Western administrators in several institutions. The example of the other schools, said Chu, had emboldened P'ei-hsin students to present the principal with an ultimatum. Another indication of effective publicity was an article providing details on seven student storms by Hsiao Ch'u-nü, Socialist Youth Corps leader, instructor at Shanghai University and Whampoa Military Academy, and co-editor of *Chung-kuo ch'ing-nien*.[72] Hsiao urged students to use the summer vacation to make the damaging evidence known throughout China. Even so, the support structure was not yet in place, and the second revelation of Chu's essay is the dependence of students on external aid. Chu confessed that most P'ei-hsin students had quickly retreated from active defiance; he pled for unity in goals and strategy as he concluded: "I hope . . . that all fellow students will rise up in support of their comrades in the church schools. . . ." The second manifesto of the Holy Trinity students complained that the principal paid no attention to their demands and protests.[73]

Not until the summer of 1924 did New Youth and party leaders begin to build a campaign apparatus. In June the Canton Student Union organized a Restore Educational Rights Committee and on June 18, the committee drew up a manifesto subsequently published in *Hsiang-tao* (July 2) and *Chung-kuo ch'ing-nien* (July 5). Recounting once again the spring storms at the Christian schools and stating that the cries for help resembled flying snow flakes, the manifesto called on students to rise up in a united movement to secure the following minimal demands: (1) all schools opened by foreigners must submit to government registration and inspection or be closed, (2) the academic program shall be directed by Chinese teachers, (3) no religious instruction or exercises shall be part of the regular program, (4) students shall not be deprived of the freedom to publish, assemble, organize, or hold discussions.

In mid-July a group of Trinity students who had transferred to Canton Normal College and had organized a youth corps to resist cultural aggression issued a proclamation reiterating the evils of colonial education and pleading for expansion of societies to fight cultural imperialism.[74] The list of organizations to whom the newly-formed youth corps sent its proclamation indicates the communication links that had been forged and the organizational structure that was already in place. The circular telegram appealed to branches of the National Student Union throughout China and to a variety of other student associations such as the New Student Society in Canton, the Foochow Young Student Society, the Hangchow Young United Progress Association, and so forth. The telegram was also addressed to those parochial students who had gone on strike in a half dozen middle schools, to the Fengtien Educational Rights Association, to the labor unions of China, and to *Hsiang-tao* and other newspaper offices.

Ch'en Tu-hsiu editorialized that the demand by the National Association for the Advancement of Education for registration was not the same as restoration of educational rights and youth must take the initiative in ousting the foreigners if the government and the educational world were unwilling.[75] The National Student Union at its 6th annual meeting in August, 1924, recapitulated the themes currently popular in radical periodicals: the common cause of the militarists and their imperialist supporters, the necessity of waging war against both, the ulterior motives with which capitalists sponsored missions, the friendship of the U.S.S.R. in contrast to the avarice of the bourgeois powers, the national necessity of closing all foreign and parochial schools.[76]

Finally, on August 13, while the Student Union congress was in session in Shanghai, approximately a hundred persons gathered to re-establish the Anti-Christian Federation. K'o Po-nien and Wu Chih-hui, who had nine days earlier exhorted members of the Student Union to become activists in the revolutionary cause, addressed the inaugural meeting. The five member executive committee that was installed included K'o, Kao Erh-po, who was secretary of the propaganda bureau of the Kuomintang Shanghai branch, T'ang Kung-hsien and Chang Ch'iu-jen, both of whom joined the CCP sometime before 1927, and Hsu Heng-yao, whose affiliation is unknown. They drew up a constitution and an ambitious program of research, publication, and conferences. Within a few days, the federation put out the first edition of its biweekly, *Fei Chi-tu-chiao t'e-k'an* (The Anti-Christian Special) and issued a proclamation decrying the new and dangerous social emphasis of the church, which could penetrate society to its depth.[77] The manifestoes and spate of articles generally repeat the arguments already formulated and do not require summarization, but it is worth noting that *Fei Chi-tu-chiao t'e-k'an* went out as insert of *Chueh-wu,* supplement to Shanghai *Min-kuo jih-pao* and that many of the contributors were activists and publicists already mentioned. Both their work pace and their inter-relationships are impressive.

Significant was the fact that by the fall of 1924 a number of organizations had been founded specifically to campaign for educational rights and to oppose Christian evangelism: the Corps to Resist Cultural Aggression, Restore Educational Rights Movement Committees, and the Anti-Christian Federation, all grouped under the Great Anti-Imperialist League. Professional educational associations, the Young China Party, the KMT and the CCP with their affiliated youth corps had incorporated the issue into their programs and the National Student Union had given priority to the recovery of a national monopoly over education. With so many participating groups, broad support was assured, but coordination in tactics and goals was far from realization.

Chapter V

The Move to Restore Educational Rights: First Stage

With the benefit of hindsight, historians can delineate the decisive events in China during 1924-1925: formation of a United Front by the Kuomintang and Chinese Communist Party and their preparations for a drive against the militarists and imperialists. Prerequisites to successful revolution were mass support to legitimize party rule, military force to overthrow the warlords, and a party ideology to attract and commit activist leaders. Scholars have, therefore, quite rightly concentrated on such activities as the establishment of Whampoa Military Academy and the creation of a party army, Sun Yat-sen's fleshing out of the Three Principles of the People and the multiplication of propaganda outlets, the training of cadres and the expansion of support organizations.

Counter activities and diversions within both parties were, however, abundant. Sectors of both parties objected so vigorously to the United Front and other policies that they refused full cooperation. Comintern agents as well as Sun Yat-sen negotiated with various warlords regarding temporary cooperation or even a coalition. And in late 1924 Sun undertook a trip north to seek an agreement with the Peking government on the convening of a broadly representative national assembly to unify China. Numerous patriotic Chinese, furthermore, accepted service in the Peking administration with the hope of reforming and strengthening China. In 1924, a Chinese nationalist predicting the military and political success of the KMT within three years might have been accused of wishful thinking. To operate on such an assumption required an act of faith. Not before the May Thirtieth Movement did the Northern Expedition of 1926 seem a viable move.

Since the appeal of the Educational Rights Movement cut across generational and political loyalties, it is not surprising that in 1924 the movement mirrored the uncertainties and divisions of China. Some supporters tried to work through the Peking government and the Ministry of Education; others anticipated success only within the context of total revolution. Certain individuals were like Sun in that they employed the rhetoric of revolution but showed a readiness to negotiate for less than complete takeover. Student groups and radical organizations frequently advocated strikes, demonstrations, and confrontations, while educators emphasized publicity and lobbying as techniques. Nor was there agreement on the optimum fate of the Christian schools.

During the initial stages of the campaign, various approaches were used and the arguments in the manifestoes, articles, and resolutions showed great variety. Though educators and political activists tried to benefit from each other's exertions, they gave little attention to coordinating their efforts. The movement, while gaining publicity, was operating on separate levels. By the spring of 1925 the campaign seemed to have reached a plateau and many were wondering what should be the next stage. What tactics would bring concrete results? Exactly what were the immediate and the long-range aims of the movement? Criticisms of the techniques and goals of other advocates of educational rights were voiced in a number of articles. Soon thereafter, the tragedy of May 30, 1925 brought anti-imperialist nationalism to full tide and altered the prospects for violent overthrow of the Peking regime. The Educational Rights Movement would be revitalized as one aspect of the nationalist revolution.

TACTICS AND THEMES

Upon the launching of the movement in the summer of 1924, the Anti-Christian Federation, the Educational Rights Association, the Student Union, and other youth groups concentrated on publicity and the establishment of branch organizations in all major urban centers. The immediate challenge was to awaken all students and especially students in the Christian institutions to the evils resulting from the cultural aggression of the missionaries. In reasserting the sovereignty lost in the unequal treaties, China must eventually regain a national monopoly over education.

KMT and CCP leaders and periodicals continued to provide support. On the recommendation of the Fan ti-kuo-chu-i ta t'ung-meng, the KMT declared the anniversary of the signing of the Boxer Protocol a National Humiliation Day; September 7 would mark the beginning of an Anti-Imperialism Week. Commemorations were accordingly held in Canton, Peking, Wuchang, Hankow, and elsewhere. Articles in *Hsiang-tao* and *Fei Chi-tu-chiao t'e-k'an* praised the anti-imperialism of the Boxers and condemned those "running dogs" lodging in the "kennels" (schools) of the foreigners. Leo Karakhan, Soviet Ambassador to China, urged the Anti-Christian Federation to suppress Christian pastors, hirelings of the imperialists and militarists.[1]

Chueh-wu not only sent out *Fei Chi-tu-chiao t'e-k'an* but it also printed articles on anti-Christian activities several times a week during the late fall and established a regular column entitled "News of the Anti-Christian Federation". Individuals were urged to send articles, letters, information about the Christian institutions and campaign activities to Li Ch'un-fan (K'o Po-nien) of Shanghai University.[2] In addition to the periodical founded by the Shanghai Anti-Christian Federation in August, 1924, the Kwangtung Anti-Christian branch edited *Fan Chi-tu-chiao chou-k'an* (Anti-Christian Weekly) beginning in February, 1925; publisher was the Canton office of the KMT's *Min-kuo jih-pao,* which sent the supplement to its regular constituencies and to mission schools and presses.[3] The Shanghai Anti-Christian Federation and the Communist Chung-kuo ch'ing-nien she (China Youth Society) collaborated in publishing on December 10, 1924, *Fan tui Chi-tu-chiao yun-tung* (The Anti-Christian Movement). This small volume, which reprinted several earlier articles and speeches, circulated widely among educated Chinese and the following year the YMCA issued an English language edition to acquaint missionaries with the campaign literature. Important centers of activity were (1) in Shanghai, Fu-Tan University and Middle School, Ta Hsia University and Shanghai University (2) in Canton, Kwangtung University and the First Middle School (3) in Changsha, Hunan First Normal School (Chung Shan University) and (4) in Wuchang, the National Wuchang University (formerly National Normal University).

With such an outpouring of materials, the propaganda inevitably became repetitive and some of the material was actually used several times over. The introduction to *Fan tui Chi-tu-chiao yun-tung,* for example, was a shortened version of Yang Hsien-chiang's (Li Hao-wu) essay in *Fei Chi-tu-chiao t'e-k'an* (September, 1924) and it was later altered slightly to become the first article in *Fan Chi-tu-chiao chou-k'an* (February, 1925).⁴ Much of the material in *Fan Chi-tu-chiao chou-k'an,* as a matter of fact, was reprinted from *Chueh-wu* and *Chung-kuo ch'ing-nien.*

Though no argument against Christianity and the parochial schools was neglected, the emphasis of the left-coalition literature as a whole was somewhat different from that of 1920-1922 and even of early 1924. The left KMT leaders, K'o Po-nien and Liao Chung-k'ai, both stressed that they supported an anti-Christian movement rather than an anti-religion one.⁵ For them, the shift from an intellectual to a political goal was complete. The enemy was the Christian missionary enterprise as the vanguard of imperialism instead of the Christian religion as the deterrent to progress and freedom of inquiry. A curriculum outline for Communist Party schools recommended that cadres use Christian schools as a concrete example of imperialist oppression in their propaganda.⁶ Many of the articles placed the Educational Rights Movement in the framework of world socialist revolution as well as the Chinese national revolution; they used Marxian class categories to explain the predestined overthrow of the capitalists and their "running dogs".

Chou En-lai saw Christianity as originating in a revolt of commoners against Judaism but stated that the church had quickly become the instrument of the dominant class in controlling and oppressing the masses.⁷ First employed by the Roman rulers, the church successively served the Papacy and the feudal nobility, then the Protestant capitalists, according to Chou. When Christianity began to decline in the West during the 19th century, the church turned to collaboration with the imperialists; it hoped to regain influence by convincing Asians and Africans that they must adopt the Christian civilization of the West in order to move into the modern world. In Chou's view, however, the oppressed were awakening; both Christianity and imperialism were doomed with the approach of the age of national liberation. Ts'ai Ho-sen, an editor of *Hsiang-tao* and lecturer at Shanghai University, emphasized the premeditation with which captialists fostered proselytism and concluded that only the science of socialism could overturn the enemies of progress.[8]

Such a Marxian approach was utilized frequently by radical writers, with some essayists including specific illustrations of the middle class orientation of Christian missions. One author interpreted a YMCA regulation requiring proper dress for admission as discrimination against the workers; another, who had attended a mission school for two years, condemned the principal's promise of heavenly reward for the poor as a capitalist technique to keep the oppressed quiet and submissive. One of the founders of the Hangchow Anti-Christian Federation noted the YMCA's use of a letter of introduction from the Shanghai Vice Chairman of the Chamber of Commerce to municipal leaders in soliciting aid for a mass education program; the YMCA, he concluded, was dependent on and tool of the Establishment. A former Christian, who was secretary of the Educational Rights Committee of the Canton Student Union, offered "evidence" of Christianity's acting as precursor of the imperialists, friend of the warlords, and prop to the traditional social system. Illustrations of the latter included a friend's being required to swear obedience to her husband in the Christian marriage ceremony and quotations from Paul's epistles.[9]

Though this holism of the radicals scared off non-revolutionaries, it was simultaneously a source of strength. The revolutionaries not only linked the Educational Rights Movement to the drive against foreign capitalists and Chinese militarists; they reinterpreted Chinese history and international relations so that the imperialists became the source of all China's failings. The Boxers were presented as warriors against imperialism rather than as traditionalist peasants. December 25 was to be designated a Day of Humiliation, on a par with May 9th, date of the acceptance of the Twenty-one Demands, and September 7, date of the Boxer Protocol.[10]

Another linkage was suggested by citing the authoritarian statements and regulations of missionary administrators as symbolic of the imperialists' treatment of China under the unequal treaties. Though all nationalistic Chinese were sensitive to the personal and national humiliations suffered by China, the intense repugnance expressed by certain left-wing writers provides an insight into one source of their radicalism. The author of an essay entitled "Kou-hua ti chiao-yü" (Dog-like Education) argued that practically all Chinese education had been taken over by foreigners either directly in the mission schools or by the dependence of Chinese schools on foreign financial assistance such as the Boxer Indemnity funds; the "dog-like" education was triply insulting because it assumed that Chinese were uncivilized and needed Western tutelage, because Westerners secured funds abroad by picturing the Chinese as less than human, i.e., as having the culture of dogs and pigs, and because missionaries treated Chinese as inferiors in the Christian institutions. He condemned those Chinese who "wagged their tails" in order to secure foreign aid; we want justice, not charity, he said.[11]

Since the Educational Rights Movement was locked into the course of Chinese history and even of world history, the crusade was all-encompassing. More than one manifesto ended on a note similar to that sounded by the Shantung anti-Christian branch: "Fathers and mothers, brothers and sisters of China, it is for the defense of our civil rights, of our national civilization, of our country, of our race, that we rise up. Do as we do and enroll in the Anti-Christian Federation."[12] Others embraced the cause of the weak and oppressed of the whole world. This purist approach helped resolve doubts about the possible utility of social services offered by the Christian church.

Broadening the cause to include the fate of the Chinese nation and race placed the apologist or non-participant in the awkward position of being indifferent to China's welfare. Often it served to increase the commitment of the activist. Consider the difficulty of nationalistic Christians in replying to an appeal that went out as Christmas Week began:

"Can you stand the sound of Christmas carols? Can you be indifferent to the decoration of Christmas trees in churches? Can you see the end of our nation without saying anything?" [13]

By mid-December, 1924, branches of anti-Christian or educational rights associations had been established in most of the government institutions of higher education and in many of the leading middle schools. At least some of these branches had regular fortnightly meetings to discuss issues and tactics. Though data on the exact role of the original associations in the founding of branches is elusive, there is some evidence of coordination. During the late fall of 1924, "News of the Anti-Christian Federation" in *Chueh-wu* frequently featured information about the founding of branch associations, with the December 3 issue listing seven cities where comrades were said to have organized branches and the December 9 issue stating that a youth went from Shanghai to Ningpo in order to call an organizational meeting. Several of the founders published anti-Christian articles in *Chueh-wu* and other journals. It seems likely that few branches of the Educational Rights Movement had been organized in Christian colleges and senior middle schools though they often had student unions or student government associations. The campaign leaders, until the May Thirtieth Movement, generally regarded parochial students as individuals to be awakened rather than as activist colleagues. An editorial in *Chueh-wu,* November 25, 1924, recommended that some of the enlightened students enroll in the mission schools, since little could be expected of the rice Christians and careerists there. This attitude, along with the need to raise the consciousness of all intellectuals, was one reason for the continued emphasis on publicity, both informational and hortatory.

Various techniques were used to keep the issue before the reading public. One was to draft frequent manifestoes and to telegraph these to the major newspapers and to branches of the professional educational associations, student unions, etc. Another was to solicit testimonials and commendations that could be reproduced in the campaign periodicals. In the first issue of *Fan Chi-tu-chiao chou-k'an,* for example, the editor stated that he had received two to three hundred letters of support during the past few days and regretted that he could publish only a portion of them.

Editors were especially desirous of statements by Christian apostates and by current or former parochial school students. In addition to proclamations by striking students, *Fan Chi-tu-chiao chou-k'an, Chueh-wu,* and *Fei Chi-tu-chiao t'e-k'an* published accounts of humiliating experiences in the Christian schools and explanations for apostasy or withdrawal. The utility of such reports was that they amassed specific detail which helped substantiate the broader accusations. Also persuasive were the bitterness and passion of most confessions. Entering the church or a mission school set a youth apart from Chinese society; in the foreignized atmosphere of the institution, he was under heavy pressure to accept the values and mores of Christian civilization as defined by Westerners; he was subject to the authority of individuals from another race and culture. Having accommodated himself, a youth could hardly reverse himself and admit his error without emotional scarring. It almost required simplification of issues and exaggeration of evils. An article by a St. John's student seems practically a textbook expression of identity crisis. "I formerly was befuddled as if drunk," he wrote; "I was Europeanized so that I thought that to learn English was everything. When I first entered this prestigious university therefore, I was happy, but I soon woke up to the dark slavish life I was leading. This is a school for rich sons of capitalists or warlords who squander money aping the foreigner. Furthermore, we receive a slavish education in which the only thing that counts is doing well in the Bible course and in which the English instruction is barely sufficient for a comprador's position." [14]

In addition to such anti-Christian testimonials, the associations sought the sanction of influential individuals and disseminated their statements. Particularly during Christmas week prominent educators and political leaders were asked to speak. On December 25 Tsou Lu, president of the Kwangtung University (later Chung-shan University) and director of the KMT Youth Department; Liao Chung-k'ai, member of the Central Executive Committee of the KMT and senior political officer at Whampoa, and Chou Fo-hai, a party propagandist who was also teaching at Kwangtung and Whampoa, addressed a rally at Kwangtung University, with Whampoa cadets participating.[15] The Shanghai federation invited Chang Sung-nien, a Peita professor who was known as an exponent of dialectical materialism and the philosophy of Bertrand Russell, to speak on "The Organization of Christianity in the World and in China."[16] Among those solicited for the December 25 convocation at Shanghai University were Shih Ts'un-t'ung, one of the founders of the CCP and of the Socialist Youth Corps and a member of the university faculty, and Liu Ch'ing-yang, organizer of the Tientsin Association of Women Patriotic Comrades and a leader in the National Student Union. An interview with Chou En-lai published in *Fan Chi-tu-chiao chou-k'an* and a speech by Wu Chih-hui to the Shanghai Anti-Christian Federation have already been cited.

The enduring magic of Sun Yat-sen's name despite his bleak prospects in the early 1920s is revealed by a controversy in which both Christian and non-Christian attempted to identify their cause with him. Sun had, of course, accepted Christianity during his youth but had later ceased to associate himself with the church. As he contrasted Russian aid with Western obstructionism, he became increasingly critical of the West and at a meeting of Lingnan students during the customs controversy of December, 1923, he berated the U.S. for its naval demonstration; America, he said, was acting as a cat's paw for British imperialists. In 1924 the Student Union claimed to be following Sun's program in its demand for a national monopoly of education. In February, 1925, however, the son of Sun Yat-sen, Sun Fo, publicly criticized the Anti-Christian Movement and expressed the hope that Christians would join the KMT.[17] Upon Sun's death in March, 1925, the family requested a Christian funeral service. In addition to the public ceremony, therefore, a private Protestant service was held in the chapel of Peking Union Medical College with Liu T'ing-fang, head of the Yenching School of Theology, presiding and Hsu Ch'ien, an old associate of Sun and an advocate of Sinified Christianity, delivering a eulogy.

Liu's funeral testimonial, Hsu's memorial, and subsequent articles by Christians argued that Sun had remained true to Christianity as he devoted his life to fulfilling the revolutionary teachings of Christ; the church should follow Sun and try to recover its revolutionary spirit; those who wished to carry out Sun's will should study and apply Christian principles. *Fan Chi-tu-chiao chou-k'an* and party members replied promptly: the Christians' espousal of Sun's cause was only for propaganda purposes; Sun had abandoned Christianity when he became a revolutionary because he knew the church was the running dog of imperialism; to fight against imperialism with its oppression of the masses was to oppose its tools; to follow Sun was to strike out against Christianity.[18] T.V. Soong tried to find a compromise position in a statement explaining the decision to hold a Christian service; Sun, he said, accepted the teachings of Christ, not "the fettering dogmas of clerical institutions."[19] The teachings of Christ had no relation to attempts of so-called Christian nations to enslave China and oppress the masses.

Though Christians obviously felt at a disadvantage, the quarreling over Sun's mantle continued. The first memorial service for Sun in Canton was a religious assembly held by the Lingnan Student Council on the evening after Sun's death. In April, when anti-Christian groups accused Chungking church leaders of lacking patriotism and threatened to disrupt Easter services, the Christians countered by transforming the Easter celebrations into a memorial for Sun Yat-sen.[20]

As guidance for Anti-Christian Week, 1924, K'o Po-nien, Chung-kuo ch'ing-nien she, and the Anti-Christian Federation recommended a variety of special efforts: rallies, street demonstrations with distribution of handbills, circular telegrams to all major newspapers, special anti-Christian editions of magazines.[21] In addition, activists should attend the Christmas programs and services to disperse leaflets and ask questions. All literature, K'o cautioned, should back up accusations with documentary evidence and material should be designed for popular consumption as well as for students. There is no question about the literary deluge in December and the rash of public meetings. As previously mentioned, Chung-kuo ch'ing-nien she and the Shanghai Anti-Christian Federation reprinted some of the more popular essays in a booklet that received wide circulation. *Chueh-wu, Hsiang-tao, Hsin hsueh-sheng,* and *Chung-kuo ch'ing-nien* increased the space devoted to the campaign, in some cases including a regular column on anti-Christian activities, in some cases publishing special editions. Hangchow reported a rally of some three hundred at which several Christians apostatized. The U.S. consul in Canton relayed to local officials his alarm over the dangers of such agitation while the convocations and propaganda became so widespread that U.S. Ambassador Jacob Schurman requested reports from consuls about anti-Christian activities in their areas.[22]

CONFRONTATIONS AND STUDENT STORMS

Despite the publicity, direct confrontations appear to have been few and to have occurred principally in Hunan. Elsewhere, there are only scattered reports of public clashes: a heated discussion at a Canton YMCA with the meeting breaking up in disorder, a speech outside a Canton church and a thwarted attempt to distribute circulars during the Christmas service; agitators entering mission schools in Hangchow and Ningpo to disrupt festivities and dispense literature. Little or no violence occurred.[23] Among the participants in Canton were groups of Whampoa cadets and Liao Ch'eng-chih, son of Liao Chung-k'ai and a student at Lingnan.

Campaign leaders might concur on the need to sensitize Chinese to the evils of cultural aggression but they had reached no agreement on the actual tactics for ending foreign tutelage. One article urged destruction of buildings and forcible take-over of parochial schools, though such calls for use of force were rare before the May Thirtieth Movement.[24] Much of the publicity at the beginning of the 1924-1925 academic year was designed to dissuade parents from sending their children to mission schools and to encourage youth to refuse to enroll in Christian institutions. Others demanded immediate government registration of all educational institutions with closure of unregistered schools after a designated date; parochial students should be penalized in matters of citizenship rights, scholarships, recognition of their degrees, and admission to national schools.

Even while advocating "student storms" in the mission schools, agitators were unclear as to the purpose other than publicity. The political activists sometimes found themselves cheering from the sidelines when student storms did arise, since the rights recovery associations had not yet extended their network to include the Christian institutions. Such appears to have been the case at middle schools in Kaifeng and Chungking where clashes occurred in November, 1924.[25] Though both conflicts began with protests over compulsory Bible study and demands for a liberalized curriculum and social code, a contributory factor was the character of the school administration. In each instance, the principal had a reputation as a strict disciplinarian who insisted that his school remain a house of study, not a center for social action. The "storms" led to student withdrawals amid considerable publicity, but the missionary educators showed little inclination to alter school policies. The "storms" brewed no tempests in neighboring schools.

The major "student storm" center in the winter of 1924-1925 was Hunan. Here, the greater sophistication and coordination of the campaign foreshadowed the post-May Thirtieth period. There were good reasons for the advanced revolutionary nationalism in Hunan. Unrest had been exacerbated by the disastrous flood of 1924 and by the recurrent warfare of militarists contending for control of a crucial province. With Hunan First Normal College and its attached schools at the center, a network of radical organizations had been nurtured by Mao Tse-tung, Ts'ai Ho-sen, Hsia Hsi, Hsia Ming-han and others. Among these associations were the Hunan Student Union, Socialist Youth Corps, and Committee for Diplomatic Support, all of which joined the educational rights and anti-Christian branches in fostering a rights recovery campaign. Liu Shao-ch'i and Hsia Hsi, furthermore, had worked as KMT recruiters in Changsha so that many of the KMT branches had a left-wing orientation. Mao, like most of the Hunan radicals, made no secret of his antagonism toward Christian missions, Mao lambasting compatriots for not realizing that England was a greater threat to China than Japan and the most villainous of all was the U.S.A., leading patron of educational missions.[26]

Several Young China Party members active in the Educational Rights Movement had also propagandized in

Hunan. Yü Chia-chü and Ch'en Ch'i-t'ien had taught at Hunan First Normal College in 1920-1921 and Yü had returned to Changsha in mid-1924 to lecture on the urgency of bringing all education under national control and on the necessity of ending all religious indoctrination in schools; subsequently he helped organize provincial branches of the Educational Rights Association. Whether connected with Yü's activities or not, graduates of Yale-in-China's middle school began to have difficulty gaining admission to national universities because the school was not registered. President Edward H. Hume acknowledged that the experience contributed to noticeable restlessness among his Yali students as the fall semester began.[27] Another Young China Party member, Shu Hsin-ch'eng, had taught in Presbyterian schools in Hunan and had been director of social services for the Changsha YMCA. After coming into conflict with mission administrators over dismissal of a student, Shu angrily withdrew from the Presbyterian church as well as from his position with the mission. He became a prolific writer in the educational field, with many of his works stressing the function of education in developing talented, patriotic citizens.

These young intellectuals in Hunan had a long anti-Christian tradition on which to build. During the 1860s and 1870s Hunan had been a major source of scurrilous anti-Christian pamphlets and the locale of frequent outbursts against foreign and Chinese Christians. So formidable was Hunan's reputation that Protestant missions did not establish a residence in the province until 1900; since that time, expansion had been rapid, accentuating, perhaps, the impression that Christian missions threatened to inundate Chinese society.

In this environment it is not surprising that a strike at Yale-in-China (Yali) over an apparently inconsequential incident escalated into a conflict closing Yali and half a dozen mission middle schools in Hunan.[28] The relationship between the trigger incident and the issues emerging during the confrontation is, in fact, so tangential that the storm can only be explained as the result of long-standing resentment toward administrators who were foreign, Christian and authoritarian, plus the politicization of parochial students, and the aid of outside agencies.

The precipitating event, furthermore, varied from school to school.

At a football game between Yali and another Christian college in early December, 1924, a fracas broke out and a Chinese instructor who was trying to separate two students lost his temper and struck the Yali student. The Yali Student Union interpreted the physical assault as an insult to the whole student body and demanded that the instructor apologize and bow three times at a formal assembly. It was probably not coincidental that the Chinese teacher was a returned American student and that the union required that he humble himself at a chapel service. Though President Hume reluctantly acceded to the demand, he also sought to restore faculty disciplinary control; in particular, he forbade further student assembly meetings without the presence of the faculty advisor and he banned the posting of placards defaming the school or faculty members.

Ill will and defiant gestures compounded the troubles and in a heated exchange the student leader stated that in any conflict he would always obey the Student Union rather than the school administration. President Hume thereupon expelled the leader, placed two others on probation, dissolved the student legislative committee and took away the seal with which it validated proclamations. A secret night meeting of the student assembly voted a strike in support of its suspended leaders and on December 12 over one third of the student body left school. The two hundred striking students included a large percentage of the middle school enrollment, many college underclassmen, but few of the college juniors and seniors. After closing the school gates, the school administration decreed that individual students would be permitted to return only upon signing a written apology.

Each side in the conflict sought external aid. President Hume wrote to the parents of the striking students giving his version of the storm and asking parents to urge their sons to return under the conditions set by the college. On December 13, the students, who had voted an assessment on each pupil and had designated a committee to coordinate activities, circulated throughout the city handbills requesting support against "the foreigner who wants to make slaves of us". The Anti-Christian Federation held a rally the following day, and assistance was shortly forthcoming from many quarters: the local and provincial Student Union, the Anti-Imperialist League, Committee for Diplomatic Support, Chiao-yü chu-ch'üan wei-chih hui (Society to Regain a Monoply over Education), the professional educational associations, labor unions, and party branches.

Both the focus and the locale of the conflict broadened immediately. As Hume reported with dismay on December 17, this outburst seemed different from previous ones in which the wisdom of the more serious students had quickly prevailed over the emotionalism of the disaffected. Scouts having been sent to other parochial schools in the vicinity, strikes broke out at half a dozen middle schools and some were forced to close. Several thousand students signed a declaration that they would never enter a Christian institution and that they would work to oust Christian education from China. Yali's academic and administrative problems became symbols for the whole range of issues in the Educational Rights Movement. The Yali student assembly had originally demanded that (1) the expelled student be reinstated, (2) the student government be re-established, and (3) Yali immediately register with the government. Within a few days leadership had passed to the supporting associations and the negotiations for settlement could no longer be confined to the Yali administration, the students and their parents.

Much of the publicity, furthermore, had shifted from negotiable demands to manifestoes against parochial education. Instead of requests for changes in Yali and registration, students vowed to prevent registration and end the encroachment of Western civilization. One placard claiming 16,875 signatures read in part:

> "Arise! Perceive your enemy!!! Down with Christianity! The military execute with a sword, and you can see the blood but Christianity kills you without your perceiving it!! . . . . They put up chapels and open schools, seducing us Chinese into these places to 'worship' there or study their foreign tongues, and later to go off to their

lands. This way they enslave us! Beware!! Then they have Associations [YMCA] and what kinds of places are these? They induce us to go out and frolic, to see free pictures. . . . They are just like the trap-birds of the Red Light district of Shanghai, who only lure you to your doom with fine appearances!!! . . . They come to us really being hired agents of their rich Governments. . . Thus they deceive and dupe us, Comrades. December 25, 1924." [29]

Other declarations equated Yali's shameful treatment of its students with the "many outrages on our national sovereignty and on our Chinese race by the Americans". [30] *Chueh-wu* called on all Chinese to join the battle against imperialists and militarists, for the strike at Yali was not simply a problem involving a particular school or south China, but the whole nation. [31] One indication of the influence of earlier publicity campaigns is the common body of knowledge and the identical wording of slogans used; more than one declaration, for example, cited Turkey's ousting of foreign education and the need to follow her example. References to the Washington Conference and to Japanese colonial education in Manchuria also appeared.

The campaign leaders demonstrated both ingenuity and sophistication in their tactics. They organized T'ui-hsueh lien-ho-hui (Drop-Out Federation) of students vowing to withdraw from mission institutions and, to strengthen such determination, they published the names of those signifying this intent. They also threatened to expose in newspapers the names of all students refusing to join the protests; one either admitted denationalization and cowardice or committed oneself to the national cause. The association made personal representations to the provincial Department of Education for transfer certificates to national institutions for all drop-outs. The Society to Regain a Monopoly over Education sent parents of mission school students circulars condemning Christian education and urging them to withdraw their offspring. In addition to public meetings, letters to the editor, handbills and manifestoes, the organizations dispatched news of the storm to youth groups throughout China. The Hunan Student Union, for instance, telegraphed the Peking Ministry of Education demanding closure of all Christian schools and then sent copies of the telegram to numerous educational institutions and student unions.

The campaign was supposed to climax in a mass rally on December 25 but the Changsha Defense Commissioner forbade the demonstration with dire predictions of another Boxer Rebellion. Some of the heat went out of the drive after Yali administrators were persuaded by city officials to back down from their original terms for reinstatement of the students. Though Yali and several of the middle schools managed to reopen for spring semester, enrollment had dropped by as much as one third.

Both the storm and its repercussions are informative. The settlement at Yali opened rifts within the faculty. President Hume, with the sanction of the foreign faculty, had initially insisted that the Yali administration would dictate the conditions for return of the strikers. For Westerners, honor, "the American sense of fair play", and the necessity of restoring discipline made compromise with the three student leaders seem impossible. Chinese Christians and municipal officials, on the other hand, argued that Yali could not regain the good will of the community without concrete indication of its desire for reconciliation; the strikers, having publicly committed themselves, could hardly return without some face-saving proviso. When President Hume acknowledged that Chinese and Americans were likely to approach a conflict differently and then agreed to certain minor concessions, some missionaries were sharply critical and accused Hume of reneging on his public stand. Even Hume concluded that the susceptibility of Chinese in yielding to demands made in the name of nationalism meant that the era when Chinese assumed control of the Christian institutions must be approached with great care and deliberation.[32] Such a widely accepted deduction was to contribute to delay in meeting the demands of the Educational Rights Movement.

A number of weaknesses in the movement became evident. Though the strikes were given national publicity and expressions of support came from many quarters, the storms remained confined to Hunan. The strikers were, furthermore, largely middle school students. The younger middle school students, less fully socialized into the Christian academic community than the college students, were more responsive to pleas for loyalty to the student generation. College upperclassmen, on the contrary, were cognizant that participation might jeopardize career opportunities or the chance to study abroad. Not enough had been done to incorporate parochial students as colleagues in the campaign so that many strikers were happy to have the token concessions enabling them to return to Yali. Coordination among the supporting organizations was inadequate and differences over tactics and specific goals remained. Perhaps most important of all, the youth associations lacked the political power to effect their program. The Hunan Department of Education, for example, was so fearful of international complications that it modified the Drop-Out Federation's request for transfer certificates for students withdrawing from mission schools; instead, it sent out approximately three-hundred letters to schools recommending that they accept drop-out students.[33]

SCHISMS

Though publicity continued to pour forth, a certain hesitancy and a desire for reassessment became manifest early in 1925. Yun Tai-ying in *Min-kuo jih-pao* urged closer ties between the KMT and the youth movement, while the Educational Rights Committee of the Kwangtung Student Union stressed the need for alliance and cooperation with the Kwangtung Educational Association and the Kwangtung Anti-Christian Federation in order to stimulate the campaign.[34] With sarcasm and irony, *Hsiang-tao* rebutted those "imperialist newspapers" which pointed out the good works of missions and viewed the Anti-Christian Movement as simply the creation of agitators. "This is a joke! This only reveals the stupidity of the imperialists. . . !"[35] Just as imperialists used schools to oppress their colonial masses, so they were using education to corrupt the spirit and deceive the thought of the Chinese masses. Chinese should realize that the anti-imperialist and anti-Christian campaigns were one; the Anti-Christian Movement, according to the author, was a "manifestation of the clash of international imperialists and the oppressed Chinese masses". The Third National

Congress of the Socialist Youth Corps advocated establishing anti-Christian cells in the parochial schools themselves so as to awaken Christian students and increase their participation.[36]

Following the death of Sun in March, 1925, and the subsequent controversy over his attitude toward Christianity, divisiveness increased. An article in *Shih-shih hsin-pao* (China Times) recommended reliance on diplomatic negotiation to regain educational rights and on improvement in the quality of national schools to offset the attraction of the foreigners' institutions.[37] Radicals contrasted their no-compromise line with that of educators, some of whom even seemed to appreciate the mission schools as a supplement to the national system, they said; parochial education had to be ended, not merely regulated. When Hsing-shih she condemned Bolshevik influence and the use of violence in the campaign, *Fan Chi-tu-chiao chou-k'an* replied promptly. The Hsing-shih she faction, according to the spokesman from Canton, was just a group of professors and returned students who looked down on everyone else; too many people who talked revolution were afraid of violence. While the Anti-Christian Federation worked for the revolution of the masses, the Hsing-shih she tried to destroy the people's movement. The Kwangtung Anti-Christian Federation, he wrote, has some four hundred members from all walks of life and it is wrong to call it a communist organization just because some communists may have joined as individuals.[38]

Despite the protestations, *Fan Chi-tu-chiao chou-k'an* and the regular meetings of the Kwangtung Anti-Christian Federation had been discontinued by May. Few student storms were reported by the Christian schools during the spring. Exceptions were storms at an academy in west Fukien and at Foochow Anglo-Chinese College, but even here factionalism came into play. When college administrators refused to grant a holiday for Canton Martyr's Day on March 29, the Anglo-Chinese College students threatened to strike and the college closed temporarily. An extremist group within the Fukien Student Union thereupon resorted to violence in an attempt to disrupt or prevent reopening of the institution. They sent menacing letters to parents warning of punishment if they sent their sons back to school and they assaulted several students and teachers who ventured outside the campus compound. Arrest of the ringleader quickly produced a lull in the agitation. Threats and an attempt to set up a rival institution were also part of the storm at the academy in West Fukien. Missionary educators reported a time of "heart searching and great bewilderment."[39] The campaign elsewhere, though far from spent, seemed relatively quiescent when the May Thirtieth tragedy burst upon the scene.

One of the difficulties had been the lack of coordination between the activities of the professional educators and those of radical nationalists. The educators, of course, also differed among themselves over the issue of political activism and over the utility of private schools. Even so, the professionals' demand for Chinese control of national education had become more insistent during the fall and winter of 1924.

In championing a national monopoly over education, Young China Party leaders turned to the professional educational associations. They considered the compromise proposals passed by the Association for the Advancement of Education in July 1924, hollow. The motions lacked teeth in that they did not set deadlines for registration and they placed on the government the burden of proof that education was being used as a means of aggression. At the October meeting of the National Federation of Educational Associations, therefore, Yü Chia-chü, Ch'en Ch'i-t'ien and Li Ju-mien lobbied for more specific and more stringent resolutions. Two groups of motions relating to parochial schools were passed, each providing a rationale in its preface.[40] The motion forbidding schools to propagate religion, conduct any religious activities, or differentiate in the treatment of converts and non-believers stated that the goals of education were to cultivate the whole personality and to create social harmony. Evangelism was not in accord with the purposes of education and, furthermore, it caused confusion in society and deterred progress. The second set of resolutions condemned the "Control of education in China that has been maintained by foreigners" and stated that: "Education is the most important function of the civil administration of a nation. . . . Each nation has its own policy for the education of its people. The racial characteristics and national ideals of foreigners are different from those of our country." In the following ways, therefore, the conduct of education by foreigners injured the nation: (1) it was an infringement on a sovereign national right; (2) it impeded national unity since foreigners could not express Chinese national character; (3) it created submissive pupils who loved another country better than their own; (4) since the education was used for political and religious purposes, it often did not attain the requisite standards.

The federation, therefore, proposed that foreigners be required to register their schools and accept government supervision and guidance, the schools be required to abide by national regulations in constructing their educational program, hiring teachers, setting tuition fees, and conducting school ceremonies. Unregistered schools should be closed and graduates of such schools penalized. Finally, foreigners should be allowed to found no new schools and within a definite time limit the schools should pass under Chinese control. Though these motions had no legal force, the National Federation was spokesman for a prestigious sector of society; since it was often charged with quasi-governmental functions, its recommendations carried weight. The Ministry of Education, which already had on the books similar registration requirements, was put on notice that the time for enforcement had arrived.

In February 1925 Young China Party personnel contributed articles for a special educational rights issue of *Chung-hua chiao-yü chieh*.[41] Their arguments typified those of nationalistic educators who scorned attempts to separate politics and education. The stress was on the creation of a national community. In contrast to the emphasis of 1921-1922, freedom of belief and the incompatibility of religion with science and progress were minor themes. Repeatedly they insisted on the reality of distinctive national character and the function of education to socialize the citizenry; the future of China depended on developing a sense of national identity and loyalty.

Much of the discussion centered on explanations as to why the missionaries could not perform the task: the missionaries had a low opinion of Chinese culture, as witnessed by the image of China conveyed in the West; foreigners, who were not the product of the Chinese heritage, could not convey the Chinese spirit. Though Western civilization was alien to China and Christianity was not essential to her modernization, the missionaries insisted on including Christianity in the curriculum and even recommended that the spirit of Christianity pervade every aspect of academic life. Most of their teachers were, in fact, evangelists rather than professional educators. The missionaries had little appreciation for Chinese nationalism as they had demonstrated time and again with their restrictions on students' patriotic activities, their neglect of Chinese language and history, and their pro-Western interpretation of recent international relations. For the nationalist educators, voluntary religious activities and Sinification of the textbooks and the curriculum in the mission schools would be inadequate. Though some of the liberal educators continued to accept these goals for the Educational Rights Movement, the Young China group believed that education could fulfill its national purpose only if the mission schools eventually came under Chinese direction.

The focus for the Young China faction was China even though several leaders had studied abroad and all had considerable knowledge about the West. When the European experience was referred to, the goal was not to place the Chinese revolution in the context of world history but to validate their insistence on education as a national monopoly and on the separation of religion and schools. Thus, the authors cited the French separation of church and state, the American use of education to create a loyal citizenry, and the imperialists' regulation of all schools in their colonies. Quoting from Paul Monroe on socialization through education and from recommendations in *Christian Education in China,* they found the two in conflict as far as China's national goals were concerned. They expressed fear that China would have two educational systems working at cross purposes if the Burton Commission's recommendation for greater coordination through the China Christian Educational Association were realized. The struggle toward national self consciousness appeared to require a simplified history and a one-dimensional education.

Perhaps as a consequence of their own Westernization, they often opted for legal justification. The unequal treaties, they said, gave foreigners the right to establish schools for their own nationals, not for Chinese citizens; the demand for restoration of sovereignty in education was simply an expression of the right of any independent nation.[42] It did not require hatred of foreigners nor did it have to await revision of the unequal treaties. Whereas the radical literature had stressed the issue of imperialism, *Chiao-yü tsa-chih,* in reporting on the student storms in Hunan during December, stated that the major cause was the failure of the mission schools to register with the government and abide by national regulations.[43]

The tactics as well as the argumentation of Young China leaders relied heavily on the legal approach. In February of 1925 Yü Chia-chü stated that the campaign was still at the talking stage; the immediate tasks were to explain and publicize the issues, to organize branches of the Educational Rights Association, to open national institutions to students withdrawing from parochial schools, and to persuade the Ministry of Education to hold the schools to the registration requirements.[44] Other moves should await the multiplication of the educational rights branches. Ch'en Ch'i-t'ien recommended, in addition, a policy of non-cooperation with the Christian schools; not only should students withdraw, but Chinese should refuse to work for the institutions, Chinese educational organizations should deny membership to Christian educators, and athletic associations should not permit mission schools to compete. Neither the government nor individual Chinese should provide financial aid. Parochial students should balk at attending religious services and classes.[45] Their's was an elitist approach, as exemplified by conservative historian Liu I-cheng, who reminded students that they were a privileged minority and therefore had a unique obligation to act responsibly in working for national reform.[46]

The weakness of the educator's position was that the Peking government was more responsive to the will of the militarists than of the intellectuals. The central administration, furthermore, lacked the self-confidence and the desire to offend the foreign powers and it lacked the authority to control education at the local level.

For this reason, many intellectuals were turning to political parties that promised to strengthen and unify China. A serious dilemma remained, one not yet squarely faced by many educators, including most members of the Young China Party. If and when China acquired an effective central government, who would dominate educational policy, the politicians or the educators? The general assumption was that the professionals would establish the guidelines and be responsible for putting them into practice in the schools, while the government would provide the funds and the legal sanctions. Ch'en Ch'i-t'ien, one of the minority who recognized the idealism of this premise, condemned his colleagues who insisted on educational independence and expected freedom from party or political control.[47] In a country where most people expend all their minds and energy on family and individual problems and do not even know the nature of the nation, he said, one must take a national viewpoint; education must serve the nation first and foremost. Until the May Thirtieth Movement, when nationalist priorities dimmed all other issues, however, most professional educators viewed national education as their province. They might found public interest organizations but their tactics were publicity and lobbying; they were, as a rule, not prepared to join forces with those taking direct action.

CHRISTIAN RESPONSES

Despite the divisions among advocates of educational rights and fluctuations in anti-Christian activity before May Thirtieth, a number of Christian organizations and individuals concluded that the campaigns should be taken seriously and should receive a direct response. They, like the professional educators, however, assumed that they would control the timing and the nature of the educational changes. Their counsels, furthermore, were no more unified than that of their critics.

Many of the responses were directed at a Christian audience, for Christians were still searching among themselves for the proper role of Christianity in national salvation and for a Christianity congruent with modern science. They, as indicated above, also had easier access to Christian periodicals than to those of the New Culture Movement. Among the most articulate defenders of

Christianity was *Chen kuang tsa-chih,* which devoted its January, 1925 issue to criticism of the Anti-Christian Federation. Partly as a forum for answering the challenge, Chinese Christians founded their own Chinese language educational journal, *Chung-hua Chi-tu-chiao chiao-yü chi-k'an* (China Christian Education Quarterly), in March, 1925. Among the goals listed by the editor, Ch'eng Hsiang-fan, were the indigenization of Christian education in China and the exchange of views between Eastern and Western educators.[48] Articles on such topics as nationalist education and Christianity, the compatibility of Christianity and nationalism, the reform of Christian schools, the special contribution of Christian education to the reconstruction of China, and the reasons for continuing faith in parochial education composed the first two issues. *Sheng-ming* and *Chen-li,* exponents of the Social Gospel, included essays on the significance of the Anti-Christian Movement and nationalism for Christianity and on the ethical questions raised by capitalism, socialism, industrialism and science in their January, February, and March numbers.

At the University of Nanking, students organized a club for the study of comparative religion.[49] During the spring of 1925 sessions were devoted to the Anti-Christian campaign at a conference on Chinese Christian education held in New York City and at a meeting of the National Christian Council in Shanghai.[50] The English language *Educational Review* carried editorials on the campaign in January and April, 1925. Most of these discussions were unlikely to come to the attention of the critics and they disclose, furthermore, that the Christians lacked the consensus necessary for a coordinated response.

There were, nevertheless, several attempts at dialogue with those outside the Christian community. On April 10, 1925, a group of Chinese Christian educators used *Min-kuo jih-pao* as a forum for a justification of parochial education.[51] In 1924 the China Christian Educational Association had made a bid for membership in the National Association for the Advancement of Education, a proposal that encountered considerable opposition from members and that proved meaningless since the latter association became moribund in 1925. A number of Christians were, however, already individual members of the association and they publicly defended parochial schools at regional meetings; they also shared in the parliamentary maneuvers to moderate the more radical resolutions directed at mission schools. Chu Ching-nung, Ch'eng Hsiang-fan, and Fan Yuan-lien asserted that they were patriotic Chinese and that as such they were working to sinify Christianity; a sinified Christianity posed no threat to China; rather, China needed the ethic of Jesus and could benefit from properly registered parochial schools.[52]

Adopting a somewhat different tack, representatives of various religions banded together in Ch'üan-kuo ko-tsung chiao hsin-t'u kuo-min hui (National Association of Believers of All Religions); though their immediate concern was the enfranchisement of clergy, they intended, they said, to cooperate in combating Bolshevism, anarchism, and Anti-Christianism.[53] Wang Tsu-chen, a Roman Catholic who had sparked earlier opposition to recognition of Confucianism as a state religion, was one of the initiators. The association resembled its forerunner in its loose organization and reliance on publicity.

In content, the rejoinders ranged all the way from impatient scolding of undisciplined, ignorant youth to agreement with many of the criticisms and even to recommendations that the more moderate demands of the educational associations be accepted.[54] A small minority viewed the campaign as a temporary phenomenon, part of the revolt by Chinese youth against all authority. The student storms and unruly behavior, according to one writer, confirmed the fact that China was not ready for full sovereignty; why did not students who professed concern over academic standards protest against the chaos and fiscal starvation of national schools instead of attacking the mission institutions, noted for their discipline and responsible administration? Some blamed Bolshevik agitators, particularly Borodin and Karakhan, but they apparently had little specific information about the activities of Comintern agents or the Chinese Communist Party. Also in the minority were those at the other end of the scale, those who advocated voluntary religious activities and speedy assumption of control and ownership by Chinese.

A frequent explanation given for the anti-Christian

opposition was lack of knowledge or understanding of true Christianity by the critics. The remedy was for the church to cultivate a dedicated and informed membership which could refute the critics and their discourse. Christians must expand their avenues of publicity and increase contacts with government educators and students.

When religion had to be defended in terms of its service to the nation, however, it was in trouble. Chinese Christians and Western missionaries averred that nationalism and Christianity were not in conflict; yet they could not agree on the proper political stance for Christian institutions and their members. Representative of the point of view of many Westerners was a statement by the Apostolic Delegate, Msgr. Celso Constantini. In a message to the Chinese Catholic Youth Association on January 25, 1925, Constantini said:

> "Religion does not in any way curtail their [Christians'] civil rights and could not in any way wound their lawful patriotism; on the contrary, it sanctifies it by the example of the Divine Redeemer who wept over the ruin of Jerusalem . . . [As to missionaries], they pay a sincere homage to Chinese patriotism. . . . They recognize the established authority and teach others to recognize it, . . . but they do not meddle with the interior nor exterior affairs of the nation."[55]

Specifically, this meant that Catholic youth could participate in politics as individuals, but the youth association, like the church, should remain aloof.

Although such guidelines appeared commendable, their implications raised controversies. Most Chinese and quite a few Westerners admitted that so long as Christians and the right of evangelism were protected by the unequal treaties, religion and politics would be linked; accordingly, the privileges should be phased out.[56] In contrast to the radical view, however, missionary spokesmen acknowledged no deliberate collusion between diplomat and evangelist; rather, anti-foreignism and incompatibility of juridical traditions during the 19th century had been the source of the linkage. Chinese and Westerner, furthermore, did not concur on the timing or the process of treaty revision, another way of saying that they frequently differed over whether the initiative should come from China or the Powers. Even if evangelist and convert agreed in principle that religious organizations should obey the constituted authority and should not engage in politics, Chinese Christians were discovering that the reality of such compliance brought their national loyalty into question. Increasing numbers asserted that the principle was not applicable in a revolutionary environment.

With notable exceptions, Chinese and Western Christians had by 1924-1925 recognized that the registration question had to be faced; the benefits of autonomy no longer offset the losses of non-registration. The matter finally engaged the serious attention of individual institutions and of the China Christian Educational Association, with the latter appointing study committees, scheduling discussion panels, and editorializing in the *Educational Review* and *Chung-hua Chi-tu-chiao chiao-yü chi-k'an*. The crucial requirements were majority control by Chinese and voluntary religious activities. Whereas the first requirement engendered debate over the tempo of devolution, the very nature and purpose of parochial education were at issue in the second. In January, 1925, and again in October, 1925, the *Educational Review* seemed favorably inclined toward registration but maintained that the educators should not let themselves be stampeded into anything; they should take the time to protect the integrity of Christian education.[37] Missionaries should seek out talented and dedicated Chinese Christians who could be sent abroad for advanced training and they should recruit Chinese for middle-level administrative positions that would provide experience. Both missionaries and students should give greater attention to Chinese language study. So that more courses could be taught in Chinese, additional textbooks should be composed or translated; so that courses could gain relevancy through Chinese examples and concepts, research in China should be fostered. Even if administrators moved expeditiously in these preparations, however, the Sinification of parochial education would be gradual.

For those Chinese who questioned whether Christian

institutions would be granted so much time, whether, indeed, all missionary executives met the high standards set for Chinese, replies were forthcoming. Self-support and self-control were depicted as interdependent. How could Chinese expect mission boards and their representatives to provide funds without a say as to their disposition? Increased Chinese contributions would create a sense of proprietorship, thereby warranting increased Chinese responsibility. Chinese, it was said, were singularly responsive to political and family pressures whereas the Westerners were insulated from such influences and could more easily insist on the primacy of the educational and religious goals of the schools. A stable political setting and a corpus of self-reliant Chinese were preconditions for the transfer of control.[58] Thus, the National Christian Council, meeting ten days before May 30, 1925, could only agree that the issues of extraterritoriality and Western control deserved study; a month earlier the China Christian Educational Association had also appointed a committee to investigate the matter.[59]

The problem of religious requirements appeared even more elusive of speedy resolution. Chinese and Westerners readily acknowledged the need for revising the religion courses and improving worship services. Some even agreed with President Hawks Pott of St. John's University that most of the students were satiated with religious activities morning, noon, and night, seven days a week, so that a reduction in quantity and a rise in quality would lead to better results. Convinced that the shortcomings of the religious work were the source of much of the antagonism, they often pushed into the background the issue of compulsion. Accordingly in 1924-1925, Christian educators were reiterating with a new urgency the recommendation of *Christian Education in China* that carefully planned, graded courses in religion be instituted and that only trained and successful instructors be assigned the religion courses. Too many schools had operated on the assumption that any missionary or minister was qualified to teach religion and had delegated the responsibility to the one whose schedule permitted. At conferences the sessions on the teaching of religion and the place of religion in education were filled to overflowing. The China Christian Educational Association commissioned committees to draw up new religion texts and a series of revised Sunday School leaflets was printed.⁶⁰

When the question of eliminating requirements in religion surfaced, the debate took on a different character. In the spring of 1925 students at a Chungking Christian middle school balked at the time devoted to the Babylonian and Assyrian wars in the Old Testament course and the mission promptly agreed to restructure Bible study. When, however, the students went on strike against the religion requirements, the mission spokesman blamed communist propaganda and resentment of foreign trade; he concluded:

> "In order to accomplish our purpose, I believe our religious emphasis must be even more marked and more clearly understood by the people." ⁶¹

Some Chinese Christians were willing to make all religious activities voluntary in order to meet registration requirements and ventured to take this stand publicly. They maintained that compulsion alienated many students and that interesting, high quality offerings would continue to attract large numbers.⁶² Whether or not a majority of the Chinese Christian educators held this view before May Thirtieth, it would be difficult to judge on the basis of written documentation, but some commentators thought that this was actually the case.⁶³ Despite notable exceptions, the overwhelming proportion of missionary writings disavowed such a position. They contended that the inculcation of religion and morality was what distinguished parochial education from public and was its reason for being. To deny parents the right to send their children to institutions where they would receive Christian instruction would be an infringement on religious freedom. Missionaries would be betraying a trust if they supported secular education with monies donated for evangelistic purposes.

The China Christian Educational Association pinned its hopes on persuading the Ministry of Education to delete the clauses on religion in the registration regulations. Its last word before May Thirtieth was to urge institutions to make those adjustments not in conflict with the special function of Christian schools; it could not recommend registration under the current religious restrictions. The executive board in April 1925 requested the Council on Religious Education to prepare a constructive program for religious education on a non-compulsory basis. Once this was done, discussion of the matter could be resumed.[64] All the study committees on Chinese control, Western privilege, and religious indoctrination were overtaken by the events of May 30, 1925.

Chapter VI

May 30, 1925, and the Educational Rights Movement

The British police who fired on demonstrators in Shanghai's International Settlement May 30, 1925, could hardly have foreseen that their action would generate significant changes in China's power structure. Even the students, who had hoped to gain publicity by defying Municipal Council restrictions on public protests, could not have anticipated the profound consequences. The killing of a dozen Chinese and wounding of twice that number, however, sent shock waves reverberating through China's cities and across the seas. In its impact on the history of republican China, the May Thirtieth Movement can only be compared with that of May 4, 1919. Unlike May Fourth, however, the immediate repercussions were almost exclusively political. What had originated with protests over a Japanese foreman shooting a Chinese textile worker had escalated with the arrest of students publicizing the incident and had become the occasion for a nationwide anti-imperialist movement in response to the "Nanking Road Massacre" of May 30th.[1]

Both the KMT and the CCP were able to use the movement to enlist new supporters, especially among urban workers and students. Amid demands for immediate political unity and abrogation of the unequal treaties, the voices of liberals advocating gradual cultural change subsided. The question of treaty revision, moreover, came to the forefront in a manner that placed many foreigners on the defensive and further undermined their will to insist on imperialist privilege. Because attaining unity and sovereignty appeared dependent on the KMT-CCP coalition and its National Revolutionary Army, the political parties bade fair to gain a monopoly over the nationalist issue. Their decision to launch the Northern Expedition in mid-1926 grew out of May Thirtieth's evidence of the power and appeal of Chinese nationalism and the dramatic expansion in party membership.

These shifts necessitated numerous adjustments. Relations between the parties and the students, between the parties and those educators who had envisioned an educational program free of politics, between cadres in mass organizations and military commanders--all were modified. Growth and potential success strained the fragile United Front of the KMT and CCP as each maneuvered for dominance. Expansion also strained the resources of the parties so that they experienced an acute shortage of trained reliable leaders. Multi-class patriotic organizations that could help discover activists and provide them with leadership experience, that could promote the solidarity of youth, peasants and workers became ever more important assets. Among such societies were branches of the Educational Rights Association and the Anti-Christian Federation. Both, like the Student Union, the Communist Youth Corps, and numerous mass associations, developed a more effective organization and increasingly gained in vitality and militancy; both reflected the political transition in their spurts of activism and in modification of tactics.

By altering relations between Chinese and foreigners, the May Thirtieth Movement affected the educational rights campaign in yet other ways. Numerous fissures within the Christian community became evident. Chinese Christians, in general, were disappointed by the Western reaction to the May Thirtieth tragedy so that the gap that had appeared during the 1922 and 1924 campaigns widened. Chinese converts found themselves increasingly critical of Western Christendom while defensive about their own nationalism. Among Westerners, liberals and conservatives moved further apart. Diplomats, businessmen, and missionaries often viewed the scene from quite different perspectives. Though condemnations by educational rights advocates implied a homogeneous Christendom, the community was so deeply divided that prompt unified response to May Thirtieth proved impossible.[2] Scars remained when, after lengthy discussions in China and correspondence with the home supporters, schools finally moved toward meeting national registration requirements and a number of mission organizations formally renounced the special privileges accorded Christians under the unequal treaties.

THE NANKING ROAD MASSACRE OF
MAY THIRTIETH AND ITS AFTERMATH

During the spring of 1925 the educational rights campaign had appeared to be receding and even the National Student Union had declined in popularity as the radicalism of its leadership outdistanced that of most students. May Thirtieth altered the environment, however. The radical nationalism of the Student Union became an asset rather than a liability. The political parties saw in May Thirtieth an opportunity to incorporate the student movement into their drive against imperialism and militarism and they seized it. The esteem still accorded scholars meant that student participation lent respectability and offered a degree of protection to the expanding mass campaign.

Since the beginning of the year, labor unrest in Japanese textile mills in Shanghai and Tsingtao had grown and as the workers, under radical tutelage, had gone on strike, the incidence of violence had risen. The second National Trade Union Conference, meeting in Canton during the first week of May, had resolved that the economic struggles of the workers should be turned into political struggles. Opportunity to implement this policy presented itself on May 30 because of three developments: the shooting of the Chinese textile worker in Shanghai, subsequent arrests of student protesters with a trial date of May 30, and the decision by the Shanghai Municipal Council to push forward four proposed by-laws. Included were increases in wharfage fees, restrictions on printed matter, and regulation of child labor. Numerous Chinese not only opposed the by-laws but questioned the authority of the foreigners to legislate on these matters. On May 27, Shanghai University students urged a massive demonstration for May 30 to bring the cause before the public despite bans on the press and assembly. On May 28 the Central Committee of the CCP recommended that anti-imperialist slogans such as "Shanghai for the Shanghaiese" be joined to the condemnations of Japanese brutality and economic aggression. The events of May 30th are history.

Within hours of the tragedy, CCP cadres, KMT organizers in Shanghai, and Shanghai and National Student

Union leaders were meeting to plan the next course of action.³ The CCP, with its Central Executive Committee located in Shanghai, was able to call an emergency meeting of its leaders the same evening of the incident; Ch'en Tu-hsiu, Li Li-san, Liu Shao-ch'i, Ts'ai Ho-sen, Yun T'ai-ying all gathered at the home of Chang Kuo t'ao to develop a synchronized response. A simultaneous strike by workers, students, merchants and gentry was called. To coordinate and guide the workers, Li Li-san, Liu Shao-ch'i, Ts'ai Ho-sen and Ch'ü Ch'iu-pai set up the Shanghai General Labor Union on May 31st. This GLU under communist leadership soon took the initiative away from the more moderate Shang-hai kung-t'uan lien-ho-hui (Federation of Labor Unions) as it came to represent some 117 unions and 218,000 members. It called an immediate general strike and June 1st saw most Shanghai shops closed, workers walking off their jobs, and some fifty thousand students abandoning classes. An umbrella agency, Kung-shang-hsueh lien-ho-hui (Federation of Workers, Merchants, and Students) was founded on June 4 to provide overall direction. Dominated by radicals, it was composed of representatives from the Shanghai and National Student Union, the General Labor Union, and the Federation of Street Unions.⁴ Ch'ü Ch'iu-pai edited a newspaper *Je-hsieh jih-pao* (Bloodshed Daily) issued by Kung-shang-hsueh lien-ho-hui during the peak of the movement.

As word of the tragedy flashed to Peking, Canton, Wuhan, Nanking, Changsha, Foochow and other centers, students and youth workers fanned out to organize demonstrations, boycotts, and strikes. One bonus of the self-conscious student sub-culture with its organizational network was the fact that youths could launch a protest movement within hours. Students left Shanghai May 31 to convey details of the massacre to other educational centers and by June 2 they were busily organizing sympathy protests in Canton and elsewhere. Only a day after receipt of telegrams from Shanghai, Nanking students were posting placards and holding student meetings. Chengtu students were distributing extra editions of Chinese newspapers carrying the story and were outlining their strategy. During the month of June, no less than 38 cities and towns saw politicized urban Chinese in action.⁵ Most colleges and many middle schools in these cities hastily ceased academic work so that students could devote full time to a campaign against the unequal treaties. Students, because of their prestige and education, assumed primary responsibility in the areas of propaganda and enforcement of the boycott against Japanese and British goods. They also solicited strike funds from urban Chinese and raised monies through theatrical renditions of May 30th, through peddling postcards depicting the atrocities, and through selling goods donated by sympathetic merchants.

Ma Ch'ao-hui, a KMT representative sent to Shanghai to organize student branches of Sun-wen-chu-i hsueh hui (Sun Wenist Study Society), had called a separate meeting on the night of May 30. Among those present were Yu Jih-chang, YMCA secretary, and Yun Tai-ying, CCP member active in the KMT Youth Department. Reports, however, make little mention of this rally or of Ma's activities in the days following. Ever since the outbreak of labor troubles in Japanese textile mills, February 1, 1925, the CCP had been multiplying and consolidating its ties with Shanghai students. The result was that it was much better positioned than the KMT to assume leadership. Chang Kuo-t'ao, in describing the exhausting pace of activities by CCP cadres, points out that the Kuomintang was still so disoriented by the death of Sun that the CCP was able to assume direction of the movement in numerous centers.[6] Even in Canton, KMT initiatives were delayed because of warfare with militarists contesting control of the Pearl River delta. On June 20, however, the Central Executive Committee of the KMT inaugurated a boycott of British, Japanese and American goods and a general strike of British and Japanese institutions and businesses in Canton and Hong Kong. To enforce the boycott, student and party cadres formed corps to visit Chinese shops, harange the owners and inspect shelves for contraband goods. Public bonfires consumed thousands of dollars worth of imports. A blockade effectively cut off intercourse with Hong Kong, where land values began to fall and numerous banks and businesses were saved from bankruptcy only by loans from London. In preparation for a mass demonstration in front of the Anglo-French concession on Shameen Island, June 23, all flags were to fly at half-mast.

Feeding the fires of nationalism were new incidents and Chinese casualties in Shanghai (June 1, 2, 3), in Hankow (June 11), at Shameen in Canton (June 23), in Chungking (July 2) and in Nanking (July 31). Over one hundred Chinese were killed, while in contrast fewer than half a dozen foreigners lost their lives. The rash of atrocities seemed to belie any explanation of May Thirtieth as an isolated and tragic miscalculation by a British officer. Chinese argued that foreign imperialism was the culprit and the whole system of unequal treaties and foreign privilege had to go. Mocking an infamous sign at the entrance to a Shanghai public garden, Peking students erected a warning at the Court of Justice: "No admittance to dogs, Japanese and Englishmen."[7] Major journals issued pamphlets and special editions urging a national rights recovery campaign. Though Settlement authorities temporarily closed such radical centers as Shanghai University, T'ung-te College of Medicine, and Ta-hsia University, the turbulence could not be damped down.

A broad anti-imperialist movement with strong anti-Western overtones was sweeping China's cities and both the KMT and the CCP benefited. Imperialism and warlordism became inextricably linked. Riding the nationalist tide, the KMT-CCP United Front regime declared itself the "National Government" of China on July 1, 1925. Kung-ch'an chu-i ch'ing-nien t'uan (Communist Youth Corps), which claimed less than 3,000 members in early 1925, boasted of 9,000 members in September 1925, while the party itself expanded from approximately 1,000 to almost 6,000. During the month of July alone some seventy new unions were organized in Shanghai under the auspices of the General Labor Union.[8] Though many party members came from the proletariat, the CCP greatly increased its influence among students as a new policy of group recruitment allowed it to incorporate numerous student societies. The KMT encouraged local student unions to operate as party branches and reinforced its links with young intellectuals through a great variety of patriotic and anti-imperialist associations. Despite the fact that party workers among youth usually propagandized in the name of the KMT and *San min chu-i,* a high proportion of the cadres were radicals; often they were communists holding membership in the KMT.

Thus, the left wing assumed control of the Executive Committee of the National Student Union at its 7th Congress in July.

MAY THIRTIETH, ANTI-CHRISTIANS AND CHRISTIANS

Manifestoes immediately after the May Thirtieth fusillade did not focus on Christianity or parochial education. In their protests against imperialism, the unequal treaties, and foreign privilege of all kinds, Chinese did occasionally include Christianity and mission schools; the latter were, after all, closely associated with imperialism in the minds of many Chinese. Over a thousand demonstrators, for example, converged on the Shanghai General Chamber of Commerce and the Federation of Street Unions, meeting on the afternoon of May 31. The assembly, chaired by a Student Union leader, passed ten resolutions, one of which opposed all foreign-run schools. "Down with the religion of Jesus" was among the slogans chanted by parading Peking students on June 3; this, despite the fact that parochial students were part of the procession.[9] Most of the onus was, however, directed at British and Japanese cruely and at the unequal treaties.

In the rapidly changing scene, though, the finger was soon pointed specifically at Christians and Christian schools. The Shanghai Executive Branch of the KMT declared that the shooting "ought to make all Christians and Anglo-Saxon lovers of freedom and independence ashamed," while the Canton Department of Education backed up the KMT boycott and general strike with an order forbidding any college or school in south China from teaching religion or holding religious services.[10] Even Peita professors identified the actions of Westerners as the actions of Christians and sent a telegram to Pope Pius XI bidding him use his power over Christians to prevent their massacring Chinese. Resolutions passed by the National Student Union Congress in late June deliberately associated Christianity, May Thirtieth, and imperialism when they condemned the *Christian* Municipal Council of Shanghai, the British *Christian* sailors and the *Christian* Mixed Court.[11] They singled out the YMCA and other Christian organizations and officers as the "hawks and hounds" of the imperialists. Claiming to represent seven million students, the Congress dispatched a letter to President Tuan Ch'i-jui demanding immediate abrogation, not simply revision of the unequal treaties; such action should encompass a ban against religious evangelism in China and a complete Chinese monopoly over education.

With a call for establishment of educational rights committees by all student unions and for cooperation between branches of the Student Union and the Anti-Christian Federation, the Congress marked the revival of the Educational Rights campaign. The resurgent influence and popularity of the Student Union are hardly surprising. As revolutionary patriotism acquired legitimacy, the union was the logical national voice for students and its reorganization along democratic-centralist lines meant that it could quickly concert the response of urban youth. Why, however, the highlighting of Christianity and Christian education?

Part of the explanation was that Christian education represented the most visible form of imperialism for university-based New Youth and they were, in the hot summer of 1925, little inclined to make fine distinctions among Westerners. Christian missionaries, after all, had often equated Christianity with Western civilization in their attempts to associate progress with Christian teachings. The operative slogan of May Thirtieth was "Down with Imperialism" but students could be expected to focus on matters closest to their interests, that is, educational and ideological issues. In appealing to New Youth, therefore, party propagandists defined the slogans to include, "Down with Christianity." Christian missionaries joined capitalists and militarists as the minions of imperialists in the exhortations of *Chung-kuo ch'ing-nien* to students.[12] An evangelist who had considered himself popular among Chinese was assaulted to cries of "Down with Capitalism!" "Kill the foreign devil!" He wrote from Soochow " . . . to be a foreigner is a very risky thing just now. When I was attacked, I was riding in a ricksha. I passed a crowd of [demonstrating] students and they seeing only a foreigner made a rush. . . I was slapped in the face by a student."[13]

Other factors came into play, however, and radical revolutionaries for the moment, reaped the advantage. Patriotic Chinese closed ranks for a few brief weeks. May Thirtieth was for them a moral issue, not a legal one; innocent youth demonstrating in the cause of the nation had been murdered by privileged foreigners. Nanking Road validated the belief in the virtue and righteousness of China's national cause. The injured, innocent youth, furthermore, were students, respected as the elite of the nation and deferred to as the offspring of the ruling classes. One incident illustrates both their special status and the general acceptance of the rectitude of their cause. Upon discovering that the Commercial Press had printed a propaganda sheet for the Shanghai Municipal Council, students visited press headquarters and obliged it to print thousands of leaflets stating that the council's propaganda sheet simply echoed the rumors and unfounded tales of the English. They warned news vendors against selling newspapers which had included material from the council's sheet and lifted the ban only after the journals had made substantial contributions to strike funds.[14] The Chinese Students' Alliance in the U.S., many of whose members were mission school graduates, addressed a letter to the U.S. Secretary of State: "Pardon us for saying that the time has passed when China can be treated as an outlying colony. . . . She has her sovereign rights which she expects other friendly nations to respect. . . . A change of heart is called for. . . ."[15] The alliance then launched a campaign among overseas Chinese to raise funds to aid the strikers. The near unanimity of Chinese revulsion is attested to in *China's Case,* a pamphlet circulated within China and overseas. Authored by such eminent intellectuals as Hu Shih, Ting Wen-chiang, and Lo Wen-kan, former head of Peking Supreme Court, it could hardly be termed an expression of radical views. Yet, even while acknowledging that they lacked all the facts concerning the Shanghai massacre, they wrote of "scores of unarmed Chinese citizens" being killed, of a "defenseless crowd" being repeatedly fired upon point blank. Did such actions require investigation to determine guilt? They then went on to discuss the crucial issue pointed up by May 30: "The Shanghai International Settlement has become a sovereign state governed by an oligarchy . . . in the interest of the foreigner alone." No government could suppress the popular agitation until justice was done.[16]

May Thirtieth appeared to epitomize all the injustices of the unequal treaties and to require their summary repudiation. In the language of the proclamations, these were not normal times, but times that called for national sacrifice; careerism and personal interests must be put aside.[17] Radicals, for whom the revolutionary cause was paramount, had little difficulty with such an argument. Chinese communists, Comintern and USSR representatives found their support of the revolution and Chinese nationalism in happy coincidence with their struggle against Western capitalism and imperialism. The Soviet Proletarian Students' Association, various workers' organizations, and Red Army groups sent messages of sympathy and encouragement as well as funds. In Moscow, Chinese and Russians joined in street demonstrations against imperialism.

The discrepancy between the response of Soviet envoys and that of Western emissaries sharpened the image of the USSR as China's friend and the West as imperialist enemy. Promptly after the shooting, Ambassador Karakhan sent a letter of condolence on behalf of the Russian people to the Peking Ministry of Foreign Affairs. Deliberately cultivating the educated elite of Peking, he gave a well-publicized address in which he ridiculed those foreigners who would delay treaty revision until the Chinese "put their house in order"; he commended, rather, those Chinese who assailed imperialism as the prime source of China's weakness and disunity. A current photograph shows him surrounded by admirers from Peita and preceded by a student conspicuously carrying Karakhan's hat as a mark of esteem. Western and Japanese diplomats, expressing regret for loss of life, rejected a finding of British guilt by the Chinese Foreign Ministry and requested a multinational investigation before assigning responsibility; meanwhile, they warned the ministry against letting a xenophobic movement get out of hand.[18] Until August, furthermore, they insisted on separating the issue of the unequal treaties from negotiations for settlement of the May 30th incident; discussions of the broader issues of extraterritoriality and tariff should await a return to normalcy, they maintained.

The actions of Christian educators themselves contributed to the resurgence of the Educational Rights Movement while the role of parochial schools in the May Thirtieth Movement was frequently cited as proof of their denationalizing influence. In mid-June the Chinese press expressed resentment over the apparent indifference of the missionaries to China's destiny and asked whether they were truly the agents of their governments that they should nct say a word. Though the public response of Westerners was not always as immediate as that of the Chinese, the Christian community had not actually been silent. The difficulty was that it spoke with many voices and it acted in a variety of ways. Unlike the Chinese, most Westerners were slow to view the tragedy as evidence that summary repudiation of the unequal system was requisite.[19] Major controversial issues were 1) the question of whether a school was a house of study or an instrument of social and political reform, 2) the division of authority between students and administrators and between Chinese and Westerners, and 3) the proper political role of religious institutions and of aliens having extraterritorial rights.

Students in most of the Christian colleges and many middle schools responded with patriotic outrage to news of May Thirtieth. Teachers and staff members frequently encouraged students to give expression to their nationalist sentiments in the hope that charges of denationalization might thereby be laid to rest.[20] When friction occurred, it was more apt to be over the form and duration of patriotic expression than over participation itself. Students in the Christian schools in Peking, Shanghai, Nanking, and other cities actively engaged in demonstrations, in organizing protest assemblies, and in issuing manifestoes. They canvassed the churches to raise strike funds. Shanghai Baptist College students initiated a letter writing campaign "to present to our foreign friends in Shanghai and elsewhere the course of events that led to the Nanking Road atrocity."[21] Certain institutions had Christian student unions which were separated from but affiliated with the National Student Union. At Yenching University and Shanghai Baptist College, for example, student activists cooperated with the local Student Union leaders in organizing the strike and boycott. Shanghai Baptist College and Middle School students stated that their strike action was taken in accord with the recommendation of the Shanghai Student Union and in conjunction with 64 schools and labor and merchant organizations.[22]

To coordinate their protests, Roman Catholic students in Peking organized their own branch of Chiu-kuo hui (National Salvation Association), as did Kwangtung Christians. In a public telegram, the latter gave their version of the Shakee incident and condemned "this BUTCHERY abhorred by God and Man". They promised support for the strike and boycott and resolved "to send telegrams for the information of true believers throughout the world, asking them to stand by the right and come to our help, and . . . write to all churches in the Province asking them to pray for the nation in its difficulty and to expose the sins of imperialism from their pulpits, asking all Christians to have nothing to do with imperialism so that they may repent."[23] In Wuchang, the Christian institution, Huachung University, made its large meeting hall available for student assemblies.

The Yenching faculty joined in a public statement deploring both the incident and the readiness of foreigners to rely on force.[24] To prevent further estrangement and misunderstanding, they recommended greater sympathy with China on the part of the foreign-owned press and a willingness to revise the out-dated treaties. But the Yenching manifesto concluded with a request to the students that their activities be orderly and dignified so as not to bring dishonor upon the institution and that their activities interfere as little as possible with their studies. The parting of ways came over the latter issues.

Most of the mission schools expected their students to return to academic responsibilities after a few days of political activism; thereafter, patriotic work should take the form of extracurricular activities and should be centered on the campus. The students had made their views known to those with the authority to settle the matter; they should resume their role as students and concentrate on their primary obligation: studying, attending class, completing the semester's examinations as preparation for future civic duties. Thus, President Matilda Thurston considered Ginling fortunate when the students consented to return to classes after three and a half days and to confine further participation in the student movement to after-class hours.[25] At Fukien Christian University a Christian Student Union was hastily formed; representatives persuaded the students that if they went out on strike they would cease to be students and would lose the right to remain on campus.[26] Other institutions closed precipitately, suspending or postponing examinations and graduation exercises; in this fashion they hoped to avoid incidents leading to campus storms and to prevent the institution from becoming embroiled in political controversy.

Chinese generally found the measures taken by mission schools and their students unsatisfactory. Though the students had shown themselves responsive to Chinese nationalism, many still tried to compartmentalize their political and academic roles. Radicals, on the other hand, were more apt to operate in terms of an integrated role as student and citizen; the evils were so fundamental that the academic community and its institutions could not hope to carry out their educational responsibilities unless they also acted as agents of change. Students at Peita and Tsing Hua took their duty as revolutionaries so seriously that they formed a Students' Batallion to provide military training for those destined to be the vanguard and nucleus of the future nation in arms. KMT leaders, who, after the establishment of the Nanking government would adopt policies resembling those of the Christian administrators, generally accorded primacy to patriotic activism during the summer of 1925.

The Anti-Christian Federation accused Aurora of suppressing the May Thirtieth Movement by forcing students to withdraw if they ceased to attend class. Yali, which closed June 6, was likewise condemned for preventing its students from participating in patriotic movements. The principal of Trinity Middle School in Wuchang, it was said, revealed the true attitude of Christians toward Chinese nationalism when he used troops to confine his students to campus and deter them from parading in the city streets.[27] Students at a Tientsin middle school contrasted the reluctance of the English principal to suspend classes for patriotic demonstrations with the declaration of a half-holiday when the principal returned from furlough; the English had finally displayed their real colors on May 30th, stated the strike declaration of the students.[28] Overlooking the fact that many students and some faculty members in Christian institutions had actively supported protests, the National Student Union Congress passed a sweeping resolution: "In the mission schools no student is allowed to have any freedom of action or freedom of thought. . . . Their students are not allowed to participate in patriotic movements."[29] The Congress thereupon determined to pursue the Anti-Christian and Educational Rights campaigns with renewed vigor.

Chinese Christians were stung by such accusations. The Christian general, Feng Yü-hsiang, distinguished between British Christians and true Christians; in July, he wrote an open letter to the latter calling on them to join him in condemning British brutality and demanding equality in Sino-Western relations. He cabled strenuous protests to the Peking government and he issued an appeal to British workers, published in *Workers Weekly,* organ of the British Communist Party. In common with many Chinese, he shifted toward greater emphasis on anti-imperialism, ordering twice-daily lectures to develop an increased awareness of Western aggression among his soldiers and requiring all army personnel to don black arm bands of mourning. Thousands of students withdrew from mission schools, particularly institutions run by British missions. In Peking, representatives from the Christian Student Union sought to found an independent Christian school. Having gained the support of Chien Yu-wen, Yenching professor and advocate of an independent Chinese church, delegates from five British schools approached Feng Yü-hsiang for financial aid and secured a promise of a donation.[30] According to *Fei Chi-tu-chiao hsun-k'an,* mission school students in the Wuhan area withdrew when administrators tried to restrict their political activities and formed a branch of the Drop-out Federation that collaborated with the Anti-Christian Federation.[31]

Even some of the Chinese administrators and teachers questioned the wisdom of insisting on fulfillment of academic responsibilities as if the times were normal. The head of the Fukien Christian University Chinese department along with a recent graduate of Fukien Christian University became influential members of the Educational Rights Movement shortly after the student body voted not to join the May Thirtieth strike.[32] Liu T'ing-fang, president of the China Christian Educational Association, pleaded with his missionary colleagues to try to understand the mood of the students and the seriousness with which they viewed the patriotic movement and their civic responsibilities.[33] Missionaries, he said, must realize that Chinese did not identify patriotic activities with indiscipline; they should cease to apply the solutions of the past to the present, cease to accuse nationalists of Bolshevism, and instead aid the students in assuming their civic obligations. They would be wise to cultivate the student activists and provide them with the necessary freedom of action; evidence of the concordance of Christianity and nationalism could prove the artificiality of associating communism and irreligion with China's welfare. Under the editorship of Liu, *Shengming* put out a special English-language issue in June, 1925 with the hope of conveying to Westerners something of the mood and the thinking of Peking Christians.

The second controversial issue, the question of authority, easily acquired racial and political implications. Missionary educators were accustomed to authoritarian control over their institutions. In this they were not unique. Both Chinese and Western mores had dictated that students show deference toward their mentors and despite occasional student storms, teaching techniques and institutional structure had accentuated the gap between generations. When New Youth rejected traditional values and disputed the commitment of their elders to the national interest, however, the authority of administrators eroded. During the early 1920s strikes and disorders had, if anything, been more prevalent in the public schools than the private.[34] Christian administrators who had prided themselves on the greater discipline of their students, were ill prepared for the challenge accompanying May Thirtieth, were slow to appreciate the changes wrought by the growing revolutionism. Though they had fostered student self-government associations, they had done so in the expectation that the father generation would retain control over curriculum, faculty recruitment and promotion, budget, and all essential educational matters. They had not anticipated a political role for student unions.

The potential for trouble was accentuated by the racial duality of the Christian academic communities. Chinese staff members were clustered in the lower ranks with a dual salary scale for Chinese and Westerners, and with Westerners chairing practically all departments except Chinese language and literature.[35] No Christian college had a Chinese president in 1925. Some middle schools were under Chinese leadership but in many cases administrative independence was limited by fiscal dependence; a number of the outstanding middle schools were attached to Christian colleges and subject to their supervision. The fact that a high percentage of the Chinese staff at the Christian schools were alumni and had studied under their current colleagues deterred the growth of an egalitarian relationship. Even before May Thirtieth some Chinese had taken exception to the missionary's monopoly of power and expressions of resentment had surfaced. May Thirtieth nationalism challenged the legitimacy of Western authority itself.

Most famous was the confrontation at St. John's University. The incident was so widely publicized in educational rights literature that the details bear repeating.[36] As a school with alumni in prominent diplomatic and governmental posts and with a consistent record of sending graduates abroad for advanced study, the institution commanded prestige and influence. Its president was the Rev. F.L. Hawks Pott, who had been head of St. John's for over 35 years; at meetings of the China Christian Educational Association and other missionary organizations, Pott's speeches had been characterized by rationality and moderation. Though he had insisted on the religious goals of the school, he had simultaneously insisted that they should not be permitted to compromise educational standards. On the other hand, St. John's reputation depended heavily on the excellence of its English language training and those who criticized the foreign atmosphere of the mission schools often cited St. John's. More than most of the Christian colleges, St. John's continued to reflect the personality of its architect. Hawks Pott, as a teacher, a Westerner, and a member of the senior generation, was not accustomed to having his word questioned; he did not expect defiance of his instructions by either students or faculty.

On June 1, 1925, St. John's University and Middle School students decided to strike in accord with the resolution of the Shanghai Student Union. That same evening Pott called a faculty meeting to discuss the university response to the students' move. With the aid of votes by junior Chinese faculty members, a majority agreed to recess classes for one week despite Pott's opposition. Pott acceded, provided the students make the campus, not the city, the locus of their patriotic activities and engage in no violence. The students chose as one expression of the national humiliation a daily assembly with a salute to the Chinese flag flying at half mast. When, however, the students raised the U.S. flag as well as the Chinese flag to half mast, Pott ordered both flags lowered and turned over to him on the grounds that the U.S. took no stand on the movement. The students thereupon produced another Chinese flag which they proposed to raise; Pott refused permission and took the flag. Outraged, the students accused Pott of insulting the national flag and called an assembly to decide on their next move. Pott, for his part, convened the Western faculty and announced that the university and the middle school would close, the students should leave campus immediately and no meetings could be held.

On June 3 some 550 students signed a declaration vowing never to return to St. John's. They formed a Drop-out Federation, which accused Pott of forbidding patriotic activities and which aired their version of the incident. Resentful over not being consulted by Pott and desiring to identify with the nationalistic students, a large portion of the Chinese faculty resigned and issued a public statement expressing mortification over their deficiencies. Students and teachers cooperated in founding a new institution, Kuang Hua University.

Pott, nevertheless, remained unshaken in his belief that discipline had to be enforced and that the administration could not permit the students to involve the institution in politics. In mid-August 1925, he dispatched a letter to parents and guardians in which he stated that a decision to send a son to St. John's signified assent to school rules by both parent and son.[37] According to regulations: 1) student self-government would be encouraged but the university authorities would have exclusive jurisdiction over administration, curriculum and discipline; no outside body such as the Student Union would be allowed to control the institution; 2) one objective of the school as established by the church was the propagation of the Christian truth; all students must abide by the requirements concerning religious courses and activities though no one was compelled to become a Christian; and 3) when students went on strike and refused to attend classes, the school would close and require the students to leave; the institution existed to fulfill an educational function and could not allow activities which interfered with discipline or made the school a center of political propaganda. St. John's reopened in the fall of 1925, but with a greatly reduced enrollment.

Though Pott was more patriarchal in his public stance than many missionary educators, his administrative practices and tactics were far from unique. President Hume, who in January, 1925, had accepted a compromise settlement with Yali students despite criticism by colleagues, issued a notice to the Yali student body on September 9, 1925 with essentially the same regulations as Pott's.[38] In a resolution adopted after May Thirtieth, the Senate of Shantung Christian University stated: "We are convinced that students and staff alike can best fulfill this purpose [goals of Christian education] by giving diligent attention at all times, to the regular studies of the university. We are in sympathy with the legitimate expression of patriotism but we would strongly urge our students to devise ways of rendering constructive service to their country. We expect them to refrain from interference with their class-work which would be opposed to their own good, to the highest interests of the university, and to the welfare of the nation at large."[39] The head of Hsin-hsueh shu-yuan (New Learning School) in Tientsin ordered students to desist from patriotic activities and return to classes after a ten-day strike in June, 1925. When the students replied that they must do their patriotic duty and stick by their comrades, the principal called on "all my good Protestant pupils" to come to his side. Instead, the student body walked out and drafted a vicious censure of the principal and the "enslaving" and "unchristian" education of mission schools.⁴⁰

The question of authority at the institutional level often became identified with the issue of sovereignty at the national level. Many Chinese Christians reacted very personally to the tragedy of May Thirtieth and displayed great sensitivity to any implication of Chinese inferiority or any doubt concerning their patriotism. Chafing over their secondary status in the mission schools, Chinese educators likened it to the inferior position of China in the international community and such an interpretation reinforced their readiness to side with students in confrontations over authority. A missionary reported that some Chinese Christians in Amoy felt under such pressure to demonstrate their patriotism that they severed all relations with foreign colleagues and joined in public criticisms of them.⁴¹ Proclamations spoke of hurt pride over the fact that foreigners treated Chinese as if they were the same as cows and horses.⁴² At Soochow University a student interrupted class to ask the American instructor for his position on the May Thirtieth incident, while the Chinese faculty and staff sent a note to missionaries demanding that they do more than express sympathy toward the students and regret for the wrongs of imperialism. "We find ourselves unable to have faith in words which are not validated by corresponding deeds," they said. "Furthermore, we desire to know whether or not such statements represent the consensus opinion of all missionaries in China."⁴³ In conclusion, they indicated that their attitude toward and relationship with foreign evangelism in China would depend on the missionary response.

Differing reactions corresponding with national origin were dramatically highlighted at Lingnan University following the Shakee incident.⁴⁴ Misunderstandings had emerged even before the June 23 demonstration in Canton was planned. Alexander Baxter, university vice-president and a Britisher, spoke for those who thought that the institution should not allow its students to engage in political action and that the school should not take a stand by flying its flag at half-mast. Chinese members of the Lingnan University Council protested a proposal to close the school early, saying that it would be interpreted as a move to prevent student participation; they asked that the college issue a formal condemnation of the May Thirtieth incident.

Early on June 23 Westerners watched some three hundred Chinese students, faculty and staff leave Lingnan for the parade. By afternoon word had arrived that one teacher and one student from Lingnan had been among the 52 Chinese killed; five Lingnan students had been hospitalized. Returning students reported that they had been marching peacefully along the canal separating the Shameen concession from the city when Anglo-French troops opened fire. Based on these reports, the Lingnan staff issued proclamations deploring the incident and censuring the Shameen perpetrators.

Baxter, despite the fact that he signed one of the statements, had become persona non grata with the Chinese and was requested to leave. He departed for Hong Kong, where he heard the British version blaming Whampoa cadets for the opening volley. Baxter thereupon publicly disavowed the Lingnan resolutions. To the outrage of Chinese, he went on to say that he had learned subsequent to signing that firing started from the Chinese side. Chinese accused Baxter of rating British word above Chinese; Lingnan students condemned him as a traitor who had disgraced the college and even alumni felt compelled to insert newspaper notices dissociating themselves from Baxter. Vice-President Baxter was forced to resign and was permanently reassigned elsewhere. Though the other Britisher on the faculty was not on campus at the time of the incident, anti-Western sentiment became so intense that he was given a three-year transfer and many of the American teachers spent the summer vacation in the Philippines.

The college managed to reopen in the fall, but only a portion of the students returned. One student, an active Christian, related how he had been made the butt of attacks in his neighborhood during summer vacation; anti-Christian leaders had circulated posters stigmatizing him as a foreign slave and a Chinese traitor.[45] On boarding a steamer to return to Lingnan in September, he had been arrested and jailed until the magistrate ordered his release. During 1925-1926 Lingnan would continue to be caught up in the nationalist maelstrom despite its two martyrs at Shakee and its conspicuous participation in an elaborate state funeral for all the 52 victims on October 3, 1925.

When it came to the third issue, that is, the question of whether a political stance was appropriate for missionaries and Christian institutions in China, divisions sometimes also coincided with nationality. For Chinese who viewed May Thirtieth as an offense against human justice, there could be no island of neutrality; the necessary response was clear. Westerners were deeply divided and more sensitive to the political and legal implications of involvement by individuals and institutions enjoying extraterritoriality. Christianity in China, furthermore, was represented by dozens of organizations, many of them responsible to mission societies and church denominations in the West. The unanimous and instantaneous response desired by Chinese was not forthcoming.

The best that concerned Westerners could do in the immediate aftermath of the tragedy was to join likeminded individuals in issuing proclamations and supporting student protesters. In Peking in early June, for example, Westerners cooperated with Chinese in separate statements by YMCA and YWCA secretaries, the Yenching faculty, the Church of Christ, and the staff of Peking Union Medical College Hospital.[46] Most of these expressed regret for loss of life, condemned use of military force, and recommended investigation of the incident. Several asked if the unequal treaties were not in need of revision, but they were not the broad puristic condemnations of imperialism awaited by Chinese. Five hundred Chinese Protestants published in the *North China Star* (July 18, 1925) a letter to the Shantung missionaries asking why they had not spoken out clearly and publicly.[47] Why had they not supported the cause of justice in their journals and in advice to their governments? Instead of disarming current anti-Christian agitation, their silence belied denials that they were the vanguard of imperialism. Other Chinese, perhaps misled by the continuing prestige of scholars in China, exaggerated the ability and willingness of missionaries to exert influence on home governments. Wu Lei-ch'uan of Yenching University stated that China would cease to have room for foreign missionaries if they continued to rely on treaty protection and to talk of separation of church and state instead of urging their governments to alter their China policy.[48]

Many missionaries, however willing to speak out individually and informally, remained hesitant to sign formal statements issued in the name of a specific Christian organization.[49] In some cases, the reluctance was based on the belief that religious organizations should not become involved in politics; in other instances, the argument was that the membership must be polled first. Mission school administrators found it inappropriate for institutions with extraterritorial rights to become havens for anti-government or political activities.

Pope Pius XI responded to the appeal from the Peita faculty with the hope that the May Thirtieth affair could be settled "in a spirit of mutual understanding in conformity with the principles of *justice,* of *equity,* and of *Christian* charity."[50] No mention of the unequal treaty system was made and no change was indicated in the church's stance that political questions were of no concern to Catholic missionaries, who should remain aloof from all Chinese political movements. Though Chinese Catholics were encouraged to manifest their patriotism in a dignified and reasonable way, Christian schools should not be the locus of anti-government demonstrations and academic discipline should be enforced. Apostolic Delegate Constantini addressed a letter to Catholic Youth of China, July 19, in which he stated that they could best serve China by spreading the Christian gospel. In a later statute members of the Catholic Youth of China were forbidden to affiliate with a political party. To the request of Amoy Christians that the missionaries address the diplomatic corps regarding a just settlement, the local council of the Reformed Church of America replied that an international investigative commission had been established and this obviated the necessity of a special petition on their part.[51]

As new incidents fed nationalism and the movement broadened, small groups of missionaries began to question the validity of their apolitical posture and the continued usefulness of the unequal treaties.[52] On July 13, one hundred seventy Americans in north China applauded

W. E. Borah, chair of the Senate Foreign Relations Committee, for advocating an end to extraterritoriality and all armed intervention in China. They expressed the hope that the U. S. government would adopt the same position and they commended the nationalist movement as a sign that Chinese citizens were taking an interest in public affairs and thereby laying the foundation for democracy. In August, eighteen missionaries of the Church of Christ in China sent a letter to U. S. Ambassador J. V. A. MacMurray renouncing their extraterritorial privileges and expressing the desire to be governed and protected solely by Chinese law. A group of Methodist missionaries at the summer resort of Kuling notified their Chinese colleagues that they had already communicated to the U. S. Secretary of State the urgency of treaty revision. They stated, further, that there was "no Christian justification for the aggressive, arrogant and superior attitude which has characterized the dealings of many Westerners with Chinese." Acknowledging that some missionaries had previously shared this Western attitude, they looked forward henceforth to a new and equal relationship. By January 1926, eighteen missionary societies in the U. S. and Great Britain had publicly endorsed the abolition of extraterritoriality and the renegotiation of the treaties on the basis of equality; some had taken the further step of renouncing special treaty privileges and opposing the use of force on behalf of evangelists.

Reactions by Western business and diplomatic personnel varied from irritation over what was designated self-righteous meddling to doubt about the legality of renouncing special rights.[53] U. S. Department of State representatives pointed out that the American government had the obligation to protect all its citizens in accord with existent treaties; missionaries could best obviate the necessity for use of force by prompt compliance with the recommendations of the U. S. consul in times of unrest. Newspaper editorials expanded this demurrer with the comment that missionaries could not abrogate extraterritoriality without also giving up all other treaty rights, including the right to reside in China and proselytize; furthermore, those who felt free to ignore the policy and instructions of their government were inciting lawlessness. In Hankow, which contained a significant

Western enclave, the Chamber of Commerce cabled the Department of State protesting the advocacy of treaty revision on the grounds that Comintern agents, not the unequal treaties, were the source of trouble.

Even the U. S. ambassador charged the missionaries with expediency and rejected the implication that either China or the U. S. could abrogate the treties unless there were prior negotiation and agreement in concert with other powers.[54] Premier Stanley Baldwin told parliament that there should be a settlement of the May Thirtieth incident and a return to normalcy before the issue of treaty revision was discussed.[55] According to a recurrent theme, the Chinese would interpret unilateral concessions as a sign of weakness and would be emboldened to press for additional concessions; the present disorders were ample proof that conditions in China did not warrant treaty revision and that dependence on the Chinese government for protection would endanger foreign lives and property.

For many Chinese, missionary recognition of the significance of May Thirtieth for the treaty system was too limited and too late; it came after they had already formulated their impressions of the Western response. Negative reaction in business and diplomatic circles, forcefully expressed in the *North China Herald* and elsewhere, more than offset any belated readiness by missionaries to alter the basis of Sino-Western relations. Chinese Christians accused the foreign press of trying to divert attention from the issue of Chinese independence by waving the red herring of Bolshevism; the true source of the movement was not Bolshevism but failure to carry out the promises of the Washington Conference, according to Chinese teachers at Yali.[56] Kuo Ping-wen, founder of Southeastern University in Nanking, stated that the movement was the patriotic expression of the Chinese people and that every other influence was incidental.[57] For the American public he reproduced an English-language poster displayed in many Chinese cities:

"The Student Movement
Is
NOT Bolshevik
NOT Anti-Christian
NOT Anti-Foreign
But a Cry for Humanity."

Frustrated by Western division and procrastination, Chinese Christians formed separate municipal Christian unions to speak for them.[58] They collected strike money, issued manifestoes condemning the unequal treaties, and cooperated with nationalist organizations. In Nanking Chinese Christians organized a Society to Promote the Abrogation of Unequal Treaties while the June 15, 1925 issue of *Chiao yu pan yueh-k'an* (Christian Semi-monthly) was entitled "Abrogation of Unequal Treaties Number" and opened with an editorial by Wang Chih-hsin: "Chinese Christians are also Chinese citizens."[59] Other Chinese Christians founded their own patriotic societies. A Shanghai Christian Student Union raised money for strikers and dispatched letters to the Municipal Council of the Shanghai International Settlement denouncing the Nanking Road Massacre.

In an appeal to Christians throughout the world, the Peking Union of Chinese Christian Churches solicited understanding of the implications of May Thirtieth for the church in China. Though courteously worded, the statement made it clear that responding to the tragedy in terms of legalities only compounded bitterness and misunderstanding; the issue was treaty revision to restore Chinese sovereignty, not just the settlement of the single incident of May Thirtieth. At a mass meeting on June 14, Chinese Christians in Peking drew up a manifesto stating: "Such flagrant violations of the Golden Rule of our Christian religion cause us to question how real is the control of Christian principles over the national conduct of Western nations who are maintaining a host of Christian missionaries in China at the annual expense of many millions of dollars. Much as we appreciate the individual expression of good-will and fraternity which we believe is the inspiration of the missionary movement, we must in all candor point out that unless the Christian conscience of the West has enough power to arouse its governments to the need of an early revision of these unequal treaties, and to root out the attitude of superiority and unbrotherliness that lies back of them, we see little positive good in the future that Christian missionaries from the West can accomplish in our land. . . ."[60]

Executives of the National Christian Council disseminated a formal pronouncement on behalf of the council on July 16, 1925. The group, under Chinese leadership but with the concurrence of the liberal Western representatives, contended that the church was implicated in the May Thirtieth incident in spite of itself and should, therefore, make its attitude clear; the church, furthermore, had an obligation to intrude in political matters when human rights and morality were violated. Not only did the council condemn the unequal treaties but it sent a letter to the Shanghai Municipal Council requesting that there be an impartial investigation and there be Chinese representatives on the municipal council and any court of inquiry. A flurry of criticism greeted the actions of the council executives.[61] Mission colleagues condemned them for exceeding their authority and for engaging the church in political activities to the detriment of evangelism.

The YMCA, which was also under Chinese leadership, openly supported the May Thirtieth Movement.[62] Yu Jih-chang, secretary of the China YMCA, cabled John R. Mott, secretary of the YMCA's International Committee, urging that he protest to the "highest authorities." The YMCA periodical, *Ch'ing-nien chin-pu* announced that it would not carry British advertising and it published manifestoes expressing outrage. The YMCA press also prepared study pamphlets on the unequal treaties, consular jurisdiction, and extraterritoriality. Publicly commending the boycott, staff members of the Shanghai YMCA helped to raise money and organize meetings for strikers. The Peking YWCA made its sentiments known by setting up a street concession to serve free tea to demonstrators. In order to acquaint English speakers with the views of Chinese, the magazine of the National YWCA issued a special supplement to *The Green Year* on July 1, 1925.

Despite prompt public support by individuals from the Western community and despite subsequent advocacy of treaty revision by mission organizations, relations between Chinese and Western Christians were severely strained by the May Thirtieth Movement.[63] A sufficient number of missionaries refused public condemnation or hedged on the abrogation of the unequal treaties to provide fuel for those eager to revive the educational rights and anti-Christian campaigns. To disentangle themselves from the Western presence, some congregations left their denominations and organized independent churches or joined the Church of Christ in China. Other Chinese accepted Christian teachings only on a private and individual basis, while for a vocal group, work for social and political justice became the primary function of Christianity and the church. Christians in Wuchow formed the Kwangsi Chinese Christian Promotion Society, which issued a proclamation stating: "The saying that missionaries and doctors are vanguards of the Imperialists proves to be a fact undeniable. Fragrances and stinks must be separated. . . ."[64] Within a year after May Thirtieth, YMCA membership for the city associations had declined 13% and income was down 15%; many of the YMCA service clubs and Bible societies in government institutions had closed. Attendance at many urban churches had fallen off.[65] Pupils in Protestant schools in Hunan and Hupei joined in the revival of anti-Christian propaganda after the Student Union Congress of July 1925. A Christian and a mission school graduate stated that he had gone to America hoping to learn more about Christianity as the source of Western strength; he now understood that the real Western ideals were materialism, nationalism, and militarism; to restore China's respect, he would henceforth preach these ideals, not Christianity."[66]

THE POLITICIZATION OF THE EDUCATIONAL
    RIGHTS MOVEMENT

The changes that May Thirtieth wrought became part of the groundwork for the Northern Expedition. Tactics included a new emphasis on a united front of all nationalists against the common enemies: the imperialists and the militarists. Student, labor and peasant unions should all join the fight. Like many facets of national life, education was to be "partyized" *(tang hua)*. Even as the parties arrogated to themselves the nationalist issue, however, factionalism intensified. The dominance of the political parties, their competition, and the new tactics, all found expression in the Educational Rights Movement.

In 1925-26 the Young China Party, the CCP, and groupings within the KMT agreed that the drive against imperialism and militarism was the first order of business. Though the Western Hills faction and the Young China Party were later to reject rapid social change, their leaders in 1925-26 advocated social and economic reform and they too worked to build a popular base. Certainly some groups were more radical than others, but during the brief interim between May Thirtieth and the Northern Expedition the labels of right wing or left are not very informative. The major sources of disagreement between the KMT leadership and members of the Young China Party and the Western Hills faction were personal rivalries and the issue of cooperation with the CCP, not the struggle for national unification under the banner of *San min chu-i*.

Thus it was that individuals from all factions sought initially to use the rights recovery campaign. Availing themselves of the ground swell of anti-imperialism, they incorporated the Anti-Christian Movement into the drive for political unification. There might be some jockeying for influence among the students, but the factions did not differ significantly in their propaganda targeting the mission schools. Only as the United Front began to break up did there emerge sharp conflicts over goals and means. The question was not whether education should serve the individual or the nation but rather which political clique should determine educational goals and content.

The hope of professional educators for reform by cultural transformation had already begun to languish by 1924. May Thirtieth brought the death warrant. Cultural reform via education had proved illusory so long as disorder and disunity undercut the educational system. Despite their continuing prestige, the educators lacked the means to implement their educational programs. Frustrated members of the National Association for the Advancement of Education demanded in the spring of 1925 that the Ministry of Education set a three-year limit for meeting registration requirements; the Ministry's answer was a promise to take the matter under advisement. In November, 1925, the Ministry did issue new and more detailed registration regulations and did urge compliance, a move which the Peking Anti-Christian Federation promptly condemned as inadequate and overly lenient.[67]

The dilemma that May Thirtieth presented to the older generation of educators was graphically expressed by Fan Yuan-lien, former president of Peking Normal University and current director of the China Foundation for the Promotion of Education and Culture (U.S. Boxer Indemnity Fund). In 1921 as Minister of Education, Fan had criticized mission schools for their neglect of Chinese studies and their requirement that non-Christians participate in religious activities. Speaking on June 16, 1925 at Peking Normal University, Fan commended the students for their protests against the May Thirtieth tragedy; he was proud, he said, that Chinese no longer endured foreign insults without resistance; the Chinese people were proving that they had spirit and a sense of nationalism. On the other hand, he cautioned the students against hoping that demonstrations and strikes could solve China's problems. The solution was a long-term one; it required that education cultivate moral character, national consciousness, and technical ability. He concluded: "Now, gentlemen, these certainly are very exasperating times!"[68] The exasperated students were offered no task for the present, nor any indication as to how or when the nationalistic education would be implemented.

One of the last articles in *Hsin chiao-yü* before it ceased publication in October 1925, repeated the familiar arguments about the need for national education to create citizens but it continued to defend a legal approach. The Ministry of Education should establish a special committee to foster restoration of educational rights, said the author; the National Congress should pass legislation for recovery of educational sovereignty.[69]

By this time many educators had lost faith in such tactics; the voices of those championing the separation of politics and education were muffled by the chorus demanding that national interests take precedence over all. Ch'en Ch'i-t'ien tried vigorously if unsuccessfully to persuade the National Association for the Advancement of Education to exclude representatives of parochial schools from membership; he and other nationalists did secure a resolution advocating special assistance to students and teachers withdrawing from church schools. After May Thirtieth both the National Association for the Advancement of Education and the National Federation of Educational Associations included military training and the fostering of national consciousness among their educational goals.[70] Recommending centralized control and patriotic content for education, the National Association for the Advancement of Education adjourned its last annual meeting in August, 1925. The National Federation ceased to function after its October convention at which speakers delineated education in terms of its national role; it should include military instruction and it should foster a sense of the racial distinctiveness of the Chinese and a knowledge of the humiliations suffered by China at the hands of the imperialists. Not only was there little discussion of education for the individual or a school system free of politics, but the educational associations could no longer find a role for themselves on the national stage. The New Culture Movement was over. Nationalists like Tseng Ch'i, Ch'en Ch'i-t'ien, and Li Huang turned to the Young China Party rather than the educational associations to try to achieve their ends.

After the loss of a sense of direction during the spring, both the Student Union and the Anti-Christian Movement gained new popularity and relevancy with May Thirtieth. Anti-religion became a supplementary theme to the cardinal theme of anti-imperialism just as the Anti-Christian Campaign became a part of the struggle for national sovereignty and unity. During the preliminary stages a few demonstrations, a spate of publicity had been useful, said the National Student Union, but the emphasis should now be on organization, coordination with other nationalist societies, and broadening of the support structure.[71] As new branches of the Anti-Christian Federation were founded, the Student Union should offer aid and cooperation in implementing their program.

Students should make a special effort to carry the campaign to the workers and peasants, for the damage inflicted by Christian missions extended beyond urban mission schools and churches.[72] During the summer and winter vacations students should undertake lecture tours and send out drama troupes to explain to the laborers and farmers the ways in which the imperialists and capitalists used Christianity to oppress them. The villager should be made to realize that the hospitals, clinics, recreation and literacy programs of the missions were simply bribes to deceive them. Only if the masses joined in the Anti-Christian Movement would Christianity in China be eradicated. To implement these united front activities, the National Student Union set up a special Bureau of Workers and Peasants and voted to co-opt worker and peasant representatives into student organizations. They established contacts by founding "Common Peoples' *(p'ing-min)* schools to arouse the masses in the struggle against capitalism and imperialism. Mao Tse-tung stated that "after the May 30th Incident and during the great wave of political activity which followed it, the Hunanese peasantry became very militant."[73] He claimed to have organized more than twenty peasant unions. Valuable as these experiences were, students continued to concentrate most of their work in the cities, where they made special efforts to broaden the student base. Most May 30th activists had little success in penetrating the countryside during 1925.

Student Union policy called for isolation of mission schools, though not of parochial students. Parents should continue to be discouraged from enrolling their sons and daughters in Christian institutions and teachers should refuse to teach in them. Those students who had dropped out or had been expelled from mission schools because of political activism were hailed as heroic martyrs; every effort should be made to help them and to encourage new withdrawals: economic assistance, transfer certificates, open admission to national schools, and the organization of units of the Drop-Out Federation which would be affiliated with the Anti-Christian branches. The Christian schools and the YMCA should not be permitted to use athletic and recreational programs to bid for popularity; hereafter, Christian institutions should be excluded from regional athletic meets.

Special efforts should be made to incorporate students remaining in parochial schools.[74] As a result of May Thirtieth, a united front including these students seemed possible. Much of the campaign literature henceforth differentiated between the students and the administrators in the Christian institutions, or between the Westerners and the Chinese. The students were less frequently condemned as denationalized; rather, it was pointed out that many of the mission students had wished to participate in the May Thirtieth Movement. As one manifesto stated: "The odor of blood revolted even the students of the Christian schools grouped under the sign of the cross."[75] School officials had, however, applied strong-arm methods designed to prevent the students from joining their colleagues. The incidents at St. John's and elsewhere were often cited as proof that the church was the handmaiden of the imperialists who opposed Chinese unity and sovereignty.

With the realization that mission school students might join the united front against imperialism, the Student Union recommended specific tactics for working among them. Agents should enroll in mission schools, in the YMCA, and other Christian associations in order to build a faction to overthrow the ruling minority and Sinify the institutions. Liberal and sympathetic teachers and students in the mission schools should be contacted and assisted in awakening the student body. These activists should encourage the students to make demands such as the freedom to organize student unions, improvement of the course of study, abolition of compulsory religious instruction and worship, the right to inspect the financial accounts, and the emancipation of students. During Christmas week and evangelistic campaigns especially, the students should be active: asking questions of lecturers, distributing anti-Christmas cards, publicizing the massacres of Chinese by Christians at Shanghai, Shameen, and Hankow, disrupting celebrations, etc. Special Student Union delegates should work to induce Christians to leave the church and the names of those who recanted should be publicized; articles by drop-outs and apostates should be solicited.

The tactics were detailed and graphic, but simultaneously, the union recognized the need to place their actions within the context of the nationwide war against imperialism. Acknowledging that students could not conduct the nationalist campaign alone, the Student Union in Setember 1925 ended the strike called after the Nanking Road Massacre and tried to forge links with other classes and associations.[76]

ROLE OF THE POLITICAL PARTIES

Though the precise role of the parties is difficult to determine, these new directions of the anti-Christian campaign coincided with tactical changes by the United Front. Extensive, if scattered evidence of party ties, especially with the CCP and radical members of the KMT can be cited. Yun T'ai-ying, a member of the Executive Committee of the Communist Youth Corps and head of its Propaganda Department, delivered the opening address at the Student Union Congress in August 1925, and argued that all the student goals could be subsumed under the slogan "Down with imperialism!" In his speech, Yun was reiterating an earlier call by the CCP Central Committee for consolidation of the anti-imperialist united front.[77] According to one source, Yun subsequently assumed leadership of the student union at Wuchang, one of the first urban centers to implement the new tactics.[78] *Hsiang tao* also sent up a call for a Chinese united front of workers, students and merchants against the imperialists' united front of journalists, diplomats and Christian missionaries.[79] Popular assemblies representing workers, peasants, students, merchants, and soldiers met on the exercise field of Kwangtung University to acclaim the legitimacy of the Canton government and the merit of its platform.

With blatant elitism but not very orthodox Marxism, *Chung-kuo ch'ing-nien* welcomed the decisions of the student congress and sketched a historical framework for the new approach.[80] The revised anti-Christian tactics were hailed as the crystallization of years of intrepid struggle and the inauguration of a new phase in the revolutionary movement. Tracing the nationalist revolt against foreign imperialism from the T'aip'ing Rebellion through the Boxer Uprising to the May Fourth and May Thirtieth movements, the author blamed the failure of the first two insurrections on poor leadership. In 1919, however, the students became the counsellors of the people, bringing them a new understanding of revolution. Henceforth, he said, the students and workers would coordinate their efforts, the workers lending their arms and the students their brains. The period of abstract theory was over and revolution was assuming concrete form in which all campaigns would become part of the great national drive against imperialism and militarism.

The article concluded by re-emphasizing the need for tighter organization.

To incorporate the peasants, the Hupei provincial committee of the KMT recommended that anti-Christian propaganda include material illustrating the rural economic hardship caused by the church, while the CCP Central Committee urged propagandists among the peasantry to use every opportunity to depict the Christian church as the vanguard of imperialism. The church, in collaborating with the imperialists' exploitation of the peasantry, shared responsibility for the decline of the village economy, it was said.[81] Those Catholic missions which supported their activities through money-lending and land holding were, therefore, doubly oppressive as foreign usurpers and as pawn brokers and landlords. In 1925 the First Congress of Peasant Unions of Kwangtung adopted the slogans: "Oppose the usurpation of land by the church!" and "Oppose the church's collusion with foreign bullies to oppress innocent people!" To displace parochial institutions, it advocated founding secular rural schools. After May Thirtieth, the Canton government reneged on a previously negotiated sale of government-owned wasteland near Chiang-men to the Maryknoll mission while tenants on church land in coastal Kwangtung engaged in a rent strike.[82]

At the KMT Second National Congress in January, 1926, the party reiterated the themes that had come into prominence after May Thirtieth.[83] It was somewhat critical of the elitism and exclusivism of the student movement and reminded the students that they must emphasize revolutionary and mass culture, must stress anti-imperialism rather than anti-religion, and must secure the cooperation of the parochial students rather than treat them as the enemy. The Central Committee of the CCP at its plenum in July, 1926, echoed the need for an anti-imperialist united front in all anti-church activities. As guidance for commemorating anniversaries and national days, its Propaganda Department was instructed to assemble for distribution appropriate propaganda aids. Discussion outlines and reference materials were requested for Anti-Christianity Week and Anti-Imperialism Week along with such dates as May First, May Fourth, May Thirtieth, and Double Ten.[84]

For members of the Young China Party, the experiences of the summer of 1925 confirmed their belief that national sovereignty and unity must take precedence over all other issues and that education was central to attaining these goals. Viewing those students who withdrew from parochial schools as national martyrs, members of the Young China Party and Hsing-shih she devoted considerable effort to helping these youth gain entry to Chinese institutions. They also took much of the initiative in ostracizing parochial schools from athletic meets and other intercollegiate events.[85] In June, 1925, *Hsing-shih chou-pao* put out a special issue on the role of the Christian schools during the May Thirtieth Movement in which it highlighted the fracas at St. John's University. In October, 1925, the weekly published *Kuo-chia-chu-i yen-chi* (Collection of Lectures on Nationalism) by Tseng Ch'i, Li Huang, Yü Chia-chü, and Ch'en Ch'i-t'ien.[86] Most essays reiterated old themes: the utility of education in creating a nation and therefore the necessity for an educational system staffed and controlled by Chinese, the importance of normal schools in cultivating teachers who would instill commitment to national goals. To promote their cause, the party founded some 30 societies and numerous periodicals in addition to *Hsing-shih*. Among those supported was *Fei Chi-tu-chiao hsun-k'an* (Anti-Christian bi-weekly), a short-lived magazine which put out its first edition on November 1, 1925, and lasted about two months. The initial home of the magazine was Ta Hsia University, which had served as an important base for anti-Christian operations in Shanghai ever since its founding in 1924.[87]

The tone and general import of the articles in *Fei Chi-tu-chiao* do not differ markedly from those of the Student Union, CCP or KMT organs, all of which reflect the changes characterizing the post-May Thirtieth phase of the campaign. Such concordance despite factionalism and enmity is indicative of the nature and personnel of the national revolutionary movement. Most of the leaders, whether of the KMT, CCP, or Young China Party, belonged to a well-educated elite. Most had attained maturity within a common intellectual environment and had been politicized in the treaty ports by the same international incidents and analogous personal experiences. As a generation, they spoke the same language and agreed on the enemies of the moment: imperialism and militarism. Though urban oriented, they relied on populism in legitimizing authority. Mass mobilization was, for the majority, a strategy for political revolution, with social transformation remaining a somewhat nebulous goal.

Thus, *Fei Chi-tu-chiao* prompted students to go to the villages to awaken the peasants to the crimes of the church and, like the Student Union, KMT, and CCP organs, it urged the founding of anti-Christian branch associations in building a mass base.[88] Pleas for tighter organization and coordination appeared regularly. While sharply critical of the role of Christian institutions during May Thirtieth, Young China also accepted the possibility of a united front including parochial students. Anti-imperialism had become the all-pervasive theme. Whatever the hostility of the Young China Party toward the CCP, propagandists in all three parties espoused the Leninist interpretation of imperialism and denied Bolshevik instigation or control of the anti-Christian campaign.[89] Instead of reiterating the defects of Christianity as a religion, as Li Huang had done earlier, *Fei Chi-tu-chiao* authors underscored the cultural aggression of Christian missions. They repeated the slogans and reprinted proclamations of anti-Christian and educational rights committees in league with the Student Union and United Front. The Young China Party in its weakness, however, could not carry the campaign to a new phase; it could try to benefit from the popularity of the issue but it lacked the political strength to become a carrier movement for the campaign.

The dependence of the anti-Christian and educational rights campaign on the United Front is indicated by the difficulty of the Student Union in implementing the strategy proposed at its July Congress. Propaganda in the form of manifestoes, essays and pamphlets for the literate continued to preoccupy the students so that there was a recrudescence of anti-Christian literature during August 1925. Typical was an August 1 declaration by the Peking Anti-Christian Federation stressing the centrality of the anti-Christian campaign to the struggle against imperialism.[90] The manifesto closed with the three slogans that were to become the battle cry:

"Down with Imperialism!" "Down with Foreign Aggression against our Education!" "Let the State Recover its Monopoly over Education!"

Efforts were made to help those who had left the Christian schools in the course of the May Thirtieth Movement.[91] Ta Hsia University and National Southeastern University (later National Central University, Nanking) pledged to enroll special quotas of drop-out students but Peking students failed in their attempt to found a new institution as the St. John's drop-outs had done. In Foochow the educational rights committee of Fukien Student Union negotiated with the Department of Education for admission of drop-outs without entrance examinations and for reduction of tuition fees for the needy.

Though Christmas week, 1925, brought a brief flurry of anti-Christian activities, missionaries in numerous cities expressed satisfaction that the holiday season had passed without major incident; some mistakenly began to anticipate a return to normalcy. Only in a few areas did activities move beyond the realm of publicity during late 1925 and early 1926. The principal exceptions were cities under direct control of the United Front government. Despite advocacy of a united front including the peasants, party organizational work in the countryside was not yet well-developed and the elitist students, as a rule, had great difficulty communicating with the peasants. There is a report of an Anti-Catholic Propaganda Corps founded by a peasant union in southwest Kwangtung, but rural China's role in the anti-Christian campaign was minimal until the Northern Expedition.

In the cities, the stalemate was partly due to the fact that both missionaries and regional commanders had become concerned about the international complications of renewed violence. Some of the churches restricted their Christmas festivities and the YMCA kept a low profile. Sun Ch'uan-fang, who became military leader in Kiangsi, Anhwei, Fukien, and Kiangsu in late 1925, warned students against political activities. Pledging protection of missionaries, he specifically condemned anti-Christians and made his point by arresting and subsequently executing the head of the anti-Christian branch of the Fukien Student Union.[92] Warlord governors in Shantung, Hunan, and Hupei employed similar repressive tactics and in Shanghai plans for an anti-Christian demonstration in February 1926 were short-circuited by a police raid. Pointing up the importance of respecting the treaty rights of foreigners, Tuan Ch'i-jui in November, 1925, banned anti-Christian activities and directed Peking authorities to suppress all such disturbances.[93] Protests from anti-Christian organizations were forthcoming and the Minister of Education was accused of bowing to foreign pressure in not enforcing registration requirements. The massacre of dozens of Peking students demonstrating against imperialists and their Chinese collaborators on March 18, 1926, vividly illustrated, however, the risks of agitation in warlord territory.

CAMPAIGN STRATEGY IN SWATOW, CANTON, AND SZECHWAN

The months before the launching of the Northern Expedition in June, 1926 were, nonetheless, not without significance for the Educational Rights Movement. The network of anti-Christian and educational rights associations was expanding and contacts inside the parochial schools were being established. Even in interior provinces such as Kwangsi, Shensi, and Szechwan, anti-Christian publications and federations began to appear, while a major center such as Shanghai boasted of twenty anti-Christian branches with some three thousand members.[94] Though such an infrastructure would not come into full play until the National Revolutionary Army began to move north, events in Swatow, Canton, and Szechwan during 1925-26 presaged the strategy of the educational rights campaign once it was incorporated into the Northern Expedition. Swatow provides a specific instance of the interest and guidance of party leaders, while Canton and Szechwan illustrate the interaction of factional competition with the campaign.

The two eastern expeditions during the spring and fall of 1925 brought east Kwangtung, including Swatow, under the control of KMT troops. One consequence was that religious buildings, Buddhist as well as Christian, were requisitioned for use by the armies; this became fairly common practice as the National Revolutionary Army needed housing for soldiers or office space for newly formed governments and the military command. More significant was use of the educational rights and anti-Christian organizations in nurturing contacts with the educated sectors of society. Accompanying the military units from Whampoa were propaganda corps and political commissars such as Liao Chung-k'ai, a leader in mass mobilization until his death in August, and Chou En-lai, party representative and head of the political department of the First Division of the First Army. Their task was to enlist the populace in the revolutionary struggle, to found support organizations, and to structure a government under party tutelage.

In coming to Swatow, the revolutionaries came to one of the oldest mission locales. It had been designated a vicariate apostolic under Missions Etrangères of Paris in 1914 and was a major center of English Presbyterian mission work in China. In addition to three Christian middle schools, a Baptist seminary, and sixteen primary and secondary institutions, there were a Presbyterian hospital and a home for abandoned wives maintained by Catholic sisters. Swatow quickly became a center for educational rights ferment despite the fact that most of the teachers and principals in these schools were Chinese. Aided by activists and a former instructor, a group of students and teachers at Nanchiang Middle School took control of the institution during the spring of 1925 and cut fiscal ties with the English Presbyterian Mission Board. The Baptist seminary closed during the May Thirtieth Movement and did not attempt to reopen in the fall.[95]

By December 1925 Chou En-lai had become special commissioner of the East River district of Kwangtung and was directing the founding of municipal governments, labor unions, and support organizations. In this capacity he called a meeting of representatives from the Swatow Christian schools and urged that they end all association with foreign missions, eliminate all religious work, issue a formal declaration condemning imperialism and cultural aggression, and provide instruction in *San min chu-i*.[96] They should rebuild their schools as revolutionary institutes. Chou also took the initiative in establishing a Shou-hui chiao-yü ch'üan yun-tung wei-yuan hui (Committee of the Movement for Restoration of Educational Rights). The composition of the executive board is indicative of the social sectors that the KMT-CCP United Front sought to enlist through the Educational Rights Movement; it included one member each from the Hsueh-sheng lien-ho hui (Student Union), Chiao chih-yuan lien-ho hui (Faculty and Staff Association), Chiao-yü hui (Educational Association), Shih tang pu (Municipal party bureau),[97] and the nationalistic society entitled Wai-chiao hou-yuan wei-yuan hui (Committee for Diplomatic Support).

Fruit of Chou's efforts was a well-organized demonstration on Christmas Day, with students and labor union activists distributing leaflets attacking the YMCA as a denationalizing agency and the "running dog" of capitalists; foreigners, they said, effectively controlled education in Swatow. Regulations for government registration of foreign-supported schools came out five days later; they stipulated administrative control by Chinese and recruitment of a predominantly Chinese faculty, cessation of religious proselytism, and adoption of a government-mandated curriculum; no new schools were to be founded without government permission.[98]

Contributing to the Lingnan and Szechwan troubles in 1926 were the gains made by the CCP and the pro-Soviet faction in the KMT after May Thirtieth. In its power base, the left became increasingly differentiated from other KMT sectors as it concentrated on propaganda and mass organizations. The CCP was able as a result of the Hong Kong strike during the May Thirtieth Movement to incorporate thousands of proletarians into the party. Through its dominance of the General Labor Union, it came close to acquiring autonomous control over mass organizations of workers in Canton. Often acting independently of the KMT, the Strike Committee had its own treasury, organized rival branches of Kwangtung workers, armed its own strike pickets and even set up a strike court to try violators.

Two reports on interviews with Borodin and visits to the Canton Strike Committee headquarters shortly before the launching of the Northern Expedition illustrate the work of radical students in politicizing the laborers.[99] Both reporters were guided by a former Shanghai Baptist College student who had joined the KMT left and both commented on the parties' dependence on student cadres.

In the dormitories provided for strikers, short-term courses were offered on "What is imperialism?", "The history of the imperialist invasion of China", and "The labor movement in China and the world". Anti-Christian posters, lists of British crimes against China, facsimilies of Sun Yat-sen's will, and other campaign placards with the crossed hammer and sickle decorated the walls of the dormitories and classrooms. The reading tables held pamphlets on "The Shakee Massacre", "The Unequal Treaties", the "Communist Manifesto", and "Elementary Course in Imperialism". When asked whether the labor movement had gotten out of hand in the case of the extravagant demands of the Lingnan University Labor Union and others, Borodin replied that the strength of the Chinese communists and the KMT left lay with the working class program; the workers and also the peasants had to be organized, educated, and protected. In contrast, he stated, "the Christian Church is doing next to nothing toward bettering the social condition of the Chinese masses."

Kwangtung University, a major left-wing center, served upon occasion as the headquarters of *Hsin hsueh-sheng,* the General Labor Union, the Kwangtung Student Union, the Communist Youth Corps, the Anti-Christian Federation, and the Movement to Restore Educational Rights.[100] As indicated by the example of Swatow, the two Eastern campaigns enabled the left to extend its influence beyond Canton by founding peasant associations, workers' unions, women's and youth groups in the areas brought under the governance of the then United Front regime.

The KMT, while cultivating support organizations, was building its army and expanding its influence via military actions; this was particularly true of the KMT faction associated with Chiang Kai-shek. Even in the army, however, the left was not lacking in influence. The Whampoa Academy depended heavily on arms and instructors supplied by the Soviet Union. If relatively few Whampoa cadets held membership in the CCP, communists frequently staffed the political department. After the assassination of Liao Chung-k'ai in August 1925 and the departure of Hsiao Yuan-ch'ung to join the Western Hills group, Chou En-lai and Pao Hui-seng effectively ran the Whampoa Political Department.

The assassination of Liao also shifted the balance in the Canton government and in KMT counsels leftward. Hu Han-min, implicated in the assassination, was ousted from the Canton government and shortly thereafter, some fifteen leading opponents of collaboration with the CCP, i.e., those who issued the Western Hills protest in November, departed for Shanghai and Peking. Indicative of the power of the radical factions was the Second National Congress of the KMT held in January 1926. About ninety of the two hundred fifty plus representatives held dual membership in the KMT and CCP. Authority was delegated to a Central Executive Committee Standing Committee in which communists held three of the nine seats; with the Left KMT they had a majority.[101] CCP members headed the Organization and Peasant Departments while Mao Tse-tung was acting chair of the Propaganda Department. The bureaus for labor, youth, overseas Chinese, women, merchants, and even the Kuomintang Central Party headquarters had communist secretaries.

Though Wang Ching-wei, Chiang Kai-shek, and the communists all upheld the United Front, their coalition was rent with tensions and rivalries. Many in the Kuomintang resented the influence of Borodin and felt threatened by the inroads of the communists. Chinese businessmen were increasingly restive undr the strike. In December, 1925, several faculty members resigned from Kwangtung University in protest over the politicization of the institution. In the early months of 1926 competition between the Sun Yat-senist Society and the Communist Youth Corps at Whampoa openly surfaced. Chiang and other Kuomintang leaders might be eager to wind down the Hong Kong-Canton strike in order to launch the Northern Expedition, but Borodin and Chinese communist leaders found the environment conducive to raising class consciousness and expanding their organizational network. The USSR, furthermore, had little desire to terminate a boycott that had brought British trade to a standstill. They argued that a Northern Expedition would be premature.

To keep the military as his preserve and more broadly to check communist influence, Chiang in 1926 executed the March 20th coup.[102] He declared martial law in Canton and arrested both Soviet advisers in the city and communist political advisers in the party army; the headquarters of the Strike Committee and the union were temporarily closed. Though Chiang subsequently apologized to the Russian advisers with the explanation that his coup was directed against uncooperative individuals rather than the Russian-CCP presence, the balance of political forces in the revolutionary camp was altered. Wang Ching-wei, after denouncing Chiang, left the country and thereby permitted Chiang to dominate the May meeting of the KMT Central Executive Committee. The latter accepted Chiang's recommendation that the United Front be continued but that CCP members be precluded from posts as KMT department heads and that communist membership on KMT committees be limited to one-third. Outspoken Russian critics of Chiang departed for Moscow. Chiang and his military supporters had won a skirmish with Wang and the civilians. The Northern Expedition would go forward.

The communists, on the other hand, continued to prevail in propagandizing and organizing workers, peasants, and youth. Mao Tse-tung assumed direction of the sixth class of the Peasant Movement Institute and intensified the Marxist orientation of the faculty and curriculum. The political training of the National Revolutionary Army remained a communist stronghold and by the launching of the Northern Expedition, Chou En-lai dominated the political work of the First Army, Li Fu-ch'un of the Second, Lin Po-ch'ü (Lin Tsu-han) of the Sixth, and Huang Jih-k'uei of the Seventh. In the expanding labor unions and peasant associations, the leadership generally came from the young, the radical, and the elite; they were recruited through student movements.

Conflicts at Lingnan University in Canton during the spring of 1926 and at West China Union University in the fall mirrored this rivalry within the United Front. Accord on the goals and tactics of the Educational Rights Movement was lacking even though the Second KMT Congress had exhorted Chinese to follow Turkey in asserting independence and had demanded closure of all foreign and mission schools not conforming to government regulations.[103] Early in 1926 Lingnan faculty members and Student Union members of a KMT branch at the university helped organize a labor union of college workers and private employees.[104] The union on March 9 presented the college administration with a forty-eight hour ultimatum containing comprehensive demands: wage increases of 30 to 60 percent with overtime rates, an eight-hour day, free medical care, a union shop in which the union regulated hiring and dismissal, retirement on half pension, etc. Union leaders extended the strike deadline when college authorities requested more time to assess the financial implications and consented to negotiate only with workers employed by the college, not with those employed by staff members or sub-contractors. Still, no settlement could be reached.

Similar impasses had recently resulted in radical takeover of Kung-Yi Medical School and the closure of Canton Hospital and Stout Memorial Hospital in Wuchow. Fearful that this might be the intent of the Lingnan activists, President James M. Henry appealed to the Labor Bureau of the Canton government to arbitrate. The Lingnan union, after consulting with the city union, reluctantly agreed to the procedure and accepted a compromise contract. With the help of student cadres, the left wing had established a tie with Lingnan workers and increased its membership. The Labor Bureau, on the other hand, had not supported the more radical union demands and the school remained under Christian administration.

Lingnan's troubles had barely begun, however. New disturbances soon occurred and these revealed even more clearly the factional contest.[105] At a meeting of the Canton Student Union on April 4, 1926, three KMT members of the Lingnan Student Union embarrassed other Lingnan students by publicly criticizing the college; a fracas broke out. With the blessing of the college administration, Lingnan students voted overwhelmingly in favor of expulsion of the three students, an action promptly executed by the college council.

The repercussions were manifold and reached into higher party councils. The Lingnan Labor Union, stating that one of the students was its official adviser, demanded an explanation and threatened a strike. The Kuomintang appointed four staff members and one student from its Lingnan branch to intercede on behalf of the students; their argument was that the conflict reflected the contest between rightists and leftists within the Kuomintang and the Student Union so that the college was playing politics in siding with the rightists. The Ministry of Education sent a recommendation that the students be reinstated pending further investigation and asked for a prompt report after reconsideration by the college council. Party newspapers condemned the college officials for authoritarian persecution. In appeals for a united front against imperialism, numerous Kwangtung groups declared their support of the expelled students, "sacrificial victims of our revolution"; the Lingnan students struggling against cultural aggression should not have to fight the battle alone.[106]

Finally, with Sun Fo mediating on behalf of the Kuomintang Central Executive Committee, a face-saving settlement was reached. President Henry wrote a letter to the Ministry of Education explaining that the initiative for the expulsion had come from the students, not the college council. The three students were reinstated for two days with the understanding that they would leave permanently. After returning to campus with banners, drums, and a worker escort, the three departed quietly the following day. At least one of the KMT faculty members, Wei Chueh (Sidney Kok Wei) apparently lost his job after acting as spokesman for the Lingnan Student Union leaders. Subsequent conflicts were to be even more difficult of resolution. Lingnan was disrupted by a strike of its labor union in November, 1926, and then in April, 1927, the school closed because of a joint strike by the Union of Non-teaching Staff and the Labor Union. Some of the staff demands bordered on the utopian, with the political motivation outweighing the economic threat.[107]

Pinpointing the exact contribution of United Front factions and individuals to the Lingnan storms is not easy. Public references and appeals almost invariably cite the Kuomintang rather than the CCP, and the line between the left Kuomintang and the CCP was ill defined. Except when specific individuals or organizations are mentioned, the contribution of the CCP is elusive; the CCP, furthermore, had its own divisions and disagreements.

Mikhail Borodin indicated in an interview with President Henry in May 1926 a desire for better coordination of union activities and implied that tighter control would reduce the arbitrariness of some of the demands and tactics. At one point, he even took credit for the fact that the anti-Christian activities of Christmas, 1925 had been more moderate than those of Christmas, 1924.[108] The Labor Bureau again acted as mediator in the November, 1926 strike. On the other hand, the Canton General Labor Union was a communist stronghold and the tactics that the Lingnan unions employed were to be repeated by student radicals and workers along the route of the Northern Expedition: presentation of an ultimatum in the expectation that rejection would lead to a strike and takeover of the institution. Agents provocateurs and resident party members would provide the necessary entree and the unions would function in close association with radical student groups and city unions.

Precipitating the storm in Szechwan was British bombardment of the Yangtze port of Wanhsien following a dispute with the local warlord Yang Sen over shipping activity. Once again the magnetic power of anti-imperialism and the extensive network of political and youth associations were demonstrated in the rapid popular response. Both Kuomintang and CCP cadres had been organizing workers' unions and youth groups in Szechwan since the early 1920s. As president of Chengtu Higher Normal Institute, Wu Yü-chang had made the school a center for progressive youth and he was in 1925 both head of the Kuomintang Szechwan branch and mentor of the local CCP. Fruit of these efforts was active participation in the May Thirtieth Movement with an effective boycott of British shipping along the Yangtze ports. By the time of the Wanhsien incident on September 5, 1926, rival labor unions existed in both Chungking and Chengtu and student propagandists and labor activists from contending factions had clashed in the streets. Chung-Fa hsueh-hsiao (Sino-French Institute) founded by Wu was training revolutionary cadres and Chu Teh and Liu Po-ch'eng, two communists who spoke the Szechwan dialect, soon arrived for organizational and propaganda work.[109] With such provocation and political groundwork, it is hardly surprising that protests and demonstrations erupted in the principal cities of Szechwan. Coordinating activities was a Great Anti-British Alliance.

Students in West China Union University, a joint British-American enterprise in Chengtu, issued a derisive anti-British pamphlet and joined other students in dispensing anti-imperialist handbills.[110] They were reprimanded by the school administration. With the aid of party activists, members of the student body tried to close down the university. Two days and nights of agitation preceded a referendum in which a slight majority voted to keep the school open. The struggle was not over, however. Approximately a third of the students withdrew and cooperated with party cadres in organizing a strike of workers in foreign and mission institutions. Promise of a food allowance helped make the strike so effective that classes at West China Union University had to be suspended.

With the threat of disorder in several cities, higher officials now intervened.[111] The provincial military commander, General Teng Hsi-hou, applied pressure to end the strike while Chiang Kai-shek responded to an appeal from Chinese Christians with a formal promise of protection. In the light of Chiang's actual authority in Szechwan, such a guarantee amounted to a pious hope, and this was speedily illustrated when the warlord Liu Hsiang sided with the left Kuomintang. His forces raided the party and labor headquarters of the Kuomintang right, forcing most of the leaders underground; they disbanded the armed labor corps and shattered the General Labor Organization. The situation continued to deteriorate as competition among warlord and party cliques intensified.[112] In Chungking tombs of foreigners and Christians were plundered. West China Union University's enrollment declined sharply, for students were reluctant to be associated with a foreign, Christian institution. The West China Christian Educational Union ceased to function and eventually it was suspended because, it was said, Chinese Christians neither identified with nor supported it. By early 1927 most British and American citizens had vacated Chungking and Chengtu; West China Union University was left with only nine foreign staff members.

Communist leaders in 1925 along with more recent communist historians have interpreted the May Thirtieth Movement as inaugurating the first revolutionary civil war of 1925-1927. Certainly, it is difficult to conceive

of the launching of the Northern Expedition in July,
1926 without May Thirtieth in the background. Continuities existed in the fervid nationalism of the propaganda,
in the techniques of mass organization, and in the goals
of the United Front. The KMT and the CCP learned
the lessons of May Thirtieth well even if they came to
interpret them differently.

As Nicholas R. Clifford points out in his study of
Shanghai during May Thirtieth, however, Ch'ü Ch'iu-pai
claimed much more for the movement. Writing three
weeks after the incident on Nanking Road, Ch'ü exulted:
"May Thirtieth! There can be no doubt that this marks
the beginning of the revolution of the Chinese People!"[113]
Few historians, whether communist or not, whether
writing before or after the establishment of the People's
Republic of China, have accorded such importance to
May Thirtieth. The May Fourth Movement of 1919,
according to communist historiography, signifies the first
stage of the new democratic revolution. Among Western
historians, also, May Fourth is often interpreted as the
cultural breaking point between old and new China; it
was May Fourth that sanctified the tradition of student
activism, a tradition that still inspires ambitious youth
and tempts political parties.

Even so, May Thirtieth was crucial to the Chinese
revolution in its own way. May Fourth awakened New
Youth and gave them a sense of community; in their
unions and associations, in their periodicals, students
fashioned channels of communication. May Thirtieth
politicized youth and linked them with structured political
parties having access to military force. The struggle
against imperialism and militarism became one in the
May Thirtieth lexicon. Though still concentrated in
urban China, the May Thirtieth Movement incorporated
mass organizations much more integrally in the nationalist
campaign than May Fourth and many of these unions
proliferated as the Northern Expedition got under way.

To point out the significance of May Thirtieth is not
to deny May Fourth its due. The desertion of the intellectuals was essential to cultural revolution. Overthrowing
an established government and altering the international
balance of power, however, required organization, military
force, and ideological security. The differences between

the intellectuality of the 1920-1922 Anti-Christian Movement and the structure, tactics, and goals of the Educational Rights Movement in 1924-1928 illuminate the differences between May Fourth and May Thirtieth.

Chapter VII

The Educational Rights Movement Incorporated Into The Northern Expedition

In embarking on the Northern Expedition in July, 1926, both the Kuomintang and the Chinese Communist Party acknowledged that popular support was essential to legitimize authority. They designated the military units initiating the campaign, the "National Revolutionary Army," and their propaganda cadres couched *San min chu-i* in terms of the national welfare of the people. More than the warlord armies, in fact, the Kuomintang army was successful in conveying the image of a national force rather than a regional one. The Whampoa Academy, which trained many of the officers for the army, attracted idealistic youth from throughout China and some care was taken to insure that political workers who accompanied the National Revolutionary Army units spoke the dialect of the people "to be liberated." Fear of invading troops might be mitigated somewhat if the army could be presented as the people's own rather than as outsiders. In Fukien, for example, female propagandists using the local tongue knocked on doors to persuade families to come out to welcome the National Revolutionary Army. Even more important were relations between the army and the populace when the party government was striving to establish its authority following conquest.

The army political workers thus had a dual responsibility: first to raise the national consciousness of the recruits so that they were not just mercenaries trying to fill their rice bowls but participants in a patriotic crusade; second, to instruct the soldiers in proper conduct toward the masses so that they would not become a scourge on the land. Despite some violent incidents, the early National Revolutionary Army did acquire a reputation as a disciplined force which paid for services and respected the needs of the people in so far as possible during warfare. Until the dissolution of the Kuomintang-Chinese Communist Party coalition, the National Revolutionary Army was not plagued by the desertions and sabotage characteristic of many warlord armies.

Both parties anticipated that mass campaigns would be significant in the drive to overthrow militarism and imperialism and to unify China. As indicated above, party branches, youth societies, and nationalistic associations had proliferated, most publishing their own periodicals. Institutes for training cadres had been established and expanded.[1] Between the formation of the United Front in 1924 and the launching of the Northern Expedition in 1926, the nationalistic overtones of Chinese communism had grown more pronounced as the populism of the Kuomintang had gained new prominence.

Notwithstanding these commonalities, the dominant factions in the parties diverged in their dependence on and use of mass campaigns. What the leaders in both parties learned from the experiences of the Northern Expedition accentuated their distinctive political styles. By 1928 the similarities between the Kuomintang and the Chinese Communist Party were less striking than their disparities. If Chiang Kai-shek did not hold uncontested power and the strategies associated with Mao Tse-tung had not yet gained dominance in the Chinese Community Party, each party was by 1928 moving along lines that would alter its basic thrust. The Chinese Communist Party of the late 1930s seems far removed from the Chinese Communist Party of the 1920s. The same is true of the Kuomintang. For the Kuomintang, the Northern Expedition appeared significant because it brought victory and a brief chance to attempt unification and modernization of China. Perhaps its greater long-term significance may be found in what happened to these two competitors for the right to define the new China.

KMT AND CCP POLICIES TOWARD MASS MOVEMENTS

While acknowledging that divisions within each party and independent initiatives meant that neither was entirely consistent, one can, nevertheless, generalize about their differing policies toward mass organization.[2] Leaders of the National Revolutionary Army were happy to have individual propagandists infiltrate enemy armies and incite desertion or evasion of combat. As the armies moved north, the political workers recruited guides and porters; they tried to persuade merchants and peasants to bring their grain and foodstuffs into the open market instead of shuttering their doors or fleeing. But the Kuomintang depended principally on military victories rather than on mass uprisings preceding the National Revolutionary Army. Once a city was seized, support groups organized parades, demonstrations and public meetings to solicit popular acceptance of Kuomintang and National Revolutionary Army rule. Political cadres often assumed responsibility for reviving the functions of local government under party tutelage and for procuring the goods, services, and income necessary to continue the momentum of the Northern Expedition. In territory conquered by the Chiang faction, the cadres' mission was not so much social revolution as the imposition of order and control. Not class struggle but an all-class union became the theme.

Chinese Communist Party leaders, for their part, sought to profit from the lesson of the Hong Kong strike, namely, that the party could expand its influence by cultivating unions of workers, youth, and peasants. Outside the permissive atmosphere of the Canton regime and the concession area of Shanghai, however, wholesale organization and general strikes invited repression by the warlord governments. It was possible to locate activists and to place a few in key positions; cadres did frequently precede army units in order to establish contact with sympathetic groups and to begin unionization. Massive unionization, city-wide strikes and attacks on foreign concessions were, however, more typical of the post-liberation period than of the pre-liberation one. In the view of many in Chiang's faction, such economic disruption, political disorder, and international incidents placed the military campaign in jeopardy rather than promoted it.

The differing approaches to mass mobilization and party rule can be illustrated by examining the course of the Educational Rights Campaign during the Northern Expedition. In warlord territory, student storms and demonstrations were sporadic and coordination was minimal. In areas where the Chinese Communist Party-left

Kuomintang prevailed, the activists were usually able to exert sustained pressure on Christian institutions; also characteristic was unionization of workers and staff members in the schools, with identical demands for student and worker participation in administration. In other liberated areas, especially those captured by the First Army, the course of the campaign was more erratic. The anti-Christian rhetoric might be equally strident but the life span of the campaign was generally shorter; insistence on three-thirds rule (student, faculty, staff) was less common. These differences hardened as the competition between Chiang and the left wing intensified and Chiang courted the business and international communities. Upon the break-up of the United Front and the ousting of Soviet advisers, the Educational Rights Movement as a mass campaign ended. The prospects for those reformers anticipating a mass-based government under Kuomintang rule were not auspicious.

Both loose discipline within the Kuomintang and divergent attitudes among party leaders toward anti-Christian activities contributed to the erraticism and variability of the campaign in Kuomintang territory. Since missions and imperialism were inextricably intertwined in the minds of many Chinese, the anti-imperialist theme of the Northern Expedition inevitably carried anti-Christian overtones. But certain individuals in the Kuomintang believed that the benefits derived from mission schools, hospitals, orphanages and so forth should not be lightly dismissed and they desired continuation of such institutions so long as they were brought under government supervision. A number of this persuasion had attended Christian institutions in China or the West, though relatively few were practicing Christians.

Sun Fo, for example, had previously declared that the party principles of his father were not anti-religious and that he did not find Christianity and Chinese patriotism antithetical.[3] In 1925 he voiced concern about infringements on religious freedom and in 1927 he wrote a public letter to the former president of Lingnan University expressing appreciation of its work and stating that China welcomed supplementary education by Americans and Christians so long as it was subject to Chinese regulations and consistent with national educational policy. In the course of the Northern Expedition, however, Sun also urged Chinese Christians and the Christian church to "stand with the people", that is, support the nationalist revolution under KMT leadership; the future of Christianity in China would depend on their taking such a stand.

Wei Chueh (Sidney Kok Wei), a former Lingnan student and faculty member, had lost his job at the university after acting as Kuomintang spokesman during the spring storm over expelled students. As a member of the departments of education and of foreign affairs in the Canton government in December 1926, he issued a policy statement that left considerable leeway for variant interpretations.[4] The southern government, according to Wei, was not in principle anti-foreign or anti-Christian, but education in a time of revolution should be revolutionary. While demanding an absolute national monopoly over education and complete separation from religion, he indicated that Christian schools might have a place in new China if they conformed with government requirements, were administered by Chinese, and made all religious activities voluntary.

In 1926 Chiang Kai-shek commemorated the Double Tenth and the fall of Wuchang to the National Revolutionary Army with a proclamation that sounded much like a campaign speech. His 33 point platform included regulation of mission schools and recovery of a monopoly over public instruction; he singled education out as one of the tricks imperialists used to destroy the nation, and he advocated strengthening the unions of workers, peasants, merchants, and students while guaranteeing the exercise of their political rights.[5] As Chiang became increasingly apprehensive about the repercussions of international incidents, however, he tried to distinguish between opposition to imperialism and opposition to religion and religious establishments; he cautioned against violent attacks on foreigners and foreign property while continuing to advocate a national revolution to end warlord rule and the unequal treaty system. Such a narrow path was not easily trod and, furthermore, many believed that such distinctions were incompatible with national revolution. Other Kuomintang leaders, Tai Chi-t'ao, Wu Chih-hui, and Kao Er-po, held leadership positions in the

Anti-Christian Movement. They supported the Canton government directive to provincial departments of education exhorting them to continue to exert pressure on private schools (November 1926).[6]

Competition among factions and personalities could produce rapid fluctuations in policy, with allies and subordinates following their own devices. It would be a mistake to assume that youth organizations of either the Kuomintang or the Chinese Communist Party were simply following the dictates of the party. The anti-Christian and educational rights movement had a genuine popular base among students and young intellectuals and, under the inspiration of the revolutionary environment, youth often took initiative on their own and pursued their own group interests. The long-standing anti-Christian tradition and widespread antagonism toward foreigners provided tinder for brief localized flare-ups, especially when politicized soldiers entered the scene. At Huachow, Kwangtung, for example, a dispute arose over a soldier's drying his coat on Maryknoll church property; rocks were thrown, and then some 300 to 400 soldiers and civilians sacked the church.[7] Even Chinese Christians, exasperated by Western procrastination and insensitivity, sometimes adopted extremist positions and lent support to radical demands and coercive tactics.

Under these circumstances, the fact that differences in the Educational Rights Movement coincided with the separate prongs of the military drive north is confirmation of the continuing role of the political parties. A comparison of the campaign in Fukien with that in Hunan and Hupei reveals distinctions that are subtle but real.

EDUCATIONAL RIGHTS CAMPAIGN IN FUKIEN

The First Army, which took the east coast route toward the Yangtze Valley, included relatively few communist officers and even in its political department, the number of communists had been reduced after the March 20th coup. Evidence of organizational work in the vanguard of the army comes from a controversy at a private middle school in Amoy. When the principal tried to forbid student membership in the Kuomintang and to restrict participation in political activity, the students gained support from the provincial party committee; eventually some forty students were dismissed for participation in the Kuomintang.[8] After the National Revolutionary Army arrived, party branches and activities came out into the open and a committee of teachers, students and party officials in the school insisted that they have a say in educational policy.

Initial missionary reports, nevertheless, told of orderly occupation and limited disruption of church work as the troops drove north. The secretary of the Reformed Church in America mission commented favorably on the conduct of the National Revolutionary Army soldiers when they entered Changchow on November 7.[9] Instead of relying on raw military force to control the populace, he wrote, the party plastered the city with posters and sent out lecturing bands to explain its goals and to cultivate public opinion and support. Similarly, a month later in Foochow, municipal leaders, youths, and southern troops cooperated so that the assumption of control brought minimal disturbance. Fukien Christian University students asked for and received a three-day holiday in order to educate the masses in *San min chu-i*. With optimism, they joined other students in agitating for registration of mission schools; they distributed handbills advocating recovery of educational control in every institution established by foreigners, and in a communication to the Fukien Christian University Board of Managers, they urged immediate steps to secure registration.[10]

In both cities, the atmosphere quickly turned sour, however. In Changchow an anti-Christian campaign under student leadership was soon underway. Speeches and placards denounced Christianity as the agent of imperialism. Demands for required memorial services honoring Sun Yat-sen and for required study of *San min chu-i* and revolutionary politics became common. Christmas Day brought an anti-Christian procession led by soldier-students from a military training academy.[11]

By mid-January, 1927, the situation in Foochow and Amoy had grown ugly. The Board of Managers of Fukien Christian University had rejected President John Gowdy's attempt to resign in favor of a Chinese head. While assuring the students of eagerness to obtain government recognition, the board promised only to watch for every opportunity to secure more favorable regulations.[12] A Chinese teacher, scarcely able to speak for emotion, accused the foreigners of not understanding the vital necessity of immediate action or of not caring.

Revival of the shopworn but still incendiary story that missionaries had murdered orphans touched off violence. According to reports, a group of students and soldiers excited a Foochow crowd with the claim that Spanish Dominican sisters had killed and cooked baby children in their Holy Childhood orphanage; mutilated cadavers were said to have been discovered as proof. When the crowd got out of hand, about thirty missionaries, novices, and orphans sought refuge on an English ship bound for Hong Kong. Some of the agitators, however, boarded the ship and at the Amoy stopover, they were able, with the aid of the local populace, to seize several orphans and a Spanish missionary as hostages. In Foochow, meanwhile, pillagers, including NRA soldiers, looted YMCA centers, churches, hospitals, a girls' school, and mission residences as well as the orphanage. A party newspaper carried an article about the capture of a servant carrying two sacks of mangled corpses and the discovery of a rotisserie on which the babies were roasted; it called for a massacre of missionaries and their converts. Evacuation of missionary wives and children to the Philippines speedily followed.[13]

Such an outburst, evoking memories of the anti-Christian tradition of the 19th century, appears to have found little favor with the party and government hierarchy.[14] The article on the murder of orphans was said to have been mounted on a wall board alongside a proclamation by Ch'en Yu-jen (Eugene Ch'en), Foreign Minister of the Canton government, urging respect for foreign lives and property. Without official party sanction and support, the anti-Christian drive rapidly receded. Chinese in the Christian institutions felt betrayed by both Westerners and the radical nationalists; though relieved from immediate stress, they were said to be too depressed to take any initiatve.

By March, 1927, however, pressures were again building. Members of the Association to Restore Educational

Rights had made contact with faculty and students in Christian schools and had encouraged them to found an organization to oppose cultural aggression. Former chancellor Ts'ai Yuan-p'ei, who was in Foochow as a member of the Kiangsu-Chekiang-Anhwei Joint Association designed to mobilize support for the National Revolutionary Army, helped contact several instructors who had studied in Peking and were currently employed in mission schools, according to President Gowdy. The educational rights advocates as a whole split into the radicals, who urged immediate government takeover of the schools and elimination of all religion courses, and the moderates who wanted immediate government registration and voluntary religious courses. Radicals in the parochial schools included: Ch'en Hsi-hsiang, who was an alumnus of Fukien Christian University and a member of its Chinese language department; the head of the University's Union Normal and Middle School; the head of Wen Shan Girls' Middle School (ABCFM), and a teacher at Hwa Nan College.[15]

The Fukien Christian University faculty, hoping to strengthen the hand of the moderates and to avoid a strike, finally voted in favor of registration on March 18. In a series of dramatic confrontations on the 21st, Ch'en charged university administrators with lack of good faith and introduced two municipal officials, who delivered fiery anti-Christian speeches and intimated that the government planned to transform the school into a Sun Yat-sen Memorial University. The moderates, for their part, imported the Commissioner of Education, who denied that the government intended to confiscate private property. Only by a series of parliamentary and extra-parliamentary maneuvers did the moderates circumvent a student vote inviting the government to assume control.

On March 24, a joint meeting of the Educational Rights Association and the Fan wen-hua ch'in-lüeh ta t'ung-meng (Great Alliance against Cultural Aggression) attracted faculty and students from half a dozen mission schools as well as National Revolutionary Army members and other political activists. Extremists placed a dunce cap on the head of a Chinese clergyman (also a returned student) and tied his hands behind his back but were unsuccessful in persuading him to recant. The rally culminated in a parade, first to various Christian centers to urge participation and then to political and party headquarters to petition the government to take possession of the schools. A strike call went out at Fukien Christian University; several mission schools closed temporarily and others dismissed the radicals on their staff. Somewhat surprisingly, the storm blew over and by late spring most of the schools were able to resume academic work, though with reduced enrollments. The rapid abatement is all the more remarkable in that the Fukien Christian University Board of Managers vetoed the faculty vote for registration.

Once again the activists had miscalculated in their expectation of official support while their intemperance had narrowed their base. The petitioners of March 24 gained access only to subordinates and secretaries and their demands elicited no concrete action. Instead of sanctioning nationalization, the Commissioner of Education indicated that the government would concentrate on revising registration regulations. Professor Ch'en, who apparently was a party member, received a lateral transfer and left town along with some of the student radicals.[16]

The Western administrators, for their part, came to appreciate the intensity of Chinese feeling on the educational rights issue and the pressure being placed on Chinese Christians in the moderate camp. Despite opposition from mission officials, the presidents of Fukien Christian University and Hwa Nan insisted on resigning in order to make way for Chinese leadership; they also argued that national sentiment necessitated registration if the schools were to survive.

EDUCATIONAL RIGHTS CAMPAIGN IN HUNAN AND HUPEI

In Hunan and Hupei, by contrast, the campaigns were sustained for weeks and even months so that the disruption of the Christian institutions was much more severe. Party spokesmen, while rarely invoking violence against foreigners, were disposed to condone such incidents as the inevitable accompaniment of revolution. With students and workers demanding policy-making roles, the attempt to organize political power through mass associations sometimes threatened to inundate the issue of educational rights. Neutrality or an apolitical stance was accorded even less tolerance than in Fukien. Similarities also existed, however, for most of the action followed rather than preceded the arrival of the National Revolutionary Army; tactics called for a united front with Chinese in mission institutions, and the party coalition discovered that the popular organizations were not simply puppets to be manipulated at will.

As the Northern Expedition began, the National Student Union and the Central Committee of the Chinese Communist Party passed several resolutions on the student movement. The eighth Congress of the National Student Union, meeting in Canton, heard addresses by the heads of three KMT departments; Kan Nai-kuang for the peasant department, Ho Hsiung-ning (Mrs. Liao Chung-k'ai) for the women's department, and Ting Wen-fen for the youth department.[17] In response to KMT and CCP criticisms of the isolation of the student movement from the masses, the congress resolved to coordinate cultural and political revolutionary movements; in response to party criticisms of the student movement's lack of unity, the congress called on its members to combat individualistic ideas and work for the solidarity of the student movement.

The Second Enlarged Plenum of the CCP Central Committee, meeting from July 12 to 18, 1926, noted the importance of the student movement to the national revolution.[18] The May Fourth and May Thirtieth movements had revealed that most students were susceptible to revolutionary propaganda despite their bankrupt, petty bourgeois background, it said; thus, students should be considered second in importance only to the workers and peasants. Maximum service to the revolution, however, required both broad, inclusive participation and unified organization under the leadership of Chinese Communist Party cadres. The committee recommended a united front which included not only communist and left Kuomintang youth but also the Kuomintang right, Young China Party members, and Christian students. To attain such cooperation, cadres should stress unity in organization and action without demanding ideological conformity; they should expound minimal revolutionary slogans and policies and in concrete situations offer only those proposals acceptable to the majority. They should lead struggles advancing the students' own interests as well as the political revolution.

As far as leaderhip was concerned, the party seemed confident that its comrades could dominate the hierarchies of the student associations so long as they participated actively in various extracurricular organizations and collaborated with the left Kuomintang. Since most student unions were run by executive committees, the cadres did not need to monopolize the associations and should not try to do so. Perhaps because of the Communist Youth Corps' radicalism and loose discipline, the Chinese Communist Party at this time took over direction of the student movement from the corps in order to incorporate the movement into the revolutionary campaign.

The Central Committee specifically mentioned Anti-Christianism in its resolutions on the student movement and also in those on the peasant movement. Attacks on parochial education should not be confused with attacks on mission school students; the latter were, on the contrary, to be drawn into the united front. Attacks on the church as the vanguard of imperialism and the opiate of the people should not provoke actual conflicts drawing international intervention.

This careful delineation of tactics and the reaffirmation of the united front by party executives stand in contrast to a propaganda piece issued by the political department of the Fourth Army a month later.[20] Divisions of the Fourth Army, fighting their way through Hunan and Hupei toward the Wuhan cities, probably included a higher proportion of Chinese Communist Party political workers and soldiers than any of the other National Revolutionary Army units. Their manifesto is an inflammatory denunciation of Christianity and all its works. Chinese should flee from missionaries and Christians as they would from cholera or other pestilence; do not approach Christians nor let them approach you, urged the authors. Listing the ways the imperialists had used Christian missions to wring concessions from China, the propagandists scored the anachronistic schools producing foreign slaves. An immediate anti-Christian counterattack was in order. They acknowledged that the Canton authorities recommended protection of missions and Christians but maintained that this was only a provisional policy until the government was more firmly established; in reality, they said, the majority of the Canton leaders had disclosed their true attitude by failing to suppress incendiary placards against religion or outbreaks against churches. The contrast between the two documents might be attributed to the different goals of a policy statement by central authorities and a propaganda leaflet employing verbal overkill; nevertheless, the contradictions found expression in student activities in Hunan and Hupei.

Despite the fact that the National Revolutionary Army took Changsha in July, 1926, Hankow and Hanyang in September, and Wuchang in October, most of the Christian schools in these cities opened for the fall semester, some even registering increased enrollments. As in Fukien, they expressed satisfaction with the orderly assumption of control. Hsiang-Ya Hospital and an emergency hospital set up for National Revolutionary Army soldiers in a nearby clubhouse worked out a friendly cooperative relationship and Commander-in-Chief Chiang even requested the services of a Hsiang-Ya American physician to have an impacted wisdom tooth pulled.[21] On the other hand, rumors flew thick and fast and the occasional incidents easily became cause for alarm. Soldiers and party officials in smaller cities now and again confiscated mission compounds and middle schools for housing and office space.

If the conquest were to differ from the familiar warlord prototype, party civilian workers had to move in quickly to establish control. As Chiang Kai-shek and the military commanders departed Changsha to continue the campaign north, the Chinese Communist Party and left Kuomintang transferred cadres to the area to organize a mass power base and implement the united front policy. Student organizations as well as peasants' and workers' unions multiplied and student storms were soon brewing. Hupei, having come into the fold later than Hunan, often followed a step behind its southern neighbor and events in Wuhan were complicated by sharpening competition between the left coalition and Chiang Kai-shek. Even so, an overall pattern emerges.

Early in October the Hunan Student Union held a provincial assembly which substituted a policy of cooperation with parochial students for the previous one of enmity; it invited all students to unite under the slogan, "Struggle for the Revolution". The Kuomintang provincial Youth Bureau printed thousands of handbills entitled "Welcome to Parochial Students Joining the Revolutionary Front" and distributed them throughout the province. Another handbill issued by the Anti-Christian Federation in Changsha concluded; "Save the oppressed [students in Christian schools]! Christian School Students! Leave those schools where you suffer!" Working through party and student union members in mission schools, the Changsha and Wuhan Kuomintang convened parochial students in meetings outside their institutions. According to a Kuomintang report on Changsha, the students did not at first realize that they had been made the slaves of foreigners, but after several meetings the truth dawned and they were ready to demand the reorganization of their school.[22] At Liuyang, Hunan, pupils in the Wesleyan boarding school were summoned to a meeting held at Peasant Union headquarters; here they were provided with a list of demands to present to the principal.[23] Coordinating committees were established; for example, the joint executive committee for the Hupei Student Union and the T'ui-hsueh lien-ho-hui composed of former parochial students.. The overall umbrella organization was Fan wen-hua ch'in-lueh ta t'ung-meng, reported to embrace over 120 member societies, including the provincial party bureau, the provincial teachers' association, student union, labor union, peasants' association, merchants' alliance, etc.[24] An executive committee at the provincial capital provided directives to branches at various centers.

As pressures mounted, Chinese Christians reacted in diverse ways. Some who had long chafed under foreign domination welcomed the opportunity to Sinify their faith and its works. Two Chinese Methodist ministers were paraded at bayonet point down the streets of Changsha; one renounced Christ and one refused. One of the strike leaders at the Liuyang middle school was a preacher's son on scholarship. Even though YMCA leadership was overwhelmingly Chinese, its headquarters were plastered with posters labeling it the vanguard of imperialism. Kuomintang members were given to understand that it was not politic to retain membership in the YMCA or attend its meetings. With the mayor withdrawing as head of the finance and membership campaign, Wuhan contributions fell so sharply that the YMCA school had to close. A staff member of the YMCA Bible institute in Changsha resigned to help guide the anti-Christian campaign, while the YMCA's plans for expanding programs for workers had to be abandoned in the face of official hostility and declining revenues.[25] Hsu Chi'en, a Christian activist and member of the left KMT-CCP regime in Wuhan, commended Hua Chung University students on the occasion of their founding a student union in December, 1926; parochial schools, he said, must join the revolutionary struggle and must conform to government regulations if they were to survive.[26]

Certain Protestants organized Wu-han Chi-tu-t'u ke-hsin yun-tung (Wuhan Christians' Reform Movement) and on January 1, 1927, issued a manifesto dissociating themselves from imperialism and a foreign-controlled church.[27] We wish, they said, to clarify our stand on the side of those fighting to save the country, i.e., the Kuomintang, the National Revolutionary Army and those upholding *San min chu-i*. We shall work to bring the Christian schools under the supervision of the Chinese government, in accord with the Chinese educational system, and under the control of a Chinese church (that is, not mission boards or a foreign-dominated church). The national revolutionary program is consonant with Christ's teachings, continued the manifesto, and those missionaries who put their own country before Christ and are unwilling to support the revolution should leave. Several mission school girls enrolled in the Wuhan political institute established by Mme. Sun Yat-sen to train women propagandists. Bobbing their hair to proclaim their revolutionism, they helped organize and direct the Wuchang Women's Union.[28] National Christian Council leaders lithographed a poster depicting Christians attacking the forces of evil: aggression, cruelty, ignorance, etc. Despite denials of any anti-foreign implication, the outcry by missionaries and the western press necessitated withdrawal of the flyer.[29]

Student storms in Hupei and Hunan mission schools

during 1926-1927 resembled earlier ones in that the issues of government registration, religious requirements, and Chinese control were prominent. Protests over lack of movement in these realms carried legitimacy for many Chinese and could be expected to increase as they gained the backing of the new local authorities. Often the students also questioned the authoritarianism of the administration and the priority accorded academic responsibilities over political or patriotic ones.

In other ways, the storms differed from earlier ones and many of the departures are attributable to the revolutionary environment. Demands broadened to embrace the participation of the student union in all policy decisions of the school, the duty of patriotic activism on the part of all teachers and students, and required courses in *San min chu-i* taught by government-approved instructors. The parties tried to ensure that the educational system would serve their political purposes. In Hankow, for example, the government ruled that the following material should be included in all school curricula: history of the political and social revolutions of foreign nations, the unequal treaties, the "actual" political and economic situation in China, popular education and the psychology of the masses, history of the Chinese revolution and the revolutionary parties, the emergence of youth, and so forth.[30]

Students, on the other hand, sometimes seized the initiative and served their own interests; party workers found upon occasion that their task was not so much to incite the students as to mediate between them and school administrators. Some of the storms, erupting in institutions already under Chinese control, had little to do with educational rights. Almost completely out of the action were the professional educational associations, as the students allied with recently founded unions. Staff unions, servants' unions, and nurses' unions, created in the drive to incorporate the masses in the revolution, could be as effective in closing a school as the students.

Missions were, finally, subject to disruptions arising out of the movement of troops, or a hiatus in political control, or transfers of government headquarters. Anti-foreign incidents having little to do with either religion or education inevitably affected the missions and their schools. Like Buddhist centers and other private schools and hospitals, their facilities might be pressed into service without regard for ideology or ownership. At Chiuchiang, Kiangsi, Roman Catholic clergy were permitted to hold 8 o'clock mass but cadres and soldiers used the chapel the rest of the time. The Franciscan high school in Wuchang was occupied and turned into a military cadet school. Earl Browder, who was a member of an International Workers' delegation to China in early 1927, told of a meeting in Wuhan with delegates of the Chinese Textile Workers Union, their picket corps, and the youth organization. The locale was an American church, "which was the only building in the neighborhood large enough for the gathering. The altar had been transformed with red flags and large pictures of Lenin, Sun Yat-sen and Marx. The meeting was opened by singing 'The Internationale' which was joined in lustily by men, women, and children!"[31]

In Hunan one sequel to nationalist conquest was the increasing frequency of holidays to allow for student participation in political activity. Students aided in publicizing party goals, in staging festivities celebrating the new revolutionary era, and in organizing unions and providing public support for strikers. In Changsha, for instance, a massive demonstration commemorated the anniversary of the Bolshevik Revolution. Monitored by students and small groups of soldiers, some seventy unions and guilds led a lantern parade in a colorful and orderly march through the city. Mission school servants, having been tutored earlier in the day by students and teachers, joined in the chorus of "Down with imperialism!" "No more hunger, no more poor!"[32]

Student strikes were soon in the offing, with the middle school students taking the leadership. By late fall a dozen or more Christian middle schools and junior colleges in Changsha, Liling, Yochow, Iyang, Liuyang, and Hsiang-t'an had experienced student storms.[33] The demands in most cases were familiar: abolition of all required religious activities, progress toward registration, and revision of the curriculum to include revolutionary culture, but several student unions also insisted that they must have the right of prior sanction for the hiring of any new school officials or the expulsion of any students. In some schools they asked for dismissal of specific individuals considered unsympathetic to Chinese nationalism or insulting in their attitude toward Chinese. The response of most principals was to close down the school in order to disperse the students but such reaction met with no favor among political activists. The Hunan Student Union requested that the provincial government order Hupin (Lakeside) College to readmit dismissed students and that it warn all schools to remain open or face government takeover. The Hunan Great Alliance Against Cultural Aggression requested the provincial department of education to mediate the disputes, to permit no school to close without adequate reason, to assume control of Hung-tao School which had expelled its students, and to give aid to students under suspension.[34]

At Yali a compromise settlement reached with the Middle School Student Union in late October proved temporary.[35] Approximately a month later, the students presented a list of much more radical demands and this time they gained the support of the student nurses who were generally of middle school age and educational level. Whether the youths intended the ultimatum to produce a confrontation rather than negotiation or whether they had been carried away by revolutionary idealism would be hard to tell, but the school officials saw no possibility of acceding to the complete list: Kuomintang members to control the teaching of the social sciences, dismissal of any teacher displeasing two-thirds of the students, termination of aid to the YMCA, decrease in tuition and room fees but improvement in recreational facilities, and extensive powers to the Student Union. The Student Union should be represented at faculty meetings, have a say in library purchases, exercise veto power in the dismissal or demotion of a student, receive a school subsidy, etc. The nurses added that they would accept orders only from their union chief while they joined in pressure to replace Chinese members of the Hsiang-Ya Medical Board with individuals more sympathetic with the Kuomintang program. Students occupied certain school buildings and picketed non-participants.

When the Yali college students went out in a sympathy strike, the faculty voted on December 9 to close academic departments for the remainder of the term. Though the hospital remained open, two of its executives who had kinsmen in the Peking government were forced to resign and leave Changsha under threat of violence; the unionized workers asked for increased wages and benefits and for control of hiring and firing by city union officials.

While the revolutionary nationalist atmosphere contributed to the simultaneity and similarity of Hunan's student storms during the autumn of 1926, the Student Union, party cadres, and Great Alliance against Cultural Aggression provided guidance and support. According to one source, outside students helped draw up the demands presented to Yali, organized a sympathy demonstration, and sent a warning to the university that they would resort to further action if satisfactory concessions were not forthcoming.[36] Newspaper publicity helped build esprit de corps and also induced commitment as activists wrote letters to the editor listing those who failed to participate. A sharp attack on I Fang Girls' School cited the Yali strikers as heroes and assured them that they would gain victory if they only continued to hold out. Internal leadership at Yali apparently came from a middle school teacher who organized a Kuomintang branch at the institution and who subsequently directed the Changsha anti-British boycott organization.[37] At Wesleyan Boarding School for Boys in Liuyang, striking students had the support not only of the peasant union, but the labor union, KMT cadres, and outside student organizations. When the school administration closed the school, these groups took over the property and used it for a propaganda training school.[38]

Not all, however, were happy with the disruption of education and other aspects of civic life. Government and private schools as well as parochial schools were in turmoil as a result of the political activism of the students and their demands for a share in administration. Though the provincial minister of education assured the mission schools that the party had no desire to destroy them or to take them over, he apparently had only limited control over the student movement. I Fang Girls' School had been founded by descendents of Tseng

Kuo-fan, had already registered with the government, and was staffed by Chinese; neverthless, it was denounced and severely disrupted.³⁹ Interestingly enough, the striking students themselves insisted that the schools should be forced to reopen and admit dismissed students.

The subsequent history of the anti-Christian and educational rights movements was even more deeply affected by factionalism and contradiction. Policies varied from place to place and from time to time, dependent upon who held authority when. Registration requirements, for example, differed according to province, with some of the regulations more extreme than others and with provincial governments frequently not having worked out procedures for enforcing the requirements. Though certain Christian schools had belatedly shifted to voluntary religious activities and had increased Chinese representation in the administration, they discovered that competing chains of command made registration far from a simple matter. That scarcely a Christian institution emerged unscathed indicates that the issue spoke to nationalists throughout China. That the course of the movement directly reflected the rivalry between the Chiang faction and the left coalition is further evidence of the importance of the party as a carrier movement.

Events in Changsha during 1927 correlated with the vicissitudes of the Chinese Communist Party. Upon the occupation of British concessions in Hankow and Kiukang in January and February, plus threats against Socony property in Changsha, most Westerners fled to Shanghai. Some minor looting of mission property occurred but the perpetrators apparently were paupers taking advantage of the turmoil. Party cadres were preoccupied with organizing intellectuals, workers, and the peasants in the surrounding countryside. Illustrative of their success in building a new political structure was the fact that ere long negotiations had to be conducted through union leaders. One such union leader, a Yali gardener, was frequently called upon to parley with soldiers seeking housing and to intercede with city union leaders in negotiations with the school servants.

By April the radical tide was running strong and the YMCA, the Bible school, the Red Cross hospital and numerous other mission institutions had been pressed into service as union headquarters or social centers, government offices or military residences. To preclude occupation by army units, the Chinese caretakers for Yali permitted the installation of a cadet school on campus. The Changsha Teachers' Union, under left-wing leadership, resolved "To apply new 'Revolutionary Education' in all schools. . . . To eliminate Christian education. . . . To get rid of all imperialist teachings and apply the Russian. . . . To have teachers take part in the political movement. . . . To expel all anti-revolutionaries."[40] Mission school teachers who wished to join the municipal teachers' union were not allowed to attend church or read the Bible, were required to study *San min chu-i*, and were obliged to obey all union rules. Despite Soviet attempts to moderate policy in order to hold the Wuhan coalition together, Hunan leaders initiated a program of confiscating the property of the rich; individuals who had gained wealth through their association with Christian institutions were favored targets.

Then, on May 21, 1927 (Ma Jih) came General T'ang Sheng-chih's coup with the execution of numerous communists, the closing down of union centers, and the imposition of martial law. Overt anti-Westernism and anti-Christianism declined and a few missionaries returned to their Hunan posts; some mission buildings were evacuated and there was even talk of reopening certain schools. General T'ang, however, ordered all junior and senior schools closed for a period of reorganization. Upon reopening, school principals were to be held responsible for the political attitudes of both the staff and students, guaranteeing that there were no communists in either group. It soon became apparent, however, that the general could promise protection but he lacked the control to ensure it. Underground communist organizations survived; incidents continued to occur, and a sense of unease pervaded the populace. Authority in Hunan changed hands several times during the last six months of 1927 as the ill-fated Autumn Harvest Uprising in September was succeeded by Nanking's challenge to T'ang in October and by an unsuccessful attempt at a communist putsch in December. The populace were, of course, the principal victims.

The campaign in the Yangtze Valley during the first quarter of 1927 was characterized, meanwhile, by a higher incidence of violence than earlier and by radicalism among students and employees. Scholars continue to disagree with respect to the exact source and significance of these characteristics. As military victories enhanced the power of Chiang Kai-shek, numerous individuals, including members of the left KMT, sought to offset or undercut his influence. The conflict came into public view when the left KMT-CCP transferred the Canton government and party headquarters to Wuhan while Chiang opted first for Nanchang and later for Nanking. The left coalition concentrated on specific centers such as Chang sha, Wuhan, and Shanghai, where it worked to build political enclaves under its control. With these bases, it hoped to dominate a civilian government that would be accepted as the legitimate national authority. According to Mao Tse-tung, the government of a local base should consist of a magistrate and representatives of the revolutionary mass organizations: the peasant association, trade union council, chamber of commerce, women's association, teachers' and staff members' association, student union, and party executive committee; implicit was a revolutionary restructuring of political power.[41] Simultaneously, the popular level of civic consciousness should be raised through anti-imperialist appeals and promises of economic benefits.

Most of the Wuhan leadership apparently hoped that this national democratic stage of revolution could be accomplished with minimal violence, though a few like Mao argued that a brief reign of terror was necessary and good for true revolution. Even those who wanted to curtail violence in order to preserve the coalition recognized that their strategy carried potential for mob action and accepted the risk. Ch'en Yu-jen (Eugene Ch'en), Foreign Minister of the Wuhan government, stated in an interview, March 18, 1927, that the Anti-Christian Movement was not an essential feature of the Nationalist movement and that the government did not favor closing down schools; on the other hand, he reminded his interviewer that China was in the midst of a popular revolution when people were forced into extreme positions. Under the circumstances, some disturbances, property loss, and personal distress were inevitable; time would remedy such matters.[42]

Both Ch'en and Borodin insisted that there could be no middle ground during a life and death struggle; the church should embrace the revolution; it should stir up the masses and organize them so that they demanded their fair share of productivity.[43] Its educational work should contribute to radical transformation of China. The church at best was thinking in terms of philanthropy, of agricultural schools, and of the morality of peaceful times, but China did not presently need soup kitchens or transcendental values; she required revolution. So long as the church retained its association with the imperialists, she was the enemy. Borodin bluntly remarked that an attack on the religion of the people would be a colossal mistake for a peasant movement; he wanted it understood, however, that his saying that the party dared not touch popular religion was not the same as saying that compromise with cultural aggression or with the unequal treaty system was possible. For Borodin, as for many Chinese, the Christian church was an alien institution to be distinguished from the faith of the masses.

None of the above nor other available documentation definitely answers the question of whether violent confrontations were deliberately provoked and if so, on whose authority.[44] Some have argued that Liu Shao-ch'i, Li Li-san and Su Chao-cheng, who were all engaged in organizing Wuhan workers during early 1927, hoped to provoke British atrocities in order to feed nationalist passions and justify repossession of British concessions. According to this interpretation, political cadres incited street crowds to seize British concessions in Kiukiang and Hankow during January and February. Certain scholars, on the other hand, dispute the existence of a conscious policy advocating violence and explain the events as the actions of excited mobs which got out of hand. Still others see the incidents as autonomous but deliberate actions by individual subordinates.

An eye-witness account of the take-over of the British concession in Hankow pointed out the contradictory impulses: a group of student propagandists from the Central Political Academy haranguing a crowd in front of the Hankow customs house and working them into a frenzy as they enumerated British injuries to

China, inflammatory posters such as one deliberately linking the enemy warlord leaders with the British. In this poster, signed by the Propaganda Department of the Hupei KMT committee, three Chinese were being crushed by a heavy weight bearing the Union Jack insignia; their blood flowed into a bucket below, where the English lapdogs, Chang Tso-lin, Chang Chung-chang, and Sun Ch'uan-fang greedily lapped it up.[45] The Western reporter pointed out, on the other hand, that he and other foreign civilians standing on the fringes of the melees met with no hostility. When Chiang Kai-shek made his triumphal entry into Hankow on January 12, red-colored leaflets proclaimed: "We are against not the British people, but British imperialism. The former are our good friends while the latter is our deadly enemy. Therefore our anti-British movement is quite different from anti-foreignism in a narrow sense. Bear this in mind and do not go astray." The author concludes that the attack was not planned except perhaps in the minds of "a few irresponsible students of a school directly under the Propaganda Department of the Kuomintang."

NANKING INCIDENT OF 1927

Whatever the source, turbulence and in some cases near anarchy became more widespread during the early months of 1927. The time-worn slander that priests had gouged out the eyes of babies surfaced in Wuchang and forced the closure of a Catholic dispensary. In Foochow, a Chinese cleric who was a returned student became the object of attempts to persuade him to recant: he was placed on a platform with a dunce cap on his head and his hands tied behind his back; when he refused to renounce his faith, he was paraded through the streets with occasional slaps to the face. Near Hankow, members of the Peasant Union captured and maltreated two Roman Catholic priests. Even so, the Foochow pastor escaped without serious injury and the two Catholic priests were released on government orders.[46] Missionaries and Chinese Christians, attempting to protect school and church property, were manhandled in several instances, while buildings left untended even briefly became fair game for looters, soldiers, or cadres. On the whole, however, the number of foreign lives lost and the amount of foreign property destroyed seem remarkably small for a dense population enduring civil war and revolution. Alarm, apprehension, and rumor far exceeded actuality. No matter what the origin, the incidents and reactions to them reveal much about relations between Chinese and Westerners. The Nanking Incident may be examined as the one having the greatest impact on the missionary community and significant consequences for the KMT-CCP coalition.

On March 23, 1927, most northern troops departed Nanking. Though some Western women and children had left the city on consular recommendation, most foreigners had anticipated the same orderly take-over by southern troops as in Hangchow and had stayed at their posts. Ginling students, relieved that they had not been molested by the retreating northerners, prepared a welcoming banner for the National Revolutionary Army.[47] Units from the Second, Sixth, and Fortieth Army Corps began to move into Nanking early on the morning of March 24. Attacks on foreign residences quickly followed. Soldiers with fixed bayonets invaded Western compounds. Under threat of being shot, foreigners turned over their belongings; homes, consulates, and business firms were looted; nine buildings were burned. Resistance provoked physical assault and in a few instances death. Among those wounded were the British Consul General and a Presbyterian missionary at Ming Te Girls' School; among those killed were two Roman Catholic priests and Vice-President John Williams of the University of Nanking. As buildings were repeatedly invaded, disappointed latecomers resorted to wanton destruction upon discovering little of value left; street mobs rushed in to glean anything overlooked by the soldiers.[48]

Most of the Westerners congregated at the University of Nanking, the British Consulate, or Standard Oil Company on Socony Hill. In mid-afternoon when a general assault on Socony Hill appeared imminent, British and U.S. ships laid down a barrage of shells to drive the attackers back and the foreigners escaped to nearby warships. Looting rapidly subsided. Under threat of a second bombardment and with the mediation of the Chinese Red Cross (Swastika Society), Chinese soldiers and police escorted foreigners from the other two centers to the waiting vessels, which set sail for Shanghai.

Though much has been written about the Nanking Incident, scholars do not agree on responsibility for the violence or on the motivation of the instigators.[49] Was it simply the bubbling up of anger against imperialists among nationalistic troops, their officers, and political commissars? Was it a deliberate attack planned by officials of the left wing? If deliberate, was the intent to discredit Chiang Kai-shek and the National Revolutionary Army, to provoke foreign military intervention, or simply to involve the populace in a take-over of foreign holdings? Similar questions have been asked about the violence occurring in Shanghai almost simultaneously. What does seem clear is the fact that the anti-imperialist outbursts were initiated by individuals under left-wing influence, in the case of Nanking, soldiers from the Sixth Army Corps and probably from the Second and Fortieth Army Corps. What is more important in the case of Nanking is the reaction of United Front leaders, Chinese Christians, and foreigners to the incident.

Responses, though not strictly along national lines, often corresponded with the historical framework of the viewer. The shadow of the Boxer Rebellion influenced the perceptions of many. Even while recognizing the changes in outlook of both Chinese and foreign political leaders since 1900, Westerners were sensitive to the possibility of a massive anti-foreign eruption. On consulate order, the Yangtze Valley was quickly denuded of missionaries. Chinese who recalled the Boxer Rebellion were more apt to conjure up images of an international expeditionary force occupying the capital and to be fearful of joint action by the powers. Other Chinese placed the Nanking Incident within a context formed by the May Thirtieth, Shakee, and Wanhsien tragedies. They contrasted the Western reaction to the loss of half a dozen foreign lives on March 24 with foreign reaction to the killing of dozens of Chinese during the 1925 incidents.

If the casualties were not high, reportedly six Chinese and seven foreigners died while twenty or so individuals were wounded, the terror experienced by Nanking residents was real. Individuals were repeatedly assailed by successive waves of Chinese and each presented the specter of death. Rumor and foreboding contributed to the sense of major tragedy. Whether the Nanking Incident was an isolated episode or the signal for a general drive against foreigners and their property was not immediately clear. According to initial communiques, numerous missionary wives had been raped and hundreds of Chinese shelled and, though neither allegation proved to be true, exaggerated accounts of the losses on both sides continued to circulate.

Nanking missionaries who had experienced the trauma of March 24 issued public statements from their refuge in Shanghai.[50] They rejected both suggestions that northern troops had perpetrated the attacks and explanations that uncontrollable mobs were responsible. Rather, they insisted that soldiers in National Revolutionary Army uniforms had taken the initiative, some asserting that numerous looters spoke with Hunan accents. They were convinced that the assaults were premeditated and, though they acknowledged that the officers had difficulty disciplining the troops, they believed the attackers were acting under orders; some officers, they said, joined in the foray. Chinese proposals for an investigatory commission to establish guilt seemed pointless to them, therefore. Like Chinese after May Thirtieth, they interpreted requests for inquiry as a technique to evade responsibility for injury to unarmed victims.

Nanking missionaries acquired a heightened sense of their own national and racial identity. Pearl Buck articulated the feelings of many: "We had taken sides against our own race again and again for their sakes, sensitive always to injustices which others had committed and were still committing. But nothing mattered today. Neither the kindness nor the cruelty. We were in hiding for our lives because we were white. . . . There was no use quibbling now . . . and I turned toward my own countrymen."[51] Though they voiced gratitude to loyal Chinese friends who had given aid at great personal risk, shock and a sense of betrayal pervaded many of their declarations. They demanded that Chinese Christians choose the side of right and condemn their fellow nationals. Like Chinese Christians after May Thirtieth, they overestimated the influence of Christians on public policy as they expressed their conviction that Chinese who really disapproved of the anti-foreign and anti-Christian agitation could find ways to make their influence and goodwill effective. They were almost unanimous in blaming left-wing radicals for the incident and some even went so far as to single out the political commissar of the Sixth Army, Lin Po-ch'ü (Lin Tsu-han), and his civilian propagandists as the organizers.[52] While some assured fellow Westerners that such actions were not representative of the majority in the Kuomintang, others saw the whole Nationalist movement defamed if its leaders refused to repudiate anti-foreign incidents and punish the guilty.

The vehemence of the reactions was certainly a function of the terror recently experienced. A sense of disillusionment and humiliation, however, added intensity. Many of the Nanking missionaries had on February 1, 1927, waived protection by gunboats and unequal treaties; they had sent a public cablegram to the U.S. government asking renunciation of force and prompt re-negotiation of treaties on the basis of equality, and they had been criticized as idealists by government representatives, businessmen, and sectors of the missionary community. Six weeks later they were saved by a naval barrage and escaped to the Shanghai International Settlement. "We stand discredited before the world," declared the refugees.[53] Compounding the indignity, the *Peking-Tientsin Times* had the day before the Nanking Incident, blamed anti-foreign outbursts on misguided missionary pacifists who had nourished nationalism and radicalism among their students and who had lost all national pride as they talked of learning from the East. The *North China Herald* expressed the hope that "sane" missionaries would speak out on the necessity of protection instead of being intimidated by liberals with their heads in the clouds; its heading for a story that the American Board Mission in Peking had voted in favor of immediate abrogation of the treaties was "And None So Blind as Those. . . ."[54]

An acrimonious controversy erupted between the National Christian Council and missionary critics.[55] The National Christian Council had been pressing for prompt treaty revision and had in October, 1926 issued a series of resolutions calling for negotiation of new treaties on the basis of equality and for an end to all special privileges for the Chinese churches and missions. Some of its leaders were engaged in conversations with the southern government about the registration requirements for private schools. Already, disagreement with the liberal theology and the political activism of National Christian Council leaders had led to condemnations in English-language newspapers and to withdrawal from membership by the conservative China Inland Mission. At one point a group of conservatives labeled the Western members of the council's executive committee "ecclesiastical Bolsheviki" and urged their deportation. An old China hand wrote a letter to the *North China Daily News* in which he dubbed the National Christian Council a pest to be exterminated and accused the Council of readiness to sacrifice the whole mission investment for "some sort of mongrel church". Frank Rawlinson might play his liberal views to the gallery in *The Chinese Recorder,* but he did not represent missionaries as a whole, asserted the writer; in fact, 75% or more of the missionaries would speak out against the abolition of extraterritoriality, if they had not been intimidated by the "riff-raff of China's students".[56]

In April, 1927, some thirty missionaries drew up a formal protest against the actions of the National Christian Council. Accusing the council of causing divisions within the Christian community, the critics condemned the council for engaging in political activity, for inaccurately representing the views of many missionaries, and for exceeding its authority by acting without prior consultation with its constituency. The National Christian Council countered that it had issued official statements only after counselling with cooperating organizations and that its actions had often been misrepresented in the press, the latter treating statements by individual members as official pronouncements. Whatever the merit on either side, the split in the ranks of the Christians had been publicly exposed, with the conservative critics including such prominent missionaries as the presidents of the University of Nanking and St. John's University and the National Christian Council identified with Chinese Christians and a few liberal missionaries.

The stance taken by the Nanking refugees aggrieved

some Christians for other reasons. North China missionaries, who lacked direct experience with the Nanking violence, were more capable of placing the incident within the revolutionary context of China. Wanting to continue to believe in the Kuomintang as the hope of liberal nationalists, they were reluctant to allow the Nanking Incident to tarnish the image of the National Revolutionary Army. They were also troubled lest reports of anti-foreignism and anti-Christianism reduce Western support for China missions. According to Hallett Abend of the Peking *Leader,* he was reprimanded by three missionaries on the paper's board of directors for featuring the story of the Nanking Incident.[57]

The missionaries had cause for concern. Financial contributions by American Protestants were already in decline; the number of students choosing a missionary career in 1926 was less than half that of six years earlier, and such influential magazines as the *Atlantic Monthly, Harper's,* and *Current History* were carrying articles critical of missionaries and questioning the rationale for foreign missions.[58] James A. Walsh, editor of the Maryknoll periodical, *Field Afar* restricted publicity about violence and disorder because, he said, "the whole Chinese situation . . . has had a tendency to make people question the value of spending money for missions in that country."[59] A *New York Times* editorial of December 10, 1926, wondered about the future of China missions in light of the fact that missionaries were wearing out their welcome in China. Articles in *Asia* deplored the loss of life at Nanking, but asked whether California were guilt-free of racism or the U.S. immune to gangster violence. "The presence of Christian missionaries in China during the past century by virtue of reliance upon force has been a shameless denial of the fundamental teachings of Jesus Christ," according to the associate editor.[60] Comparative anthropology had entered upon the scene and convictions of Manifest Destiny were eroding. Even *The Chinese Recorder* had recently published an article by Pearl Buck entitled "Is There a Place in China for the Foreign Missionary?"[61] Though she concluded on a positive note, her enumeration of faults was enough to give pause to any advocate of evangelism: denominationalism, arrogance in the conviction that they possessed a monopoly over truth, lack of effort to understand Chinese culture, demand for gratitude in return for their sacrifices, confounding Western civilization with the simple teachings of Christ, and so forth.

Following the Nanking Incident, missionaries vacated interior China. Only five hundred out of eight thousand Protestant missionaries remained at their posts by July 1927. Catholic priests, lacking family responsibilities, were somewhat more apt to try to weather out the turmoil, but consuls exerted great pressure on Catholic sisters to withdraw. Of the refugees, approximately one third congregated in coastal ports awaiting the opportunity to return while two-thirds quit China. The enrollment in Christian middle schools declined to about half of the total for 1922; church membership had fallen, and church income from Chinese sources was declining.[62] Reassurances about the future of evangelism in China seemed imperative.

Christian spokesmen in North China endeavored to offset the alarming headlines and reduce the damage on the home front. President J. Leighton Stuart, with characteristic optimism, cabled the Yenching Board of Trustees: "Chinese and foreign teachers and students are working together harmoniously, strengthened by the present disturbances. . . . A splendid opportunity presents itself to practice international fellowship and Christian principles."[63] The North China Mission of the American Board at its annual council meeting in April urged missionaries on furlough to establish a bureau to counteract sensational news and entreated the parent body to publicize the essential friendliness of Chinese and encourage as much optimism as possible regarding Chinese nationalism.[64] They reminded their churches that the attacks were perpetrated by an atypical minority. While Nanking missionaries were coming to terms with the conviction that their lives had been saved by gunboats and naval barrages, other missionaries were insisting that their governments refrain from further military intervention and abandon foreign privilege.

Chinese reactions to the Nanking Incident also varied, though in comparison with the Westerners they generally covered a different range of the spectrum. A stance overlapping that of Western liberals outside the battle area was taken by the Chinese Students' Christian Association in the U.S., which issued a formal statement of regret and sympathy to the friends and relatives of Dr. John Williams of the University of Nanking; they labeled his murder the act of a misguided extremist and cautioned against response with force, which would incite mob violence and would undo missionary work; they voiced their belief that the Chinese people were not anti-Christian. A group of east China business associations cabled regret and simultaneously a plea for patience on the part of Americans.[65] Taking a different tack was the North China Council of the Congregational Union.[66] Its letter to the U.S.A. National Council of Congregational Churches deplored the American use of force in response to the actions of a few radicals, who represented neither the Chinese people nor the Kuomintang; such recourse to gunboat policy further undermined confidence in the U.S. While admitting that many missionaries had quit their stations under duress, they reasoned that the transfer to Chinese control had been orderly and was achieving the long desired goal of devolution; matters could only improve.

Non-Christian Chinese also condemned the Western military response, which was initially reported to have caused numerous Chinese casualties. They insisted, furthermore, that an investigation to determine responsibility for the attacks on foreigners would have to be undertaken before apologies or punishments were in order. On March 31, Ch'en Yu-jen, Minister of Foreign Affairs at Wuhan, issued a report stating that preliminary investigations indicated that "reactionary and counter-revolutionary elements" instigated the attacks on foreigners and that the Nationalist forces only entered Nanking at 5:30 p.m. While his government denounced the violence, it protested even more strenuously the bombardment said to have caused the loss of a hundred Chinese lives for every foreign life.

Great Britain, the U.S.A., Japan, France, and Italy presented identical notes to Ch'en and to Chiang Kai-shek; they asked for punishment of both the perpetrators and the responsible commanders, reparations, apology by the Commander-in-Chief and a guarantee against repetition of such outbursts in the future. Ch'en reiterated his expressions of regret and offered compensation but insisted that punishment and apology would be premature. He suggested, in fact, an international investigation of the violence at Shanghai and Shameen in 1925 and at Wanhsien in 1926 as well as that at Nanking and he concluded that the best guarantee against future incidents would be to eliminate the cause, i.e., the unequal treaties.[67] In an article headlined "[Nanking missionaries] Preach 'Other Cheek' But Welcomed Gunboats," the Chinese Student Association in America accused the Nanking missionaries of having lost their heads as well as their religion in trying to coerce Washington into a policy of armed force.[68] The students condemned the hypocrisy of missionaries who asked patriotic Chinese to repudiate the conduct of those responsible for the Nanking Incident but who themselves did not repudiate the conduct of Westerners perpetrating numerous outrages.

Westerner and Chinese appeared to have reversed roles since the May Thirtieth reactions. Missionaries were now insisting that the guilt was clear and that morality required Chinese to speak out on the side of right while Chinese regretted the loss of life but called for an impartial inquest. Nothing in the responses took cognizance of the irony of role reversal nor indicated enhanced understanding and sympathy.

Spokesmen for the Western business community in Shanghai were even more vociferous than the missionaries in their cries of outrage. *The North China Daily News* headlined an article on the Nanking Incident, "'Nationalism' Reveals Itself at Nanking. Foreigners Murdered and Houses Looted by Chiang Kai-shek's Rabble."[69] According to the editor, what was sweeping China was not a true Chinese nationalist movement, but a new form of Boxerism provoked by the Russians, by teachers, students, and discontented laborers, and by riff-raff bought off by the Soviets. In April, 1927, the newspaper published a special supplement entitled "China in Chaos" and designed for circulation in the U.S. and England. Composed primarily of news clippings, its stated purpose was to enlighten the Western public and especially British statesmen, neither of whom allegedly understood the actual situation in China or the character of the Chinese governing class; both should be disabused of the erroneous notion that settlement of China's troubles by negotiation was possible. The conciliatory Hankow agreement of February 19, 1927, it labeled "The Great Betrayal" and it urged, not diplomacy, but military intervention. Contending that most Chinese would actually appreciate an international operation to rescue them from "their frenzied and unscrupulous tyrants, Red agitators, and professional exploiters", the editor expressed the hope that London would avoid further diplomatic mistakes by listening to the opinion of sane and experienced residents in China.[70]

Neither London nor Washington listened, however. Dorothy Borg has argued that, on the contrary, the immediate historical background of the Nanking Incident influenced the U.S. Department of State in deciding against a major increase in troop strength and/or joint intervention; the anti-imperialist agitation following previous incidents, plus Western public debate over treaty revision, encouraged a policy of restraint by the U.S. government.[71] Certainly China had gained the attention of the news media and of Washington officials between 1925 and 1928. The president of the American Federation of Labor had, shortly after May 30th, written to the Department of State saying that American workers favored a policy of dealing with China on the basis of equality.[72] Through the International Workers' Aid Society, such prominent intellectuals as Henri Barbusse, George B. Shaw, Upton Sinclair, and Clara Zetkin, had given both financial and moral support to the May 30th strikers.[73]

The magazine, *Asia*, had presented a variety of arguments against intervention and in favor of renunciation of the unequal treaties. Editor L.D. Froelick quoted with obvious approval a call for U.S. initiative in mediating the May 30th settlement; later he urged America to make a majestic gesture similar to the remission of Boxer Indemnity funds: unilaterally renounce the treaties. He rejected military reprisals after the Nanking Incident because they would only injure American economic interests, would be in defense of an outdated and unequal system, and would undermine the Nationalist movement, which was China's best hope for peace and order. The commentator, Elmer Davis, rejected the argument of

Frank Kellogg, Secretary of State, that treaties approved by the U.S. Senate could not be abrogated by unilateral action. Ample precedent for such abrogation existed, according to Davis, and the sooner the U.S. replaced the unequal treaties with treaties negotiated as equals, the better it would be, "If you are going to judge policy by results rather than intentions, . . . the Russian policy was successful while ours was, and still is, a flop. We still back and fill, falter and hesitate." From Canton in February, 1926, the associate editor of *The Nation* described the economic hardships of Hong Kong after the Shakee tragedy and the anti-British boycott.[75] Far from condemning the revolutionary government, however, the article's theme reflected its title, "Canton--Hope of China". British arrogance and British insistence on special privilege, not Russian influence, had made the strike. Only by renouncing the unequal treaties, as Russia had done, could the West hope to moderate the revolution. *Asia* and *The Nation* represented, of course, the liberal view, but other sectors of the press interpreted the events of 1925-1927 as a great national revolution with which the U.S. should be in sympathy, especially in the light of its revolutionary heritage. May 30th, furthermore, had clarified the high price which defense of the treaties carried.

Though proof of precise influence by the press and public opinion on Congress and on U.S. foreign policy would be difficult to establish, Borg concludes that the cry against intervention could have been heard from varying sources by even the casual reader. In 1927 President Calvin Coolidge reiterated the thesis that China was undergoing a revolution and that in such an environment, the norms for protection of foreigners and their property could not always be achieved or demanded.

A similar evolution of views and a similar divergence between British "old China Hands" and the home front, between English businessmen and missionaries in China seems to have occurred. During the inquiries after May 30th, two missionaries had testified that the circumstances on Nanking Road did not appear to have warranted opening fire on the demonstrators. The reaction of the Shanghai Municipal Council representatives was that the missionaries had a right to their private opinion, but they owed to the Western community the obligation to keep their mouths shut and maintain a solid front.[76] In England, Professor Arnold J. Toynbee noted a rising public interest in China after May 30th.[77] The English, he said, had begun to realize that Great Britain had very significant investments in China and that these were in peril; they could only be saved by getting rid of the unequal treaties altogether. Further, according to Toynbee, China had as much right in the 1920s to demand a change in the system as the British had had a century ago. As early as mid-June, 1925, the head of the China desk of the British Foreign Office, S.P.P. Waterlow, had written: "It is really time we did something to overhaul a system which has not changed since the middle of the 19th century and which involves real Chinese grievances.".[78] He, like Toynbee, acknowledged that the unequal treaties were obsolete. Former Prime Minister Lloyd George stated in 1926: "The Chinese are struggling for the elementary and fundamental rights of every free and self-respecting nation. [The program of the Nationalist government] was not Bolshevik; it was a sound practical program, and to go to war with a man whose policy is of that kind would be an outrage."[79]

Following Chinese take-over of British concessions in Hankow and Kiukiang in early 1927, the British adopted a conciliatory stance. Their proposals for settlement expressed willingness to modify the municipal administrations of British concessions, abandon the mixed court for British plaintiffs, and meet other Chinese demands such as taxation of British residents. The proposals also stated: "His Majesty's government are prepared to accept the principle that British missionaries should no longer claim the right to purchase land in the interior, that Chinese converts should look to the Chinese law and not to the Treaties for protection; and that missionary educational and medical institutions will conform to Chinese laws and regulations applying to similar Chinese institutions."[80] Despite some military build-up in Shanghai and construction of barricades around the International Settlement, conflict between the National Revolutionary Army and foreign troops would be largely avoided when the city came under radical and then KMT control. Protests against the KMT's abrogation of the treaty tariff after its assumption of power were verbal, not martial, and the issue was eventually settled by negotiation.

FACTIONALISM AND RADICALISM

The Nanking Incident further aggravated relations within the Chinese Communist Party-Kuomintang coalition and was a backdrop for Chiang Kai-shek's anti-communist purge in Shanghai in April. Maneuvering for the control of the coalition had been activated by Sun's death in 1925 while Chiang's coup of March 20, 1926, had sharpened the competition; subsequently the National Revolutionary Army's drive for control of the Yangtze Valley intensified the contest during the early months of 1927. As the conquest of territory expanded, as tax resources and administrative responsibilities multiplied, government membership acquired increasing importance. It became imperative to work out the terms of Kuomintang-Chinese Communist Party cooperation in the national government as well as in the party United Front. Ideological, tactical, and personal differences were a source of conflict both within the parties and between the parties.

That much argumentation centered on which faction had remained true to Sun Yat-sen only beclouded the actuality of a basic power struggle. Ch'en Tu-hsiu in March used the pages of *Hsiang-tao* to denounce those Kuomintang members who had abandoned Sun's policies and were now opposing rather than cooperating with the Soviet Union, the Communist Party, and the labor and peasant movements. Chiang accused the communists of undermining the coalition by failing to abide by Sun's conditions for the United Front; friendship with the U.S.S.R. did not mean accepting the dictates of the Comintern, he said; nor did Sun condone class warfare or Kuomintang membership for communists defying party leadership.[81] Chiang talked of impeaching members of the left-wing government in Wuhan on the grounds of disloyalty to *San min chu-i*. Though Sun's mantle was important enough to squabble over, it actually cloaked a struggle for control of the Chinese revolution.

Two fundamental issues were military-party relations and the relative emphasis to be accorded social revolution and national revolution. Translated into tactical terms, the first question generated quarrels over the locale of the capital and the release of funds to the military. The Chinese Communist Party and left-Kuomintang had chosen Wuhan, the locus of their influence, while Chiang had sought to transfer the government and party center to a city he could dominate, initially Nanchang and later Nanking. Perturbed by Chiang's use of the military to enhance his political power, the Wuhan faction demanded subordination of the military to civilian authority.[82] Specifically, the Third Plenum of the Kuomintang Central Executive Committee, held in Wuhan March 10-17, 1927, and boycotted by Chiang partisans, abolished Chiang's position as chair of the Central Executive Committee and established as supreme authority a seven-man Presidium of the Political Council, to which Chiang was not elected. The Central Executive Committee took direct control of military funds and revived the Kuomintang Military Council in an attempt to make the Commander-in-Chief answerable to party leadership. Wuhan was the scene of anti-Chiang rallies. In areas under Chiang's command, Kiukiang and Nanchang for example, he removed Wuhan sympathizers from the municipal councils and dissolved trade union councils; several communist activists were assassinated.

With the contest growing ever more open and brutal, radicals deemed it crucial that Shanghai not become a Chiang stronghold. How to accomplish this presented a quandary, however. Many looked to the power of the masses despite the ideological and tactical problems. Mass organizations might provide an important political base for the left, but catering to the economic aspirations of peasants and proletarians was threatening the United Front. Radical land redistribution policies were not popular with those National Revolutionary Army officers who came from gentry families; idealistic labor demands alienated the business community and disrupted the economy necessary to support the Northern Expedition and southern government. By the spring of 1927 Wuhan was forced to issue unbacked paper money, speeding up an inflationary spiral already in motion.

For Chiang Kai-shek's political ambitions, radical social reform appeared doubly threatening. It could erode the loyalty of the officer corps and stall the northern campaign; in addition, it increased the risk of foreign intervention. As a rule, Kuomintang anti-imperialist policy had tried to diminish the likelihood of an international military expedition by concentrating its attack on a single foreign power at a time, primarily Great Britain, and by minimizing the use of violence against foreign persons and property. Mass demonstrations and workers' strikes, however, could not be so regulated that they always conformed to these guidelines. Anti-imperialist youth had little patience with such niceties, while Marxists were committed to class categories rather than national identities. Especially in the battle for Shanghai did the danger of foreign military action seem threatening. Japan had already indicated that she would oppose with force any take-over of her concessions and the Shanghai Municipal Council had announced that it would take all necessary measures to maintain law and order. Early in the year the foreign powers began to amass troops and gunboats and by mid-March, 1927, some thirty thousand foreign soldiers had assembled in the Shanghai area.

Despite the growing polarization, neither camp within the coalition could boast of concord in policy or personnel; neither appeared a sure winner in a direct confrontation. Chiang, as of March, possessed neither overwhelming troop strength nor undisputed authority among those critical of Wuhan; on the other hand, he did have certain advantages, not the least of which was his single-minded ambition. He derived doctrinal and strategic flexibility from the fact that for him the personal drive for power and the goal of national unification coalesced. The Wuhan fraction included no leader of comparable political astuteness and desire. Wang Ching-wei, though ambitious and influential, had already proved indecisive when challenged; typically, he was at the time in self-imposed exile in Europe and his return on April 1 probably misled the left regarding its strength rather than added to it. Neither Ch'en Tu-hsiu nor Li Ta-chao was at Wuhan headquarters during the Shanghai uprising and both were more able as party builders than as political fighters. Amply endowed with political acumen and ambition, Mao Tse-tung still lacked the requisite prestige and power base.

Though the real political pilot in Wuhan was Borodin,

he worked under a dual disadvantage: (1) he was a foreigner at a juncture when Chinese were becoming ever more sensitive about foreign dictation; documents seized April 6, 1927, in a raid of the Soviet Embassy in Peking fed these fears; (2) he was obliged to implement Comintern instructions and as a consequence, his latitude for adjusting strategy to the Chinese environment was limited. This remained true despite the fact that Moscow made such contradictory demands as maintenance of the United Front while intensifying mass involvement. Of central importance was the Chinese Communist Party's failure to control the gun; a dramatic demonstration of this weakness was Wuhan's attempt to prevent Nanking from coming under Chiang's control by courting General Ch'eng Chien; instead, General Ch'eng obeyed Chiang's evacuation order and Chiang's troops took over. In another instance, Hunan peasants were left without protection after their union had executed the landlord-father of a KMT general.[83] Despite bloody suppression by the general and union pleas to Wuhan for aid, no troops could be sent against the army leaders; too many National Revolutionary Army officers were the sons of gentry. Local landowners retaliated, furthermore, by refusing loans to peasants at spring planting time, while Wuhan was unable to provide government credits.

The March labor uprisings in Shanghai occurred in the midst of this deadly contest and their story has been told numerous times. Perhaps one explanation for the widely variant interpretations is the fact that different revolutionaries had different goals in calling a general strike, seizing police and garrison posts to secure arms for workers, and organizing a municipal council. Some leaders and many laborers undoubtedly believed that they were preparing the way for liberation by the National Revolutionary Army; certain radicals, on the other hand, apparently viewed the establishment of a revolutionary regime as a deterrent to control by Chiang. Though some anticipated that the likelihood of foreign military action could be reduced if prior preparations enabled the National Revolutionary Army to enter peaceably, others may have entertained the idea of provoking foreign intervention in order to force the revolutionaries to close ranks.[84]

An interpretation offering sundry motivations, some of them contradictory, may well be more accurate than attempts to find coherent and unified policies being pursued by either camp. One reason for believing this is the upsurge in student storms and labor activism in the mission institutions during March. The student movement of the spring of 1927 lacked the tragic drama of Shanghai labor and so has drawn limited attention; yet it can aid scholars in unraveling the complex events leading to the dissolution of the United Front.

The majority of the storms occurred during the last week of March, many of them breaking out between March 23 and 25. The wave of strikes was not confined to Shanghai; it hit many of the cities where the contest between Chiang and the left was intensifying. An explanation that emphasizes the initiative of politicized students and workers caught up in an emotionalized anti-imperialism has some merit, for local issues often precipitated the conflicts. With the United Front defining mission school students as allies rather than objects of attack, members from the Christian community became active organizers and participants. The simultaneity of the storms and the similarity of demands and tactics, however, bespeak coordinated guidance as well. For radicals in Canton, Ningpo, Hangchow, Wuhan, Changsha, and Foochow as well as Shanghai, competition with the Chiang faction was crucial, and the anti-imperialist issue became a weapon in the struggle. Revolutionaries associated with the Communist Youth Corps and with propaganda work, in particular, believed that negative reaction to Chinese casualties during the Nanking Incident made an upsurge in the anti-imperialist movement possible. In Canton for example, the unions' militia planned a massive demonstration to protest the killing of "tens of thousands" in the bombardment.[85]

Pointing to a push to the left in the Educational Rights Movement was a March 18 ultimatum by the United Front government demanding that all mission institutions meet its registration requirements by April 1 or close.[86] In addition to the typical regulations concerning religious activities and Chinese control, the ultimatum stated that all students should be required to participate in all patriotic celebrations and meetings convened by the revolutionary party. Public demonstrations to increase the pressure for compliance were organized. Also in March, the Communist Youth Corps received instructions from the Communist Youth International reiterating tactics for incorporating the Christian community into the United Front: individuals from the corps were to befriend members of the institutions, identify activists who might be recruited into the Communist Youth Corps, and assist in organizing left-KMT branches and political study groups.[87] The use of the ultimatum as a tactic, the insistence on the legitimacy of political concerns in academia, and the emphasis on a united front including students, staff, and workers in mission schools--all were to characterize the March outbursts.

Lingnan, Ningpo Methodist College, Fukien Christian University, Hua Chung University, Hangchow (Christian) University, St. John's, Shanghai Baptist College and numerous middle schools experienced attempts by Chinese to take over the institution or to close it down. Political activists prescribed that workers as well as students share in the administration of the school. The institutions, furthermore, should cooperate in the revolutionary struggle; insistence on separation of education and politics was simply a reactionary strategy employed by militarists and imperialists. Many of the ultimatums replicate desiderata set forth by the Shanghai College Student Union: the hiring and firing of faculty members must have the approval of the school's student union; the student union shall have representation on the school's executive council; the budget shall be open for public inspection; no student shall be expelled without the union's sanction.

To insure that the schools serve the revolutionary cause, the protesters frequently stipulated that courses in *San min chu-i* be required and that instructors in these courses be acceptable to the party; instructors declared reactionary, imperialistic, or militaristic by the student union should be prohibited from teaching. Students should have complete freedom to organize, publish, assemble, strike, and engage in political activity and they should not be penalized academically for fulfilling their national responsibilities. Finally, there were two groups of demands expressing the specific interests of students and of youth. One covered improvement of academic and recreational facilities, coeducation throughout the school system, reduction of fees, and grading on the basis of notebooks instead of examinations. The other sought freedom from all institutional regulation of personal life: no inspection of letters, student control of sports, dormitory, and dining facilities, and freedom in selection of spouse.[88]

Such demands went far beyond the registration regulations of even the more radical southern governments and it is doubtful that they had been authorized by responsible officials in Wuhan. Tu Hsiu-ching, a recent recruit to the Chinese Department of Hua Chung University and a member of the Chinese Communist Party Hunan Provincial Committee, helped initiate the attempt to take over the school. When, however, the protesters gave the administration a two-day deadline for meeting their demands, the president informed Foreign Minister Ch'en Yu-jen, whereupon student representatives stated that they had erroneously written two days when they meant two months. When school officials decided to close the school rather than accede, Ch'en urged them to continue operation and offered support in the effort.[89] In mid-March both Ch'en and Borodin granted interviews to missionary educators in which they offered assurances that China had a place for the parochial institutions, though they also insisted on the necessity of participation in the revolutionary movement. Ch'en acknowledged excesses by students and workers but interpreted them as the inevitable accompaniment of revolution and urged that the administrators try to hold things together without closing or deciding to reduce mission education.

Radicals were little inclined to accept compromise positions. Though Ningpo Methodist College had already passed under Chinese governance and had made religious work voluntary, agitators demanded a controlling voice in school administration for party and student union representatives; closure of the school by the Chinese directors precipitated a takeover by radical activists. Chapels in Ningpo were wrecked; Bibles and hymnbooks were destroyed. Kuang Hua students organized a move to occupy St. John's, which had suspended academic work and was serving as a refugee camp for missionaries from the interior; they were deterred by British troops guarding the campus.[90] Extremists in Hangchow and Foochow colleges launched campaigns that closely coincided with the radical outbursts in Nanking and Shanghai, the Foochow storm beginning with a city-wide demonstration on March 24 and the Hangchow one following immediately upon the Nanking Incident.[91] The insurgents were able to take possession of the YMCA headquarters and a Christian hospital though not of the colleges. In hopes of saving a middle school in Shenchow, Hunan, Chinese Christians assumed control and indicated that they would operate without American aid. But, according to one of the teachers, the move had come too late.[92] Hostility had been building for a long time as missionaries ignored requests to share authority with the Chinese faculty and to allow a more equitable relationship. The party ordered the Chinese teachers to close the school; a few days later, fire partially destroyed the school building.

A distinctive feature of many of the spring storms was the activism of the clerks and laborers hired both by the foreigners on a private basis and by the schools. Union organization of non-academic personnel had been especially vigorous during the early spring and as the mass societies expanded, the line between the general anti-imperialist, anti-militaristic movement and the Educational Rights Movement faded. On March 30 students helped organize and lead a massive demonstration in Shanghai for retrocession of the foreign concessions. Concurrently, the recently unionized laborers at Shanghai Baptist College presented an ultimatum that led to the strike on April 1; armed workers briefly closed the gates of the compound and took control of the campus; they locked the power house and classrooms and cut off supplies to faculty and students.[93] In Changsha a meeting of union representatives voted to occupy the YMCA and YWCA property and after insisting on immediate government and party approval, proceeded to do so.[94] The YMCA building was turned into a "People's Club House" under radical auspices. At Lingnan, the non-teaching staff formed a union and on March 15 asked immediate implementation of a long list of demands; failing to secure agreement, they struck on March 25 and shut down the library and many offices. The older Workman's

Union called a slowdown a few days later and then a minor fracas involving an ex-student acting as union adviser precipitated a walk out by all the workers. The school closed down, upon which many Chinese and Western faculty members left campus in anticipation of further trouble. When pickets and strikers pummeled some of those exiting the campus, the Department of Public Safety provided an armed escort. The workers, on the other hand, were said to have been able to continue the strike because of funds provided by the Canton General Labor Union.[95]

Since the workers and clerks were primarily concerned with improving their economic status, recruiters initially emphasized wages and working conditions. According to a later party criticism, however, the directing party members of many unions were not workers, but students and intellectuals.[96] The goals of the latter were political as well as economic, for they were trying to build revolutionary outposts for the party. The nature of the union demands would seem to confirm subsequent party critiques. Though the economic packages requested were so expensive and so far above the norm that no institution could have been expected to acquiesce, they were generally presented in the form of an ultimatum. In addition to salary increases, the Staff Union of Lingnan asked for such benefits as: a closed shop with union control over hiring and dismissal plus a minimum of one year's salary for individuals terminated with union approval; a $7\frac{1}{2}$ hour day, a year's furlough with salary after five years' service, free medical care, housing, furniture, and water, continuation of salary for one month if an individual absented himself for special reasons, observance of all holidays declared by the government, special union quarters with a kitchen and a cook, and so forth.[97]

The workers and clerks seem, in some instances, to have been genuinely surprised and dismayed when the administration decided to close the institution rather than meet the demands. Whether the students, alumni, and teachers who acted as initiators and organizers were so naive would be hard to say. Certainly, the storms had little relation to the immediate goals of the Educational Rights Movement. Lingnan had, in January, 1927, concluded a reorganization agreement providing for control by a Board of Directors based in China and including a Chinese majority; alumni prominent in the Student Union and members of the nationalist movement participated in the reorganization negotiations and were elected to board membership.[98] Shanghai Baptist College had made religious activities voluntary and was in the process of restructuring its administration when the storms broke. Admittedly the actions were belated and were introduced under duress so that even Chinese Christians resented the manner in which the institutions moved toward Sinification. The purpose of the union strikes, however, was not to restrict foreign and Christian dominance in education so much as to enable a small faction within the institution to mobilize labor while taking control.

Dissension within the United Front over the radicalism of the student movement paralleled controversies over radicalism in peasant and proletarian policies. Just as certain individuals took exception to Wuhan's policy of restricting the social revolution in order to maintain the United Front, so certain individuals closely associated with propaganda and youth organizations repudiated attempts to restrain their activities. Among these were P'eng Shu-chih, Ts'ai Ho-sen, Jen Pi-shih, and probably Yun Tai-ying.[99] They put great store in the organization and politicization of students and the urban masses because they believed the strategy would serve the anti-imperialist, anti-militarist campaign in multiple ways. The demoralization of northern soldiers and their defection was perhaps the most obvious goal, but the cultural and economic agents of capitalism could also be demoralized and defeated. Witness British acquiescence in the occupation of their concession in Hankow. The autonomy and authority of military leaders within the Kuomintang camp might be curbed as revolutionary bases acquired political legitimacy. But Communist Party officials accused the Communist Youth Corps under Jen's leadership of considering itself more progressive than the party and of being overly concerned with the educational and cultural sectors. Several cadres in propaganda and youth work came under party criticism for their radicalism and in some instances were labeled Trotskyists. Such uncertainty and divisions over policy allowed room for radical uprisings but doubtless also contributed to the rapid demise of the Educational Rights Movement.

The polarization of the United Front into two mutually hostile groups was still incomplete in the spring of 1927 and both the Wuhan and the Nanking regimes remained troubled by internal frictions. Chiang Kai-shek's Shanghai coup of April 12, 1927, nevertheless, laid bare the priorities of the two camps. By this point in the Northern Expedition it becomes possible to apply the terms "right" and "left" with some accuracy. Each faction had made use of anti-imperialist nationalism and of mass organizations, but for Chiang the overriding aim was national unity under KMT leadership. The military was his political power base as well as the means to achieve his national goals. While soliciting support from numerous quarters, he tailored his tactics to maximize the influence of the military. The goal for the CCP was also political power but the means was social revolution. Despite influence in the National Revolutionary Army through political commissars, the left was unable to rely on the army as its instrument. Attempts to gain the loyalty of military commanders were often undercut by its social policies and class ideology.

For the historian, the Nanking Incident, the storms in the mission schools of Kwangtung, Hunan, and Hupei, and the anti-Christian outburst in Fukien illustrate the differing approaches of the factions. For the actors in 1926-1927, the episodes brought home the consequences of their tactics and also influenced their choices. The foreign powers had responded to the Nanking Incident by reinforcing their troops and their naval strength in the Shanghai region, while world-wide publicity threatened to blemish the National Revolutionary Army's reputation. Though diplomatic negotiation had followed the seizure of the British concession in Hankow, United Front leaders could not predict foreign reaction if their much larger investments in Shanghai were endangered. The actions of popular organizations in the Changsha and Wuhan areas had reduced the role of foreigners in schools, churches, and commercial establishments, had brought power to labor unions, and had enabled peasants to make demands on landlords. But the immediate results in many cases had been disruption of education, reductions in the flow of food to the cities, and political confusion.

Chiang Kai-shek's response was growing disenchantment with the utility of mass movements that incurred risk of foreign intervention and disrupted the economy and the social structure; increasingly, he opted for compromise with warlord leaders willing to acknowledge the Nanking government. In the Wuhan regime indecision and dissension prevailed as the CCP seemed unable to resolve the contradictions of its policies. Social revolution through popular uprisings by students, workers, and peasants was not leading to political control and stability. The most effective force for mobilizing the articulate urban populace was nationalism, still closely identified with the KMT. Not only was the CCP burdened by its association with a foreign power but it had helped link the KMT and nationalism by emphasizing *San min chu-i* in its propaganda and by employing the KMT label in many of its activities. Without a primary identification with Chinese nationalism and without an effective military apparatus, the CCP needed the left KMT. The breakup of the United Front, even in its reduced form at Wuhan, could only result in a loss for the CCP. Both Chiang and the CCP leadership would pay court to the left KMT, the CCP by moderating the social revolutionary strategy, Chiang by accentuating national unity and sovereignty based on military success. The radicals' bid for control in the Shanghai Uprising of late March and the launching of the "party purification" drive by Chiang in mid-April left little doubt that the battle lines had been drawn.

Chapter VIII

Demise

SHANGHAI COUP AND THE DEMISE OF THE
1920s STUDENT MOVEMENT

For student activism as well as for the United Front, Chiang Kai-shek's Shanghai coup of April, 1927, marked a turning point. Except for isolated storms, the student movement, including anti-Christian campaigns and educational rights activities, declined precipitately with the inauguration of the "party purification" drive on April 12, 1927.

Before striking out at the left, Chiang had solicited moral and financial backing from a broad range of groups: Shanghai merchants, members of the Kuomintang center and the Western Hills faction, National Revolutionary Army commanders, leaders from the underworld labor organization known as the Green Gang and from the recently founded Kuomintang labor union, Ch'üan-kuo kung-hui lien-ho-hui (National Labor Federation), and finally certain prominent intellectuals. In rapid order, he suppressed the Shanghai provisional government and closed the headquarters of political associations, unions, and student organizations; he disarmed picketing workers and authorized a raid on the political department of the Shanghai KMT branch, headed by Kuo Mo-jo, an avowed Marxist who joined the CCP shortly thereafter. Arrests and executions of leftist leaders, including party and union cadres, students and young intellectuals soon followed. Even the Shanghai General Chamber of Commerce was transformed as local businessmen who had shown political independence were displaced by a party-appointed committee. The establishment of a Kuomintang government at Nanking on April 18 and orders for the ousting of communists and "reactionaries" from all military and civilian units formalized the drive.

Members of the Nanking regime publicly accused the communists of sabotaging the Northern Expedition and using gullible workers and students for their own political purposes. Sounding the theme of unity against imperialists and militarists, they urged all patriots to join in following the true principles and policies of Sun. Specifically on education, Chiang accused the left of deliberately lodging soldiers and political workers in schools so as to disrupt teaching; all troops were ordered to evacuate schools by June 6. If the imperialists had no right to teach their doctrines in schools, neither did the communists, said Chiang; he believed in party education, but only the governing party of China was entitled to control education and instill its tenets.[1] The Nanking Minister of Foreign Affairs and the Central Educational Council offered assurances of religious freedom and protection of foreign property and lives; anti-imperialist and anti-religious activities should not infringe on religious freedom. China had need of private schools so long as they complied with the regulations and ideology of the party government.[2]

Chiang admonished students to return to their studies and stop wasting time demonstrating in the streets and trying to play the role of counsellor to the government; teachers should resume the direction of education. At radical centers, school administrators were displaced by officials with instructions to clear out communist and "reactionary" students and teachers. The military commander of Hunan and Hupei ordered middle and higher schools closed for a term while reorganization was undertaken. A loyalty oath was sometimes a prerequisite for admission and "putting the school environment back in order" became the operative slogan.[3]

In Szechwan on March 31, 1927, the military governor Liu Hsiang turned on the left just as he had lashed out against the Kuomintang four months earlier.[4] At what had been billed a giant anti-imperialist rally in Chungking, thousands had gathered to denounce militarism, imperialism, and Chiang Kai-shek; suddenly, Liu Hsiang's agents opened fire on the speaker's platform. They killed the chairperson and several other communist leaders and in the melee that followed, more than two hundred were shot or trampled to death. Ruthless repression brought quiet submission of the students. The Chinese Communist Party in Szechwan became almost defunct and attempts to rebuild the provincial Kuomintang could be conducted only under the aegis of local militarists. West China Union University, which had been functioning at a reduced level under Chinese leadership, soon benefited from the altered political environment. Students began to return to campus and at University Day on April 19, 1927, several government speakers expressed appreciation of the school's work and disputed the charges of the Anti-Christian Movement.[5]

Among students, confusion, fear, and suspicion reigned. The leadership ranks had been thinned as executions silenced several top leaders of the National Student Union, including the chairperson who was a Chinese Communist Party member; other activists were in detention awaiting an uncertain fate. Communist Youth Corps members, who had been in the forefront during the Shanghai uprisings, were hard hit by the purges. Since leftists had acquired dominance in many student associations, the effect was devastating for the student movement. Political radicalism in areas under Nanking's tutelage henceforth carried great personal risk with Wuhan offering scant protection. The left lacked the means to shield its comrades in many cities, but, in addition, Wuhan was desperately striving to keep the United Front alive. Rent by factionalism and almost paralyzed by the contradictory requisites of social revolution and of cooperation with the left Kuomintang, the Chinese Communist Party provided little guidance. Revolutionaries surely were dismayed as Ch'en Yu-jen of Wuhan called on them to distinguish between anti-imperialism and anti-foreignism; after the Nanking Incident, furthermore, Ch'en ordered protection of Christians and warned students and workers against attacks on Christian churches and other foreign property.

Among the older generation outside the United Front, Young China Party members had been especially adamant about terminating all education under foreign influence though they preferred legal sanctions to confiscation. They, like the leftists, considered government registration and supervision insufficient to end cultural aggression.[6] But they too lost political influence after the Shanghai coup and could offer little assistance to the student movement. They too were condemned by Kuomintang leaders for having led students astray. Several of their leaders, furthermore, suffered political eclipse during the Northern Expedition. Some were in trouble for supporting the warlord, Wu P'ei-fu, while others had been publicly critical of Chiang; on several occasions, *Hsing-shih* had censured the KMT for advocating "partyized" education.[7] Thus, in 1927 Tseng Ch'i was arrested by the Kuomintang in Shanghai and subsequently fled to Japan. Li Huang, after offending Chiang, took refuge in the French concession and Yü Chia-chü turned to editing an encyclopedia of education. *Hsing-shih* ceased publication after 1927. Students might occasionally gain support from local leaders of any of the three parties and a storm might arise, but those demanding more than the registration requirements no longer had the benefit of a national carrier movement.

Factionalism, combined with the atmosphere of suspicion, brought about a break-down of discipline within the Student Union. Since even allegations of communism or reactionism could bring arrest, certain individuals began to use the tactic for personal or political purposes. At Hua Chung, for example, middle school pupils denounced as anti-revolutionary a college student who had protested against their demonstration and they had him arrested; retaliating, the college students labeled anti-revolutionary a pupil who criticized Wuhan's foreign policy and had him arrested. Even the acting president of Hua Chung, Wei Cho-ming (Francis Wei) was seized as a communist by Chinese authorities upon his arrival in Shanghai and secured release on bail only after intervention by colleagues.[8]

At a Christian hospital in Taiku, Shansi, a clerk belonging to the Kuomintang unknowingly registered a patient later accused of communism; fearing that he would be arrested for harboring a communist, he left his position and fled for home. The hospital cashier was imprisoned for eighteen days during investigations.[9] In the name of four outstanding students, the student party branch at Hangchow (Christian) University issued a letter attacking ten other students as communists. When the letter proved to be a forgery, four students were arrested and almost a third of the student body was expelled because of involvement.[10] Tung Lin (William L. Tung) at

Fu-tan University attributed an accusation that he was a communist to the jealousy of a rival Kuomintang member; students were sadly bewildered by the rapid turn of events, according to Tung.[11] With political activism of any kind entailing such danger, many youths sought the anonymity of studies.

Even before the purge, evidence of student disillusionment and fatigue had begun to accumulate. This depression, along with the chaos and intimidation caused by "party purification", is significant in explaining the swift decline of student activism. Students had been dismayed by the divisiveness within the revolutionary camp. They saw their puristic hopes for a new China belied by the troubles of the Wuhan government, the indiscipline of army units and mass organizations, and the feuding of Chiang, Wang Ching-wei, Ch'ü Ch'iu-pai, Ch'en Tu-hsiu, and other leaders. Some had reached the saturation point and had lost their taste for endless parades, demonstrations, and patriotic meetings. Exhibiting the characteristic weakness of student movements, they began to retreat into the quietude and security of studenthood.

Many examples of student ambivalence and naivete concerning their role as political activists might be cited. As mentioned above, ultimatums condemning institutions in the harshest terms and demanding drastic restructuring were frequently followed by requests to the government that the school be forbidden to close or forced to reopen. At St. John's and other colleges, students and faculty cooperated in organizing tutorial institutes and correspondence courses during strikes and official closure. Lingnan students, dismayed by the closing of their school, initiated the organization of classes for middle school pupils in a Canton church and the renting of a floor in a new hotel, where preparatory and college students could reside, study, and attend lectures.[12] Faculty members mimeographed semester assignments and mailed them to students, who took their final examinations at various locales in Hong Kong, Amoy, Swatow, and Canton. Despite the sharp confrontation between the labor union and the administration at Shanghai Baptist College, the school soon reopened with the foreign faculty commuting from the International

Settlement. Others held special summer schools to enable pupils to make up credits lost because of strikes and many students gratefully took advantage of these opportunities.

In their writings, John Israel and Chang Kuo-t'ao cite examples of idealistic youth left rudderless.[13] Chiang Hsien-yun, an honor student in Whampoa's first class and a Chinese Communist Party member, desperately believed in the United Front as essential to the revolution and he had shuttled back and forth between Nanchang and Wuhan attempting to clear up misunderstandings. Plunged into depression by his failure, he requested active service and was killed on the firing line. Hu Ch'iu-yuan, a teenage prodigy at Wuhan University, joined the Communist Youth Corps and rose to prominence as youth leader and publicist, even consorting with celebrities at central party headquarters. To his dismay, he discovered that the revolutionaries were human, subject to petty jealousies and personal ambition; Wuhan rule seemed to be bringing economic hardship and administrative chaos instead of peace and prosperity. Hu and his colleagues quit the Communist Youth Corps and returned to their studies. "The silent withdrawal of students like Hu was a step toward the downfall of the Wuhan government," says Israel. And also the ebbing of political activism by students, it might be added.

Wang Fan-hsi, a provincial cadre from Peking, expressed his disillusionment over the indulgences of CCP officials in Canton and the continuous conflicts he observed in Wuhan. Even more frustrating for him was the fact that by mid-summer, 1927, the CCP leadership was in such disarray that it neither consulted with nor provided a role for party workers. "We were like abandoned concubines . . .," he wrote.[14] Though he remained a party stalwart, he seized the opportunity to study in Moscow with palpable relief. Joining him in the decampment were some seven or eight hundred cadres, the majority being either students or intellectuals. Such retreats into martyrdom by Chiang, into academics by Hu and colleagues, or into external refuges by Wang and comrades expedited the decline of the student movement.

The issues of the Educational Rights Movement,

furthermore, no longer appeared so clear cut as formerly. Though the radicals had not attained their goals, many changes desired by the moderates were in progress. Fleeing interior China after the Nanking Incident, missionary educators had hastily turned over executive positions to Chinese Christians. By mid-1927, therefore, Chinese were serving as principals, acting presidents, and heads of administrative committees in many mission institutions. Numerous schools had a Chinese majority on the board of managers; some had voted for voluntary religious activities, and a few were in the process of seeking government registration. Even within the China Christian Educational Association the tide was swinging in favor of registration. The non-denominational Church of Christ in China convened its first general assembly in October, 1927, and voted acceptance of a minimal constitution deemphasizing Western tradition and sectarian theology.[15] School registration and voluntary religious worship were endorsed by the largely Chinese membership. Amid much publicity, Pope Pius XI had, on October 28, 1926, consecrated six Chinese bishops, the first Chinese priests to be raised to the episcopate since the seventeenth century. A Maryknoll Father who requested his superior to seek compensation for a looted mission through the U.S. State Department was informed that Vatican policy now discouraged such diplomatic intervention.[16]

Sinification was actually to take longer and to be less complete than indicated in 1927 but for the moment the missionaries, who had been labeled instruments of cultural aggression, were absent from most campuses and churches. Chinese Christians, many of whom shared the goals of the moderates, would bear the brunt of any continued campaigning. If occasional outbursts over special issues were still possible, radicals would find it difficult to inspire more than short-term involvement by the majority.

Further obscuring the scene was the support accorded Nanking by several intellectuals esteemed by youth. Ts'ai Yuan-p'ei, Li Shih-tseng, and Wu Chih-hui initially joined Chiang's coalition, Li arguing that Sun's teachings were more suitable for China than those of Marx or Proudhon, Ts'ai instructing youth that they could best demonstrate their patriotism by studying, not by incessant strikes and demonstrations.[17] Both parties had resorted to violence on occasion, so that, despite dismay over the "white terror" in Shanghai, many were as yet unsure whether Nanking was abandoning revolutionism. The decision by Wang Ching-wei and other KMT members of the Wuhan government to break with the CCP in July, 1927, meant the end of the United Front. Since a major issue was Moscow's use of the CCP to carry out the U.S.S.R.'s revolutionary and national designs, the KMT consolidated its position as champion of Chinese national sovereignty. Wang Ching-wei's turn toward Nanking both intensified rivalry for leadership of the KMT and encouraged social reformers to keep alive their faith in the KMT. In the highly complex struggle, the battle lines were unclear. Even Chiang Kai-shek had not yet entirely escaped from his image as the "red general".

The rapid decline of the Educational Rights Movement, therefore, reflected the synchronous erosion of support at the base and shifts in party policy. The hand of the Kuomintang can be discerned in the simultaneous demands for expulsion of communists from youth organizations by Shanghai students from numerous schools; on the May Fourth anniversary thousands supported resolutions censuring the Wuhan regime. The Shanghai Educational Association condemned those who had misconstrued Sun's policies in order to arrogate power to themselves; patriots, they said, should side with Chiang Kai-shek and the revolution and against those who had seduced youth and misled honest nationalists. A new Shang-hai hsueh-sheng ko-ming t'ung-chih hui (Shanghai Society of Revolutionary Student Comrades) published an open letter summarizing the glorious history of the student movement which had created a new Chinese civilization; if the gains made by the southerners were not to be lost, however, students must insist on purification of the movement and must oust the bandits who were trying to destroy education and to take political control.[18] Even Shanghai's primary school students issued a manifesto incorporating a fascinating potpourri of requests; they wanted school uniforms modeled on Sun's dress, a visit by Chiang so that they could do him homage, textbooks written by competent scholars and bearing the white-starred red and blue flag of the Kuomintang Republic on the cover, improved recreational facilities and more field trips, better pay for teachers, and greater social freedom; they concluded with assurances that they were pure of all communist contagion and faithful to *San min chu-i*.[19]

At Lingnan, where striking workers had remained on campus despite official closure, government troops invaded the compound and arrested three student leaders on communist charges. The Canton city government ordered the labor bureau, the police, and the education department to help the college effect a settlement.[20] With conservatives gaining control of the Nanking Student Union and other branches, the National Student Union Executive Committee, still dominated by the left, decided to transfer headquarters from Shanghai to the more congenial environment of Wuhan. Educators remarked on the apathy of youth. A Kuomintang leader admitted, on the other hand, that the radicals were so powerful in certain schools that the students were unwilling or unable to carry out the purge.[21]

Though the student movement had gone dormant, occasional brief campaigns occurred between 1927 and 1931. Neither the KMT nor the CCP was entirely consistent in its policies toward student activism and mission institutions; furthermore, party factions might foster student storms in defiance of the center. Even in Nanking the reimposition of discipline was complicated by the student movement tradition with its readiness to dispute authority and to allot priority to patriotic activities; furthermore, municipal party headquarters sometimes overrode attempts by the Educational Council to restrict student agitation.[22]

The Central Committee of the CCP censured intellectuals for opportunism in August, 1927, but during the Canton Commune, December 11-13, 1927, radical youth leaders again came to the forefront; anti-Christian propaganda was revived as part of their anti-imperialist drive.[23] Party and military cadres requisitioned missionary residences, hospitals, and schools for their own use and advised all missionaries to leave as a safety measure. A decree by the Canton soviet government berated all missionaries as imperialists, who initiated foreign penetration of China, as capitalists, who deprived the populace of money and land, as charlatans, who misled the people with false doctrines; the schools and all their works were simply devices for the implantation of a foreign civilization. Even during the brief days of the Canton Commune, however, contradictions surfaced. American instructors at Lingnan could satisfy their curiosity by roaming the streets of Canton without harm; when the Canton Soviet fell, the Chinese secretary of the local YMCA helped the Russian consul and his family escape.[24] After the communist's debacle, the party again rebuked the students, who were said to have dominated the Canton regime. Arguing that the petty bourgeois intellectuals had demonstrated their lack of loyalty and dependability, the party decided to recruit peasants and workers into the Communist Youth Corps at the expense of students. In Hunan, where the fortunes of the Chinese Communist Party fluctuated widely during 1927, anti-imperialist activity ebbed and flowed. Coordination of student protests was poor while the Educational Rights Movement lacked internal momentum. Pressures on Yali and other Christian institutions seemed more a function of party needs at the moment than of a drive for educational and national autonomy.

Though Kuomintang opinion regarding student political action was divided and was subject to change upon external threat, Nanking officially insisted on an end to student activism. The educational council, replying to the Shanghai Student Union in July, 1927, informed the students in no uncertain terms that they should return to their studies and let the teachers run the schools and the party look after politics.[25] Educational policy, decisions on tuition fees, the selection of teachers and dismissal of students, all were the province of the faculty and administration, according to the commission; if students wished to express opinions on these matters, they should do so in written statements signed by responsible persons. Students were free to engage in extracurricular activities only if they did not interfere with the educational process, did not contravene Kuomintang and government policies, and did not constitute arbitrary and domineering actions against any student. As for the Student Union's demand for the restoration of educational rights and abolition of religious education, the educational commission claimed that it had already issued regulations requiring the registration of private schools and the separation of religion and education; these would be enforced, so the matter was not difficult of solution. The formal answer of the educational commission to the Shanghai students acquired wider legitimacy as it was distributed to provincial educational bureaus.

One of the most prominent opponents of student activism was the former head of Peita, Ts'ai Yuan-pei. As a leading member of the Central Educational Council and then as chancellor of *Ta-hsueh yuan* (University Council, which replaced the Central Educational Council), Ts'ai was Nanking's de facto minister of education from May, 1927, until August, 1928. Consistent with his 1922 essay advocating independence of education, Ts'ai wanted a school system controlled by educators and free of both political and religious influence. An educational conference called by Ts'ai in May, 1928, rejected "partyized" *(tang hua)* education in favor of education infused with the spirit of *San min chu-i*. Students should limit their concerns to educational matters; the party should stay out of educational administration and the students should stay out of party affairs. Accepting the cultivation of national citizens as a primary goal, the educators recommended reducing both the use of English language texts and the number of hours devoted to English language study. [26]

Educational authorities such as Ts'ai, nevertheless, assured the China Christian Educational Association that the Chinese government had no desire to confiscate school property and that they would not support campaigns that tried to destroy private institutions under the slogan, "Restore Educational Rights". Mission schools would be subject to the same regulations as all other private schools and so long as they registered they were free to continue operation.[27] The registration requirements promulgated by the national educational conference in May, 1928, were more detailed than previous ones.[28] Information on budget, curriculum, equipment, library holdings, and faculty had to be presented, but the purpose of these was to set minimum academic standards rather than to impose any particular hardship on private institutions. Permission from the government was required for the founding, discontinuance, or alteration of a private school. In April, 1928, Ts'ai met with Christian educators and helped reach agreement on a statement of educational mission which omitted the word Christian but was acceptable to the educators: "education in a spirit of love, service, and sacrifice".[29] Colleges could offer academic courses on religion as electives within the philosophy department. Since the provincial governments were responsible for regulating middle schools, the registration requirements for them varied considerably; in many cases, the provincial authorities ruled that parochial middle schools could not offer religious education during regular class hours.

Even these regulations were not strictly and immediately enforced. When St. John's, which had decided against registration, proposed to reopen in September, 1928, the National Student Union and the Shanghai Student Union protested vigorously and requested preventative action by the government. The government, however, chose to avoid direct confrontation and St. John's opened without incident to a small and carefully screened student body.[30] Other institutions were able to obtain extensions of the deadline for registration while continuing operation.

Ts'ai's policies on education and student movements brought him strange bedfellows. Out of fear that immature youth would be seduced by the communists, Hu Han-min and Tai Chi-t'ao favored restrictions on student political activism; the communists were accused of offering such snares as money, women, entertainment, and absurd promises of student control in order to create their own instruments of destruction. According to Tai, many of the storms glorified as youth movements had really been used only to further personal interests.[31] Yeh Ch'u-ts'ang, who as a member of the youth and propaganda departments had once encouraged students to give eight hours a day to political work, declared political activism incompatible with social order and national reconstruction; youth should concentrate on preparing for future service to the state. In Chiang's messages to students, the words: discipline, obedience, unity, and morality appeared with increasing frequency. Such a disparate group persuaded the Kuomintang Central Executive Committee to abolish the party youth bureau in

February, 1928, to bar primary and secondary pupils from politics, and to rule that college students might join parties and student movements only as individuals, not as branch units.³²

Not all Kuomintang leaders subscribed to such a restrictive policy, however, and an equally disparate group recommended continuation of the youth movement.³³ Wang Ching-wei and the "Reorganization" *(Kai-tsu p'ai)* faction argued that the social revolution remained unfinished and required mass involvement; youth were essential as propagandists and organizers. While agreeing that student participation was needed for completion of the Northern Expedition's drive against imperialism and militarism, Ch'en Kuo-fu urged tight party control. The party should not default to the communists in the leadership of the youth movement and simultaneously it should call a halt to excesses. Employing this argument, Ch'en persuaded the same executive committee that had abolished the youth bureau to establish a Committee for Training the Masses under his direction. He began to draw up elaborate plans for a national youth association and for student-led mass organizations, all regimented by the party and indoctrinated in *San min chu-i*. Faced with contradictory proposals from Ts'ai and Ch'en, the Central Executive Committee effectively tabled the issue of student political activity by recommending further study.

Kuomintang ambivalence, Nanking's tenuous hold outside the Yangtze Valley, plus the party's willingness to use popular protests in case of threat to national security - all contributed to erratic outbursts of the Educational Rights Campaign during 1928 and 1929. Procrastination by mission societies and school boards on the question of registration also helped generate storms. The Tsinan Incident, as John Israel has pointed out, illustrates the Kuomintang's attempt to benefit from a revival of the student activism so recently damped down.³⁴ It also offered parochial schools an opportunity to seek a new role in the national movement. Even so, KMT reaction to protests against Japanese military maneuvers in Tsinan illustrates the change in KMT policy toward the student movement. When denunciations of and demonstrations against foreign aggression enhanced the KMT nationalist image, the party leaders sanctioned student activism, though they tried to keep the reins tight. Once the National Revolutionary Army moved north of the Yangtze, however, the student movement had largely ceased to have the role of incorporating the populace into the Northern Expedition. One reason was that the organization of students, workers, and peasants was underdeveloped in these northern warlord regions. Another was party policy. Tai Chi-t'ao, the head of the new Political Training Department of the National Revolutionary Army, defined the function of the political commissars as keeping the National Revolutionary Army soldiers properly motivated and indoctrinated, not as arousing the masses.

On April 7, 1928, Chiang announced renewal of the Northern Expedition and his troops headed for Tsinan, capital of Shantung and railway terminus. Although the Japanese had already reinforced their guard along the rail route from Tsinan to the port of Tsingtao, they poured four thousand additional soldiers in to protect the alleged two thousand Japanese civilians in Tsinan. Newspapers and party periodicals protested vehemently against Japanese imperialism and student associations quickly followed suit. By May 3 when clashes between Chinese and Japanese soldiers occurred, students were geared for action.[35] Shanghai students announced a three-day strike while they organized a boycott of Japanese goods and the National Student Union began preparations for a nation-wide boycott. Schools in numerous cities called protest meetings.

But the signals sent by the Kuomintang were contradictory; on the one hand, party speakers kindled indignation and informed the Japanese that they could not ban lawful protests; on the other, they restricted commemoration of May's revolutionary holidays and arrested youths for inciting disorder. They seemed on constant alert lest radical elements capture the campaign. Chiang, for his part, had already chosen to avoid contest with the Japanese and had rushed his troops through Tsinan without occupying it. Even though the Japanese general imported additional men "to chastise the lawless Chinese soldiers" and to maintain Japan's prestige, even though he bombarded sectors of the city to rout out remaining National

Revolutionary Army troops, Nanking looked to a diplomatic settlement. The Kuomintang turned critic of the boycott it had helped instigate.

Outside Shanghai, students were generally restricted to campus protest meetings and violently worded manifestoes.[36] Street parades and the organizing of workers for mass demonstrations were forbidden. The teachers and students of the Central Party Affairs School in Nanking, for example, petitioned the government to oppose the Japanese, lift the ban on mass movements, and send students north to do battle; in a manifesto "to the Peoples, Press, and Parliaments of All Friendly Nations", they denounced the May Third Action as "the unprecedented and most tragic incident . . . in the history of mankind"; they asked that world opinion condemn "this international outrage and inhuman conduct" and demand the immediate withdrawal of all Japanese troops.[37] But despite these rumblings, Nanking students launched no coordinated mass movement.

With Chang Tso-lin dominating eastern Chihli (Hopei after 1928), public protest placed careers in jeopardy. The province lacked a functioning provincial student union; the Peking Student Union had been outlawed, and students were required to sign a pledge to abstain from political activities. Peking students staged a 24-hour walkout that led to early closure of many schools for summer vacation, but the proud Peita could not assume leadership as on May 4, 1919. Yenching, on the contrary, took advantage of its semi-extraterritorial status to act as a focus for protests by private schools. Anticipating their role in the anti-Japanese demonstration of December 9, 1935, Yenching students organized a rally of parochial and private school students and they led in conspicuous observance of National Humiliation Day on May 9.[38] They were offering evidence of incorporation into the national and intellectual community. With Japan as the enemy, they had the blessing of university administrators for their attempts to disprove charges of denationalization.

In Tsinan and Amoy also, parochial students were politically active.[39] Cheeloo University students had cheered the arriving National Revolutionary Army and had declared May 4 a holiday to celebrate liberation. Talmage College students joined in the protests of the Amoy Student Union. But in both cities the movement quickly dissipated under Japanese terrorist tactics. Bypassing Amoy officials, the Japanese themselves arrested and detained four Koreans for making public speeches. Alleging anti-Japanese activity, Japanese soldiers invaded and searched Cheeloo University buildings, frisked students, and even used the campus for gun emplacements. Kuomintang support was not forthcoming and as a matter of fact, Amoy authorities posted orders from Nanking forbidding strikes, parades, and street propaganda. Amoy students had to confine their activity to the campus. Many Tsinan residents quit the city temporarily and Cheeloo eventually decided to suspend work for all but the senior class and the hospital staff.

Many Christian institutions, of course, did not participate in the anti-Japanese protests. A few were still so insulated from Chinese politics and student life that their pupils were willing to give priority to studies. Regionalism came into play with the result that the troubles of North China appeared secondary to more immediate concerns. The Tsinan Incident revealed a Christian educational community in transition toward Sinification, a transition occurring at a different rate in various institutions.

Also in transition were relations between the Kuomintang and New Youth. Protests against the Peking warlord cabinets under the banner of anti-imperialism and antimilitarism had been persuasive and had carried conviction for many. After 1928, however, nationalist protests against the Kuomintang divided loyalties, for the Kuomintang seemed, at least until 1935, the best hope and the necessary instrument for opposition to Japanese imperialism. The Tsinan Incident had probably eased the National Revolutionary Army drive toward Peking, as once again Chinese nationalists had identified with the KMT, defender of China against foreign aggression.[40] In June, 1928, Peking acknowledged KMT rule and in December, 1928, Chang Hsueh-liang flew the KMT flag in Mukden. The era of party dictatorship under KMT rule had begun and most Chinese nationalists hoped for the best.

Even so, relations between the Kuomintang and activist intellectuals deteriorated. The on-again, off-again sanction of political activism gave New Youth the feeling of being used. Leftists, furthermore, were highly critical of Chiang for negotiating with the Japanese over Tsinan instead of fighting it out, a reaction by Chiang and a response by radical nationalists that would be repeated with the Mukden Incident of 1931 and with Japan's attempt to set up a North China Autonomous Regime in 1935. Resolutions passed by the National Student Union in October, 1929, contained thinly veiled criticisms of the Kuomintang. Tai Chi-t'ao's response was abrupt closure of the union's annual conference.[41]

Despite the moderation of Kuomintang policy toward parochial schools, particularly after Chiang's marriage into the Christian Soong family in December, 1927, the registration question continued to be troublesome. Chinese, including most Chinese Christians, considered the registration requirements minimal and reasonable. Many missionary educators also acknowledged the necessity of registration if the schools were to be acceptable to Chinese nationals and their graduates not penalized. Mission societies and Western school boards, on the other hand, traditionally gave high priority to evangelistic goals and were free from the immediate pressures of the Chinese environment. In more than one instance, they refused to accept recommendations by school faculties and China-based boards for immediate reorganization and registration. Having given assurances of registration during the height of the Educational Rights Campaign, missionary educators as well as Chinese Christians were disconcerted by the delay.

The experience of Hangchow (Christian) University illustrates the rift that had opened between the sponsoring groups.[42] In the summer of 1927 President Robert F. Fitch had resigned to make way for Chinese leadership and the faculty and field board had approved the changes necessary for registration. Following a year of negotiation and controversy, the American board of trustees refused to sanction voluntary religious worship and instruction. The field board, upon rejection of its cabled pleas for reconsideration, then voted on July 5, 1928 to close the institution pending reorganization.

The dispute had become so heated and so public that forty percent of the students had already applied for transfer and Fitch felt obliged to offer a formal explanation. In an article in the *Shanghai Times*, Fitch admitted the differences between the school administrators in China, himself included, and the U.S. trustees, but tried to present the trustees' viewpoint. The overtones of his concluding paragraph convey some of the anguish: "The Trustees have felt obligated to a different course of action, to pay the full price for the maintenance of their convictions, in the hope of a broader policy in the future. Since they are willing to pay so heavily, it is also due to them to give . . . as fully and as clearly as possible, the force and what is to them the reasonableness of their position [sic]." [43] The Reformed Church mission in Amoy went through a similar trial, with Chinese students and faculty criticizing lack of progress toward the registration of Talmage College and the boys' primary school; they rebuked the missionary educators for failing to persuade the home society that registration was imperative. [44]

Despite these controversies, the clashes of 1928-1929 were more closely related to the local scene than to any national policy. Sometimes among the decisive factors were the attitudes of district party members and government officials. When West China Union University tried to register with the Szechwan provincial government in January, 1928, the response was, in effect, "What's the rush? Do you wish to register under Nanking's or Peking's rules?" [45] In contrast, several brief disturbances erupted in 1928-1929 in Fukien where left KMT cadres and other radicals were working to build a third party. [46] Youths distributed anti-Christian propaganda at the Christmas festivities held by Talmage College and Changchow Boy's Primary School in 1928; a Chinese preacher and his assistant were publicly humiliated and briefly imprisoned by individuals reported to be KMT members, though not government officials. A few months later, when directed to attend church services rather than a postponed athletic meet, Talmage students went out on strike; school officials declared a three-week holiday after the students secured support from other schools and the municipal magistrate. Students with outside contacts initiated several confrontations with the newly appointed Chinese president of Fukien Christian University during 1928-1929. During the eight days that the Red Army held Changsha, July 28-August 5, 1930, street mobs, often with one or two communist cadres in the lead, looted and burned mission property. According to one author, however, these incidents did not represent official policy; they were the acts of the poor masses, either encouraged by the permissive attitude of the CCP toward attacks on "reactionaries'" property or channeled by CCP leaders toward imperialist targets.[47]

Cheeloo was the one institution that experienced a lengthy campaign reminiscent of previous years, with striking students and workers and with participation by provincial party and government officials. Even here, however, national support for the movement was not forthcoming and Nanking eventually directed local leaders to effect a settlement. In the conflict at Cheeloo lasting from October, 1929, to mid-February, 1930, the radical minority and the moderate majority were frequently at odds, but Cheeloo's failure to achieve registration benefited the radicals. The left KMT may also have benefited from the fact that the NRA had avoided contest with the Japanese in Tsinan, for this contributed to Nanking's limited authority in Shantung and to the radicals' ability to use the nationalist issue. Shantung was the locus of several demonstrations against Christian evangelism during 1929 and numerous parochial schools were shut down. Local party authorities in Tsinan reportedly forbade members to join the church and threatened to expel Christians from the KMT unless they renounced their faith.[48]

Though Cheeloo had promoted Chinese within the administration and had made religious activities voluntary, the negotiations for registration had been lengthy and tedious. The autumn of 1929 brought a growing impatience with what some Chinese interpreted as dilatoriness by the college. A parade on October 27 and a student assembly on October 28 preceded a vote to strike in order to compel registration. A newly-founded Cheeloo Arts College Reorganization Committee requested immediate appointment of a permanent Chinese dean of the College of Arts and Science. Though its letter was courteously worded, an appendix stated that the dean should be a well-known educator with a Ph.D. from a Chinese institution and should be neither a member of the current university staff nor an adherent of any religion.[49] (No Chinese university at that time granted a Ph.D.)

Despite the initiation of negotiations between the Reorganization Committee and college authorities, the students quickly moved to demands for resignation of the Chinese president and threats of arson if the resignation were not instantaneous. A brief respite succeeded the president's departure, but radicals were able to renew the strike as the Board of Managers convened to consider a replacement. Handbills urged restoration of educational rights, and Cheeloo was designated an organ for "cultural aggression and destruction of the Chinese race . . . . the headquarters of the imperialists in North China", an obstacle to progress that should be eliminated. Strikers locked the classrooms and posted pickets. When the Cheeloo administration voted additional changes to facilitate registration, the radicals raised their demands once again with eleven new stipulations. Agreement was eventually reached through the mediation of the provincial party committee and the government educational bureau.[50]

At Christmas time, however, the party propaganda department, where the radicals were concentrated, renewed the agitation. As in the strikes of the spring of 1927, college workers formed a union and presented an ultimatum calling for sweeping improvements in wages and benefits plus a closed shop. Strikers cut cables to shut down the electrical plant and pickets flying Kuomintang colors sealed off the hospital. After the second Chinese head of the institution resigned within two months, the school closed. Orders from Nanking were necessary before the strikers left campus and the municipal authorities helped work out a compromise settlement in mid-February. The university, without a president, a vice-president, or a dean of arts and science, allowed the medical students to continue work but made no attempt to reopen until the fall of 1930. The new president, a former Vice-Minister of Education, completed registration in December, 1931.[51]

By this time all of the Protestant colleges except St. John's had either registered with the Nanking Ministry of Education or were in the process of registering. Many of the middle schools had passed into Chinese hands and had severed ties with the church. Of those that continued as parochial schools, the majority, like the colleges, had already registered or were in negotiation with government authorities.[52] Foreigners continued to hold administrative and faculty positions, though the proportion of Chinese grew; dependence on foreign funds continued, though the percentage of the budget derived from Chinese sources increased. Because English-language training continued to be an important drawing card for the schools, it remained central to the curriculum.[53]

Registration, of course, meant the end of compulsory religious activities and courses even if not the end of conscious indoctrination. Study of *San min chu-i,* rather than Christianity, was now required of all, and a ritual including obeisance before a portrait of Sun Yat-sen draped with the KMT flag and a reading of Sun's will was part of the weekly routine. In an attempt to insure that education served the needs of the nation, the KMT government began to monitor textbooks, set forth detailed requirements for various curricula, and establish quotas for majors in different fields. Self-government associations, discrete to each school, were to replace the National Student Union. With the inauguration of the New Life Movement in the mid-1930s, a qualified Neo-Confucianism became the new orthodoxy.

Both anti-Christianism and anti-Westernism were toned down after Chiang Kai-shek's public espousal of Christianity in 1930 and Japan's invasion of Manchuria in 1931. Some of the Christian schools shared in the Boxer Indemnity Funds and even received government subsidies for certain programs. Christians, Chinese and Western, served as advisers to Nanking, particularly in the ill-fated rural reconstruction projects. Though the KMT government had had some initial success in prevailing on the Western powers to accept modifications of the unequal treaty system, KMT pressure on the West lessened as Japanese imperialist pressure mounted. The Chinese had assumed control over their tariffs and had regained a few minor concession areas; Chinese participated in the government of the Shanghai International Settlement. But foreigners retained their extraterritorial privileges. After the Mukden Incident, however, Nanking turned to the West in search of support; Japanese infringements on Chinese sovereignty became a more pressing issue than the unequal treaties. The concept of a special relationship between China and the U.S.A., whatever its merits or factual basis, had been fostered by missionaries during the Open Door years and was now being revived.[54]

CONCLUSION

The realities of the 1930s seemed a far cry from the dreams of the social revolutionaries, the anti-imperialist nationalists, and even the liberal educators of the 1920s. What had happened to their hopes and why? And for the articulators of the hopes, for the campaign warriors, what was the significance of the 1920s? Had China truly changed direction during the 1920s and then reversed herself?

A few comparisons and quotations may lead us toward some answers. In 1922 Hu Shih, Ting Wen-chiang, founder of the China Geological Survey, and T'ao Meng-ho, Peita Professor of Sociology, proposed to Chung-hua chiao-yü kai-chin she that religious education be forbidden in all kindergartens and elementary schools.[1] Seven years later the KMT government decreed that such a prohibition of religious education be enforced in all primary and junior middle schools. Though the specific goal was the same, the contrast in the justification of and the effectiveness of the two moves is instructive.

Professors Hu, Ting, and T'ao argued that elementary school children had not yet reached the age of discretion; until experience and education had prepared them to make a reasoned judgment, teaching a specific doctrine was an infringement on intellectual and religious freedom.[2] Their 1922 resolution, a recommendation by educators to a professional association, had little practical effect except to contribute to the literature of the Educational Rights Campaign. In 1929 the KMT had defined *San min chu-i* as the one acceptable ideology for Chinese citizens; all schools should institute required courses on Sun's precepts. The KMT's motivation for opposition to religious education was not freedom of thought so much as intolerance of a rival canon. Since the KMT viewed itself as custodian of the national orthodoxy, it was unwilling to permit educators to control education. Not professors, but the government had issued a ruling and Nanking had the political backing to enforce at least outward obedience to its decree. Schools refusing to abide by the ruling would not be granted government certification. By 1929 the typical liberal position: separation of church and state, separation of education from indoctrination in a specific dogma, was not acceptable; it was, in fact, rarely enunciated. The operative policy was, instead, that typical of nationalistic, authoritarian regimes of the 20th century; citizens must be nationalized and socialized in the one correct teaching.

Perhaps as informative as this contrast is one revealing the evolution of the student movement during the 1920s. On May 19, 1919, the Peking Student Union issued a "Manifesto for a General Strike", which opened with the words: "'Externally preserve our sovereignty and internally eliminate the traitors!' This is the repeated demand we students make of the government and the incessant call to our fellow citizens since the May Fourth Incident."[3] The Manifesto concluded: "We students have been educated and self-cultivated so long that we will advisedly follow our national traits of wisdom, virtue, and courage and will not, by exceeding accepted rules of action, shame our national history. We shall behave according to our own natural ability and innate knowledge, and do not care whether you [Peking government] understand or censure us at the present but wait for the judgment of posterity." Distress over the Peking government's response to the May Fourth demonstrations prompted a Peita student to commit suicide; a note in his pocket read:

> "With such severe internal and external troubles, China may soon be a dead nation. . . . What a pitiful sight to see the students rise up empty-handed, risking their lives for national salvation without the least selfishness or conceit and free from any ulterior motives! With the realization that I am witnessing the passing of a nation and the enslavement of her people, I have decided that I would rather be a free ghost than a living slave. My fellow citizens, be brave and struggle for your country! I have finished my life."[4]

Seven years later the Eighth Congress of the National Student Union looked back at the heroism and idealism of May Fourth and resolved: We must "remedy the weakness of the undefined and romantic cultural movement of the May Fourth period".[5] New Youth would create a scientific revolutionary culture suitable to the nationalist revolution and spread it among the masses; they would combat decadent Oriental culture, the religious culture of the imperialists, and the individualistic ideas of the West. A solidified student movement would join the peasants and workers in supporting the [Canton] National Government and the Northern Expedition. The political and cultural revolutionary movements had become one; compartmentation was impossible.

The transition from the May Fourth Movement and the Anti-Christian Movement, 1920-1922, to the May Thirtieth Movement, the Educational Rights Movement, and the Northern Campaign was reflected in the altered mood and perspective of young activists. Gone, or certainly in recession, were the diversity, cosmopolitanism, and openness of the New Culture Movement. Faded were the hopes of liberals for gradual cultural change through education. Individualism now carried connotations of selfishness amidst the pervasive desire for national unity, strength, and sovereignty. As in traditional China, politics and ideology had been reunited. The increasing responsibilities of the modern state and the inherent populism of nationalism and republicanism, in fact, made the interdependence of ideology and politics appear even more crucial than in dynastic China. The Student Union may have been advocating a revolutionary culture in conformity with political and social revolution while the KMT was moving toward a hybrid ideology to stabilize society and unify the state, but both agreed that education should be an instrument of the nation. Education in the hands of foreigners preaching a deviant doctrine amounted to cultural imperialism.

Iconoclasm and anarchism had given way before the need for discipline, power, and psychological security. Just as the CCP and the KMT had formed the United Front, from which each expected to benefit, so the student movement and the political parties had entered into a marriage of convenience in which each side hoped for greater effectiveness. The Educational Rights Movement was the offspring of this marriage. The differences between the brief, amorphous, intellectualistic Anti-Christian Movement of 1920-1922 and the Educational Rights

Movement with its concrete goals, confrontational tactics, duration, and united front of Chinese against Westerners were characteristic of the evolving student movement during the decade. They can be accounted for first, by the maturation of Chinese nationalism under the influence of Leninist doctrines and the May Thirtieth Movement and second, by the linkage between the student movement and the political parties.

As China moved into the mobilization stage of nationalist movements, the parties nurtured and coopted various nationalist groups and tangential causes. The Educational Rights and Anti-Christian organizations, along with numerous other youth societies, served the United Front in diverse ways. As transmission belts for the parties, they expedited the mobilization process; they also provided wider access for propaganda and support activities such as parades and boycotts. At a time when party membership was multiplying and leadership was in short supply, the Educational Rights Movement helped spot activists and gave them political experience. Though the number of cadres who could assume leadership in labor unions and peasant associations failed to keep pace with party expansion, the allied organizations could furnish supplementary guidance. They became, for a minority, an avenue to party membership, with some of the recruits rising in party ranks during later years. Having developed the technique of working through multi-group alliances in the 1920s, the CCP continued to employ this tactic during the following decades. Such organizations as the National Liberation Vanguard of China and the National Salvation Association during the student movements of the 1930s and the Association for Protesting against American Atrocities and the Anti-Hunger, Anti-Civil War Movement during the civil war of 1946-1949 served purposes similar to those of the Anti-Christian and Educational Rights associations in the 1920s.[6]

Even so, continuities with May Fourth and indeed with imperial China survived. None of the student movements was the manipulable creation of the parties. Scholars still had great prestige in China and intellectuals were often categorized as a separate class or sub-class. As a basis for recruitment and bonding, academic networks continued to be effective. Elitism was still integral to the attitude of the educated. Compare the 1919 pronouncements with the 1926 Student Union resolutions in which the union talked of uniting with the masses but presumed that the New Youth were the ones who would create the revolutionary culture and carry it to the people. Implicit, of course, was the assumption of both Confucius and Mao Tse-tung that transformation of human consciousness was intrinsic to political change. New China required new men and women.

The May Fourth tradition, consolidated by the Anti-Christian Movement, the May Thirtieth Movement, and the Educational Rights Movement, had strengthened New Youth's sense of their special status and special responsibility. Even if the events of the 1920s had not strengthened the position of intellectuals in the political arena, a student sub-culture, ever ready to criticize the elders when they failed China, survived. The seeds of generational conflict were always present so that alliances between power groups and student movements were always fraught with tension.

Despite the ever-present potential for friction, governing political parties committed to modernization needed the scholars. So long as ideology and politics were joined, the ruling party required doctrinal legitimization and could not employ the scholars simply as technicians. It was much easier, however, to find a satisfactory role for New Youth in the drive for power than in the exercise of power. Both the KMT and the CCP were to discover this once they became the responsible authority. Then, the intricate power relationship between the student-movement tradition and the establishment would come into play. Failure of the ruling party to provide a regularized route to power for intellectuals would provoke the confrontational tactics of the May Fourth tradition. Though the CCP proved more adept than the KMT at incorporating newly politicized groups, relations between party and the intellectuals were, in both cases, fragile, and even at times stormy. Intellectuals had in the course of the 1920s developed a sense of intellectual autonomy which they cherished. Restrictions on intellectual freedom were tolerable only under duress.

The ruling party might seek to use the May Fourth

tradition only to discover that it could not control the student movement of the 1930s or 1960s any more than it could in the 1920s. The KMT might seek to make use of the students as exponents of nationalism as in the 1931 protest against the Japanese invasion of Manchuria, only to find that it was losing control of the nationalist issue when it compromised with the aggressor rather than defended Chinese sovereignty. During the December Ninth Movement of 1935-1936 against Japanese imperialism, the CCP proved to be the principal beneficiary. As during the 1920s, the CCP leadership echelon organized and guided multigroup committees and societies representing diverse organizations, thereby broadening support for the protests and widening their contacts despite the party's illegal status.[7] Though the party out of power, their desire for a united front against the Japanese coincided with the demands of the student nationalists. Later, as the responsible authority in the 1960s, however, the CCP leaders tried to use the Red Guards for their own purposes and they learned again that student movements had a life of their own. Student demands, like the platforms of revolutionaries out of power, tended to opt for the utopian. Utopianism, however, was a luxury which a reigning party could ill afford.

Nineteenth-century China was a society in tension: administrative decline and domestic economic strains had produced intellectual ferment leading to challenges to Chu Hsi orthodoxy. To these internal pressures were added external ones. Christianity and Christian missions contributed to the erosion of the Confucian consensus so vital to the integration and cohesion of dynastic China. Such was true whatever the missionaries' lack of success in converting China to Christianity. Not only by offering an alternative ideology and by undermining gentry authority, but simply by manifesting a different life style, evangelists were a disruptive force. They founded schools, hospitals, and other institutions which they touted as substitutes for, not supplements to Chinese institutions. And indeed, some of the institutional concepts and structures introduced by the missionaries were later adopted by reformist China. In making demands on China, the missionaries were, of course, joined by other representatives of the expanding West. This meshing of foreign and indigenous pressures eventually forced China to abandon the Middle Kingdom view of the world for an international arena of sovereign and competing states.

During the early twentieth century, Chinese patriots turned increasingly to nationalism as surrogate for the old consensus. Nationalism should inspire the group loyalty essential to parties seeking political unification and social reintegration. For a people no longer characterized by commitment to the same fundamental beliefs and values, nationalism became the cement to hold China together. Having been built on numerous humiliating experiences, both personal and national, Chinese nationalism had a high negative content. It also had awesome emotional power.

Christian missionaries, who of all Westerners had penetrated furthest into Chinese life, along with Christian institutions designed to alter Chinese society, were prime targets for Chinese animus. During the decade of the 1920s, when the language of Chinese nationalism crystallized, Christianity and Christian missions played an important role. The anti-capitalist and anti-Christian connotations of Leninism had great appeal and the association of these with imperialism was strengthened by the Anti-Christian and Educational Rights Movements. For many Chinese, Christianity could never again be dissociated from imperialism. The broadening of the definition of imperialism to include cultural aggression as well as political and economic infringements on sovereignty would continue to influence China's relations within the international community. That political and economic self-determination was deemed essential might be expected: equally essential and even more arduous was the task of building a strong and new national identity.

Nationalism, despite its ability to inspire intense loyalty, was an inadequate substitute for a holistic ideology. For nationalism, in Tom Nairn's phrase, was Janus-faced, one face looking forward and one backward.[8] Political unity and centralization of authority, industrial and agricultural growth were the goals of Chinese nationalists. Yet in 20th-century China, where the uneven rate of change had generated revolutionary pressures and where the traditional linkage between ideology and politics remained attractive, pursuit of these national goals often seemed destructive of the heritage. Chinese during the New Culture Movement and even before were forced to ask: If tradition is attacked and abandoned, what is the basis for the nation? Wherein lies the distinctiveness of China? "As human kind is forced through its [modernity's] strait doorway, it must look desperately into the past, to gather strength wherever it can be found for the ordeal of 'development'." [9]

Few Chinese discovered a successful formula for harmonizing "national essence" with political and economic development programs. Hu Shih, influential as advocate of *pai hua,* lost support when he recommended change by inches and drops. His prescription for reform evolving out of Chinese history while importing from the West, failed to garner many followers. Liang Shu-ming, however much he shared the radicals' concern for the plight of the peasantry, was ineffectual as he tried to combine the techniques of a status society with the values of a metaphysical religion. Even the KMT faltered when it sought to provide content to nationalism via the New Life Movement. However nationalistic the rhetoric of the New Life Movement, its emphasis on the superficialities of Confucian social ethics set up few positive reverberations.

Chinese Christians, attempting to Sinify Christianity during the 1920s and 1930s, enjoyed no great success. Partly, their attempts to speak for a national Christianity were belied by the reluctance of Western missionaries and mission societies to cut the apron strings. But they also faced the question: What does Sinification of Christianity mean beyond fiscal and administrative independence? Chao Tzu-ch'en, Wu Lei-ch'uan, and Hsu Pao-ch'ien tried to demonstrate the similarities and the compatibilities of Confucianism and Christianity: the emphasis on moral excellence, concern for the welfare of humankind, commitment to the perfect society or the Kingdom of Heaven on Earth. They hoped to demonstrate that acceptance of Christianity did not necessarily mean denial of their own heritage. In the process, both Christianity and Confucianism lost uniqueness. Even more damaging was the fact that defending Chinese Christianity in terms of Confucianism at a time when Confucianism

Conclusion

was under attack as immoral and feudalistic was counterproductive.

Mao Tse-tung and his colleagues, enmeshed in the countryside during the 1930s and 1940s, were able to build on peasant values and perspectives, overcoming the villagers' solipsism and raising their class consciousness. In a creative adaptation to the Chinese environment, Marxism-Leninism was transmuted into Maoism. Liu Shao-ch'i, in "How to be a Good Communist", drew on Confucianism as he instructed cadres to practice self cultivation, pay heed to moral rectitude, and subordinate personal interests to the greater good of society. Though Mao preached revolution and censured the gentry society and culture, he deliberately fostered and adapted aspects of popular culture such as folk opera and woodcuts. But insistence that artists and writers employ the vocabulary of the people and confine themselves to a didactic art serving the needs of socialism meant a sharp break with the Great Tradition in both form and substance. Intellectuals chafed under the restraints. Liu was later to be read out of the party and his famous essay denounced, only to be rehabilitated after the Cultural Revolution. Though the Chinese communists have been more successful than many in evolving a new synthesis, the cost has been great and equilibrium has proved elusive.

To condemn Hu Shih, Chao Tzu-ch'en, or KMT leaders who sought a middle course as denationalized sychophants or foreign puppets is to misunderstand their commitment to China. The same might be said of the wholesale condemnation of parochial students during the 1920s as "running dogs". Experience in a mission school could heighten national consciousness in a way not unlike the experience of Chinese students in Japan during the first decade of the twentieth century or even Chinese students in the West. Both parochial students and Chinese Christians demonstrated their national loyalty as they distanced themselves from Westerners after May Thirtieth and identified themselves increasingly with the student movement and the United Front.

The crux of the matter was that nationalism specified no political models or economic blueprints. And neither did Christianity. National unification and industrial development had to be translated into reality by state and party. The state and party might hope to employ nationalism to gather support for their political and economic programs, but neither they nor most Chinese found a positive role for Christianity in the process. Certain specific contributions by Christian missions might gain acknowledgment: women's education, medical and agricultural education, famine relief, etc. But for many the price had been too high to warrant recognition. The anti-Christian tradition remained alive in Republican China partly because of the incomplete Sinification of the church and its schools. More importantly, the mission institutions were inseparable from the foreign presence, which Chinese found humiliating to the individual and offensive to the nation.[10] During the 19th century Christianity had not been acceptable because it was an affront to Confucian orthodoxy and the gentry class. During the 20th century Christianity remained unacceptable so long as it was deemed counterpoint to Chinese nationalism. Christianity seemed to most Chinese irrelevant to the power-oriented goals of political unity and economic growth. After the establishment of the People's Republic of China in 1949, foreign missionaries were ousted and ties with Western churches severed. The educational and social service activities of missions became the province of the state. Mao Tse-tung had expressd the sentiment of many Chinese when he stated in September, 1949: "[China will] no longer be a nation subject to insult and humiliation. We have stood up. . . ."[11] Only by means of independence from the West, institutional support for the regime, and the privatization of religious faith has Christianity survived in China.

China Christian missions and their fate set up reverberations in U.S.-China relations. Anti-Christian radicals of the 1920s argued that the U.S. had resorted to cultural aggression through missions because it could not compete with Japan and Great Britain in economic and political realms. Without accepting the implication of malice aforethought, one can acknowledge that U.S. trade and investment in China lagged well behind that of Japan and Great Britain throughout the 19th century and well into the 20th century. In the negotiation of the unequal treaties, the U.S. acquired privileges in China by riding

Conclusion

on the coattails of those who engaged in military action. Only in the sending out of evangelists to remake China was the U.S. a strong competitor during the 19th century and did the U.S. assume leadership over all other nations during the 20th century.

Through their writings and lecture tours as well as their preaching, teaching, and social service activities, missionaries were decisive agents in the evolution of Chinese images of the West and in Western perceptions of China. At the same time, missions were value laden in ways that marked neither political nor economic expansion. Letters to sponsoring churches and mission societies as well as speeches during sabbatical home stays frequently painted a picture of heathen China that could justify home support and the missionary's sacrifice. Missionaries went out to change China. Unlike merchants or diplomats in their separable enclaves, evangelists established multiple points of contact with Chinese. This is not to say that the contributions of missionaries to perceptions on either side of the Pacific carried any greater distortions than those from other sources. It is to say that there was generally a higher level of emotional content in those contacts and portrayals associated with the missionaries.

Contrasting viewpoints were also derived from the quite different historical pattern followed by the U.S. and China during the century after the Opium War.[12] The U.S., strengthened by territorial expansion, economic growth, and political stability during most of the period, was on the way to becoming a superpower. For China, the century was characterized by political decline, social disintegration, economic hardship, and international humiliation. The international power gap, as it widened throughout the era, became the source of attitudes and assumptions conducive to friction and misunderstandings. The missionary response to the Anti-Christian Movement of 1920-1922 was not unlike the attitude pervading the Washington Conference of 1921-1922. Both acknowledged that the time had come to begin to consider changes in the unequal relationship. As preparation for these changes, the time had come to set up study committees and commissions which included Chinese membership. Missionaries, along with foreign diplomats, assumed that they would control the timing and the format of the devolution. May Thirtieth, the Educational Rights Movement and the Northern Expedition brought a new urgency to the demands for change and a greater readiness to accept the termination of the unequal treaty system and the Sinification of parochial education and Christianity. In both instances, such a change of heart was so long delayed as to create resentment. In both realms, the transfer of control was not far-reaching enough to offset the image of dependency; full sovereignty would be achieved only after 1949. The evolution of separable Chinese churches, which was accelerated after 1949, promoted a Sinified Christianity which continues to speak to a small but dedicated number of loyal Chinese.

American citizens had invested much money, effort, and time in the hope of Christianizing China. Both the ill will and good will on which the flip-flops in Chinese-American relations have been based were derived in part from the Chinese and the American experience with missions. Missionaries had contributed to the percption of a special relationship between the U.S. and China, to great expectations that were often unrealistic and unfulfilled, with the result that disappointment and resentment were generated on both sides of the Pacific Ocean. The Anti-Christian Movements, parochial education, and the Christian church in China were part of the love-hate relationship that has described Sino-American relations.

ABBREVIATIONS

ABC	American Board of Commissioners for Foreign Missions
CCP	Chinese Communist Party
CCYB	*China Christian Year Book*
CHCYC	*Chung-hua chiao-yü chieh*
Chang, TCSC	Chang Ch'in-shih, *Kuo-nei chin-shih-nien-lai chih tsung-chiao ssu-ch'ao*
CMYB	*China Mission Year Book*
CR	*The Chinese Recorder*
CYC	Communist Youth Corps
CYTC	*Chiao-yü tsa-chih*
Fan CTC	*Fan Chi-tu-chiao chou-k'an*
Fei CTC	*Fei Chi-tu-chiao hsun-k'an*
KMT	Kuomintang
KMT Archives	*Chung-kuo Kuo-min-tang chung-yang wei-yuan-hui tang-shih shih-liao pien-tsuan wei-yuan-hui*
MRL	Missionary Research Library, NYC
N.B. Theo.	New Brunswick Theological Seminary Library
RCA	Reformed Church in America
SYC	Socialist Youth Corps
UB	United Board for Christian Higher Education in Asia, China Records Project, Yale Divinity Library
WSCF	World's Student Christian Federation
Yali	Yale in China Files. China Records Project, Yale University
Y.M.C.A.	Young Men's Christian Association
Y.W.C.A.	Young Women's Christian Association

FOOTNOTES

INTRODUCTION

1. Statistics summarized in Albert Feuerwerker, *The Foreign Establishment in China in the Early Twentieth Century* (Ann Arbor, MI, 1976), pp. 39, 42, 51-53.

2. I use the periodization of Liao Kuang-sheng, *Antiforeignism and Modernization in China, 1860-1980* (Hong Kong, 1984), pp. 44-55.

3. In discussing the May Fourth Movement, I have drawn heavily on Chow Tse-tung, *The May Fourth Movement: Intellectual Revolution in Modern China* (Cambridge, MA, 1960); Benjamin I. Schwartz, ed., *Reflections on the May Fourth Movement: A Symposium* (Cambridge, MA, 1972); Joseph T. Ch'en, *The May Fourth Movement in Shanghai* (Leiden, 1971); Lin Yü-sheng, *The Crisis of Chinese Consciousness* (Madison, 1979).

4. Quoted in Paul G. Pickowicz, *Marxist Literary Thought in China. The Influence of Ch'ü Ch'iu-pai* (Berkeley, 1981), pp. 18-19.

5. New Youth refers to twentieth-century Chinese students and young faculty members congregated at modern institutions of higher education and caught up in nationalism and anti-traditionalism. The term distinguishes them from the older generation among the intellectual elite at any given time and it also indicates the break between the traditional literati and the scholars who have been heavily influenced by Western learning.

   I use the term intellectuals as it is frequently defined when referring to pre-industrial or industrializing societies; included among the intellectuals would be almost anyone who has attained a modest level of literacy and is engaged in professional or academic pursuits where literacy is an important prerequisite. This is a much broader definition than that often employed for societies where literacy is so widespread as to confer little distinction or privilege.

6. Furth, "May Fourth in History," in Schwartz, *Reflections on May Fourth*, p. 60.

7. Charles H. Corbett, *Lingnan University* (N.Y., 1963), p. 41; Edward J. M. Rhoads, "Late Ch'ing Response to Imperialism: the Case of Canton," *Ch'ing-shih wen-t'i*, 2. 1:71-73 (Oct., 1969).

8. Paraphrase from Richard H. Solomon, "From Commitment to Cant: The Evolving Functions of Ideology in the Revolutionary Process," in Chalmers Johnson, ed., *Ideology and Politics in Contemporary China* (Seattle, 1973), p. 53.

9. Chow Tse-tung, *May Fourth,* p. 49; Y.C. Wang, *Chinese Intellectuals and the West, 1872-1949* (Chapel Hill, NC, 1966), pp. 365-367.

10. Samuel P. Huntington, *Political Order in Changing Societies* (New Haven, 1968), p. 308.

11. For further detail, see Jessie G. Lutz, *China and the Christian Colleges, 1850-1950* (Ithaca, 1971), pp. 25-79.

12. Statistics summarized in Feuerwerker, *Foreign Establishment,* pp. 51-53.

Chapter I

1. Ch'en Tu-hsiu, "Chi-tu-chiao yü Chung-kuo jen" (Christianity and the Chinese people), *Hsin ch'ing-nien,* 3.3:14-22 (Feb. 1, 1920). For an abbreviated translation, see Jessie G. Lutz, ed., *Christian Missions in China* (Boston, 1965), pp. 47-50.

2. For a discussion of the anti-Christian tradition, see Paul A. Cohen, *China and Christianity: The Missionary Movement and the Growth of Chinese Anti-foreignism* (Cambridge, MA, 1963); Lü Shih-ch'iang, *Chung-kuo kuan shen fan chiao ti yuan-yin* (Taipei, 1966); Michael Stainton, "Sources of 19th Century Chinese Opposition to the Missionaries and Christianity," *Ching Feng,* 20.3: 130-146; 4:230-248.

3. John K. Fairbank, "Introduction: The Place of Protestant Writings in China's Cultural History," in Suzanne W. Barnett and John K. Fairbank, eds.,*Christianity in China: Early Protestant Missionary Writings* (Cambridge, MA, 1985), p. 8.

4. Paul R. Bohr, *Famine in China and the Missionary: Timothy Richard as Relief Administrator* (Cambridge, MA, 1972), pp. 145-183; Adrian A. Bennett, *Missionary Journalist in China. Young J. Allen and His Magazines* (Athens, GA, 1983), pp. 130-137.

5. The phrase "cocoon of extraterritoriality" comes from James C. Thomson, Jr., et al., *Sentimental Imperialists. The American Experience in East Asia* (N.Y., 1981), pp. 47, 52-55.

6. Stainton, *Ching Feng,* 20: 241. A fairly typical 20th-century summary of the various motives attributed to the missionaries is

Yun Tai-ying, "Wo-men wei shen-ma fan tui Chi-tu-chiao?" (Why are we against Christianity?), *Chung-kuo ch'ing-nien* (Chinese Youth), no. 8 (Dec. 8, 1923).

7. Pearl S. Buck, *My Several Worlds* (New York, 1954), p. 199.

8. Reiterated in the 20th century by T'ang Liang-li, *China in Revolt* (London, 1927), pp. 65-66. D.S. Sanford, who went to teach at Yale-in-China in Sept., 1924, says that in a course on current religious problems, he spent three or four weeks on the topic, Why are the missionaries here? One answer given was that missionaries could live more comfortably and cheaply in China than at home. They had ample servants and were paid salaries twice as large as those of Chinese at the same institution. See his "China's Mission Students" (mimeo. paper, Sept. 10, 1926, Yali Archives), p. 10.

9. Paul A. Cohen, "Christian Missions and their Impact to 1900," in *The Cambridge History of China, vol. X Late Ch'ing, 1800-1911,* pt. 1, ed. by John K. Fairbank (Cambridge, 1978), 563-573; Lü Shih-ch'iang, *Chung-kuo kuan shen.*

10. Catholic and Protestant versions of the incident in Hosea B. Morse, *The Trade and Administration of the Chinese Empire* (Taipei, 1966 reprint), pp. 419-427.

11. Daniel H. Bays, "Christianity and Chinese Sects: Religious Tracts in the Late Nineteenth Century," in Barnett, *Christianity in China,* p. 126; Stainton, *Ching Feng,* 20: 142-143.

12. Fairbank, "Introduction," in Barnett, *Christianity in China,* p. 11.

13. Stainton, *Ching Feng,* 20: 136.

14. Quoted in Eliza A. Morrison, *Memoirs of the Life and Labors of Robert Morrison* (London, 1839), I, 335.

15. Daniel H. Bays, "Christianity and the Chinese Sectarian Tradition," *Ch'ing-shih wen-t'i,* 4. 7:33-55 (Je., 1982).

16. Stainton, *Ching Feng,* 20: 143.

17. See Liao Kuang-sheng, *Antiforeignism and Modernization in China,* pp. 44-50, 76-79, 112-113, 235-240. I have benefited from Liao's work, though I find anti-foreignism, anti-imperialism, and anti-Christianism so closely intertwined that I disagree with his statement that Christianity did not play an important role in the development of Chinese nationalism (p. 50).

18. Quoted in Thomson, *Sentimental Imperialists,* p. 49.

19. Tom Nairn, *The Break-up of Britain. Crisis and Neo-Nationalism* (London, 1977), p. 353; Huntington, *Political Order*, pp. 302-304.

20. Chu Tzu-ch'ing, "Pai-chung-jen--shang-ti ti chiao-tzu!" (The white race--elect of Heaven), *Pei-ying* (Silhouette), 1929. Trans. in Marie-Claire Bergère and Tchang Fou-jouei, *Savons la Patrie: Le nationalisme chinois et le mouvement du Mai 1919* (Paris, 1978), pp. 121-128. The essay was written June 19, 1925.

21. Chang Kuo-t'ao, "Chung-kuo i t'o-li le kuo-chi ch'in-liao ti wei-hsien ma?" (Will China henceforth escape international aggression?), *Hsiang-tao chou-pao* (Guide Weekly), no. 6, Oct. 18, 1922.

22. An abridged English translation of one of the Hunan tracts was made by Shantung missionaries under the title, *Death Blow to Corrupt Doctrines: A Plain Statement of Facts* (Shanghai, 1870). For an analysis of the tract, see Cohen, *China and Christianity*, pp. 45-59. "Yeh-su shih shen-ma tung-hsi?" first appeared in December, 1919. For reprint, see Chang Ch'in-shih, ed., *Kuo-nei chin-shih-nien-lai chih tsung-chiao ssu-ch'ao* (Peking, 1927), pp. 23-37. Chang's collection includes many documents of the Anti-Christian Movement. For this comparison of the two tracts, I have drawn on my article, Lutz, "Chinese Nationalism and the Anti-Christian Campaigns of the 1920s," *Modern Asian Studies*, X, 398-399 (1976). Additional information about Chu Chih-hsin is available in Edward Friedman, *Backward toward Revolution* (Berkeley, 1974), pp. 132-143, 208-209.

23. Lam Wing-hung, "The Emergence of the Protestant Christian Apologetics in the Chinese Church during the Anti-Christian Movement in the 1920s," Diss., Princeton Theological Seminary, 1978, pp. 61-62.

24. Anthony D. Smith, *Theories of Nationalism* (London, 1971), pp. 244-245.

25. Edward V. Gulick, *Peter Parker and the Opening of China* (Cambridge, MA, 1973), esp. pp. 113-124; Paul A. Varg, *Missionaries, Chinese, and Diplomats* (Princeton, 1958), p. 5; Kenneth S. Latourette, *A History of Christian Missions in China* (London, 1929), p. 232.

26. Quoted in Chia-lin Pao Tao, "Peter Parker and the Cushing Mission to China," *The Thought and Word Magazine*, 8.3:35.

27. Latourette, p. 308.

28. Alan R. Sweeten, "The *Ti-pao's* Role in Local Government as

Seen in Fukien Christian Cases, 1863-1869," *Ch'ing-shih wen-t'i,*
3.6:19 (Dec., 1976).

29. Circular of Sir E. Satow, August 31, 1903, reproduced in
Morse, *Trade and Administration,* pp. 417-418.

30. Cohen, *China and Christianity,* p. 252.

31. John K. Fairbank, "Patterns behind the Tientsin Massacre,"
Harvard Journal of Asiatic Studies, 20:480-511 (1957).

32. For detail, see Lutz, *China and the Christian Colleges,* esp.
ch. III, "An Educational Alternative," pp. 50-79.

33. "Educational Department," *The Chinese Recorder,* XXXVIII,
104 (1907).

Chapter II

1. Lin Yü-sheng, *Crisis,* p. 33; Ernest P. Young, "The Hung-
hsien Emperor as a Modernizing Conservative," in *The Limits of
Change, Essays on Conservative Alternatives in Republican China,*
ed. by Charlotte Furth (Cambridge, MA, 1976), pp. 174-176.

2. Chow Tse-tung, *May Fourth,* pp. 291-293; Ernest P. Young,
The Presidency of Yuan Shih-k'ai (Ann Arbor, 1977), pp. 202-204.

3. H.K. Wright, "The Confucian Revival," *China Mission Year
Book,* 1914, p. 63; Yu-ming Shaw, "The Reaction of Chinese Intel-
lectuals toward Religion and Christianity in the Early Twentieth
Century," in James D. Whitehead, Yu-ming Shaw, and N.J. Girardot,
eds., *China and Christianity . Historical and Future Encounters*
(Notre Dame, IN, 1979), pp. 158-159.

4. Arne Sovik, "Church and State in Republican China." Diss.,
Yale U., 1952, pp. 99-100, 109-110; Young, *Presidency of Yuan,*
pp. 203-204; Jerome Ch'en, *Yuan Shih-k'ai,* 2d. ed. (Stanford, 1972),
pp. 162-163.

5. Sovik, pp. 105-108; Wright in CMYB, 1914, pp. 65-68; Cheng
Ching-yi, "Translation of Protest against the Movement in Favor
of Making Confucianism a State Religion," *The Chinese Recorder,*
XLIII, 687-692 (Nov., 1913). The assembly defeated the motion to
establish a state religion and stated only that "Citizens of the
Republic of China shall have the liberty to honour Confucius and
to profess any religion, on which no restriction shall be imposed
except in accordance with law."

6. Some vicars even made preparations for a high mass to

celebrate the coronation, though opposition to the monarchy was expressed in a Hupei Roman Catholic journal. Sovik, pp. 114-115.

7. See biographies of Hsu Ch'ien and Ma Liang in Howard L. Boorman, ed., *Biographical Dictionary of Republican China* (New York, 1968), II, 118-119, 470-473. For a negative reaction by a western missionary, see R.P. Henri Doré, "Le Confuceisme sous la Republique, 1911-1923," *The New China Review,* IV, 298-319 (Aug., 1922).

8. Chow Tse-tung, *May Fourth,* pp. 302-303; Ch'en Tu-hsiu, "Po K'ang Yu-wei chih tsung-t'ung tsung-li shu (Refuting K'ang Yu-wei's message to the president and prime minister), *Hsin ch'ing-nien,* 2.2 (Oct. 1, 1916); Ch'en, "Hsien-fa yü K'ung-chiao" (The constitution and Confucianism), *ibid.,* 2.3 (Nov. 1, 1916).

9. Biography of Wu Yü in Boorman, III, 462-465; Wolfgang Franke, *Chinas Kulturelle Revolution, Die Bewegung vom. 4 Mai 1919* (Munich, 1957), p. 26. A collection of Wu's essays was published in Shanghai in 1921 as *Wu Yü wen-lu* and reprinted in 1936. The titles of the essays are provocative, for example, "On the family system as the root of despotism," "The harmful workings of the class system as propagated by Confucianism," "Refutation of K'ang Yu-wei's thesis that traditional relations between prince and subject are not subject to abolition," "Concerning filial piety".

10. Ch'en Tu-hsu, "Ti-k'ang li" (The force of resistance), *Hsin ch'ing-nien,* 1.3 (Nov. 15, 1915); Ch'en, "Tung Hsi min-tsu ken-pen ssu-hsiang chih ch'a-i" (Differences in basic thought between Eastern and Western peoples), *ibid.,* 1.4 (Dec. 15, 1915).

11. These are the concluding words of "The Diary of a Madman". Wu Yü followed with a vicious essay entitled, "Ch'ih jen yü li chiao" (Cannibalism and the doctrine of li), *Hsin ch'ing-nien,* 6.6 (Nov. 1, 1919).

12. Ch'ien Hsuan-t'ung, "Wen-hsueh ko-ming chih fan-hsiang" (A reaction to the literary revolution), *Hsin ch'ing-nien,* 4.3 (March 15, 1918); Chow, *May Fourth,* pp. 66, 321.

13. Yun Tai-ying, "Lun hsin-yang" (On faith), *Hsin ch'ing-nien,* 3.5 (July 1, 1917).

14. Ts'ai Yuan-p'ei, "I mei-yü tai tsung-chiao" (Aesthetics as a substitute for religion), *Hsin ch'ing-nien,* 3.6 (Aug. 1. 1917).

15. Hu Shih, "Pu-hsiu" (Immortality), *Hsin ch'ing-nien,* 6.2 (Feb. 15.1919).

16. T'ien Han. Letter in *Shao-nien Chung-kuo,* 2.8 (Feb., 1921).

17. Many of the lectures and translations were included in the three issues devoted to "The Problem of Religion": *Shao-nien,* 2.8

(Feb., 1921); 2.11 (May, 1921); 3.1 (Aug., 1921). Chinese Christians translated some of the articles for *The Chinese Recorder* during 1921-1922.

18. For a detailed exposition, see D.W.Y.Kwok, *Scientism in Chinese Thought, 1900-1950* (New Haven, 1965), esp. pp. 1-30.

19. Li published under the name, Li Yü-ying. The title of his essay is simply "Li Yü-ying hsueh-sheng ti chiang-yen" (Mr. Li Yü-ying's lecture), *Shao-nien,* 2.8 (Feb., 1921). Four months later Li summarized Friederich Schleiermacher's views on religion: "Tsung-chao lun" (On religion), *Min-to,* 2.2 (May, 1921).

20. Yun Tai-ying, "Wo ti tsung-chiao kuan" (My religious views), *Shao-nien,* 2.8. Shanghai University is to be distinguished from Shanghai Baptist College, later called the University of Shanghai (Hu-chiang ta-hsueh). Shanghai University was founded in 1923 to train cadres for the KMT-CCP United Front and was controlled and staffed mainly by CCP members. *Chung-kuo ch'ing-nien* was a CCP organ and should be distinguished from publications by *Chung-kuo ch'ing-nien tang* (Young China Party).

21. T'u Hsiao-shih, "T'u Hsiao-shih hsueh-sheng ti chiang-yen" (Mr. T'u Hsiao-shih's lecture), *Shao-nien,* 2.8. T'u's lecture to the Philosophical Society was published in *Che-hsueh,* June, 1922, and later summarized in "What the Chinese are thinking about religion, the attitude of a Chinese literatus," CR, LIV, 273-276 (May, 1923).

22. *Lo-su yueh-k'an* was a short-lived magazine that served primarily to print and circularize Russell's lectures in China. See Chiang T'ing-ch'ien's transcript of Russell's lecture on religion in *Shao-nien,* 2.8.

23. Liu Po-ming, "Tsung-chiao che hsueh" (Religious philosophy), *Shao-nien,* 2.11 (May 15, 1921); Chou Tso-jen, "Tsung-chiao wen-t'i (The problem of religion),*ibid* .; Lu Chih-wei, "Tsung-chiao yü k'o-hsueh" (Religion and science), *ibid.*

24. Among the contributors were Li Ta, "Hai-fu-ting ti tsung-chiao kuan" (Hoffding's religious views) and Shen Yen-ping (Mao Tun), "Lo-man Lo-lan tsung-chiao kuan" (Romain Rolland's religious views). *Shao-nien.* In a letter to *Chueh-wu,* April 7, 1922, Shen also paraphrased Rolland's views on religion.

25. Major contributors to this issue of *Shao-nien,* 3.1 (Aug. 1, 1921) were Li Huang, Chou T'ai-hsuan, and Li Fu-ch'un.

26. Hsieh Fu-ya (N.Z. Zia), "The Anti-Christian Movement in China, A Bird's Eye View," CMYB, 1925, pp. 52-53.

27. Léon Wieger, ed. and trans., *Chine Moderne*, vol. IV, *L'Outre d'Eole* (Hsien-hsien, 1923), pp. 221-222. This action was consistent with earlier policies during Li Shih-tseng's administration. Converts to Christianity were often ostracized by their Chinese colleagues in France; sometimes their names were published in Chinese journals in Paris and their subsidies were cut. See *ibid*. and Jean M. Planchet, ed., *Les Missions de Chine et du Japon*, 1929, p. 691.

28. Absolute decline in the number of missionaries sent to China and in mission society budgets came only after 1925. There were, however, earlier indicators of trouble: the number of college students signing the Student Volunteer pledge to enter mission work fell; annual contributions did not keep pace even though endowments and investment income masked this fact until 1929; a major drive to secure funds for women's colleges in China had to be abandoned in the early 1920s, while ambitious dreams of developing several top-quality medical schools faded as it became apparent that monies were sufficient for only one, Peking Union Medical College; plans for women's colleges to parallel Fu Jen University and West China Union University came to naught. In 1924 Harold Balme of Cheeloo University characterized "efforts to secure large funds in the West" as disappointing. Balme, "Council of Higher Education," *Educational Review*, XVII, 51-52 (Jan., 1925). A Centenary Campaign by American Methodists went into the red and allocations to Central China in 1924 had to be cut back forty percent. Shirley S. Garrett, "Why They Stayed: American Church Politics and Chinese Nationalism in the Twenties," in *The Missionary Enterprise in China and America*, ed. by John K. Fairbank (Cambridge, MA, 1974), p. 287.

29. Jerome Ch'en, *China and the West* (Bloomington, 1979), p. 135; Latourette, p. 774; Feuerwerker, *Foreign Establishment*, pp. 43-47. The figure of 130 Protestant mission societies does not include numerous other Christian organizations such as the Y.M.C.A. and Salvation Army. About one-third of the total Protestant middle schools were located in the three provinces of Chekiang, Anhwei and Kiangsu. E.H. Cressy, "Christian Education in China." in *The China Year Book*, 1929/30, I, 536.

30. Feuerwerker, *Foreign Establishment*, p. 42; Eric O. Hanson, "Political Aspects of Chinese Catholicism," in Whitehead, ed., *China and Christianity*, pp. 139-141.

31. *Ibid.*, pp. 138-139; Jerome Chen, *China and the West*, p. 93; Thomas A. Breslin, *China, American Catholicism, and the Missionary* (University Park, PA, 1980), pp. 31-33.

32. Latourette, pp. 740, 780. Latourette distinguishes between Protestant communicants, 366, 527 in 1920, and the baptized non-communicants, 85, 140 in 1920. He does not make a similar distinction in the case of Roman Catholics.

33. Milton T. Stauffer, ed., *The Christian Occupation of China* (Shanghai, 1922), pp. 32-39; *The Chinese Church as Revealed in the National Christian Conference held in Shanghai, May, 1922* (Shanghai, 1922), pp. 144-147. In demonstrating growth, the latter volume uses 1913 as the base year. *Hsin chiao-yü*, 5.4:863 (Nov., 1922) published a table demonstrating the growth of pupils in parochial schools in China from 1876 to 1920.

34. A Chinese edition was published under the title, *Chung-hua kuei-chu* (China for Christ).

35. Mei Kung-pin (Mei Yuan-lung), "Chi-tu-chiao yü Chung-kuo" (Christianity and China), reprinted in Chang, TCSC, pp. 387-394. Also see a later protest: Ch'in Chien (?), "Kou-hua ti chiao-yü" (Dog-like education), *Fan Chi-tu-chiao chou-k'an,* no. 3 (Jan. 15, 1925).

36. Feuerwerker, *Foreign Establishment,* p. 42; *Christian Occupation,* pp. 429-433. Included in the statistics for Protestants are ca. 300 middle schools and two dozen institutions of higher education (junior colleges, colleges, medical schools, and seminaries).

37. A. Legendre, "La pénétration americaine de la Chine par l'école," summarized in Wieger, IV, 211-214.

38. For further detail, see Varg, *Missionaries,* esp. ch. IX, "The Crusade Runs into Stumbling Blocks at Home Base, 1919-1931," pp. 147-166.

39. "The Bible Union of China," CMYB, 1923, pp. 95-101. For further detail, see M. Searle Bates, "The Theology of American Missionaries in China, 1900-1950," in Fairbank, *Missionary Enterprise,* pp. 151-155. For the reaction of Chinese Christians, see Hsu Pao-ch'ien, "The Prospect for Christianity in China," CR, LII, 823 (Dec., 1921).

40. See, for example, "Chung-kuo chih-shih chieh tui yü Chi-tu-chiao ti t'ai-tu" (The limits of Chinese knowledge regarding Christian attitudes), *Sheng-ming,* 2.7 (March, 1922); Wu Lei-ch'uan, "Wo tui yü Chi-tu-chiao ti kan-hsiang" (My impressions regarding Christianity), *ibid.,* 1.4 (Nov. 15, 1920); Hsu Pao-ch'ien, "The Prospect for Christinaity in China," CR, LII, 818-825. G. Sherwood Eddy was a prominent Western advocate of the Social

Gospel and made several evangelistic tours of China. See his statements in *North American Students and World Advance* (NY, 1920), p. 192 and *Christian Students and World Problems* (NY, 1924), pp. 116-121.

41. The preface to "The Bible Union of China," CMYB, 1923, p. 95 contains a statement by Frank Rawlinson, editor: "The Editors feel that the Bible Union of China is of importance historically and that some description of it should be included in the *China Mission Year Book*. They made an effort to get a member of the Bible Union to prepare a statement, and also tried to get a member of the Bible Union to read and approve the statement which is herewith printed but in both cases without success." See also a protest against the "modernist" approach in a letter to the editor, CR, LIII, 725-726 (Nov., 1922).

42. Liu T'ing-fang, "China's Renaissance--The Christian Opportunity," CR, LII, 301-303 (May, 1921).

43. Hsu Pao-ch'ien, "The Prospect for Christianity in China," CR, LII, 8, 18-25.

44. "Pei-ching Chi-tu-chiao hsueh-chiao shih-yeh lien-ho-hui shuo-ming" (Statement of the Peking Christian Schools' Work Federation), *Sheng-ming,* 2.7; "The Work and Plans of the Peking Christian Student Work Union," CMYB, 1919, pp. 308-311.

45. The original name of the Life Fellowship was *Cheng-tao t'uan* (Apologetic Group). It included both Chinese and Westerners and many of its leaders were teachers and administrators at Yenching University. For further detail, see Philip West, *Yenching University and Sino-Western Relations, 1916-1952* (Cambridge, MA, 1976), pp. 19-23, 65. During its first year *Sheng-ming* included such articles as Hsu Ch'ien (George Hsu), "Christianity, the Basis for a Republic," a translation of H.E. Fosdick's writings on faith and science and of B.S. Burgess, "Christian Faith and Social Progress," plus several statements of faith by Chinese Christian liberals.

46. "Chi-tu-chiao ti she-hui hsin-t'iao" (Christian social creed), *Sheng-ming,* 2.7.

47. On the WSCF conference, see Fan Wan-hui, "Chi-tu yü shih-chieh kai-tsao" (Christ and the reconstruction of the world), *Ch'ing-nien chin-pu,* no. 50 (Feb., 1922); "Yeh-su ti p'ing-min-chu-i" (The democracy of Jesus) and "I chung hsin neng-li" (A new power), *Chung-hua kuei-chu,* no. 19 (Jan., 1922). *Sheng-ming* put out a special Federation Conference number in both Chinese and

English in March, 1922. On the National Christian Conference, see editorial, "Chiao-hui shih shei jen ti?" (Whose is the church?) and Yeh Ming-chao, "Wo tui yü ch'üan-kuo Chi-tu-chiao ta-hui chih hsi-wang" (My hopes for the National Christian Conference), *Shang-hai kuang-tung Chung-hua Chi-tu-chiao hui yueh-pao,* no. 50 (March, 1922); Ch'eng Ching-yi, "The Chinese Church," *The Student World,* XV, 27-31 (Jan., 1922). *The Student World* was the official magazine of the WSCF and all of the articles in the January issue were by Chinese Christians; most of them discussed current Chinese education and Chinese students.

48. "Shang-hai fei Chi-tu-chiao hsueh-sheng t'ung-meng hsuan-yen chi t'ung tien" (Manifesto and circular telegram of the Shanghai Anti-Christian Student Federation), in Chang, TCSC, pp. 187-188. Chang stated: "The spark which started the Anti-Religion conflagration was the special number of "Association Progress" which discussed the World's Christian Student Federation in spring of 1922. A tiny group of Bolshevik students in Shanghai read this special number, dismissed the only Christian member of their group and wrote the proclamation of the Non-Christian Student Federation, an inflammatory article which was widely circulated." Chang Ch'in-shih, "The Anti-Religious Movement," CR, LIV, 459 (Aug., 1923). Chang provides no documentation; the manifesto does specifically protest against the meeting of the WSCF at Tsing Hua University.

49. "Future Tasks of the Federation," *Sheng-ming,* 2.7.

50. "I chung hsin neng-li," *Chung-hua kuei-chu,* no. 19. "Moral power" was a term frequently employed by the evangelist, G. Sherwood Eddy.

51. Yun Tai-ying, "Wo-men wei shen-ma fan tui Chi-tu-chiao?" (Why we are against Christianity),*Chung-kuo ch'ing-nien,* no. 8 (Dec., 1923).

52. Yü Chia-chü, "Chiao-hui chiao-yü wen-t'i" (The problem of parochial education), *Chung-hua chiao-yü chieh,* XIII (Oct., 1923).

53. "The Impression of Christianity made upon the Chinese People through Contact with the Christian Nations of the West," *Sheng-ming,* 2.7.

54. Respondents included Kao I-han, professor at Peking College of Law and Political Science; Chou Tso-jen, New Culture essayist and professor at Yenching and Peita; Hu Shih; and Chang Tung-sun, ed. in chief of *The China Times;* see *Sheng-ming,* 2.7. In the same issue, see "Attitude of Non-Christian Women towards Christianity in China."

55. Ch'en Ch'i-t'ien, "Wo-men pu kai fan tui Yeh-chiao yü chi yun-tung ma?" (Shouldn't we oppose Christianity and its works?), *Shao-nien,* 3.9 (April 1, 1922); Ch'en Tu-hsiu, "Wai chiao wen-t'i yü hsueh-sheng yun-tung" (Foreign relations question and the student movement), *Hsiang-tao chou-pao,* no. 23, 163-166 (May 2, 1923).

56. University of Nanking, "Report of the President," 1918-1919, p. 3 (UB); Hangchow Christian College, "Report of the President," 1919-1920, p. 10 (Presbyterian Board of Foreign Missions, NYC); Peking University (Yenching), "Report of the President," 1918-1919, pp. 4-6.

57. Biography of Ch'ü Ch'iu-pai in Donald W. Klein and Anne B. Clark, *Biographic Dictionary of Chinese Communism, 1921-1965* (Cambridge, MA, 1971), I, 240; Pickowicz, *Marxist Literary Thought,* p. 21; Chow, *Research Guide,* p. 48. For data on other activities, see Fukien Christian University, "Report of the President," 1919, p. 2 (MRL); Peking University (Yenching), "Report of the President," 1918-1919, p. 5 (UB); Tsang Yi (?), "The Chinese Students' Patriotic Movement of 1919," *Student World,* XV, 33 (Jan., 1922); Dwight Edwards, *Yenching University* (NY, 1959), pp. 137-141; Shirley S. Garrett, *Social Reformers in Urban China. The Chinese Y.M.C.A.* (Cambridge, MA, 1970), pp. 165-166; S.K. Sheldon Tso, *The Labor Movement in China* (Shanghai, 1928), p. 79.

58. Mary Lamberton, *St. John's University* (NY, 1955), pp. 77-81; F.L.H. Pott, "History of St. John's University," in *St. John's University, 1879-1929* (Shanghai, 1929), pp. 29-30.

59. Biography of Hsu Ch'ien in Boorman, II, 119; West, *Yenching U.,* p. 38.

60. For further detail, see Garrett, *Social Reformers,* pp. 168-169, 176-177; Lutz, *China and Christian Colleges,* pp. 111, 295, 312.

61. See statements by Wu Yao-tsung, executive secretary of the Peking Christian Schools' Work Federation, in "Shui shih Yeh-su ti men-t'u?" (Who are the disciples of Jesus?), *Chen-li chou-k'an,* no. 9 (May, 1923) and by Yü Jih-chang (David Z.T. Yui), YMCA secretary and co-chair of the WSCF conference of 1922, in Wieger, IV, 164-169. Yü takes credit for coining the slogan, "jen-ko ch'iu kuo".

Chapter III

1. Chang Kuo-t'ao, *The Rise of the Chinese Communist Party* (Lawrence, KS, 1971-1972), I, 239; *Wu-ssu shih-ch'i ch'i-k'an chieh-shao* (Peking, 1959), II, 21; Ka-che Yip, *Religion, Nationalism and Chinese Students* (Bellingham, WA, 1980), p. 25. Repeated in several accounts is the statement that a prime mover was a student dismissed from Shanghai Baptist College. I have been unable to identify the student or locate information that would confirm or negate this statement. A former Shanghai Baptist College student did subsequently become an active labor organizer in Canton.

2. Chang, TCSC, pp. 187-189.

3. The first page of *Hsien-chü*, March 15, 1922, is reproduced in Ku Ch'ang-sheng, *Ch'uan-chiao-shih yü chin-tai Chung-kuo* (Shanghai, 1981), pp. 352-353; Ch'en Tu-hsiu's article, "Chi-tu-chiao yü Chi-tu-chiao hui" (Christianity and the Christian church) extended over two issues, March 15 and March 20, 1922. He later published an essay specifically on the Anti-Christian Movement in the June 20 issue of *Hsien-ch'ü:*"Tui yü fei tsung-chiao t'ung-meng ti huai-i chi fei Chi-tu-chiao hsueh-sheng t'ung-meng ti ching-kao" (Regarding the skepticism of the Anti-Religion Federation and the warning of the Anti-Christian Student Federation). In addition to his essay in *Hsien-chü*, March 15, Lu Shu published an attack on Christianity and Christian missions in *Shun-t'ien shih-pao*, see trans. in Wieger, III, *Remous et Écume*, 1922, pp. 52-54.

4. Chin later became anti-communist in outlook.

5. Laurence A. Schneider, *Ku Chieh-kang and China's New History* (Berkeley, 1971), pp. 258-272; Nicholas R. Clifford, *Shanghai, 1925: Urban Nationalism and the Defense of Foreign Privilege* (Ann Arbor, 1979), pp. xii, xiii; Jerome B. Grieder, *Intellectuals and the State in Modern China,* (NY, 1981), pp. 150-152, 302-303. Quotation is from Charlotte Furth, "Intellectual change: from the Reform movement to the May Fourth movement, 1895-1920," in Fairbank, ed. *Cambridge History of China,* vol. 12, *Republican China, 1912-1949,* Part 1 (Cambridge, 1983), 403.

6. Chang, TCSC, p. 187.

7. *Ibid.*

8. *Ibid.*, pp. 193-196. Yip, p. 23, interprets the change in name as primarily a tactical move by radicals to broaden the movement's support. Though 79 individuals supposedly signed the tele-

gram, only four names are supplied by Chang and by other sources reprinting the telegram. See the comparison of the Shanghai and Peking telegrams in Wang Chih-hsin, *Chung-kuo Chi-tu-chiao shih-kang,* rev. ed. (Hong Kong, 1959). p. 270.

9. Joseph Ch'en points out the differences between the May Fourth Movement in Shanghai and in Peking, *May Fourth in Shanghai,* pp. 11-15, 61-66, 214-220.

10. Chang Ch'in-shih, "The Anti-Religion Movement," CR, LIV, 460.

11. *Shun-t'ien shih-pao,* April 4, 1922, trans. in Wieger, III, 43-45.

12. See John Dewey. "American and Chinese Education," *The New Republic,* XXX, 15-17 (March 1, 1922). The *North China Herald* reported that college students at Yunnanfu had organized a mass demonstration to protest against the Washington Conference on March 14, "Students of Yunnanfu," *North China Herald,* April 15, 1922. Demonstrations also occurred in Peking and elsewhere.

13. Wieger, III, 32-33.

14. Liang Ch'i-ch'ao, "P'ing fei tsung-chiao t'ung-meng" (Comments on the Anti-Religion Federation), *Tung-fang tsa-chih,* 19.8: 133-138 (April, 1922).

15. Ch'en Ch'i-t'ien, "Wo-men pu kai fan tui Yeh-chiao yü chi yun-tung ma?", *Shao-nien,* 3.9;Yü Chia-chü, "Chi-tu-chiao yü kan-ch'ing sheng-huo"(Christianity and the emotional life), *ibid.,* 3.11 (July, 1922); "K'o-hsueh yü tsung-chiao" (Science and religion) and Ch'en Chien-shan, "Chin hua lun yü tsung-chiao" (Theory of evolution and religion), *Hsueh-sheng tsa-chih,* 9.6 (June, 1922); Fu P'ei-ch'ing (Fu T'ung), "K'o-hsueh ti fei tsung-chiao yun-tung yü tsung-chiao ti fei tsung-chiao yun-tung" (The scientific anti-religion movement and the religious anti-religion movement),*Che-hsueh,* VI (June, 1922); Liu Po-ming, "Fei tsung-chiao yun-tung p'ing-i" (Comments on the Anti-Religion Movement),*Hsueh-heng,* no. 6 (June, 1922); I Wei, "Tsai lun tsung-chiao wen-t'i" (Another discussion of the problem of religion, *ibid.;* Ching Ch'ang-chi, "Lun hsueh-sheng yung-hu tsung-chiao chih pi-yao" (Discussion of the need for student support of religion), *ibid.* Most, though not all, of the comments were negative in their attitude toward religion and Christian missions.

16. During March, 1922, Protestant leaders in north China gave prominent support to a nationalist boycott of Japanese goods. Whether both Japanese and Westerners were trying to deflect negative publicity, it would be difficult to say.

17. "Canton and the Anti-Christians," North China Herald, April 29, 1922; Lam, pp. 75-76, 169; Wang Ching-wei, "She-hui chiao-yü yü hsin-yang" (Socialist education and faith), Chueh-wu, April 7, 1922, and Wang, Letter to Min-kuo jih-pao, Shanghai, April 15, 1922, both trans. in Wieger, III, 83-86.

18. Yip, p. 24; biographies of Ch'en Kung-po and T'an P'ing-shan in Boorman, I, 196-201; III, 217-220. According to the North China Herald, April 29, 1922 Law College students led the meeting at which Canton students founded a branch of the Anti-Christian Federation on April 16.

19. Chang Kuo-t'ao, I, 222-223, 238-241; Tatsuro and Sumiko Yamamoto, "The Anti-Christian Movement in China, 1922-1927," Far Eastern Quarterly, XII, 134 (1953).

20. "Chiao-yü p'ing-t'an," (Educational critiques), Chiao-yü tsa-chih, 14.4 (April, 1922); for the editorial comments on student storms, see ibid., 14.1 (January, 1922).

21. Chang Ch'in-shih, "The Anti-Religion Movement," CR, LIV, 467. The collection reprinted articles by Ts'ai Yuan-p'ei, Ch'en Tu-hsiu, Li Shih-tseng, Wang Ching-wei, Bertrand Russell, Chu Chih-hsin, and others.

22. Chow Tse-tsung, Research Guide to the May Fourth Movement (Cambridge, MA, 1963), p. 113.

23. Yü Chia-chü, "Chi-tu-chiao yü kan-ch'ing sheng-huo," Shao-nien, 3.11.

24. Chang, TCSC, p. 199. Signing the statement were: Chou Tso-jen, Ch'ien Hsuan-t'ung, Shen Chien-shih, Shen Shih-yuan, and Ma Yü-tsao. The responses of Ch'en, Shen, and Li took the form of letters to the editor published in the April 7, 1922 editions of Min-kuo jih-pao and Chueh-wu.

25. "Non-Christians on the Offensive," North China Herald, April 15, 1922; Yip, pp. 27-28.

26. Chang, TCSC, pp. 199-206; Wieger, III, 42-43, 74-79.

27. See newspaper enclosures, Peking Leader, March 26, 1922; Peking-Tientsin Times, April 3, 1922 in A.B. Ruddock to U.S. Secretary of State, April 10, 1922 (U.S. Dept. of State, Archives, Decimal File, China, 893.00 404/13). Also, "Canton and the Anti-Christians," North China Herald, April 29, 1922; Yü Yung-fan, "What the WSCF Conference has Meant to China," Student World, XV, 93 (July, 1922).

28. V.K. Ting, "The Anti-Christian Movement," *China Weekly Review*, April 22, 1922; for editorial, see pp. 281-282 of same issue.

29. "The World's Student Convention," *North China Herald*, April 15, 1922; "The Anti-Christians," *ibid.*, April 22, 1922.

30. Chiang Wen-han (Kiang Wen-han), *The Ideological Background of the Chinese Student Movement* (N.Y., 1948), p. 78; Wieger, III, 432-433.

31. Ch'en Tu-hsiu, "Chi-ti-chiao yü Chi-tu-chiao hui" in Chang, TCSC, pp. 190-193; Ch'en "Wai-chiao wen-t'i yü hsueh-sheng yun-tung," *Hsiang-tao*, May 2, 1923; Lu Shu in Wieger, III, 52-54; also, several of the student proclamations of support, trans. in Wieger, III, 40-41.

32. See trans. of a printed circular issued by Chungking students, enclosed in Jacob G. Schurman to U.S. Secretary of State, April 24, 1922 (U.S. Dept. of State Archives, Decimal File, China 893.00/4404). Yun Tai-ying was at the time teaching in Chungking and working to organize branches of the Socialist Youth Corps in Szechwan.

33. "Manifesto of Peking Socialists", April 4, 1922, trans. in Wieger, III, 43-45; Ch'en Tu-hsiu, "Chi-ti-chiao yü Chi-tu-chiao hui." Condemnations of these organizations were repeated throughout the campaign. See, for example, the condemnation in the 1926 proclamation supporting expelled Lingnan students by "Sheng chiang pa-kung wei-yuan-hui" (Canton-Hong Kong Strike Committee), April 11, 1926 (Newspaper clippings on the Youth Movement and Education). Chung-kuo Kuo-min-tang chung-yang wei-yuan-hui tang-shih shih-liao pien-tsuan wei-yuan-hui.

34. Chang Ch'in-shih, "The Anti-Religion Movement," CR, LIV, 460; *Min-kuo jih-pao*, Shanghai, April 13, 1922.

35. Robert A. Scalapino and George T. Yu, *The Chinese Anarchist Movement* (Berkeley, 1969), p. 32. Anarchists or former anarchists born in the 1880s or 1890s include Li Shih-tseng, Hsieh Tzu-sheng, Ch'en Ch'i-t'ien, Yü Chia-chü, and Chang Chi.

36. Ch'en Ch'i-t'ien, "Wo-men pu kai fan tui Yeh-chiao?", *Shao-nien*, April 1, 1922.

37. Yü Chia-chü, "Chi-tu-chiao yü kan-ch'ing sheng-huo," *Shao-nien*, July 1, 1922; Li Shih-tseng in Chang, TCSC, pp. 201-206.

38. Ts'ai Yuan-p'ei, "Chiao-yü tu-li i" (On independence of education), *Hsin chiao-yü*, 4.3 (March, 1922); "Ch'üan-kuo chiao-yü tu-li yun-tung hui hsuan-yen" (Proclamation of the National

Association for Educational Independence), *ibid.,*4.5 (May, 1922).

39. Introduction of Ts'ai Yuan-p'ei by Hsiao Tzu-sheng at Peita rally, April 9, 1922, Wieger, III, 75.

40. Ch'iang Shu-ko, ed., *Chung-kuo chin-tai chiao-yü chih-tu* (Modern educational system of China), (Shanghai. 1934), p. 160.

41. Yü Chi-chü, "Chi-tu-chiao yü kan-ch'ing sheng-huo," *Shao-nien,* July 1, 1922.

42. Wang Chih-hsin, pp. 270-271.

43. A.H.Smith, "The Present Attitude of the Chinese toward Christianity," CMYB, 1923, pp. 12-17. Smith solicited the views of missionaries in various sectors of China. Those who mentioned the Anti-Christian Movement were generally optimistic; often they commented on its brevity and predicted that the faith of true Christians had been strengthened. Most made no mention of the movement while discussing the indifference of Chinese to evangelism or, on the other hand, stating: "There is a readiness to hear as never before existed." (p. 13)

44. Evangelists arriving in the 20th century, unlike the early pioneers, found a mission structure already in place so that they could quickly move into a specific position and into the mission compound society. The consequence for many was a more limited linguistic ability and greater insulation from the Chinese community than had often been true during the early and mid-19th century. This applied particularly to Protestant missionaries and Catholic sisters. For a case study, see Sidney A. Forsythe, *An American Missionary Community in China, 1895-1905* (Cambridge, MA, 1971).

45. Wu Yao-tsung, "Chung-kuo ti Chi-tu-chiao hsueh-sheng ying-tang tso shen-ma?" (What should Chinese Christian students do?), *Chen-li,* no. 10 (June, 1923).

46. CR, LI, 704-709 (Oct., 1920); LII, 38-42 (Jan., 1921); 97-101 (Feb., 1921); 177-186 (March, 1921); 818-825 (Dec., 1921).

47. "The Non-Christian Students Federation," *Sheng-ming* (March, 1922), pp. 9-10.

48. *Shang-hai kuang-tung Chung-hua Chi-tu-chiao hui yueh-pa* (May, 1922), pp. 1-3. Mott is quoted in the editorial.

49. Chao, CR, LIII, 743-748.

50. Liu Po-ming (K.S. Liu), "The Anti-Religion Movement, Christianity and Religion," CR. LIII. 748-754.

51. The symposium was later published in *The Chinese Social and Political Science Review,* VII, 103-113 (April, 1923). Chang, Wu, and Hu made a real effort to bring the movement and its literature to the attention of Westerners. They contributed articles and translations to the *Chinese Recorder, Educational Review,* and *China Mission Year Book,* but, of course, most of these appeared while the movement was quiescent. Their replies in Chinese language periodicals such as *Sheng-ming* and *Ch'ing-nien chin-pu* generally appeared earlier.

52. Wu Yao-tsung's essay, "Our Message," contained the plea that the Christian church find out more about the intellectual awakening and read its literature, that it listen to criticisms, and that it train more Chinese leaders. See CR, LIV, 486-487.

53. "The Chinese Student Mind," CR, LIII, 681 (Nov., 1922).

54. Edwin Marx, "Progress and Problems of the Christian Movement since the Revolution (1911)," CMYB, 1924, p. 94.

55. "Editorial," CR, LIII, 295-296 (May, 1922).

56. B. Burgoyn Chapman, "Compulsory or Voluntary Worship or Instruction?", *Educational Review,* XV, 240-242 (July, 1923); I.D. Ross, *ibid.,* 349-351 (Oct., 1923).

57. Edwin R. Embree Collection, "Family Journal," Aug. 22, 1922 (Yali Archives). Embree later became a trustee for Yale-in-China.

58. Hsu Ch'ing-yü in Chang, TCSC, pp. 212-240. Chao, who summarizes the contents of the booklet, gives the name as Hsu Ching-yi and provides the information that Hsu was from Changsha. Chao Tu-ch'en, "Christians and Non-Christians Reply to the Anti-Religion Movement," CR, LIII, 744-745.

59. Eugene E. Barnett speaks of the "sadly inarticulate state of the Church in the realm of Christian literature" in "The Chinese Students and the Christian Church," CMYB, 1923, p. 85. Pao Kuang-lin says few Christian periodicals, if any, reach people outside the church; see "Christian Periodicals in China," *China Christian Year Book,* 1928, pp. 372-375. In 1926 CMYB was retitled *China Christian Year Book.*

60. Wang Tsi-chang, *The Youth Movement in China* (N.Y., 1927), p. 209; Lam, pp. 68-70, 75-79, 83, 152-157. I have been unable to locate copies of *Chen kuang.* Many of the essays were reprinted in Chang I-ching, *P'i-p'ing fei Chi-tu-chiao yen-lun hui-k'an* (A collection of articles criticizing the anti-Christian literature) (n. p., 1922).

61. "Tui yü fei tsung-chiao yun-tung ti hsuan-yen" (Declaration regarding the anti-religion movement), *Kuang-tung Chi-tu-chiao hui yueh-pao,* no. 60, pp. 4-6 (May, 1922). The statement, drawn up on April 10, was signed by Chien Yu-wen, Fan Tzu-mei, Ying Yuan-tao, Yang I-hui, and Wu Chih-chien. K'ang P'o-chung, "Tui yü fei Chi-tu-chiao ta t'ung-meng chih kan-hsiang" (Impressions of the Great Anti-Christian Federation), *ibid.,* no. 61, pp. 1-3.

62. The June issue of *Sheng-ming,* for example, contained two items: a formal response to the anti-religion movement by the Committee on Publications of Sheng-ming she and a statement by a Yenching Student, Yang Wen-ch'ao; additional responses were published in September and October issues.

63. Chien Yu-wen, "Min-ts'u ti chiao-hui" (A national church), *Ch'ing-nien chin-pu,* no. 52 (April, 1922); also, his editorial, "Chiao-hui shih shei jen ti?", *Kuang-tung Chi-tu-chiao hui yueh-pao,* no. 59; Lam, p. 85.

64. Hu Hsueh-ch'eng, "Wei fei tsung-chiao ta t'ung-meng chin i chieh" (Further explanations regarding the Great Anti-Religion Federation), *Sheng-ming,* 3.2 (Oct., 1922); Hsu Pao-ch'ien, "Fan Chi-tu-chiao yun-tung yü wu-jen ying-ts'ai chih fang-chi" (The Anti-Christian Movement and our strategy for response), in Chang, TCSC, pp. 445-454; "Tui yü fei tsung-chiao yun-tung ti hsuan-yen" (Declaration regarding the anti-religion movement), *Kuang-tung Chi-tu-chiao hui yueh-pao,* no. 60.

65 Hsu Ch'ing-yü in Chang, TCSC, pp. 212-240; Liu T'ing-fang, "Wo-men tang tso shen-ma?", *Sheng-ming,* 3.9 (May, 1923); Chang Ch'in-shih, "The Anti-Religion Movement," CR, LIV, 464-465.

66. Wu Yao-tsung, "Chung-kuo ti Chi-tu-chiao hsueh-sheng ying-tang tso shen-ma?", *Chen-li,* June, 1923. Wu, "The Chinese Student Christian Movement," CR, LIV, 468-473; "Proclamation of the Young Progressive Student Society," in Wieger, III, 266-267.

67. Wu Lei-ch'uan, *Chi-tu-chiao yü Chung-kuo wen-hua* (Christianity and Chinese Culture) (Shanghai, 1936), p. 104; Ng Lee-ming, "Wu Lei-chuen--From Indigenization to Revolution," *Ching Feng,* 20.4:211 (1977).

68. Yeh Ming-chao, "Wo tui yü ch'üan-kuo Chi-tu-chiao ta hui chih hsi-wang," *Kuang-tung Chi-tu-chiao hui yueh-pao,* no. 59; "China Today," *Sheng-ming,* 2.7. The April, 1922 issue of *Ching-nien chin-pu,* which was devoted to the impending conference, contains articles by Chien Yu-wen, Fan Wan-hui, and Ch'üan Shao-wu. Their phraseology foreshadows the organization of the national

Protestant church as the Three-Self Movement under the People's Republic of China.

69. Wang Chih-hsin, pp. 273-276.

70. Chien Yu-wen, "Min-ts'u ti chiao-hui," *Ch'ing-nien chin-pu*, no. 52. Chien anticipated inclusion of Roman Catholics as well as Protestants in the Chinese national church.

71. Chao Tu-ch'en, "The Appeal of Christianity to the Chinese Mind," CR, XLIX, 371 (1918); "Can Christianity Be the Basis of Social Reconstruction in China?", CR, LIII, 313 (1922); "Wo ti tsung-chiao ching-yen" (My religious experience), *Sheng-ming*, 4.3: 5-16; "Tsung-chiao yü ching-pien" (Religion and circumstantial changes), *Ch'ing-nien chin-pu*, 30 : 30ff; *Chi-tu-chiao che-hsueh* (Christian philosophy) (Shanghai, 1926); "Feng-ch'ao chung fen-ch'i ti Chung-kuo chiao-hui" (The rise of the Chinese church in the midst of difficulties), in Chang, TCSC, pp. 460-464.

72. C.G. Sparham, "The Church of Christ in China," CMYB, 1925, pp. 124-125; Wallace C. Merwin, *Adventure in Unity. The Church of Christ in China* (Grand Rapids, MI, 1974), pp. 33-34.

73. *The National Christian Council of China, A Five Years' Review,* (Shanghai, 1927), pp. 2-3. Something of the divergence of views can be perceived in the 1924 CMYB where the Western authors reassure readers that the National Christian Council is not a "director of church activities" and does not inaugurate policies; it is a "servant" of the church and has only advisory powers. See Henry T. Hodgkin, "The Forward Program of the National Christian Council," pp. 147-153 and L.J. Birney, "The National Christian Council and the Church in China," pp. 154-157.

74. For detailed discussion, see Valentin H. Rabe, *The Home Base of American China Missions, 1880-1920* (Cambridge, MA, 1978).

75. Fan Wan-hui, "Chung-hua Chi-tu-chiao ch'ing-nien hui chin-jih ti shih-ming" (Charge to the YMCA today), *Ch'ing-nien chin-pu*, no. 55 (July, 1922).

76. Garrett, *Social Reformers*, pp. 168-172; Yü Jih-chang, "Present Tendencies in the Chinese YMCA," CMYB, 1924, pp. 161-162; Jean Chesneaux, *The Chinese Labor Movement, 1919-1927* (Stanford, 1968), pp. 204-206.

77. Tso, *Labor Movement in China*, p. 203.

78. Quoted in Hans-Ruedi Weber, *Asia and the Ecumenical Movement, 1895-1961* (London, 1966), p. 108.

79. Lynda Shaffer, *Mao and the Workers. The Hunan Labor Movement, 1920-1923* (Armonk, NY, 1982), p. 59. See also pp. 57-61, 69-70, 86-88 and Li Jui, *The Early Revolutionary Activities of Comrade Mao Tse-tung,* trans. A.W. Sarite (White Plains, NY, 1977 reprint), pp. 186-187, 202-203. Also, Kuo Ping-wen, "A Chinese Statement of the Chinese Case," *Asia,* XXV, 1037 (Dec., 1925).

80. Stanley High, "China Astir against the Foreigner," *Asia,* XXV, 707 (Aug., 1925).

81. Hanson, "Political Aspects of Chinese Catholicism", in Whitehead, ed., *China and Christianity,* pp. 142-143; Sovik, pp. 141-143. An apostolic delegate was eventually appointed in 1922.

82. Lo Ch'uan-fang, "The Future of Christianity in China," *China Critic,* IV, 29-30 (Jan. 8, 1931); Earle H. Ballou, "The Present Situation in Evangelistic Work," CMYB, 1923, p. 134; O. R. Magill, "Student Evangelism," *ibid.,* 1925, p. 198. According to one report, however, the number of those following through on pledges and joining the church increased.

83. For further detail, see Philip West, "Christianity and Nationalism; The Career of Wu Lei-ch'uan at Yenching University," in Fairbank, *Missionary Enterprise,* pp. 226-246. Also, P'eng Ch'in-chang, "Tui yü ch'a-hui ti chiao-hui kai-chien wei tzu-li hui ti i-chien" (Comments on the reconstruction of the mission church as an independent church) and Chang Ch'in-shih, "Pei-ching chiao-hui tang tso shen-ma?" (What should the Peking church do?), *Chen-li,* no. 7, 8, 9 (May, 1923). Circulation of *Chen-li* was less than 1,000.

84. The biography of Chien Yu-wen (Jen Yu-wen) on the book jacket of his *The Taiping Revolutionaru Movement* (New Haven, 1973) states: "When nationalist sympathies cut short his appointment as associate professor at Yenching University (1924-1927), he joined Feng Yü-hsiang's army as a political commissioner and from 1933 to 1946 sat as a member of the Legislative Yuan."

85. Varg, *Missionaries, Chinese,* pp. 157, 163.

86. J.V. MacMurray to R. Leslie Craigie, British Embassy, May 20, 1922 (U.S. Dept. of State Archives, Decimal File, China 893.00/4).

87. Nathaniel Peffer, "The Uniqueness of Missionaries," *Asia,* XXIV, 353 (May, 1924).

Chapter IV

1, "Kuang-chou 'Sheng-san-i' hsueh-sheng hsuan-yen" (Canton "Holy Trinity" student manifesto), *Hsiang-tao,* April 23, 1924; "Kuang-chou Sheng-san-i hsueh-hsiao hsueh-sheng fan-k'ang nu-li chiao-yü chih hsuan-yen chi ch'i-ta t'uan-ti chih yuan chu sheng" (Manifesto against slavish education by Holy Trinity College students and statements of support by other groups), CYTC, XVI (June, 1924).

2. L. Ducathay, "La Vie tenace d'une Université en Chine," *Revue d'histoire des Missions* VI, 65-66 (March, 1929); Corbett, *Lingnan,* p. 41; Ting Chih-p'in, *Chung-kuo chin ch'i-shih-nien lai chiao-yü chi-shih* (Shanghai, 1935), p. 17. Initially the secessionist institution from Chen-tan was called Fu-tan hsueh-yuan (Fu-tan Academy).

3. Eddy L. Ford, *The History of the Educational Work of the Methodist Episcopal Church in China* (Foochow, 1938), p.162.

4. "The China Field," CR, LIV, 695-696 (Nov., 1923).

5. Liu Chan-en, "Chinese Students and Religion Today," CMYB, 1925, pp. 44-45. Liu later became president of the (Baptist) University of Shanghai.

6. Ku Hung-ting, "The Emergence of the Kuomintang's Anti-Imperialism," *Journal of Oriental Studies,* XIV, 87-89 (1978).

7. Geoff Eley, "Nationalism and Social History," *Social History,* 6: 100-103 (Jan., 1981).

8. Huntington, *Political Order,* pp. 8, 12, 144-145.

9. See the discussion of P. Cavendish, "Anti-Imperialism in the Kuomintang, 1923-28," in *Studies in the Social History of China and Southeast Asia,* ed. by Jerome Ch'en and Nicholas Tarling (Cambridge ,1970), pp. 23-56.

10. Ts'ai Ho-sen. "Chin-tai ti Chi-tui-chiao" (Modern Christianity), reprinted in *Fan tui Chi-tu-chiao yun-tung* (Shanghai, 1924). I do not know where the essay was originally published but internal evidence indicates that it came out in 1922.

11. Stuart Schram, *Mao Tse-tung* (Baltimore, 1967), p. 73. Mao, in his efforts to obtain publicity outlets, nevertheless took over editorship of Yali's *Hsin Hunan* when the Yale-in-China Student Union was having difficulty in obtaining copy. Mao immediately set forth new goals for the periodical and it was banned by provincial

officials after only three issues. Jerome Ch'en, *Mao and the Chinese Revolution* (London, 1965), p. 64.

12. Chen Yü (pseud.?), "I-hou i-ch'ieh tui Hua ch'in-lueh chieh chiang i chiao-yü ti hsing-shih ch'u chih" (All future encroachments against China will be in the form of education), *Hsiang-tao, no. 22* (April 25, 1923).

13., Harley F. MacNair, *China in Revolution,* 1968 ed. (NY, c. 1931), p. 72. In September, 1923 Leo Karakhan, the newly appointed Soviet ambassador to China, was feted by numerous groups in Peking, including Peita professors and the Student Union. At a Peita banquet, the acting chancellor, Chiang Meng-lin, stressed the common goals of China and the U.S.S.R.: revolution and the overthrow of imperialism. Editorials commemorating the anniversary of the Russian revolution reiterated this theme, see *Chueh-wu,* Nov. 9 and 11, 1923.

14. "Manifesto of the First Congress of Toilers of the Far East," in Xenia J. Eudin and Robert C. North, *Soviet Russia and the East, 1920-1927* (Stanford,1957), pp. 230-231.

15. Shaffer, *Mao and the Workers,* p. 54.

16. Ch'en Yü, "Pei-ching chiao-hui hsueh-sheng ti tan-tu tui Jih shih-wei yun-tung" (Demonstration of Peking parochial students only against Japan), *Hsiang-tao,* no. 21 (April 18, 1923).

17. "Shou-hui kuan-yü yü lieh-ch'iang p'ai chien chin p'o Kuang-chou shih-wei" (Recovery of customs surplus and the Powers' sending of warships to oppress the Canton demonstration), *Hsin hsueh-sheng,* no. 11 (Dec. 16, 1923); "Kuang-tung jen-min fan k'ang ti-kuo-chu-i chih piao-shih" (Declaration of the Kwangtung peoples' opposition to imperialism), *Hsiang-tao,* no. 51 (Jan. 9, 1924). In protesting the Lin Cheng affair, the Peking Student Union and the Executive Committee of the CCP also appealed to workers and oppressed peoples throughout the world to support the fight against imperialism, source of all China's troubles. See Wieger, IV, 289-292.

18. Man Han (?), "'Wu ch'i' kuo chih chi-nien yü ch'ing-nien hsueh-sheng" ("May Seventh" national humiliation commemoration and young students), *Chiao-yü chou-pao,* no. 9 (May 15, 1924). The author states that the capitalists and militarists are the enemies, while the Chinese people and proletarians of all countries are allies. The students must "direct all the people of China in the struggle to save the nation."

19. Chang Kuo-t'ao, *Rise of CCP*, I, 216-217.

20. *Ibid.*, p. 218.

21. Ch'en Tu-hsiu, "Chiao-yü chieh neng pu wen cheng-chih ma?" (Can the educational world be unconcerned with politics?), *Hsiang-tao*, no. 18 (Jan. 31, 1923). Ch'en made frequent appeals to students, youth, and scholars to participate actively in the revolution. In "Shou-hui chiao-yü ch'üan" (Restore educational rights), *ibid.*, no. 74 (July 16, 1924), he stated that ousting foreigners from the educational system was essential to the national revolution and he urged awakened youth to accept the responsibility if the government and educators did not.

22. This is a major theme in Lee Feigon, *Chen Duxiu, Founder of the Chinese Communist Party* (Princeton, 1983); see esp. pp. 21-22, 77, 165, 232-234.

23. For trans. of CCP manifesto, see Conrad Brandt, B. Schwartz, and J.K. Fairbank, *A Documentary History of Chinese Communism* (London, 1952), pp. 71-72. For KMT declaration, see Li Chien-nung, *The Political History of China, 1840-1928*, trans. and ed. by Ssu-yu Teng and Jeremy Ingalls (Stanford, 1956), p. 453. For Changsha Anti-Christian Manifesto, see Robert E. Speer and Hugh T. Kerr, *Report on Japan and China of the Deputation sent by the Board of Foreign Missions of the Presbyterian Church, 1926* (NY, 1927), p. 135.

24. John M. Roots, "The Moscow End of Chino-Soviet Affairs," *Asia*, XXVII, 472 (June, 1927).

25. C. Martin Wilbur and Julie Lien-ying How, *Documents on Communism, Nationalism and Soviet Advisers in China, 1918-1927* (NY, 1956), pp. 105, 108.

26. Ho Ping-i, "Ti-kuo-chu-i jou-lin Shang-hai ta-hsueh ti chui-chi" (Reflections on imperialism's trampling on Shanghai University), *Hsiang-tao*, no. 96 (Dec. 24, 1924); Ting Lee-hsia Hsu, *Government Control of the Press in Modern China, 1900-1949* (Cambridge, MA, 1974), pp. 71-72; Pickowicz, *Marxist Literary Thought*, pp. 62-63. The KMT official Yü Yu-jen was nominal head of Shanghai University. In addition to the staff members listed in the text, youth leaders and party personnel associated with Shanghai University included: Ch'ü Ch'iu-pai, Hsiang Ching-yü, Chang T'ai-lei, Li Ta, Jen Pi-shih, Teng Chung-hsia, Yeh Ch'u-ts'ang, and probably Shao Li-tzu. Ting Ling and Wang Chien-hung, who studied at Shanghai University in 1923-24, were deeply influenced by the radical environment of the school. Information on Shanghai Uni-

versity has been drawn from a variety of sources, but particularly from biographies in Boorman. Ho says that some of the items seized in the Dec., 1924 raid were not revolutionary; he cites *Introduction to Social Science, Hsin ch'ing-nien,* and lectures by Sun Yat-sen. The university administrators were charged with publishing *Hsiang-tao,* according to Ho. According to another source, the publication of *Hsiang-tao,* had already been transferred to Hangchow because of a raid in Dec., 1924.

27. Chow Tse-tsung, *Research Guide,* p. 94. Under *Fu-nü sheng* (Women's Voice), Chow states: "No. 6 (Mar. 5, 1922) is a special issue for the introduction of *Shang-hai p'ing-min nü hsiao* (Shanghai Girls' School for the Plain People), which was founded ostensibly for women educators but in fact by the Chinese Communist Party for recruiting and training women cadres. Ch'en Tu-hsiu and other contributors were teaching at the school." Ting Ling was one of the early students at the school.

28. Allen Whiting says that a report (probably by Maring, i.e., H.Sneevliet) to the Comintern, August, 1922 advised that the CCP concentrate activities in Canton. "As for Peking, it was written off as a hopeless area, lacking the nucleus of a workers' movement, surrounded by backward peasants, and permeated with inactive intellectual Socialists." Whiting, *Soviet Politics in China, 1917-1924* (NY, 1954), p. 89. Some organizational and propaganda work was undertaken by the CCP and the left KMT in Peking but it had to be mostly underground because of warlord power at the capital.

29. Ch'en Tu-hsiu, "Chiao-yü chieh neng pu wen cheng-chih ma?", *Hsiang-tao,* no. 18 (Jan. 31, 1923); "Wai-chiao wen-t'i yü hsueh-sheng yun-tung," *ibid.,* no. 23 (May 2, 1923); "Yang-jen shih-li hsia chih I-chang hsueh-sheng yü Shang-hai hsueh-sheng" (Foreigners' influence over I-chang and Shanghai students), *ibid.,* no. 26 (May 23, 1923).

30. "Ch'ing-nien-men ying-kai tsen-yang tso" (What ought we youth to do?), *Chung-kuo ch'ing-nien,* Oct. 20, 1923; Yun Tai-ying, "Chi-tu-chiao yü jen-ko chiu-kuo" (Christianity and saving the country by personality), *ibid.,* Nov. 3, 1923; "Ch'ing-nien ti hsin tao-te" (The new morality of youth), *ibid.,* Dec. 1, 1923; "Wei shen-ma tang chiao-yü?" (Why undertake education?), *ibid.,* Dec. 8, 1923.

31. Wieger, IV, 277-279.

32. Cheng An (?), "Tui yü ch'ing-t'an fu-hsing ti ching-kao" (Warning against mere talk of revival), *Chueh-wu,* Feb. 26, 1924; "Hsien-tai hsueh-sheng ying yu ti ching-shen" (The spirit that

present students ought to have), *ibid.*, March 12, 1924; Shao Li-tzu, "Hsueh-sheng chia-ju Kuo-min-tang wen-t'i" (The question of students' entering the KMT), *ibid.*, March 22, 1924.

33. Chen Yü, "I-hou i-ch'ieh tui Hua ch'in-lueh chieh chiang i chiao-yü ti hsing-shih ch'u chih", *Hsiang-tao,* April 25, 1923; Mao Tse-tung, "Ying-kuo jen yü Liang Ju-hao" (The English and Liang Ju-hao), *ibid.*, Aug. 23, 1923; Hung T'ao (Pseud.?), "Wai-chiao yun-tung yü chiao-hui hsueh-sheng" (The foreign relations movement and parochial students), *Hsin hsueh-sheng,* July 1, 1923; Chung Wan-hua, "Chiao-hui hsueh-hsiao ti hsin-chiao tzu-yu" (The religious freedom of parochial schools), *ibid.*, Aug. 16, 1923.

34. Wilbur and How, *Documents on Communism,* pp. 67-68. "Fan ti-kuo-chu-i yü fei ch'u pu-p'ing teng t'iao-yüeh chin yun-tung (The movement against imperialism and against the unequal treaties), *Tung-fang tsa-chih,* XXI, 127-141 (Aug., 1924).

35. "Ch'üan-kuo hsueh-sheng tsung-hui chih hsuan-ch'uan chi-hua" (Propaganda plans of the National Student Union), *Chung-kuo Kuo-min-tang chou-k'an,* no. 13 (March 23, 1924).

36. Ch'en Tu-hsiu, "Tu-er-chi fang-chu chiao-chu" (Turkey ousts religious leaders), *Hsiang-tao,* no. 56 (Feb. 27, 1924). See Wieger, V, *Nationalisme, Xenophobie, Antichristianisme,* pp. 129-130 for the Moscow communique.

37. Pao Tsun-p'eng, *Chung-kuo chin-tai ch'ing-nien yun-tung shih* (Taipei, 1953) devotes only a brief section to the Movement to Restore Educational Rights. After mentioning several parochial school strikes in the post May Thirtieth period, he concludes that these were the manifestations of the growth of nationalism; see pp. 60-61.

38. Chow, *May Fourth,* pp. 218-226, 250-251.

39. In accord with the viewpoint of liberal educators, the Ministry of Education had in 1917 ordered students, teachers, and officers not to enlist in political parties or engage in political activities. Cyrus H. Peake, *Nationalism and Education in Modern China* (NY, 1932), p. 79. This discussion of the role of education has drawn on my essay, "Students and Politics, Revolution and Historical Continuity" in *Tradition and Modernity, The Role of Traditionalism in the Modernization Process,* ed. by Jessie G. Lutz and Salah El Shakhs (Washington, DC, 1982), pp. 191-217.

40. Chiao-yü tu-li yun-tung was founded in 1922 to advocate that educational funds be made independent of warlord budgets and military allocations. Chung-hua chih-yeh chiao-yü she, established

in 1917, published two magazines *Chiao-yü yü chih-yeh* (Education and Vocation), beginning in 1918, and *Sheng-huo chou-k'an* (Life Weekly), beginning in 1925. It also sponsored numerous vocational schools and set up a bureau to publish vocational guidance programs, textbooks, and curriculum outlines for vocational schools. In 1922 Hsin chiao-yü kung-chin she expanded and adopted the name Chung-hua chiao-yü kai-chin she (National Association for the Advancement of Education). For further detail, see Barry C. Keenan, "Educational Reform and Politics in Early Republican China," *Journal of Asian Studies*, XXXIII, 227-237 (Feb., 1974); Margo S. Gewurtz, "Social Reality and Educational Reform. The Case of the Chinese Vocational Education Association, 1917-1927," *Modern China*, IV, 157-180 (April, 1978); Andrew J. Nathan, *Peking Politics, 1918-1923* (Berkeley, 1976), pp. 12-15.

41. In 1927 the Nationalist Youth Corps adopted the name Chung-kuo ch'ing-nien tang and formally emerged as a political party. They are sometimes called the Chauvinists or the China Youth Party. Because they consciously used Young Italy and Young Turkey as models, I have preferred Young China Party in translating their name and shall refer to them by this name from 1924 on. They should be distinguished from Chung-kuo ch'ing-nien she (China Youth Society), a communist organization. For more information, see *Chung-kuo ch'ing-nien tang shih tzu-liao* (Taipei, 1955).

42. Li Huang, "My Memoirs," trans. Lillian Chu Chin, (Unpub. ms. in Special Collections, Columbia University, 1971), I, 225. Li stated: "Tseng Ch'i was determined to instill the principles of nationalism and democracy in the minds of the young intelligentsia. Therefore he was anxious that when I returned home, I should strive hard and teach for three years in the famous universities so that I could gain the trust of the best university students and introduce them to the concepts of nationalism and democracy at Wuchang University." Li also reveals that he provided students in his class with copies of *Hsing-shih* and then gave guidance to those interested in organizing branches to oppose the leftists (pp. 234-235).

43. Tso Shun-sheng, "Fa-kuo ch'e-ti ti p'ai-ch'ih tsung-chiao chiao-yü" (France's complete exclusion of religious education), *Hsing-shih*, no. 5 (Nov., 1924); "Chung-kuo chiao-jü ti chih ming-shang yü chi chiu fa" (The fatal injury to Chinese education and methods of first aid), *ibid*, no. 10 (Dec., 1924). Also, Yü Chia-chü, "Chiao-yü chien kuo" (Education to build the nation), *ibid.*, no. 13 (Feb., 1925). The following issues contain

typical discussions of nationalistic education and criticisms of parochial education: Aug. 22, Dec. 25, 1926; Sept. 24, Oct. 1, Oct. 16, 1927. Li Huang seems to indicate that *Hsing-shih* printed 1,000 copies per issue, "My Memoirs," I, 237.

44. Ch'en Ch'i-t'ien, "Wo-men pu kai fan tui Yeh-chiao yü chi yun-tung ma?", *Shao-nien,* 3.9; Ch'en, "Kuo-chia-chu-i yü chiao-yü" (Nationalism and education), *Hsin chiao-yü,* 8.1 (Feb., 1924).

45. Tso Shun-sheng, "Lun lieh-ch'iang tui Hua ti chiao-yü ch'in-lüeh" (On the Powers' educational aggression against China), *Chueh-wu,* April 24, 1924, in Wieger, V, 129-130.

46. Yü Chia-chü and Li Huang published *Kuo-chia-chu-i chiao-yü* in October, 1923 and later, in October, 1925, Hsing-shih she published *Kuo-chia-chu-i chiang yen-chi* with contributions by Li Huang, Yü Chia-chü, Ch'en Chi-t'ien, and Tseng Ch'i.

47. Paul Monroe, "Chiao-hui chiao-yü yü kuo-chia cheng-ti," *Hsin chiao-yü,* 4.5 (May, 1922), originally published as "Mission education and national policy," *International Review of Missions,* X, 321-350 (1921). For Ch'en's reactions, see "Kuo-chia-chu-i yü chiao-yü," *Hsin chiao-yü,* 8.1.

48. Shu Hsin-ch'eng, *Shou-hui chiao-yü ch'üan yun-tung* (Shanghai, 1927), p. 57; Yang Hsiao-ch'un, "Chi-tu-chiao chih hsuan-ch'uan yü shou-hui chiao-yü ch'üan yun-tung"(Christian propaganda and the Movement to Restore Educational Rights), CHCYC, XIV (Feb., 1925).

49. Ch'iang Shu-ko, pp. 157-159.

50. Chao Kuan-ch'ing, "Feng-t'ien chiao-yü ch'üan wen-t'i" (Fengtien educational rights question), *Cheng-chih chou-pao,* no. 11 (May 30, 1924); "Tung san sheng shou-hui chiao-yü ch'üan chih wen-t'i" (The question of restoring educational rights in the three eastern provinces), *Min-kuo jih-pao,* April 17, 1924; "Chiao-yü chieh hsiao-hsi" (News of the educational world), CYTC, 16.6 (June, 1924); Ch'en Tu-hsiu, "T'ou-hsiang t'iao-chien hsia chih Chung-kuo chiao-yü ch'üan" (Chinese educational rights under the terms of surrender), *Hsiang-tao,* no. 63 (April 30, 1924).

51. Shu Hsin-ch'eng, *Shou-hui chiao-yü,* pp. 45-47; Ch'en Tu-hsiu, "Huan-ying *Fengtien tung pao* fu k'an" (Welcome *Feng-tien Eastern Press's* return to publication), *Hsiang-tao,* no. 64 (May 7, 1924); Ch'en I-lin, *Tsui-chin san-shih-nien Chung-kuo chiao-yü shih* (Shanghai, 1930), pp. 346-356.

52. "Chi-lin Chang-chun wai-kuo hsueh-hsiao tiao-ch'a" (An investigation of foreign schools in Changchun, Chilin), CHCYC,

XV, (Aug., 1925); "Wai-kuo chiao-yü ti ya-p'o" (Oppression of foreign education), *ibid*.

53. Ch'en Tu-hsiu, "Yang-jen shih-li hsia chih I-chang hsueh-sheng yü Shang-hai hsueh-sheng," *Hsiang-tao*, no. 25; see also, Yü Chia-chu "Chiao-hui chiao-yü wen-t'i," CHCYC, Oct., 1923; Hung T'ao, "Wai-chiao yun-tung yü chiao-hui hsueh-sheng" *Hsin hsueh-sheng*, July 1, 1923; Mao Tse-tung, "Ying-kuo jen yü Liang Ju-hao," *Hsiang-tao*, Aug. 23, 1923.

54. Yun Tai-ying, "Chi-tu-chiao yü jen-ko chiu-kuo," *Chung-kuo ch'ing-nien*, Nov. 3, 1923.

55. For further detail, see Lutz, *China and the Christian Colleges*, esp. pp. 42-79, 205-207.

56. It should be pointed out, however, that the influence of the Christian educators and mission schools was in some ways greater than has been generally acknowledged. This is particularly true in certain specific areas, for example, the provision of textbooks, which were often reprinted by Chinese, the founding of the Chinese Medical Association, the development of research and higher education in such fields as agriculture, medicine, archaeology, journalism, music. physical education, etc.

57. Peng Ta-mu (P'eng Ta-mou), "A Chinese Student Looks at the World," *Asia*, XXVIII, 246 (March, 1928).

58. Ch'iang Shu-ko, p. 157; F.L. Hawks Pott, "Education," in China Centenary Missionary Conference, *Records* (Shanghai, 1907), pp. 74-76; A.S. Mann, "The Government and the Schools," CR, XXXIII, 104-105 (Feb., 1907).

59. K'ung Fu-cho (Fong F. Sec), "The Cooperation of Chinese and Foreign Educationalists in the Work of the Association" and "Appeal of Chinese Educationalists to the Educational Association" in (Christian) Educational Association of China, *Triennial Report*, 1909, pp. 60, 69-70; Clarence B. Day, *Hangchow University*, (NY, 1955), pp. 62-63; S.K. Tsao, "How to secure Chinese cooperation in educational work," *Educational Review*, VIII, 121-123 (April, 1916); Pott "Problems of Educational Work in China," CMYB, 1911, pp. 141-143.

60. Between 1900 and 1923, Roman Catholic societies had founded two institutions of higher education and in 1925 would add a third. Protestant societies had added almost a dozen institutions during this period.

61. *Christian Education in China, A Study Made by an Educational Commission Representing the Mission Boards and Societies Conducting Work in China* (NY, 1922). The recommendations are summarized on pp. 37-38, 45, 361-375.

62. Wu Lei-ch'uan, "Tui yü chiao-hui chung hsueh-hsiao kai-liang ti wo chien" (My opinion on the reform of parochial middle schools), *Chen-li,* 1.15 (July 8, 1923); Wu Yao-tsung, "Chung-kuo ti Chi-tu-chiao hsueh-sheng ying-tang tso shen-ma?", *ibid.,* 1.10 (June 3, 1923). Extracts from these two essays are in Wieger, IV, 145-151.

63. Ernest D. Burton, "Chi-tu-chiao hsueh-sheng tsai Chung-kuo chiao-yü hsi-t'ung chung so chan ti-li" (The place which Christian schools should take in the Chinese educational system), *Hsin chiao-yü,* 4.3 (March, 1922); "Chi-tu-chiao chiao-yü chih p'u-t'ung yuan-tse" (The general principles of Christian education), *ibid.,* 5.1 and 2 (Aug., 1922).

64. Yü Chia-chü, "Chiao-hui chiao-yü wen-t'i," CHCYC, XIII. In his chapter on the Educational Rights Movement, Chen I-lin quotes extensively from *Christian Education in China* to demonstrate the need for such a movement; he also reproduces charts showing the growth of mission schools and parochial students, see pp. 347-352, 357-360.

65. Chou T'ai-hsuan, "Fei tsung-chiao chiao-yü yü chiao-hui chiao-yü" (Against religious education and parochial education), CHCYC, XIV; Chou, "Wo kuo chiao-yü chih chi-chung t'ung-i yü tu-li" (The unification and independence of our national educational system), CYTC, XV (Dec., 1923).

66. I have been able to identify only a portion of those who published during the weeks following the Holy Trinity incident. Many did not attain the prominence to be listed in biographical dictionaries; some used pseudonyms or only given names, which I have failed to track down; a few of the latter indicated that they were parochial students.

67. K'o Po-nien (Li Ch'un-fan), "Chiao-hui ta-hsueh yü kuo-wen" (The Christian university and Chinese), *Chueh-wu,* May 17, 1924; K'o's speech at the meeting marking the revival of the Anti-Christian Federation, August, 1924, was reprinted in a widely circulated pamphlet. See "Ch'uan-chiao yü ti-kuo-chi-i" (Evangelism and imperialism) in *Fan tui Chi-tu-chiao yun-tung* (Shanghai, 1924). The pamphlet, in a somewhat abbreviated and toned-down English translation, was made available to Christians by the YMCA and YWCA. Nationalists frequently cited the widespread use of English in

Christian higher schools as proof of their denationalizing influence; it should be noted, however, that at Kwangtung University and numerous other government institutions, science courses, mathematics, and certain other subjects were taught largely or wholly in English. English language textbooks in these subjects were also common.

68. Shao Li-tzu, "Lun shou-huan chiao-yü ch'üan" (Comment on restoring educational rights), *Chueh-wu,* July 19, 1924.

69. Yang Yu-chiung, "Ch'üan kuo ch'ing-nien tang lien-ho tso shou-hui chiao-yü ch'üan ti ta yun-tung" (Youth of the whole nation ought to join in working for the great movement to restore educational rights), *Chueh-wu,* May 31, 1924.

70. Wieger, V, pp. 138, 142 for quotations from students.

71. Chu Wu-p'ing, "Hsu-chou chiao-hui hsueh-sheng fen-tou ti ching-kuo" (The struggles experienced by the Hsu-chow parochial students), *Hsiang-tao,* no. 70 (June 18, 1924).

72. Hsiao Ch'u-nü, "Ti-kuo-chu-i ch'in-lüeh Chung-kuo ti shih k'uang" (The real situation in imperialism's encroachment on China), *Chung-kuo ch'ing-nien,* June 14, 1924; High, "China Astir," *Asia,* XXV, 706-707.

73. "'Sheng san-i' hsueh-sheng ti erh-tz'u hsuan-yen" (Second manifesto of "Holy Trinity" students), *Hsiang-tao,* no. 67 (May 28, 1924).

74. "Kuang-chou fan-k'ang wen-hua chin-lueh ch'ing-nien t'uan t'ung-tien" (Circular telegram of the Canton youth corps to resist cultural aggression), *Hsiang-tao,* no. 74 (July 16, 1924).

75. Ch'en Tu-hsiu, "Shou-hui chiao-yü ch'üan," *Hsiang-tao,* no. 74.

76. [Yun] Tai-ying, "I-nien lai ti ch'ing-nien yun-tung" (The youth movement during the past year), *Min-kuo jih-pao,* Jan. 1, 1925, trans. in Wieger, VI, *Le Feu aux poudres,* 1925, pp. 78-81.

77. Shih Ts'un-t'ung replaced Kao on the executive committee when the latter left Shanghai. For the constitution and proclamation of the Anti-Christian Federation, see Chang, TCSC, pp. 376-380. I have been unable to locate copies of *Fei Chi-tu-chiao t'e-k'an,* which differs from *Fan Chi-tu-chiao chou-k'an* and from *Fei Chi-tu-chiao hsun-k'an.* Summaries of numerous articles are, however, available in Wieger, V, 239-243 and *Wu-ssu shih-ch'i ch'i-k'an chieh-shao,* III, 61-76.

Chapter V

1. The proposal to commemorate the signing of the Boxer Protocol apparently originated with several Peking parliamentarians who were members of the Anti-Imperialist Federation. The designation of Anti-Imperialism Week came at a time when Sun Yat-sen was engaged in a sharp dispute with the Canton Merchants' Corps and Great Britain. Signifying the revised attitude toward the Boxers was the Sept. 3, 1924 issue of *Hsiang-tao,* largely devoted to articles on the subject. For Karakhan's letter, see Wieger, VI, 98-99.

2. *Chueh-wu* printed over twenty articles on Christianity, Christian missions, and parochial schools during September 1924 and an equal number during December, 1924. See listing for several magazines in *Chung-hua Chi-tu-chiao hui nien-chien*, 1925, pp. 142-175.

3. *Fan Chi-tu-chiao chou-k'an* apparently put out only eight issues, Feb. 17, 1925 to May 16, 1925.

4. The articles in *Fan tui Chi-tu-chiao yun-tung* are: Yang Hsien-chiang, (Li Hao-wu), "Fan tui Chi-tu-chiao yun-tung"; K'o Po-nien (Li Ch'un-fan), "Ch'uan-chiao yü ti-kuo-chu-i"; Mei Kung-pin (Mei Tien-lung), "Chi-tu-chiao yü Chung-kuo"; Ts'ai Ho-sen, "Chin-tai ti Chi-tu-chiao"; Chu Chih-hsin, "Yeh-su shih shen-ma tung-hsi?".

5. K'o Po-nien (Li Ch'un-fan), "Fei Chi-tu-chiao chou" (Anti-Christian week), *Chueh-wu,* Dec. 9, 1924; "Liao Chung-k'ai hsien-sheng yen-chiang" (Lecture by Mr. Liao Chung-k'ai), Dec. 25, 1924, in Fan CTC, no. 3 (March 4, 1925).

6. Wilbur and How, *Documents,* p. 132.

7. "Chi-tu-chiao yü ti-kuo-chu-i, Chou En-lai hsien-sheng chiang" (Christianity and imperialism, Mr. Chou En-lai discourses), Fan CTC, no. 2 (Feb. 25, 1925).

8. Ts'ai Ho-sen, "Chin-tai ti Chi-tu-chiao," *Fan Chi-tu-chiao yun-tung.*

9. Wu Hsiao-t'ien, "Chi-tu-chiao yü wu-ch'an chieh-chi" (Christianity and the proletarian class), *Chueh-wu,* Nov. 25, 1924; [Shao] Chi-ang, "Kuan-liao tzu-pen-chia yü Chi-tu-chiao" (Bureaucrats, capitalists and Christianity), *ibid.,* Dec. 9,1924; [Ch'en] Chih-wen, "Chi-tu-chiao yü hsueh-sheng yun-tung" (Christianity and the student movement), Fan CTC, No. 1 (Feb. 17, 1925).

10. "Fan tui Chi-tu-chiao ch'uan-tan" (Anti-Christian handbill),

issued by Canton Great Anti-Christian Federation, Dec. 25, 1924, in Fan CTC, no. 3; "Down with the Foreigner," *Peking Tientsin Times,* n.d. (Clipping in Correspondence of President Edward E. Hume, 1925, Yali archives). The clipping quotes from a Changsha placard, Dec. 25, 1924. The placard concludes: "So on this date we form an Anti-Christian Festival, on the date they call Holy Birth Day Festival [sic] and we unite ourselves to form this new Union. We are already sixteen thousand, eight hundred and seventy-five names...."

11. Ch'in Chien, "Kou-hua ti chiao-yü," Fan CTC, no. 3.

12. "Manifesto of the Shantung Anti-Christian branch," Dec. 25, 1924, in Wieger, VI, 148.

13. Shou Shih (?), "Fei Chi-tu-chiao t'ung-chih tui yü Yeh-su sheng-tan chieh ying-kai pao tse-yang ti t'ai-tu" (The attitude that anti-Christian comrades should take toward Jesus' birthday festival), *Chueh-wu,* Dec. 17, 1924.

14. Ju Fang (?), "Chiao-hui ta-hsueh chien-tan chih hsieh-chen" (A simple portrait of a Christian university), *Chueh-wu,* Dec. 9, 1924.

15. "Liao Chung-k'ai hsien-sheng yen-chiang," Fan CTC, no. 3; "Chou Fo-hai chiao-shou chiang-yen" (Professor Chou Fo-hai lectures), *ibid.,* no. 5 (March 28, 1925); American Foreign Service Report no. 6, Jan. 7, 1925; Douglas Jenkins, American Consul General, to U.S. Dept. of State, Jan. 7, 1925 (Dept. of State Archives, Decimal File, China, 393.116/343).

16. See report on Dec. 22, 1924 meeting of Anti-Christian Federation Executive Committee at Fu Tan Middle School, *Chueh-wu,* Dec. 25, 1924.

17. Corbett, *Lingnan,* pp. 82-83; Wieger, VI, 163-164. For a discussion of Sun Yat-sen's attitude toward and intellectual debt to Christianity, see Donald W. Treadgold, *The West in Russia and China,* vol. 2, *China 1582-1949* (Cambridge, 1973), pp. 79-98.

18. Wieger VI, 164-166, 170-174; Hsin (?), "Sun Chung-shan hsien-sheng yü Chi-tu-chiao" (Sun Yat-sen and Christianity), Fan CTC, no. 6 (April 4, 1925); Ping Yung (?), "Chi-tu-chiao t'u k'ai-hui chui tao Chung-shan hsien-sheng ti i-i" (The significance of the Christian's memorial service for Sun Yat-sen), *ibid.*

19. Yip, *Nationalism,* pp. 64-66.

20. Corbett, *Lingnan,* pp. 86-87; quotation from "West China Missionary News", Aug.-Sept., 1925, in "Information about China", no. 13 (Yali archives).

21. K'o Po-nien (Ch'un-fan), "Fei Chi-tu-chiao chou," *Chueh-wu*, Dec. 9, 1924; Chung-kuo ch'ing-nien she, "Fan tui Chi-tu-chiao yun-tung," *ibid.*, Dec. 11, 1924; Shou Shih, "Fei Chi-tu-chiao t'ung-chih tui yü Yeh-su sheng-tan chieh ying-kai pao tse-yang," *ibid.*, Dec. 17, 1924; Wieger, VI, 143-145. In the Dec. 9, 1924 edition of *Chueh-wu*, K'o requested that contributions for a special Dec. 25 edition be sent to him at Shanghai University.

22. J. Schurman to U.S. Secretary of State, telegram of Jan. 12, 1925 (Dept. of State Archives, Decimal File, China 893.00/5945); Wieger, VI, 147-148. Indicative of the prestige of the student elite and of the sympathy of the educational establishment is the fact that some of the rallies were held in the facilities of the provincial director of education.

23. J. Schurman to U.S. Secretary of State, telegram of Jan. 12, 1925; Hsin (?), "Hsing-shih p'ai yü Chi-tu-chiao" (Awakening Lion branch and Christianity), Fan CTC, no. 8 (May 16, 1925).

24. Hsin (?), "Kuo-nei tsui-chin chih chiao-hui hsueh-hsiao feng-ch'ao" (The most recent parochial school storms in the country), Fan CTC, no. 3.

25. "Chiao-hui chiao-yü chih fan-k'ang yun-tung (The movement opposing parochial education), CYTC, XVII (Jan., 1925); "K'ai-feng chi-pien chung hsueh ti san-tz'u chieh-san feng-ch'ao" (Kaifeng Chi-pien middle school, the third shut-down storm), *Chueh-wu*, Dec. 3, 1924. External influence was not absent, however. Kaifeng had been the locale of the annual meeting of the National Federation of Educational Associations in October, 1924. Amid considerable publicity, it had passed resolutions demanding enforcement of registration requirements and banning of religious instruction in schools. KMT and CCP cadres had been working in Szechwan to organize youth groups and labor unions.

26. Mao Tse-tung, "Ying-kuo jen yü Liang Ju-hao," *Hsiang-tao*, Aug. 23, 1923. For further information about the Hunan radicals and their organizations, see biographies in Boorman and Angus W. McDonald, *The Urban Origins of Rural Revolution* (Berkeley, 1978).

27. Edward H. Hume correspondence, Dec. 13, 1924 (Yali archives).

28. Storms occurred at Ya-ko (St. James) Middle School, Changsha; Cheng Chih School, Changsha; Hsin I Middle School, I-yang; I Chih (Wells) Middle School, Hsiang-t'an; and Tsun Tao (Albright) Middle School, Li-ling. The description of the Yali storm is derived from the following sources: Correspondence of President Edward H. Hume to Palmer Bevis, Dec. 13, 14, 17, 19, 23, 1924; Jan.

13, 1925 (Yali archives); "Tsai chih chaio-hui chiao-yü chih fan-k'ang yun-tung" (More about the movement against parochial education), CYTC, XVII (March, 1925); "Hu-nan hsueh-sheng fan-k'ang chiao-hui chiao-yü chih sheng-li" (The victory of Hunan students against parochial education), *ibid.*; "Kuo nei tsui-chin chih chiao-hui hsueh-hsiao feng-ch'ao," Fan CTC, no. 3; "Hu-nan fei Chi-tu-chiao yun-tung" (The Hunan Anti-Christian Movement), *Chueh-wu*, Dec. 25, 1924; "Chang-sha Ya-li hsueh-sheng fan-k'ang nu-li chiao-yü" (Changsha Yali students resist slavish education), *ibid.*, Dec. 24, 1924; Sanford, "China's Mission Students," pp. 11-14.

29. "Down with the foreigner." *Peking-Tientsin Times*, Dec. 25, 1924 (Clipping in Hume correspondence).

30. [Cheng] Ch'ao-lin, "Tui ti-kuo-chu-i wen-hua ch'in-lueh chih yu-i kang-i--Yali pu-k'o shih chien" (Another protest against imperialist cultural invasion--the strike at Yali), *Hsiang-tao*, no. 96 (Dec., 1924); Wieger, VI, 135.

31. "Changsha Yali hsueh-sheng fan-k'ang nu-li chiao-yü", *Chueh-wu*, Dec. 27, 1924.

32. Correspondence of Edward H. Hume, Dec. 23, 1924. President John Gowdy of Fukien Christian University drew somewhat similar conclusions after strikes at his school: Gowdy, "Report to Board of Managers, 1925-26," (Am. Bd. of Commissioners, Fukien Christian University, Docs. and Letters, Houghton Library, Harvard).

33. "Hu-nan hsueh-sheng fan-k'ang chiao-hui chiao-yü chih sheng-li," CYTC, XVII.

34. [Yun] Tai-ying, "I-nien lai ti ch'ing-nien yun-tung," *Min-kuo jih-pao*, Jan. 1, 1925; "Shou-hui chiao-yü ch'üan yun-tung chih chin-hsing" (Progress of the Movement to Restore Educational Rights), *ibid.*, Feb. 10, 1925.

35. Wei Ch'in, "Ti-kuo-chu-i yü fan Chi-tu-chiao yun-tung" (Imperialism and the Anti-Christian Movement), *Hsiang-tao*, no. 98 (Jan. 7, 1925).

36. At this congress, Feb., 1925, the Socialist Youth Corps changed its name to Communist Youth Corps.

37. "Shou-hui chiao-yü ch'üan yun-tung" (The Movement to Restore Educational Rights), *Shih-shih hsin-pao*, March 28, 1925 (Newspaper clippings, KMT archives).

38. Hsin, "Hsing-shih p'ai yü Chi-tu-chiao," Fan CTC, no. 8.

39. "News of This and That," *The Shaowu Bulletin,* VI, 14 (April, 1925) (Andover Divinity Library); High, "China Astir," *Asia,* XXV, 706.

40. Shu Hsin-ch'eng, *Shou-hui chiao-yü,* p. 50; Li Ju-mien, "Chiao-hui ta-hsueh wen-t'i" (Problem of the Christian Universities), CHCYC, XIV (Feb., 1925).

41. Contributors to the special Educational Rights issue of CHCYC, XIV, were: Ch'en Ch'i-t'ien, "Wo-men chu-chang shou-hui chiao-yü ch'üan ti li-yu yü pan-fa" (The reasons for and methods by which we advocate restoration of educational rights); Chou T'ai-hsuan, "Fei tsung-chiao chiao-yü yü chiao-hui chiao-yü"; Li Huang, "Lun li chiao-yü yü tsung-chiao chiao-yü" (Discussion of ethical education and religious education); Ch'ang Tao-chih, "Tui yü chiao-hui ta-hsueh wen-t'i chih kuan-chien" (Outlook on the problem of the Christian universities); Li Ju-mien, "Chiao-hui ta-hsueh wen-t'i"; Liu I-cheng, "Lun ta hsueh-sheng chih tse-jen" (Discussion of the responsibility of university students); Shu Hsin-ch'eng, "Shou-hui chiao-hui chung hsueh wen-t'i" (Problem of recovering parochial middle schools); Yang Hsiao-ch'un, "Chi-tu-chiao chih hsuan-ch'uan yü shou-hui chiao-yü ch'üan yun-tung"; Yü Chia-chü, "Shou-hui chiao-yü ch'üan wen-t'i ta-pien" (Answers to questions on the restoration of educational rights).

42. This argument is repeated in Ch'iang Shu-ko, p. 157.

43. "Tsai chih chiao-hui chiao-yü fan-k'ang yun-tung," CYTC, XVII.

44. Yü Chia-chü, "Shou-hui chiao-yü ch'üan wen-t'i ta-pien," CHCHC, XIV.

45. Ch'en Ch'i-t'ien, "Wo-men chu-chang shou-hui chiao-yü ch'üan ti li-yu yü pan-fa," CHCHC, XIV.

46. Liu I-cheng, "Lun ta hsueh-sheng chih tse-jen," CHCHC, XIV.

47. Ch'en Ch'i-t'ien, "Kuo-chia-chu-i yü chiao-yü," *Hsin chiao-yü,* 7.1.

48. Ch'eng Hsiang-fan, "Shou-hui chiao-yü ch'üan ti chü-t'i" (The practicality of restoring educational rights), *Tung-fang tsa-chih,* 23.10 (May 25, 1926). Contributors to the early issues overlapped with those active in Sheng-ming she and Chen-li she: Liu T'ing-fang, Li Teng-hui, Chu Ching-nung, Chu Yu-kuang.

49. University of Nanking, "Report of the President," 1924-25, p. 12 (UB).

50. Shen Ssu-liang (William Z.L. Shen), "A Study of the Anti-Christian Movement," CR, LVI, 227-232 (April, 1925). Also, discussions in *Chinese Christian Education* (NY, 1925), pp. 41, 70-71, 80-85; Yü Jih-chang (David Z.T.Yui), "What attitude should the Chinese churches take?" originally published in *Chung-hua kuei-chu,* June 10, 1925, abbreviated translation in CR, LVI, 595 (Sept., 1925).

51. Wieger, VI, 177-178.

52. Dwight C. Baker, "The New China Christian Educational Association Realized," *Educational Review,* XVI, 308 (July, 1924); Sanford, "China's Mission Students," p. 9; Shu Hsin-ch'eng, pp. 75-76; Chou T'ai-hsuan, "Fei tsung-chiao chiao-yü yü chiao-hui chiao-yü," CHCYC, XIV; Chu Ching-nung, "Chung-kuo chiao-hui hsueh-hsiao kai-liang t'an" (Discussion of the reform of Chinese parochial schools), *Chung-hua Chi-tu-chiao chiao-yü chi-k'an,* 1.2 (June, 1925). Chu, a member of the KMT, was head of the Chinese department of Shanghai Baptist College in 1924 and Dean of Kuang Hua University in 1925. In addition to editing *Chung-hua Chi-tu-chiao chiao-yü chi-k'an,* Ch'eng Hsiang-fan was head of the China Christian Educational Association. Fan Yuan-lien had served briefly as Minister of Education on three occasions; he was president of Peking Normal University, 1923-1924, and of the China Foundation for the Promotion of Education and Culture (Boxer Indemnity Fund), 1924-1927.

53. Wieger, VI, 181.

54. Wu Lei-ch'uan, "Tui yü chiao-hui chung hsueh-hsiao kai-liang ti wo chien," *Chen-li,* 1.15; Wu, "Chiao-hui hsueh-hsiao yü Chung-kuo chiao-yü ti ch'ien-t'u" (Parochial schools and the future of China's education), *ibid.,* 2.20 (Aug. 11, 1924). Typical criticisms are A. Legendre in Wieger, VI, 189-191 and a later editorial in *China Press,* Oct. 9, 1925.

55. Quoted in Pascal M. d'Elia, *The Triple Demism of Sun Yat-sen* (Wuchang, 1931), p. 580.

56. "Editorial Notes," *Educational Review,* XVI, 389 (Oct., 1924); Hsu Pao-ch'ien, "Ching kao-chin chih t'i-ch'ang kuo-chia-chu-i che" (A plea to the advocates of nationalism), *Sheng-ming,* 5.4 (Jan., 1925); comments of Frank Rawlinson in *Chinese Christian Education,* pp. 70-71; R.E. Chandler, "Christian Missions and the international system in China," CMYB, 1925, pp. 253-258; "Conditions in China," Aug. 31, 1925 (Mimeo, Harvard-Lingnan Archives, Box 191), esp. the quotation from a missionary at an inland station in north China.

57. "Editorial Notes," *Educational Review,* XVII, 2-8 (Jan., 1925); *ibid.,* 332-333 (Oct., 1925).

58. J. Leighton Stuart, "Some administrative problems," *Educational Review*, XV, 363 (Oct., 1923); F.L. Hawks Pott, "Some principles contained in the report of the China Educational Commission," ibid., 218 (July, 1923); Matilda Thurston, "Ginling College," ibid., XVI, 30 (Jan., 1924); F.J. White, "Making the Christian Colleges More Chinese," *The Christian College in New China*, China Christian Educational Association Bul. no. 16 (Shanghai, 1926), pp. 34-35.

59. *The Green Year*, Supplement to the magazine of the National YWCA of China (Shanghai, 1925), p. 2; "Resolutions of the General Board, April 1,2,1925," *Educational Review*, XVII, 257-259 (July, 1925).

60. "Recommendations of the 9th Annual Meeting of the Advisory Council of the CCEA," *Educational Review*, XVI, 313-314 (July, 1924); discussion in *Chinese Christian Education*, pp. 56-57, 80-95. Ernest Burton argued that the issue of compulsion was secondary; if religion courses were of sufficiently high quality, requirements would be unnecessary.

61. "West China Missionary News," quoted in "Information about China," no. 13 (Nov. 18, 1925) (Yali archives).

62. Pao Kuang-lin, "Chin jih Chung-kuo Chi-tu-chiao hui chi ying chieh-chueh ti chi ko wen-t'i" (A few problems that the Chinese church today ought to solve). *Chen-li*, 3.18 (July 26, 1925), summarized in CR, LIV, 591-593; Shu Hsin-ch'eng, pp. 75-76; Wu Lei-ch'uan, "Tui yü chiao-hui chung hsueh-hsiao kai-liang ti wo chien," *Chen-li*, 1.15.

63. Bishop Frederick R. Graves, quoted in Lamberton, p. 113.

64. "Resolutions of the General Board, April 1,2,1925," *Educational Review*, XVII, 257-261.

Chapter VI

1. For an overall study, see Richard W. Rigby, *The May 30 Movement. Events and Themes* (Canberra, Australia, 1980). There is general agreement that four demonstrators were killed outright; the figures for the number of wounded who later died vary from 3 to 9.

2. One hundred different organizations had to be taken into account when Protestants allocated representation for the National Christian Conference of 1922. E.E. Barnett, "Cooperative Christian Activities in China in 1925," CCYB, 1926, p. 94. Roman Catholics, of course, also had their own organizations and institutions.

3. Clifford, pp. 19-21; Hung-ting Ku, "Urban Mass Movement: The May Thirtieth Movement in Shanghai," *Modern Asian Studies*, XIII, 197-205 (1979), Chang Kuo-t'ao, I, 426-432.

4. Neither the Chamber of Commerce nor the Federation of Labor Unions was represented.

5. Rigby, *May 30*, p. 63.

6. Chang Kuo-t'ao, I, 436. Yun attended both the CCP and the KMT meetings.

7. Wieger, VI, 41-42.

8. Ku, "Urban Mass Movement," p. 212.

9. Rigby, *May 30*, pp. 38-39; "Revolt Spirit Grows in Cities of China," *New York Times*, June 4, 1925, p. 2.

10. Quotation from Clifford, p. 22; Edward J.M.Rhoads, "Lingnan's Response to the Rise of Chinese Nationalism: The Shakee Incident (1925)," in *American Missionaries in China*, ed. by Liu Kwang-ching (Cambridge, MA, 1966), p. 192.

11. Italics mine for Student Union quotation. See Chang, TCSC, pp. 395-400; "Information about China," Dec. 2, 1925, issued by Foreign Missions Conference of North America (Yali archives).

12. "Chung-kuo kung-ch'an-chu-i ch'ing-nien t'uan wei fan-k'ang ti-kuo-chu-i t'u-sha Chung-kuo shih-min kao ch'üan kuo ch'ing-nien" (The Chinese CYC, in regard to imperialism's killing Chinese citizens, speaks to the nation's youth), *Chung-kuo ch'ing-nien*, no. 81 (June 20, 1925); [Yun] Tai-ying, "Pei ya-p'o ch'ing-nien ti wen-t'i" (The question of oppressed youth), *ibid.*, no. 87 (Aug. 8, 1925).

13. Latourette, p. 737; "Conditions in China," Aug. 31, 1925 (Mimeo. quotations issued by the Board of Foreign Missions of the Presbyterian Church, U.S.A.; Harvard-Lingnan archives, Box 191), p. 7. The anonymous missionary commented: "The Lord was with me and I was able to take it smilingly so that no bad results have come from it. . . . The students have everything in control. . . . They have stirred themselves to a state of perfect frenzy. . . . There is no use to argue. . . . It is a time to be very quiet."

14. Rigby, *May 30*, p. 73.

15. High, "China Astir," *Asia*, XXV, 652.

16. Rigby, *May 30*, pp. 101-104.

17. "Shang-hai chiao-yü chieh tui 'wu-sa' shih" (Shanghai educational world in regard to the "May 30th" affair), in newspaper

clipping file of KMT Historical Archives, which contains numerous published proclamations. The pamphlet, *Wu-sa hsieh an shih lu* (The true story of the bloody incident of May 30th) (no publ. data, KMT archives), is a collection of proclamations. Many of the manifestoes and other documents are available in translation, see *Peking Leader* Press, *Documents on the Shanghai Case* (Peking, 1925) (Cornell U. Wason Collection). See also the flyer issued by the Union of Students Supporting the Shanghai Case, entitled "Why We Come Out. This is not a case of passionate quarreling; it is a question of humanity against inhuman oppression" (Harvard-Lingnan, Box 191).

18. Wieger, VI, 37, 39, 194-195, 229-230; for photograph, see High, "China Astir," *Asia,* XXV, 653.

19. The privileges enjoyed by foreigners in China included: (a) extraterritoriality, whereby defendants in court cases were subject to their own national jurisdiction, not to Chinese jurisdiction, (b) foreign control of certain small portions of Chinese territory with exemption from Chinese taxation, (c) the treaty tariff plus special treatment in the case of certain internal levies, (d) the right to maintain foreign troops and gunboats at certain stations. Missionaries enjoyed, in addition, (a) the right of travel and residence in the interior, (b) the right of purchase or lease of property in the interior, (c) protection of Christian converts from persecution because of faith, and (d) exemption of Christian converts from taxes levied for temple support or other religious observances contrary to their faith. Some Chinese questioned the legality of certain of these privileges according to the authoritative text of the treaties.

20. See, for example, University of Nanking, "Report of the President," 1924-1925 (UB), p. 3; Yenching, "Report of the President," 1924-1925 (UB), p. 6; also quotations from missionaries at Yenching in "Conditions in China," Aug. 31, 1925.

21. Quoted in Thomas A. Creamer, "Hsueh-yun. Shanghai's Students and the May Thirtieth Movement" (M.A. Thesis, University of Virginia, 1975), p. 35.

22. "An Appeal for Justice by Students of Shanghai College," in "Information about China," Aug. 18, 1925 (Yali Archives).

23. Mimeo from "Tsun In" (a Chinese Christian News Sheet), signed Loung Siu Choh, for the Kwangtung Christian National Salvation Association (n.d., Harvard-Lingnan, Box 191). The fusillade in Canton opposite Shameen Island on June 23 is often referred to as the Shakee incident.

24. Li Huang, "My Memoirs," p. 236: *Peking Leader* Press, *Documents*, pp. 39-40.

25. Matilda Thurston and Ruth M. Chester, *Ginling College* (NY, 1955), pp. 50-51.

26. Roderick Scott, *Fukien Christian University* (NY, 1954), p. 36; President John Gowdy said that the F.C.U. Student Union withdrew from the local Student Union because of the latter's anti-Christian activities: Gowdy to F.C.U. Bd. of Trustees, Sept. 25, 1925 (ABC-FCU archives, Houghton).

27. "Shang-hai fei Chi-tu-chiao ta t'ung-meng ch'eng-li hsuan-yen" (Proclamation upon the establishment of the Shanghai Great Anti-Christian Federation), Fei CTC, no. 5, pp. 61-62 (Dec. 25, 1925); Hsueh Wu(?), "Wu-han pan-nien lai ti fan Chi-tu-chiao yun-tang" (The Anti-Christian Movement in Wuhan during the past half year), *ibid.*, no. 4, pp. 51-53 (Dec. 1, 1925).

28. "Wai-kuo chiao-yü ti ya-p'o" (Oppression of foreign education) CHCYC, XV (Aug., 1925); Wieger, VI, 213-215.

29. "Translation of certain Resolutions regarding Anti-Christian Movement adopted by the 7th National Convention of the National Student Union, July, 1925," in "Information about China," Dec. 2, 1925.

30. Feng Yü-hsiang, "To All Professed Christians of the World," in "The Shanghai Affair," special issue published by Chinese Students' Christian Association in North America, July, 1925, pp. 3-4 (Yali archives); D. Willard Lyon, "Topics which occupy the minds of Chinese Christians," CR, LVI, 663-664 (Oct., 1925); T'ang Liang-li, *China in Revolt*, pp. 70-71; J.E. Sheridan, *Chinese Warlord* (Stanford, 1966), pp. 157, 168, 173-174. Gen. Feng apparently made a donation, but Chen-li she, in which Chien Yu-wen was prominent, did not sanction the proposal for a new institution under Chinese control and the project died.

31. "Wu-han pan-nien lai ti fan Chi-tu-chiao yun-tung," Fei CTC, no. 4; for other reports of restrictions on parochial students, see Kuang Han [Han Kuang-han ?], "Wu-sa yun-tung chung ti Ning-po Chi-tu-chiao hsueh-hsiao" (Ningpo parochial schools during the May Thirtieth Movement), *ibid.*, no. 1, pp. 12-13 (Nov. 1, 1925).

32. Scott, p. 36.

33. Liu T'ing-fang (T.T. Lew), "To the Members of the General Board, the Three Councils, Regional Associations, and other members of CCEA," *Educational Review*, Appendix, XVII, 1-8 (1925).

See also B.S. Siao, "An Appeal to All Concerned," June 6, 1925, in *The Green Year*, pp. 11-12.

34. For an analysis of student storms, 1911 to 1922, see Yü Chia-chü and Ch'ang Tao-chih, *Hsueh-hsiao feng-ch'ao ti yen-chiu* (Shanghai, 1925), esp. III, The Total Number of School Storms and their Distribution by Period; IV, Distribution according to the Nature and Locality of the School; V, Analytical View of the Origin of Storms.

35. For further detail, see Lutz, *China and the Christian Colleges*, pp. 192-197.

36. The description of the St. John's confrontation is based on the following sources: Shu Hsin-ch'eng, ed., *Chin-tai Chung-kuo chiao-yü shih-liao* (Shanghai, 1928), III, 180-183; Lamberton, pp. 101-102; Ting Chih-p'in, pp. 122-125; Correspondence of H.P. DePree to W.I. Chamberlain, June 15, 1925 (China Mission Correspondence, Reformed Church in America, New Brunswick Theological Seminary Library). *Hsing-shih* devoted most of its June, 1925 issue to the St. John's incident. See also, Ch'iu Jen (?), "Wu-su yun-tung yü chiao-hui hsueh-hsiao" (May 30th Movement and parochial schools), *Chung-kuo ch'ing-nien*, no. 89 (Aug. 22, 1925).

37. Copy of letter in Yali archives under Hume correspondence.

38. Hume letter in *ibid*.

39. "News," *Educational Review*, XVII, 426 (Oct., 1925).

40. Wieger, VI, 213-215.

41. H.P. DePree to W.I. Chamberlain, July 23, 1925 (RCA, NB Theo). In an article summarizing essays in Chinese Christian periodicals, D. Willard Lyon wrote: "The events of May 30th and after have put an emotional content into the thinking of both missionaries and Chinese Christians, which has made it extremely difficult for either group fully to understand, much less to appreciate the attitude of the other." See "What are Chinese Christians Saying to One Another at this Time?", CR, LVI, 478 (July, 1925).

42. Lu Jen, "Ti-kuo-chu-i ti pao-chih wai-chiao-chia Chi-tu-chiao t'u yü Chung-kuo chih min-tsu chieh-fang yun-tung" (Imperialistic journalists, diplomats, Christian missionaries, and the Chinese people's liberation movement), *Hsiang-tao*, no. 125, Aug. 18, 1925.

43. "To Our Missionary Friends in China, June 10, 1925" (Copy in Hume correspondence, Yali). The statement was signed by the

Chinese members of the administrative and teaching staff of both Soochow University and the university middle school no. 1. There apparently was no direct response, except by Westerners who requested that their comments be "off the record". W.B. Nance, *Soochow University* (NY, 1956), p. 100.

44. This account is based on the following sources: Correspondence of Alexander Baxter to W.Henry Grant, June 17, 1925; Flyer issued by Kwangtung Christian National Salvation Association; "Conditions in China," Aug. 31, 1925, pp. 13-14 (probably by Baxter); China Christian Union for National Salvation, "To Our Missionary Friends in China," June 30, 1925; Correspondence of Herbert Parsons, Pres. of Bd. of Trustees, to U.S. Secretary of State, July 8, 1925; "Resolution of American staff present at Canton Christian College, June 24, 1925" (all in Harvard-Lingnan, Box 191). Also Corbett, *Lingnan*, pp. 89-94; Rhoads, "Lingnan's Response," in Liu, *American Missionaries*, pp. 184-214. See the latter for greater detail.

45. Earl Swisher, *Canton in Revolution. The Collected Papers of Earl Swisher, 1925-1928*. Ed. by Kenneth W. Rea (Boulder, CO, 1977), pp. 16-18.

46. See translations in *The Green Year, Peking Leader* Press, *Documents* and *Sheng-ming*, English issue, June, 1925.

47. Wieger, VI, 224-225.

48. Wu Lei-ch'uan, "The Shanghai Case and the Future of Christianity in China," *Sheng-ming*, English issue, June, 1925. This essay originally appeared as an editorial in the Chinese edition of *Sheng-ming*, June, 1925.

49. Several members of the R.C.A. Amoy mission, for example, drew up a statement on treaty revision, Feb. 8, 1926 and twenty missionaries signed it, but the Executive Committee of the Amoy Mission "did not feel prepared to make a statement." DePree to Chamberlain, March 30, 1926 (RCA, N.B. Theo).

50. d'Elia, pp. 580-587.

51. DePree to Chamberlain, Oct. 10, 1925 (RCA, N.B. Theo.). A statement of the kind to raise Chinese hackles was an article entitled, "Mission Schools and Chinese Politics". According to this English educator, no student below the university level was capable of forming a political opinion and even students in Chinese universities should operate in a calm and orderly manner. Mission schools and their students could play no political role; he found the incendiary aspects of the movement unchristian and regretted that so many Christians had joined in the movement; he urged his

Chinese colleagues to give the proper guidance to mission school students. H.H. Rowley, in CR, LVI, 560 (Sept., 1925). Most missionaries who argued that the church should abstain from all political involvement were more circumspect and diplomatic than Rowley, but hostile critics could make use of such statements.

52. Varg, *Missionaries, Chinese,* pp. 194-200; J.V.A. MacMurray to U.S. Secretary of State, Oct. 6, 1925, with enclosure of statement by Church of Christ in China (Dept. of State archives, Decimal File, China, 393.116/366). See also, documents in George E. Sokolsky, ch. XXVI, "Labour, Strikes, and the Anti-foreign Agitation," *China Year Book,* 1926-27, ed. by H.G.W. Woodhead, pp. 895-1016.

53. R.E. Chandler, "Christian Missionaries and the International System in China," CMYB, 1925, pp. 255-257. Varg, *Missionaries, Chinese,* pp. 196-202. See also, earlier correspondence on this issue: Robert E. Chandler and Harold S. Mathews to Jacob Schurman, Aug. 24, 1924; Schurman to Chandler, Sept. 25, 1924; Schurman to U.S. Secretary of State, Jan. 6, 1925; U.S. Secretary of State to Schurman, March 16, 1925 (Dept. of State Archives, Decimal File, China 393.116/342).

54. Paul A. Varg, "The Missionary Response to the Nationalist Revolution," in Fairbank, *Missionary Enterprise,* p. 330.

55. Wieger, VI, 231-232.

56. Chinese Members of the Faculty of the College and the Middle School of Yale-in-China, "To the Friends of China," June 17, 1925 (Hume Correspondence, Yali).

57. Kuo Ping-wen, "A Chinese Statement," *Asia,* XXV, 1035.

58. "Shang-hai Chi-tu-t'u lien-ho-hui chih kung-pu-chü tung-shih han" (Letter of the Shanghai Christian Union to the Municipal Council), *Tung-fang tsa-chih,* XXII, 20-21 (July, 1925); DePree to Chamberlain, June 15, 1925 (RCA, N.B. Theo.); Hsieh Sung-kao (Z.K. Zia), "Chinese Christian Unions," CCYB, 1926, p. 86; Eugene E. Barnett, "Cooperative Christian Activities in China in 1925," *ibid.,* pp. 111-112. E.C. Lobenstine of the National Christian Council explained to the mission boards that the unions had been organized because "the difficulty of the church becoming involved in political questions has been felt much more keenly by missionaries than by the Chinese." Letters to Secretaries of Boards of Foreign Missions, July 22, 1925 (Yali).

59. D. Willard Lyon, "What are Chinese Christians Saying to One Another at this time?", CR, LVI, 478-479.

60. Union of Chinese Christian Churches of Peking, "An Appeal to the Christian Peoples of the World, June 7, 1925" (Yali); "Manifesto on the Shanghai Incident Issued by Chinese Christians Assembled in a Mass Meeting in Peking on Sunday, June 14, 1925," *Shengming,* June, 1925 (Originally published in *Chen-li*).

61. "Chung-hua ch'üan-kuo Chi-tu-chiao hsieh-chin hui chih kung-pu-chü han" (Letter of the National Christian Council to the Municipal Council), *Tung-fang tsa-chih* XXII (July, 1925); *National Christian Council, a Five Years' Review,* p. 22; Cheng Ching-yi, "Problems and Needs of the Church," CCYB, 1931, p. 94.

62. Garrett, *Social Reformers,* p. 178.

63. Wu Lei-ch'uan, "Hu-an yü Chung-kuo Chi-tu-chiao ch'ien-t'u" (The Shanghai case and the future of Chinese Christianity), *Sheng-ming,* 5.5 (June, 1925); Wu, "Fan Chi-tu-chiao yun-tung yü kuo-chia-chu-i" (Anti-Christian Movement and nationalism), *Chen-li,* 3.39 (Dec. 27, 1925); Hsu Pao-ch'ien, "The Anti-Christian Movement, the Challenge to Christians," *New Mandarin,* 1.3: 18-21 (June, 1926). See also articles by Wu Lei-ch'uan, Hsu Pao-ch'ien, and Chao Tzu-ch'en in a special issue of *Chen-li yü sheng ming,* 1.12 (Nov. 30, 1926); these are summarized in English in *ibid.* Feb., 1927). Wu, Hsu and other Christian nationalists argued that the linkage of Christianity and imperialism could be offset only by speeding up the process of Sinification and by rapid progress toward a self-governing and self-propagating Chinese church.

64. Quoted in Diana Lary, *Region and Nation. The Kwangsi Clique in Chinese Politics, 1925-1937* (London, 1974), p. 99.

65. Garrett, *Social Reformers,* p. 178.

66. High, "China Astir," *Asia,* XXV, 652.

67. Shu Hsin-ch'eng, *Shou-hui chiao-yü,* pp. 62-63; Ting Chih-p'in, p. 120; "The New Tides of Chinese Affairs," *New Mandarin,* 1.1: 30 (Jan., 1926).

68. Fan Yuan-lien, "Hu-an yü chiao-yü (The Shanghai case and education), CHCYC, XV (Aug., 1925).

69. Ch'en Hsieh-hsun, "Shou-hui chiao-yu ch'üan ying yu ti pu-chou" (The steps necessary for restoration of educational rights). *Hsin chiao-yü,* 11.1 (Aug., 1925).

70. Shu Hsin-ch'eng, *Shou-hui chiao-yü,* pp. 61-63; Peake, pp. 90-92. Earlier the Chinese Students' Alliance in the U.S. had also passed resolutions favoring adoption of military training in Chinese schools while students at Peita and Tsing Hua had organized drill teams.

71. "Hsueh-sheng tsung-hui chieh-shu wu-sa ts'an-an pa-k'o yun-tung t'ung-k'ao" (Notice of the Student Union's ending the strike movement of May Thirtieth), CYTC, XVII (Oct., 1925).

72. Wan Yin (?), "Fan Chi-tu-chiao yun-tung ti hsin k'ou-hao-- 'Tao hsiang-ts'un li ch'ü!'" (The new slogan of the Anti-Christian Movement--"To the Countryside"!), Fei CTC, no. 4. For the National Student Union Congress resolutions detailing tactics, see Wieger VI, 217-218.

73. Edgar Snow, *Red Star over China* (NY, 1944), p. 160.

74. Yang Chia-ming, *Min-kuo shih-wu nien Chung-kuo hsueh-sheng yun-tung kai-k'uang* (Shanghai, 1927), pp. 25-26.

75. Wieger, VI, 237-238. See also, Tzu Chen (?), "Kao wei wu-sa yun-tung erh t'ui hsueh ti chiao-hui hsueh-sheng" (To parochial students withdrawing from schools in the May Thirtieth Movement), Fei CTC, no. 1.

76. "Hsueh-sheng tsung-hui chieh-shu wu-sa ts'an-an pa-k'o yun-tung t'ung-k'ao," CYTC, Oct., 1925.

77. Chang Kuo-t'ao, I, 422-444. In an earlier essay Yun had urged closer coordination between the student movement and the KMT in working for the national revolution; one indication of progress in the youth movement, he said, was the decision of the National Student Union to unite with the KMT in class struggle and in liberation of the masses, see "I nien lai ti ch'ing-nien yun-tung," *Min-kuo jih-pao,* Jan. 1, 1925.

78. Donald A. Jordan, *The Northern Expedition* (Honolulu, 1976), p. 242.

79. Lu Jen, "Ti-kuo chu-i ti pao-chih wai-chiao-chia Chi-tu-chiao t'u yü Chung-kuo," *Hsiang-tao,* Aug. 16, 1925.

80. [Yun] Tai-ying, "Pei ya-p'o ch'ing-nien ti wen-t'i," *Chung-kuo ch'ing-nien,* Aug. 8, 1925; also, Chung Wen (?), "Chin-hou chih fei Chi-tu-chiao yun-tung" (The Anti-Christian Movement from now on), *ibid.,* nos. 911 & 912 (Sept. 1, 1925).

81. Yip, p. 52; Wilbur, *Documents,* p. 299.

82. Breslin, pp. 49, 52-53.

83. Yang Chia-ming, pp. 124-130.

84. Wilbur, *Documents,* pp. 125-127.

85. "Chiao-yü chieh hsiao-hsi," CYTC, XVII (Aug., 1925); Tzu Chen, "Kao wei wu-sa yun-tung erh t'ui hsueh ti chiao-hui hsueh-

sheng," Fei CTC, no. 1; Ming Chih [Ch'en Ch'i-t'ien], "Kao Nan-yang, Fu-tan chi Tung-nan san hsiao t'ung-hsueh" (To fellow students of the three schools, Nan-yang, Fu-tan, and Tung-nan), *ibid*. In addition to Ch'en's article, three essays in the second and third nos. of Fei CTC concern the attempt to eliminate St. John's and all foreign coaches and judges from the East China athletic meet.

86. The subject of practically all of the lectures is either nationalistic education or nationalism and Chinese youth. All of them appear to have been delivered during 1925. Typical titles are: "Kuo-chia-chu-i yü Chung-kuo ch'ing-nien" (Nationalism and Chinese youth) by Tseng Ch'i; "Kuo ch'ih ti chiao-yü" (National humiliation education) by Yü Chia-chü; "Kuo-chia-chu-i yü Chung-kuo shih-fan chiao-yü chih kai-tsao" (Nationalism and the reconstruction of Chinese teacher education) by Ch'en Ch'i-t'ien.

87. All of the articles are listed under pseudonyms or given names with no family name and so it has been possible to identify ony a minority of the authors. Tseng Ch'i was teaching at Ta Hsia University during this time. Several of the articles are by Ming Chih, a pseudonym used by Ch'en Ch'i-t'ien.

88. Wan Yin, "Fan Chi-tu-chiao yun-tung ti hsin k'ou-hao--'Tao hsiang-ts'un li chü!'", Fei CTC, no. 4; "Pen k'an ti shih-ming" (Our mission), *ibid.*, no. 1; Yung Chien (?), "Fei Chi-tu-chiao yun-tung chih tsu-chih wen-t'i" (The problem of the organization of the Anti-Christian Movement), *ibid*.

89. Ku I (?), "Ch'uan-chiao yü Mei-kuo ti-kuo-chu-i" (Missions and American imperialism), Fei CTC, no. 4; Chih Ching (?), "Fan Chi-tu-chiao yü Chung-kuo min-tsu tu-li yun-tung" (Anti-Christianity and the Chinese people's independence movement), *ibid*.; Wan Yin, "Fan Chi-tu-chiao yun-tung chou" (Anti-Christian Movement week), *ibid.*, no. 5.

90. Wieger, VI, 237-238.

91. T'ang Liang-li, pp. 70-71; "Chiao-yü chieh hsiao-hsi," CYTC, Aug., 1925; Chung Wen (?), "Chieh-shao Fu-chien hsueh lien-hui chih shou-hui chiao-yü ch'üan yun-tung" (Introducing the Movement to Restore Educational Rights of the Fukien Student Union), Fei CTC, no. 4.

92. Yip, pp. 58-59; Yang Chia-ming, p. 51; see also, Anna L. Strong, "The Awakened Peasantry of China," *Asia*, XXVIII, 33 (Jan., 1928).

93. Wieger, VI, 67. The Peking Anti-Christian Federation planned a three-day campaign, Dec. 24 to Dec. 26, but recommended

only peaceful methods of protest. One source refers to a Peking Anti-Christian Weekly, but I have located no copies of it. "The New Tide of Chinese Affairs," *New Mandarin,* 1.1:30; *ibid.,* 1.2 (March, 1926). For some of the activities of Anti-Christianity Week, see Sun Heng (?), "I-chiu-erh-wu nien ko-ti 'Fei Chi chou' yun-tung kai-k'uang" (1925, each place's "Anti-Christianity Week" movement, in general), *Chung-kuo ch'ing-nien,* nos. 112, 113 (Jan. 30, Feb. 6, 1926).

94. Wan Yin, "Fan Chi-tu-chiao yun-tung chou," Fei CTC, no. 5.

95. "Shan-tou shou-hui chiao-yü ch'üan chih chi-chin" (Progress in the restoration of educational rights in Swatow),CYTC, XVIII Feb., 1926), E.D. Harvey to F.W. Williams, Dec. 13, 1926 (Yali). Nanchiang was formerly known as Swatow Anglo-Chinese College.

96. "Chou En-lai shou-hui Shan-tou chiao-yü ch'üan" (Chou En-lai restores educational rights in Swatow), *Min-kuo jih-pao,* Dec. 5, 1925.

97. CYTC has *shih tang pu* (municipal party bureau) whereas *Min-kuo jih-pao* has *cheng-chih pu* (political bureau).

98. "Shan-tou shou-hui chiao-yü ch'üan," CYTC, Feb., 1926; Garrett, *Social Reformers,* p. 180.

99. Lewis S. Gannett, "In Red Canton," *Asia,* XXVI, 491, 569-570 (June, 1926); John M. Roots, "Chinese Head and Chinese Heart," *Asia,* XXVII, 94-95 (Feb., 1927).

100. According to Wieger, VI, 69, thirty-eight teachers resigned from Chung-shan University in Dec., 1925 in protest over the influence of Borodin and other communists there. Some six hundred students were said to belong to left-wing organizations.

101. For a detailed analysis, see C. Martin Wilbur, "The Second National Congress of the Kuomintang" in *Symposium on the History of th Republic of China* (Taipei, 1981), III, 39-61. The exact number of CCP delegates at the Congress is unknown, but Wilbur seems to accept ninety as a reasonable figure (pp. 42, 55). Of the 36-member CEC of the KMT, seven to eight were CCP members.

102. Chiang Kai-shek claimed that the communists acted first with an attempt to kidnap him. Evidence to substantiate or disprove this claim is lacking, according to several scholars. Tien-wei Wu, "Chiang Kai-shek's March Twentieth Coup d'Etat of 1926," *Journal of Asian Studies,* XXVII, 585-602 (May, 1968).

103. "Manifesto of the Second National Congress of the KMT" in Milton J.T. Shieh, *The Kuomintang, Selected Historical Documents*

(NY, 1970), pp. 113, 117-119; Wieger, VII, *Boum!*, 1926-1927, pp. 20, 98.

104. Based on the following sources: President James M. Henry to W.H. Grant, March 15, 1926 and "Report--Labor Troubles, Jan. 1-March 22, 1926" (Harvard-Lingnan, Box 35); "Labor Demands submitted by Canton Christian College Labor Union, March 9, 1926" (*ibid.*, Box 191); Corbett, *Lingnan,* pp. 100-101.

105 "Ko chieh t'uan-ti yuan-chu Lingnan ta-hsueh pei-ko hsueh-sheng hsuan-yen" (Statement by all occupational groups in support of the expelled Lingnan University students), April 11, 1926 (Newspaper clippings, KMT archives); Pres. Henry to Grant, April 5, 7, 19, May 12, 1926 (Harvard-Lingnan, Box 35); Corbett, *Lingnan,* pp. 101-102.

106. See the proclamations by Sun-ta Kuang-hsi hsueh-sheng hui (Kwangsi student association at Chung-shan University), Sheng Chiang pa-kung wei-yuan hui (Kwangtung-Hong Kong strike committee), and Ko chieh t'ung-i tai-piao hui (United representative committee of all occupations), April 11, 1926 (Newspaper clippings, KMT archives).

107. Translation of letter of Lingnan Labor Union to W.K. Chung, Associate President, Nov. 2, 1926 (Harvard-Lingnan, Box 191); "Demands of the Staff Union of Canton Christian College," *China Weekly Review,* April 23, 1927.

108. John C. Griggs, "Canton's Contribution to the Chinese Revolution," *Current History,* XXIV, 876 (Sept., 1926); "Brief Interview upon the part of Dr. Henry with Mr. Borodin, Thursday, May 20, 1926" (Harvard-Lingnan, Box 192).

109. Robert A. Kapp, *Szechwan and the Chinese Republic* (New Haven, 1973), pp. 66, 75-85; Chang Kuo-t'ao, I, 543. According to the "West China Missionary News," Spring, 1925 (Yali) Szechwan was flooded with nationalistic and socialist propaganda and students hoisted a sign at one Chengtu middle school saying, "Middle School for British Commerical Expansion".

110. "Report of the Senate of West China Union University to the Board of Governors," 1926-1927 (UB); Joseph Taylor, *History of West China Union University, 1910-1935* (Chengtu, China, 1936), pp. 46-52, 84-87; Yang Chia-ming, p. 23.

111. Wu Chao-kwang, *The International Aspect of the Missionary Movement in China* (Baltimore, 1930), p. 187; Kapp, pp. 77-79.

112. Taylor, pp. 48, 84-87; Wieger, VII, 59.

113. Clifford, p. ix.

Chapter VII

1. Teng Yen-ta became Director of the Political Department of the NRA in June, 1926. According to one source, Teng promptly established a Wartime Propaganda Center in the main hall of Chungshan University and recruited more than one thousand students for two-week courses in propaganda techniques. John K. Olenik, "Left Wing Radicalism in the Kuomintang," (Diss., Cornell U., 1973), p. 136.

2. In this discussion of the Northern Expedition, I have drawn on Jordan, *Northern Expedition,* Harold Isaacs, *The Tragedy of the Chinese Revolution* (Stanford, 1951); F.F. Liu, *A Military History of Modern China* (Princeton, 1956); C. Martin Wilbur, "Military Separatism and the Process of Reunification under the Nationalist Regime, 1922-1937" in *China in Crisis,* ed. by Ho Ping-ti and Tsou Tang (Chicago, 1968), bk. I, vol. I, 203-263.

3. Vice-president Alexander Baxter to President James M. Henry, Jan. 7, 1925 (Harvard-Lingnan, Box 191); "Letter to Dr. Edmunds, March 16, 1927 by Sun Fo," *School and Society,* XXVI, 108 (July, 1927); Yip, p. 66; Wieger, VI, 163.

4. *Ibid.,* VII, 234. Wei Chueh's statement of Dec., 1926 was much more ambiguous than an essay written before May Thirtieth and before his experiences during the spring storm at Lingnan. In "National Crisis and Christianity," May 3, 1925 (Mimeo. paper, Harvard-Lingnan, Box 191), Wei expressed the views of a Christian nationalist accepting the Social Gospel approach. "We need Christian men and women who have undaunted faith in God and who will serve the cause of China through thick and thin and who will die for Christ if necessary" (p. 7). He was critical of those subscribing to Russian propaganda as well as those subscribing uncritically to Western ideals and Western ways; both, he said, meant that China was submitting to foreign domination (p. 3).

5. *Min-kuo jih-pao,* Oct. 10, 1926.

6. For the directive, see "Chiao-yü chieh hsiao-hsi," CYTC, XIX (Feb., 1927).

7. Breslin, *China, American Catholicism,* p. 52.

8. DePree to Chamberlain, Jan. 17, 1927 (RCA, N.B. Theo.).

9. "Chiao-yü chieh hsiao-hsi," CYTC, XIX (Jan., 1927).

10. Eric M. North to "Friends of Fukien Christian University," Jan. 28, 1927, quoting from a letter of Pres. John Gowdy to W.I. Chamberlain, Dec. 15, 1926 (ABC-FCU, Houghton).

11. DePree to Chamberlain, Jan. 17, 1927. DePree does not indicate whether the soldier students were from Whampoa or from one of its preparatory branches. He states, without giving his source, that in some government schools, students were threatened with having their grade marks reduced if they failed to participate.

12. Gowdy to Chamberlain, Dec. 23, 1926; Minutes of the Board of Managers of Fukien Christian University, Dec. 23, 1926 (ABC-FCU, Houghton).

13. DePree to Chamberlain, Jan. 31, 1927 (RCA, N.B. Theo.); Wieger VII, 66, 176. The accusation that Catholics were murdering babies for their eyes also reappeared in Wuchang at this time.

14. North to "Friends of F.C.U.," Feb. 28, 1927 (ABC-FCU, Houghton); DePree to Chamberlain, Jan. 31, 1927 (RCA. N.B. Theo.); Wieger VII, 175-176; Dorothy Borg, *American Policy and the Chinese Revolution, 1925-1928* (NY, 1947), p. 268; "Sha-men ta-hsueh hsueh feng-ch'ao chih yü-po" (The swell after the Amoy University student storm), CYTC, XIX (March, 1927).

15. Gowdy to North, March 30, 1927 (ABC-FCU, Houghton); biography of Ts'ai Yuan-p'ei in Boorman, III, 298.

16. Narrative based on the following sources: "Chiao-yü chieh hsiao-hsi," CYTC, XIX (May, 1927); Gowdy to North, March 30, April 11, 1927 (ABC-FCU, Houghton); DePree to Chamberlain, April 25, 1927 (RCA, N.B. Theo.); Scott, pp. 36-39.

17. Yip, pp. 69-70.

18. Wilbur, *Documents,* pp. 311-312.

19. Just a couple of weeks earlier, *Hsing-shih* had devoted a whole issue to the "nefarious influence" of the communists in higher education. See articles by Tseng Ch'i, Ch'en Ch'i-t'ien, and others in no. 89 (June 27, 1926).

20. Wieger, VII, 115.

21. Ruth A. Greene, *Hsiang-Ya Journal* (Hamden, CT, 1977), pp. 45-47.

22. Yang Chia-ming, pp. 24-26; William J. Hail, "Yali and the Chinese Revolution," *Yali Quarterly,* X, 4 (June, 1927); *North China Daily News and Herald,* Jan. 26, 1926.

23. *China in Chaos,* pub. by *North China Daily News and Herald* (Shanghai, 1927), p. 40.

24. "Chiao yü chieh hsiao-hsi," CYTC, XIX (Feb., 1927); Sanford C.C. Chen, "Twenty-seven Days in Wuhan, Jan. 1-26, 1927" (Mimeo., Yali). The Wuhan Great Alliance against Cultural Aggression was reported to receive a government subsidy of $200 @ month.

25. Garrett, *Social Reformers,* pp. 180-181; Leavens to Bevis, Nov. 26, 1926 (Yali).

26. Wieger, VII, 234.

27. Chang, TCSC, pp. 460-464.

28. Anna L. Strong, "Some Hankow Memories," *Asia,* XXVIII, 794-797, 832-833 (Oct., 1928).

29. *National Christian Council, A Five Years' Review,* pp. 34-35; Mimeo of newspaper extracts regarding the NCC Poster and manifesto (Yali). According to the extract from the *Morning Post,* London, Jan. 18, 1927 (Shanghai dateline), the Wuhan Christians' manifesto was drawn up during a meeting with Soong Ch'ing-ling (Mme. Sun Yat-sen).

30. Wieger, VII, 232-233.

31. Earl Browder, *Civil War in Nationalist China* (Chicago, 1927), p. 40. Both Browder and the other leader of the delegation, Tom Mann, were communist party members on their way home from a meeting of the International of Labor Unions in Moscow.

32. Greene, pp. 50-51; Harvey to Bevis, Nov. 30, 1926 (Yali).

33. "Chiao yü chieh hsiao-hsi," CYTC, Feb., 1927; Yang Chia-ming, pp. 24-25; Harvey to F.W. Williams, Dec. 13, 1926 (Yali).

34. "Chiao yü chieh hsiao-hsi," CYTC, Feb., 1927.

35. Harvey to Bevis, Nov. 30, 1926; W.H. Hail to Student Union of Middle School, Dec. 3, 1926; Frank Hutchins to Edward Hume, Dec. 6, 1926 (Yali); "Standing By--Statement by Trustees," *Yali Quarterly,* X, 2-4 (Dec., 1926); Hail, "Yali and the Chinese Revolution," *ibid.,* pp. 4-7 (June, 1927).

36. "Chiao yü chieh hsiao-hsi," CYTC, Feb., 1927. Liu Yueh-chih, a recent Yali graduate, was in 1926 director of the Peasant Department of the KMT provincial headquarters. Another provincial party leader who aided Yali students during the strike also worked as a cadre in the organizing of peasant and labor unions; he was executed in the Ma Jih incident of May 21, 1927. The Comintern

delegate, M.N. Roy, had spent some time at Yali shortly before the student storm.

37. Harvey to Bevis, Nov. 30, 1926; Hail, "Yali and the Chinese Revolution," *Yali Quarterly,* pp. 4-10 (June, 1927).

38. *China in Chaos,* p. 40.

39. Logan H. Roots, "Effects of 1927 on the Work of Missionaries," CCYB, 1928, p. 116.

40. Speer and Kerr, *Report on Japan and China, 1926,* pp. 381-382; Leavens to Bevis, March 5, April 4, 18, 30, 1927 (Yali).

41. Mao Tse-tung, *Selected Works* (NY, 1954), I, 43.

42. A.G. Baker, "Interview with Eugene Chen, March 18, 1927 in Hankow" (Yali).

43. *Ibid.;* Baker, "Interview with Michael M. Borodin, March 22, 1927 in Hankow," (Yali).

44. For variant interpretations, see the following: Jordan, *Northern Expedition,* pp. 118-119; Chang Kuo-t'ao, I, 562-565; Akira Iriye, *After Imperialism* (Cambridge, MA, 1965), pp. 125-133; Fujii Takama, "The Chinese Northern Expedition and Moscow," *Symposium on the History of the Republic of China,* III, 160-190. See also, the indignant protest by Chung-shan (Kwangtung) University professors and students against "British outrages" and "British barbarism": "Declaration regarding the Hankow Incident by the Sun Yat-sen University" (mimeo, n.d.; Yali).

45. John S. Littell, "The Revolutionary Spirit on the Yangtze," *Asia,* XXVII, 485-486, 529 (June, 1927).

46. Gowdy to North, March 30, 1927 (ABC-FCU, Houghton); Wieger, VII, 214; Breslin, p. 54.

47. Thurston, pp. 57-59.

48. Frank W. Price of University of Nanking to "My dear friends," April 2, 1927; quotations from cable sent by Emily Case of Ginling in letter of E.R. Bender and F.G. Tyler to "Dear friends of Ginling College," March 31, 1927 (Yali). These relate the personal experiences of two Nanking missionaries.

49. See the questions posed by Wilbur in "Military Separatism," pp. 249-250. Chang Kuo-t'ao continued to maintain that northern army troops carried out the plunder and that Gen. Chen Chien's army restored order. He also emphasized the anti-imperialist reaction to the Western bombardment; see *Rise of CCP,* I, 582.

50. "A Statement to Chinese Friends" by a group of Nanking missionaries, April 21, 1927 (4 pp. printed flyer signed by twelve missionaries); "Public Statement" (1 p. mimeo signed by twelve missionaries, n.d.) (Yali).

51. Buck, *My Several Worlds,* pp. 208, 216.

52. Lin Po-ch'ü was not actually in Nanking on March 24, 1927 according to his biography in Boorman, III, 378.

53. "A Statement to Chinese Friends," April 21, 1927 (Yali), p. 3.

54. *North China Herald,* March 26, 1927; May 7, 1927.

55. *National Christian Council, A Five Years' Review,* Appendix E, pp. 29-34; excerpts from letter by Cheng Ching-yi, May 30, 1927 and mimeo extracts regarding the NCC poster and manifesto (Yali); Wilbur Burton, "A Critical View of Christian Missionary Results in China," *Current History,* XXX, 414 (June, 1929). The title of a privately printed booklet is indicative of the acrimony: E.E. Strother, *The National Christian Council of China, A Bolshevik Aid Society,* (Shanghai, 1927).

56. Rodney Gilbert, Letter to the editor, *North China Daily News,* March 25, 1927.

57. Hallett Abend, *My Life in China, 1926-1941* (NY, 1943), pp. 50-51.

58. For further detail, see Garrett, "Why They Stayed," in Fairbank, *Missionary Enterprise,* pp. 283-310.

59. Walsh quoted in Breslin, p. 59.

60. Louis D. Froelick, "An A-B-C of the China Puzzle," *Asia,* XXVII, 456, 534 (June, 1927).

61. See CR, LVIII, 100-107 (Feb., 1927).

62. Edwin Marx, "Losses and Gains of the Church in 1927," CCYB, 1928, p. 61; Varg, *Missionaries, Chinese,* pp. 147-166.

63. Edwards, p. 198.

64. North China Mission of American Board, "Minutes of Annual Meeting," April 21-27, 1927 (ABC-N. China, Mission Archives, Houghton).

65. Reprints of these statements by Committee of Reference and Counsel, Occasional Bulletin, April 1, 1927 (Yali).

66. Council of North China Kung Li-hu Congregational Churches

of U.S., Letter dated April 20, 1927 (ABC-N. China, Houghton).

67. "The Nanking Outrages," *The China Year Book,* 1928, ed. by H.G.W. Woodhead, pp. 729-735 reproduces the exchanges. Earl Browder and the other members of the International Workers' Delegation visiting China sent a public letter to the "Troops of the Imperialist Powers in China," Hankow, April 2, 1927, which stated: "Only the other day in order to avenge the six Europeans who were killed by the paid agents provocateurs of the Northern militarists, the British and American imperialists bombarded the city of Nanking, killing over six hundred defenseless Chinese. . . . It is your duty and in your own interests that you who are yourselves being exploited should not fight against the Chinese people, but on the contrary, you must aid it in its struggle for liberation. . . ." Browder, pp. 33-34.

68. *New China,* May 14, 1927 (Yali).

69. *China in Chaos,* p. 55; also, pp. 1-2.

70. *Ibid.,* pp. 1-2, 38.

71. Borg, *American Policy,* pp. 266, 336-337, 429.

72. Louis D. Froelick, "The Personal Equation in China," *Asia,* XXV, 777 (Sept., 1925).

73. Rigby, *May 30,* p. 132.

74. Froelick, "Personal Equation," *Asia,* XXV, 778; "Along the Trail with the Editor," *Asia,* XXVII, 271 (April, 1927); Froelick, "An A-B-C," *Asia,* XXVII, 532-535; Elmer Davis, "An Inexpert Looks at Asia," *Asia,* XXVII, 339. See also, Littell, "The Revolutionary Spirit," *Asia,* XXVII, 482-486, 529-532. Littell recommends cooperation with the progressive, idealistic group within the KMT rather than armed threats.

75. Lewis S. Gannett, "Canton--Hope of China," *The Nation,* 122: 336-338 (March 31, 1926); also, Gannett, "In Red Canton," *Asia,* XXVI, 489-492, 569-570.

76. Harry F. Ward, "The White Boomerang in China," *Asia,* XXV, 939 (Nov., 1925).

77. Toynbee, "A British View of Trade with China," *Asia,* XXVII, 273-277 (April, 1927).

78. Quoted in Rigby, *May 30,* p. 150.

79. Lloyd George quoted in Tso, *The Labor Movement,* p. 41.

80. Text of the proposals in Hsia Ching-lin, *The Status of*

Shanghai. A Historical Review of the International Settlement, reprint of 1929 ed. (Taipei, 1971), pp. 190-191.

81. See *North China Herald,* April 9, 1927 for trans. of Ch'en Tu-hsiu's statement, originally published in *Hsiang-tao,* March 18, 1927. For trans. of Chiang Kai-shek's statements, see Wieger, VII, 151-154; VIII, 23-24.

82. Jordan, pp. 118-120.

83. Strong, "The Awakened Peasantry," *Asia,* XXVIII, 33-35, 64-65.

84. At least this was a proposal made by Ts'ai Ho-sen somewhat later in June, see James P. Harrison, *The Long March to Power* (NY, 1972), p. 554.

85. J. Lossing Buck, "Peasant Movements," CCYB, 1928, p. 274.

86. Wieger, VII, 234-235.

87. Section 9 of the "Resolutions on the Chinese Communist Youth Corps adopted at the [sixth] Plenum of the Young Communist International" was devoted to CYC tasks with reference to the YMCA and the Anti-Christian Movement.

88. "Shang-hai hsueh-sheng lien-ho-hui chih hsuan-yen yü yao ch'iu" (Proclamation and petition of the Shanghai Student Union), in "Chiao-yü chieh hsiao-hsi," CYTC, XIX (Jan., 1927).

89. Leavens to Bevis, March 5, May 22, 1927 (Yali).

90. "Educational Events," *School and Society,* XXVIII, 262 (Sept., 1928); Lamberton, p. 183.

91. DePree to Chamberlain, April 25, 1927 (RCA, N.B. Theo.); Gowdy to North, March 30, April 11, 1927 (ABC-FCU, Houghton); "Report of the Vice-president of Hangchow Christian College," 1927-1928 (Presbyterian Board of Foreign Missions), pp. 1-2.

92. Peng Ta-mu, "A Chinese Student," *Asia,* XXVIII, 246-247.

93. "Workers at Shanghai College Organize Union, Present Demands and Take Things into own Hands," *China Press,* May 25, 1927.

94. Leavens to Bevis, April 4, 1927 (Yali).

95. "Demands of the Staff Union of Canton Christian College," *China Weekly Review,* April 23, 1927; Swisher, *Canton in Revolution,* pp. 50-55, 61-64, 70-74.

96. "Circular Letter of the CC [CCP] to All Party Members, Aug. 7, 1927," in Brandt, *Documentary History,* p. 109. J.L. Buck states that the membership of the executive committee of the Kwangtung Peasant Union was composed mostly of non-farmers and that the staff members of the union were almost all from the intellectual class, "Peasant Movements," CCYB, 1928, p. 274.

97. "Demands of the Staff Union of Canton Christian College," *China Weekly Review,* April 23, 1927.

98. "Chiao-yü chieh hsiao-hsi," CYTC, XIX (Feb., 1927); Corbett, *Lingnan,* pp. 106-110; Lingnan University Catalogue, 1928-1929, p. 13.

99. P'eng was criticized for losing sight of the crucial importance of the military while concentrating on the repercussions of anti-imperialism after the Nanking incident; Ts'ai was reported to have proposed provoking imperialist intervention in Shanghai and Nanking in order to restore unity to the anti-imperialist, anti-militarist campaign; Ts'ai advocated strengthening and deepening the revolution even if it delayed the Northern Campaign and necessitated withdrawal from the United Front. After Chiang's March 20, 1926 coup, the CCP sent Yun Tai-ying to teach at Whampoa Military Academy; later he became political instructor at the Wuhan branch of the Central Military Academy and was given responsibility for attempting to counterbalance Chiang's influence; Yun helped organize and lead the Canton Commune of Dec., 1927, which assumed a radical stance regarding the missionaries, their schools, and works. Klaus H. Pringsheim, "The Functions of the Chinese Communist Youth Leagues (1920-1949)," *China Quarterly,* 12: 75-80, (Oct.-Dec., 1962); Chang Kuo-t'ao, I, 617, 623-624; Hsiao Tso-liang, "The Dispute over a Wuhan Insurrection in 1927," *China Quarterly,* 33: 108-122 (Jan.-March, 1968).

Chapter VIII

1. Wu Chao-kwang, pp. 187-188; Letter of Chiang Kai-shek to comrades of the revolutionary party, May 16, 1927, *Jen-min jih-pao,* May 19, 1927.

2. "Kuo-min cheng-fu chiao-yü hsing-cheng wei-yuan-hui chieh-shih shou-hui chiao-yü ch'üan chih pan-fa" (National government Central Educational Council's explanation of the method of restoring educational rights), Doc. 34 (Yali); H.C. Tsao, "The Nationalist Movement and Christian Education," CCYB, 1928, pp. 183-184.

3. John Israel, *Student Nationalism in China, 1927-1937* (Stanford, 1966), p. 16; Chang Ch'in-shih, (Neander Chang), "What of the students?", CR, LIX, 441 (1928). Later some schools were given special permission to conduct supplementary classes; in a few instances, schools simply disregarded the order and carried on regular classes.

4. Kapp, pp. 78-81.

5. "West China Union University Celebrates University Day," *Educational Review*, XX, 304 (July, 1928); *The China Year Book*, 1928, pp. 515-516.

6. In late 1926 and 1927 *Hsing-shih* was still publishing articles sprinkled with references to Western authors and policies as it argued the case for nationalist education monopolized by nationals. See Ch'en Ch'i-t'ien, "Kuo-chia yü chiao-yü (Nation and education), no. 106 (Oct. 16, 1926); Hsia Wen-yun, "Tsui-chin shih-ch'i ko-kuo ti kuo-chia-chu-i chiao-yü ti yun-tung" (The nationalist education movment of our country during the most recent period), *ibid.*, no. 149 (Sept. 24, 1927) and no. 150 (Oct. 1, 1927).

7. I Chün, "Tang-hua chiao-yü chiu shih p'o-huai kuo-chia chiao-yü, chiu shih ts'ui-ts'an min ch'üan (Partyized education is injurious to national education, is destructive of the people's rights), *Hsing-shih*, no. 108 (Oct. 30, 1926); Ying Ch'ou, "Fan tui tang-hua chiao-yü ti san ta lun-chü (Three important factors against partyized education), *ibid.*, no. 114 (Dec. 4, 1926).

8. Leavens to Bevis, May 22, 25, 1927 (Yali); John L. Coe, *Huachung University* (NY, 1962), pp. 54-56.

9. "Midnight Watch," April, 1929 (Report on the Taiku, Shansi mission by C. and A. Hausske) (Andover Divinity Library, Pamphlets and mimeos., China).

10. "Report of the Vice-President of Hangchow Christian College," 1927-1928 (Prebyterian Board of Foreign Missions), p. 3; Day, pp. 64-65.

11. William L. Tung (Tung Lin), *Revolutionary China, A Personal Account, 1926-1949* (NY, 1973), pp. 39-42.

12. Swisher, *Canton in Revolution*, pp. 57-68.

13. Chang Kuo-t'ao, I, 579-580; Israel, pp. 13-14.

14. Wang Fan-hsi, *Chinese Revolutionary*, pp. 23, 35-42.

15. "Digest of Important Actions of the First General Assembly of the Church of Christ in China" (Pamphlet, MRL). Ch'eng Ching-yi was elected Moderator.

16. Latourette, pp. 726-727; Breslin, pp. 58-59. Latourette points out that none of the Chinese bishops was entrusted with a major vicariate at the time and that nine-tenths of the bishops still were foreigners.

17. Israel, pp. 16, 124; Wieger, VIII, 32-35.

18. Ibid., pp. 2, 46-47, 452-458.

19. Ibid., pp. 47-48.

20. "Carrying On" (Brief report issued by Lingnan in 1927, MRL).

21. Chang Ch'in-shih, "What of the Students?", CR, LIX, 440-441; Wieger, VIII, 77.

22. John H. Reisner, University of Nanking, Occasional Letter, no. 9, Dec. 28, 1927 (Yali). Partly became many of the administrators in the public schools were political appointees, indiscipline was said to be even more prevalent in the government institutions of Nanking than in the mission schools.

23. Brandt, Documentary History, pp. 108-109; Wieger, VIII, 67-68. For further detail on the Canton Commune, see Harrison, pp. 138-140; Hsiao Tso-liang, "Chinese Communism and the Canton Soviet of 1927," China Quarterly, 30: 49-78. Another indication of the prevalence of fatigue as well as fear was the minimal support given the insurrectionists by all sectors of society in Canton.

24. Swisher, Canton in Revolution, pp. 91, 138-139.

25. National Central Educational Council, "Students' Demands Officially Answered" (Trans. in Yali).

26. Allen B. Linden, "Politics and Education in Nationalist China," Journal of Asian Studies, XXVII, 770-772 (Aug., 1968); Wei Chueh (Sidney K. Wei), "Education under the Nationalist Government," CCYB, 1928, pp. 200-206; Mok Poon-kan, "The History and Development of the Teaching of English in China," (Diss., Columbia U., 1951), p. 256. Wei was a member of the Educational Council.

27. "Kuo-min cheng-fu chiao-yü hsing-cheng wei-yuan-hui chieh-shih shou-hui chiao-yü ch'üan chih pan-fa" (Yali).

28. "Kai-chin szu-li hsueh-hsiao tsu" (Progress in private school organization), Ch'üan kuo chiao-yü hui-i pao-kao (Nanking, 1928), pp. 623-639.

29. "The Future of Christian Schools," CR, LIX, 394-395 (1928).

30. Lamberton, pp. 223-226; "The Recent Attitude of the Nationalist Government towards Christian Schools," Educational Review, XX, 391-392 (Oct., 1928).

31. Tai Chi-t'ao, "A Message to China's Youth," CR, LIX, 567-571 (1928); Israel, pp. 16, 25; H. C. Tsao, "The Nationalist Government and Education," Educational Review, XX, 188.

32. Ibid.; "To Provincial and Municipal Educational Authorities, University Districts and Presidents of Government Universities," ibid., 394-395 (Oct., 1928); "Order of the National Government Regarding Discipline of Students," ibid., XXI, 197-198 (April, 1929). For trans. of several of Chiang Kai-shek's speeches on the subject, see Wieger, VIII, 126-129, 163.

33. Israel, pp. 22-28; Olenik, pp. 249-262.

34. Israel, pp. 18-22.

35. For discussions and documents of the Tsinan Incident, see Akira Iriye, pp. 198-205; Jordan, pp. 156-160; The China Year Book, 1929/30, II, 881-893.

36. DePree to Chamberlain, May 25, 1928 (RCA-N.B. Theo.); Israel, pp. 19-21.

37. Teachers and Students of the Central Party Training College of the Kuomintang, Nanking, "Manifesto to the Peoples, Press and Parliaments of All Friendly Nations," May 8, 1928 (trans. in Yali); Wieger, VIII, 96-97.

38. May 9, National Humiliation Day, commemorated Yuan Shih-kai's acceptance of Japan's Twenty-one Demands in 1915. For the role of Yenching in the December 9 Movement, see Jessie G. Lutz, "December 9, 1935: Student Nationalism and the China Christian Colleges," Journal of Asian Studies, XXVI, 627-648 (Aug., 1967).

39. Charles H. Corbett, Shantung Christian University (Cheeloo) (NY, 1955), pp. 191-193; Marjorie B. Leavens to Palmer Bevis, May 31, 1928 (Yali); DePree to Chamberlain, May 25, 1928 (RCA - N.B. Theo.).

40. "The Tsinan Incident. A Chinese View," The China Outlook, June 1, 1928, pp. 4-5. One Chinese interpretation saw Tsinan as simply a bargaining chip that the Japanese were retaining in order to secure their interests in Manchuria and Inner Mongolia.

41. Israel, p. 34. The Hong Kong branch of the General Labor Union accused Chiang of "uniting the nation only to surrender it

to the Imperialists" and adopted the slogan, "Oppose the Five Demands of the Japanese Imperialists which have been accepted by the Kuomintang!", quoted in Jordan, p. 160.

42. Day, pp. 62-69; "Hangchow College Trustees Decide to Close," *Shanghai Times*, July 10, 1928 (clipping in Yali).

43. *Ibid.* The college reopened a year later. One of the complications was the fact that the provincial regulations were more strict than Nanking's; for example, all members of the local board had to be Chinese. Only later did the national government overrule the provincial administration.

44. Letter from Secretary of Talmage College Board at Board's request to state position on registration, Aug. 2, 1927; DePree to Chamberlain, Aug. 16, 1927; Cablegram from Board of Foreign Missions to Amoy Mission, Oct. 22, 1927; Chamberlain to DePree, Oct. 20, 1927; DePree to Chamberlain, June 30, 1928; Feb. 12, 1929 (RCA - N.B. Theo.).

45. "News: West China Union University," *Educational Review*, XX, 111 (Jan., 1928).

46. Fukien Christian University, "Report of the President," 1930, p. 3; 1931, pp. 1-2 (MRL); DePree to Chamberlain, Feb. 12, 1929 (RCA - N.B. Theo.); Theodore Hsi-en Chen, "The 15th Anniversary of Fukien Christian University," *Educational Review*, XXIII, 217 (April, 1931). See Olenik, pp. 253, 276 for Teng Yen-ta's attempts to organize a third party at this time.

47. Paul Clark, "Changsha in the 1930 Red Army Occupation," *Modern China*, VII, 432-439 (Oct., 1981). Clark points out that some Christian institutions (Yali and the YMCA) were spared, while certain Chinese private and government properties were destroyed.

48. Williams-Porter Hospital, Techow, Shantung, "Report for 1929," (Andover; Pamphlets, etc., China); Hallett Abend, "The Crisis of Christian Missions in China," *Current History*, XXXII, 931 (Aug., 1930); Sovik, p. 257.

49. Corbett, *Shantung Christian University*, pp. 169-173.

50. *Ibid.*, pp. 173-175; "Settlement of Arts Students' Strike," *Cheeloo Bulletin*, no. 257 (Nov. 30, 1929) (Andover).

51. Corbett, *Shantung Christian University*, pp. 175-182; K.K. Thompson, "Notes from the Shantung Christian Educational Association," *Educational Review*, XXIII, 106-108 (Jan., 1931).

52. Frank W. Price, "Registration Trends,"; *Educational Review*, XXI, 159-160 (April, 1929).

53. For further information, see Lutz, *China and the Christian Colleges*, ch. VIII, "Sinification and Secularization, the 1930s," pp. 271-321.

54. For detailed discussions, see Paul A. Varg, *The Making of a Myth* (Lansing, MI, 1968); James Reed, *The Missionary Mind and American East Asian Policy* (Cambridge, MA, 1983); Michel Oksenberg and Robert B. Oxnam, eds., *Dragon and Eagle. United States-China Relations: Past and Future* (NY, 1978); Michael H. Hunt, *Making of a Special Relationship: The United States and China to 1914* (NY, 1983).

Conclusion

1. Chang, TCSC, pp. 271-272.

2. Shu Hsin-ch'eng, *Shou-hui chiao-yü*, p. 55.

3. Quoted in Chow, *May Fourth*, pp. 139-140.

4. *Ibid.*, pp. 137-138.

5. Yang Chia-ming, pp. 57-59, 70-80.

6. For further detail, see Israel, *Student Nationalism*, pp. 131-132, 155, 177; Lutz, "December 9, 1935," *Journal of Asian Studies*, XXVI, 641-647; Suzanne Pepper, "The Student Movement and the Chinese Civil War, 1945-1948," *The China Quarterly*, 48:698-735 (Oct.-Dec. 1971); Lutz, "The Chinese Student Movement of 1945-1949," *Journal of Asian Studies*, XXXI, 89-110 (1971).

7. C.M. Wilbur, "The Influence of the Past: How the Early Years Helped to Shape the Future of the CCP," in *Party Leadership and Revolutionary Power in China*, ed. John W. Lewis (Cambridge, MA, 1970), pp. 53-54; Lutz, "December 9, 1935," *Journal of Asian Studies*, XXVI, 627-648.

8. Nairn, *Break-up of Britain*, pp. 329-363.

9. *Ibid.*, p. 349.

10. Chang Ch'in-shih, himself a Christian, had some rather blunt things to say about the status of missions and the Christian church in 1929. He called the Chinese Christian church an unrealized ideal and he accused mission boards of being primarily concerned with funds, property, and administration; they took for granted that the mission churches were Chinese churches. "For many the relationship between [Chinese] church members and missionaries appears to be that between recipients and philanthropists, or between slaves and masters." See "The Biggest Problem Before Us,"

Chen-li yü sheng-ming, 4.3 (April 15, 1929). A graduate of Lingnan stated in 1933 that the private schools, "being, relatively speaking, immune from financial disruption and political disturbance, . . . at once become a peaceful and thus a better place of learning. . . ." He remained highly critical of parochial schools, nevertheless: "While the private school is attacked for its private character and its segregational tendency as being undesirable for a nation which strives for democracy and national solidarity, the mission schools are further attacked for their religious character as educationally unsound, their foreign control as undesirable, their foreign cultural influence as unwholesome, and their separate system of organization as dangerous." Tsang Chiu-sam, *Nationalism in School Education in China since the Opening of the Twentieth Century* (Hong Kong, 1933), pp. 186-187. Also, the comments of Yu-ming Shaw, "The Reaction of Chinese Intellectuals toward Religion and Christianity," in Whitehead, ed., *China and Christianity,* pp. 175-176.

11. For extracts from Mao's speech, see Schram, *Political Thought of Mao,* pp. 109-110.

12. Michael Schaller, *The United States and China in the Twentieth Century* (NY, 1979), pp. 4-5, 24-25.

SELECTED BIBLIOGRAPHY

Abend, Hallett. *My Life in China, 1926-1941.* New York, 1943.

American Board of Commissioners for Foreign Missions. "Fukien Christian University: Documents and Letters." Houghton Library, Harvard University.

──────. "Foochow Mission" vols. XIX, XX. Houghton Library, Harvard University.

──────. "North China Mission" vol. XLVI. Houghton Library, Harvard University.

Andover Divinity Library. Pamphlets and mimeographed materials, China.

The Anti-Christian Movement: A Collection of Papers Originally Issued by the Anti-Christian Movement and Translated for the Student Y.M. and Y.W.C.A. of China. 2d. ed. Shanghai, 1925.

Asia. New York, 1922-1928. Title varies; also, *Asia and the Americas.*

Barnett, Suzanne W. and John K. Fairbank, eds. *Christianity in China. Early Protestant Missionary Writings.* Cambridge, MA, 1985.

Bennett, Adrian A. *Missionary Journalist in China. Young J. Allen and His Magazines, 1860-1883.* Athens, GA, 1983.

Bergere, Marie Claire and Tchang Fou-jouei. *Sauvons la Patrie. Le nationalisme chinois et le mouvement du 4 Mai 1919.* Paris, 1978.

Bohr, Paul R. *Famine in China and the Missionary: Timothy Richard as Relief Administrator and Advocate of National Reform, 1876-1884.* Cambridge, MA, 1972.

Boorman, Howard, ed. *Biographical Dictionary of Republican China.* 4 vols. New York, 1967, 1970, 1971.

Borg, Dorothy. *American Policy and the Chinese Revolution, 1925-1928.* New York, 1947.

Brandt, Conrad, Benjamin Schwartz, and John K. Fairbank, eds. *A Documentary History of Chinese Communism.* Cambridge, MA, 1952.

Breslin, Thomas A. *China, American Catholicism, and the Missionary.* University Park, PA, 1980.

Browder, Earl. *Civil War in Nationalist China.* Chicago, 1927.

Buck, Pearl S. *Tell the People. Talks with James Yen about the Mass Education Movement.* New York, 1945.

―――. *My Several Worlds.* New York, 1954.

Cavendish, P. "Anti-imperialism in the Kuomintang, 1923-1928," in Jerome Ch'en and Nicholas Tarling, eds., *Studies in the Social History of China and Southeast Asia. Essays in Memory of Victor Purcell.* Cambridge, 1970.

Chang Ch'in-shih (Neander C.S. Chang). *Kuo-nei chin-shih-nien-lai chih tsung-chiao ssu-ch'ao* (The tide of religious thought in China during the last decade). Peking, 1927.

Chang Kuo-t'ao. *The Rise of the Chinese Communist Party, 1921-1938.* 2 vols. Lawrence, KS, 1971-1972.

Chapman, Herbert O. *The Chinese Revolution, 1926-1927. A Record of the Period under Communist Control as Seen from the National Capital, Hankow.* London, 1928.

Chen-li chou-k'an (Truth weekly). Peking, 1923-1926.

Chen-li yü sheng-ming (Truth and life). Peking, 1926-1929.

Ch'en I-lin. *Tsai-chin san-shih-nien Chung-kuo chiao-yü shih* (History of Chinese education during the last thirty years). Shanghai, 1930.

Ch'en, Jerome. *Mao and the Chinese Revolution.* London, 1965.

―――. *Yuan Shih-k'ai,* 2d ed. Stanford, 1972.

―――. *China and the West. Society and Culture 1815-1937.* Bloomington, 1979.

Ch'en, Joseph T. *The May Fourth Movement in Shanghai; The Making of a Social Movement in Modern China.* Leiden, 1971.

Cheng-chih chou-pao (Political weekly). Peking, May, 1924.

Ch'eng Ching-yi, "The Chinese Church," *The Student World,* XV, 27-31 (Jan., 1922).

Chesneaux, Jean. *The Chinese Labor Movement, 1919-1927,* tr. H.M. Wright. Stanford, 1968.

Chia-yin chou-k'an (The tiger weekly). Peking, July, 1925-February, 1927.

Chiang Wen-han (Kiang Wen-han). *The Ideological Background of the Chinese Student Movement.* New York, 1948.

Selected Bibliography   359

Ch'iang Shu-ko, ed. *Chung-kuo chin-tai chiao-yü chih-tu* (Modern educational system of China). Shanghai, 1934.

Chiao-yü chou-pao (Education weekly). Shanghai, May, 1924.

Chiao-yü tsa-chih (Educational review). Shanghai, 1922-1928.

China Centenary Missionary Conference Records: Report of the Great Conference held at Shanghai, April 5 to May 8, 1907. Shanghai, 1907.

China Christian Educational Association. *The Christian College in New China. The Report of the Second Biennial Conference of Christian Colleges and Universities in China.* Shanghai, 1926.

The China Christian Year Book. Shanghai, 1926-1931. (A continuation of *The China Mission Year Book.*)

The China Critic. Shanghai, 1928-1932.

China in Chaos. Pub. by *The North China Daily News and Herald Ltd.* Shanghai, April, 1927.

The China Outlook. Peking, Dec. 1, 1927-July 1, 1928.

The China Mission Year Book. Shanghai, 1910-1919, 1923, 1925. (In 1926 became *The China Christian Year Book).*

China Weekly Review. Shanghai, 1922-1930.

The China Year Book, London, 1919; Peking and Tientsin, 1921-1930.

Chinese Christian Education: A Report of a Conference held in New York City, April 6, 1925. New York, 1925.

The Chinese Church as Revealed in the National Christian Conference held in Shanghai, May, 1922. Shanghai, 1922.

The Chinese Recorder. Shanghai, 1911-1930.

The Chinese Social and Political Science Review. Peking, 1919, 1920, 1922-1930.

Chinese Students' Christian Association in North America. *The "Shanghai Affair".* New York, July, 1925.

Ching Feng. Hong Kong, 1964-1983.

Ch'ing-nien chin-pu ("Association progress"). Shanghai, 1922-1928.

Ch'ing-nien chou-k'an (Youth weekly). Canton, 1922.

Ch'ing-shih wen-t'i. New Haven, 1967-1982.

Chow Tse-tsung. *The May Fourth Movement: Intellectual Revolution in Modern China.* Cambridge, MA, 1960.

───────. *Research Guide to the May Fourth Movement.* Cambridge, MA, 1963.

Christian Education in China: A Study Made by an Educational Commission Representing the Mission Boards and Societies Conducting Work in China. New York, 1922.

Chueh-wu (Awakening). Shanghai, 1922, 1924.

Chung-hua Chi-tu-chiao chiao-yü chi-k'an (China Christian educational quarterly). Shanghai, 1925-1930.

Chung-hua Chi-tu-chiao hui nien chien (China Christian Church year book). Shanghai, 1925, 1927.

Chung-hua chiao-yü chieh (Chinese educational circles). Shanghai, 1922-1927.

Chung-hua kuei-chu (China for Christ). Peking, 1922.

Chung-kuo ch'ing-nien (Chinese youth). Shanghai, 1923-1927.

Chung-kuo ch'ing-nien tang shih tzu liao (Materials on the history of the Young China Party). Taipei, 1955.

Chung-kuo Kuo-min-tang chou-k'an (The Chinese Kuomintang weekly). Canton, 1924.

Chung-kuo Kuo-min-tang chung-yang wei-yuan-hui tang-shih shih-liao pien-tsuan wei-yuan-hui (Party archives commission of the Kuomintang under the Kuomintang Central Committee), Newspaper clippings on Youth Movement, Education, May 30, 1925. Taiwan.

Ch'üan-kuo chiao-yü hui-i pao-kao (Report of the National Educational Conference). Nanking, 1928.

Clark, Paul. "Changsha in the 1930 Red Army Occupation," *Modern China.* VII, 413-444 (Oct., 1981).

Clifford, Nicholas R. *Shanghai, 1925: Urban Nationalism and the Defense of Foreign Privilege.* Ann Arbor, 1979.

Coe, John L. *Huachung University.* New York, 1962.

Cohen, Paul A. *China and Christianity: The Missionary Movement and the Growth of Chinese Antiforeignism, 1860-1870.* Cambridge, MA, 1963.

───────. "Christian Missions and their Impact to 1900," in John K. Fairbank, ed. *The Cambridge History of China,* vol. X, p. 1, *Late Ch'ing, 1800-1911.* Cambridge, 1978.

Selected Bibliography

Corbett, Charles H. *Shantung Christian University (Cheeloo)*. New York, 1955.

──────. *Lingnan University*. New York, 1963.

Creamer, Thomas A. "Hsueh-yun: Shanghai's Students and the May Thirtieth Movement." M.A. Thesis, University of Virginia, 1975.

Cressy, Earl H. *Christian Higher Education in China: A Study for the Year, 1925-26*. Shanghai, 1928.

Current History. Philadelphia, 1926-1931.

Day, Clarence B. *Hangchow University: A Brief History*. New York, 1955.

Death Blow to Corrupt Doctrines. A Plain Statement of Facts. Published by the Gentry and the People. Tr. from the Chinese. Shanghai, 1870.

Dewey, John. "American and Chinese Education," *The New Republic* XXX, 15-17 (March 1, 1922).

Doré, R.P. Henri, "Le Confuceisme sous la Republique, 1911-1922," *The New China Review* IV, 298-319 (Aug., 1922).

Duiker, William J. *Ts'ai Yuan-p'ei, Educator of Modern China*. University Park, PA, 1977

Eddy, G. Sherwood. *North American Students and World Advance*. New York, 1920.

──────. *Christian Students and World Problems*. New York, 1924.

The Educational Association of China. *Triennial Reports*. Shanghai, 1905, 1909.

Educational Review. Shanghai, 1916-1930.

Edwards, Dwight W. *Yenching University*. New York, 1959.

Eley, Geoff, "Nationalism and Social History," *Social History*, VI, 83-107 (Jan., 1981).

d'Elia, Pascal M. *The Triple Demism of Sun Yat-sen*. Wuchang, 1931.

Eudin, Xenia J. and Robert C. North. *Soviet Russia and the East, 1920-1927. A Documentary Survey*. Stanford, 1957.

Fairbank, John K., "Patterns behind the Tientsin Massacre," *Harvard Journal of Asiatic Studies* XX, 480-511 (1957).

_____., ed. *The Missionary Enterprise in China and America.* Cambridge, MA, 1974.

Fan Chi-tu-chiao chou-k'an (Anti-Christian weekly). Canton, Feb.-May, 1925.

Fan tui Chi-tu-chiao yun-tung (The Anti-Christian Movement), comp. by Chung-kuo ch'ing-nien she and Fei Chi-tu-chiao t'ung-meng. Shanghai, 1924.

Fei Chi-tu-chiao hsun-k'an (Anti-Christian bi-weekly). Shanghai, Nov.-Dec., 1925.

Feigon, Lee. *Chen Duxiu. Founder of the Chinese Communist Party.* Princeton, 1983.

Fenn, William P. *Christian Higher Education in Changing China, 1880-1950.* Grand Rapids, MI, 1976.

Feuerwerker, Albert. *The Foreign Establishment in China in the Early 20th Century.* Ann Arbor, 1976.

Ford, Eddy L. *The History of the Educational Work of the Methodist Episcopal Church in China.* Foochow, 1938.

Forsythe, Sidney. *An American Missionary Community in China, 1895-1905.* Cambridge, MA, 1971.

Franke, Wolfgang. *Chinas Kulturelle Revolution. Die Bewegung vom. 4 Mai 1919.* Munich, 1957.

Friedman, Edward. *Backward toward Revolution. The Chinese Revolutionary Party.* Berkeley, 1974.

Fukien Christian University. *Report of the President.* 1919-1922, 1925-1927 (MRL).

Furth, Charlotte, ed. *The Limits of Change. Essays on Conservative Alternatives in Republican China.* Cambridge, MA 1976.

_____. "Intellectual Change: from the Reform Movement to the May Fourth Movement, 1895-1920," in John K. Fairbank, ed. *The Cambridge History of China,* vol. XII, pt. 1, *Republican China, 1912-1949.* Cambridge, 1983.

Gannett, Lewis S., "Canton--Hope of China," *The Nation* CXXII, 336-338 (March 31, 1926).

Garrett, Shirley S. *Social Reformers in Urban China. The Chinese Y.M.C.A., 1895-1926.* Cambridge, MA, 1970.

Gellner, Ernest. *Contemporary Thought and Politics.* Ed. by I.S. Jarvie and Joseph Agassi. London, 1974.

Gewurtz, Margo S. "Social Reality and Educational Reform. The Case of the Chinese Vocational Educational Association, 1917-1927," *Modern China* VI, 157-180 (April, 1978).

The Green Year. "Supplement Concerning Events on and since May 30 in Shanghai." Issued by the magazine of the National Y.W.C.A. of China. Shanghai, 1925.

Greene, Ruth Altman. *Hsiang-ya Journal.* Hamden, CT, 1977.

Grieder, Jerome B. *Intellectuals and the State in Modern China. A Narrative History.* New York, 1981.

Gulick, Edward V. *Peter Parker and the Opening of China.* Cambridge, MA, 1973.

Hangchow Christian College. *Report of the President.* 1919-1920, 1925-1926, 1927-1928 (Presbyterian Board of Foreign Missions, NYC).

Harrison, James P. *The Long March to Power. A History of the Chinese Communist Party, 1921-1972.* New York, 1972.

Harvard-Lingnan Archives. Box 35, James N. Henry, 1926. Harvard Yenching Library.

———. Box 191, Crisis and Transition: Nationalist Uprising, Labor Uprising on Campus.

———. Box 192, Crisis and Transition: Government Registration and Transfer of Administration.

Hay, Stephen N. *Asian Ideas of East and West. Tagore and His Critics in Japan, China, and India.* Cambridge, MA, 1970.

Hsia Ching-lin. *The Status of Shanghai. A Historical Review of the International Settlement.* Taipei, 1971 reprint.

Hsiang-tao chou-pao (Guide weekly). Shanghai, 1922-1927.

Hsiao Tso-liang. "Chinese Communism and the Canton Soviet of 1927," *China Quarterly* 30: 49-78 (April-June, 1967).

———. "The Dispute over a Wuhan Insurrection in 1927," *China Quarterly* 33: 108-122 (Jan.-March, 1968).

Hsin ch'ao (New tide or "The Renaissance"), Peking, 1919-1922.

Hsin chiao-yü (New education). Shanghai, 1921-1925.

Hsin ch'ing-nien (New youth or "La Jeunesse"). Shanghai, 1916-1921.

Hsin hsueh-sheng pan yueh-k'an (New student semi-monthly). Canton, 1923-1924.

Hsing shih chou-pao (Awakening lion weekly). Shanghai, 1924-1928.

Hsu Ting Lee-hsia. *Government Control of the Press in Modern China, 1900-1949*. Cambridge, MA, 1974.

Hsueh-heng ("Critical Review"). Nanking, 1922.

Hsueh-sheng tsa-chih (The students' magazine). Shanghai, 1922-1923.

Hu Shih. "What I Believe," *Forum* LXXXV, 38-43, 114-122 (Jan., Feb., 1931).

Hunt, Michael H. *Making of a Special Relationship: The United States and China to 1914*. New York, 1983.

Huntington, Samuel P. *Political Order in Changing Societies*. New Haven, 1968.

International Review of Missions. Edinburgh, 1921-1930.

Iriye, Akira. *After Imperialism, The Search for a New Order in the Far East, 1921-1931*. Cambridge, MA, 1965.

Isaacs, Harold R. *The Tragedy of the Chinese Revolution*. Stanford, 1951.

Israel, John. *Student Nationalism in China, 1927-1937*. Stanford, 1966.

Jordan, Donald A. *The Northern Expedition. China's National Revolution of 1926-1928*. Honolulu, 1976.

Kapp, Robert A. *Szechwan and the Chinese Republic. Provincial Militarism and Central Power, 1911-1932*. New Haven, 1973.

Keenan, Barry C. "Educational Reform and Politics in Early Republican China," *Journal of Asian Studies* XXXIII, 225-237 (Feb., 1974).

──────. *The Dewey Experiment in China: Educational Reform and Political Power in the Early Republic*. Cambridge, MA, 1977.

Kiang Wen-han, See Chiang Wen-han.

Klein, Donald and Anne B. Clark. *Biographic Dictionary of Chinese Communism, 1921-1965*. 2 vols. Cambridge, MA, 1970.

Ku Ch'ang-sheng. *Ch'uan-chiao-shih yü chin-tai Chung-kuo* (Missionaries and modern China). Shanghai, 1981.

Ku Hung-ting. "The Emergence of the Kuomintang's Anti-Imperialism," *Journal of Oriental Studies*. XIV, 87-97 (1978).

──────. "Urban Mass Movement: The May Thirtieth Movement in Shanghai," *Modern Asian Studies* 13. 2: 197-216 (1979).

Kuo-chia-chu-i chiang yen-chi (Collection of lectures on nationalism), comp. Hsing shih she. 2d ed. Shanghai, 1927.

Kwok, D.W.Y. *Scientism in Chinese Thought, 1900-1950.* New Haven, 1965.

Lam Wing-hung. "The Emergence of a Protestant Christian Apologetics in the Chinese Church during the Anti-Christian Movement." Diss., Princeton Theological Seminary, 1978.

Lamberton, Mary. *St. John's University, Shanghai, 1879-1951.* New York, 1955.

Lary, Diana. *Region and Nation. The Kwangsi Clique in Chinese Politics, 1925-1937.* London, 1974.

Latourette, Kenneth S. *A History of Christian Missions in China.* London, 1929.

Li Chien-nung. *The Political History of China, 1840-1928.* Tr. and ed., Ssu-yu Teng and Jeremy Ingalls. Princeton, 1956.

Li Huang. "My Memoirs," tr. Lillian Chu Chin. 5 vols. Unpub. ms. in Special Collections Library. Columbia University, 1971.

Li Jui. *The Early Revolutionary Activities of Comrade Mao Tse-tung.* Trans. by Anthony S. Sarite. White Plains, NY, 1977.

Liao Kuang-sheng. *Antiforeignism and Modernization in China 1860-1980. Linkage between Domestic Politics and Foreign Policy.* Hong Kong, 1984.

Lin Yü-sheng. *The Crisis of Chinese Consciousness. Radical Antitraditionalism in the May Fourth Era.* Madison, 1979.

Linden, Allen B. "Politics and Education in Nationalist China, The Case of the University Council, 1927-1928," *Journal of Asian Studies* XXVII, 763-776 (Aug., 1968).

Lingnan University. "Carrying On." 1927 (Pamphlet, MRL).

Liu, F.F. *A Military History of Modern China.* Princeton, 1956.

Liu Kwang-ching, ed. *American Missionaries in China: Papers from Harvard Seminars.* Cambridge, MA, 1966.

Lutz, Jessie G. "December 9, 1935: Student Nationalism and the China Christian Colleges," *Journal of Asian Studies* XXVI, 627-648 (Aug., 1967).

──────. *China and the Christian Colleges, 1850-1950.* Ithaca, 1971.

──────. "The Chinese Student Movement of 1945-1949," *Journal of Asian Studies,* XXXI, 89-110 (1971).

_____. "Chinese Nationalism and the Anti-Christian Campaigns of the 1920s," *Modern Asian Studies* 10. 3: 395-416 (1976).

_____. "Students and Political Parties in the Educational Rights Movement, 1924-1928," in *Symposium on the History of the Republic of China*, vol. III. Taipei, 1981.

_____., ed. *Christian Missions in China, Evangelists of What?* Boston, 1965.

_____ and Salah El-Shakhs, eds. *Tradition and Modernity. The Role of Traditionalism in the Modernization Process.* Washington, DC, 1982.

Lü Shih-ch'iang. *Chung-kuo kuan shen fan chiao ti yuan-yin, 1860-1874* (The causes of opposition to Christianity among Chinese officials and gentry, 1860-1874). Taipei, 1966.

_____. "An Analysis of the Anti-Christian Thoughts of Chinese Intellectuals in the Early Republican Period," in *Symposium on the History of the Republic of China*, vol. II. Taipei, 1981.

McDonald, Angus W., Jr. *The Urban Origins of Rural Revolution. Elites and Masses in Hunan Province, China, 1911-1927.* Berkeley, 1978.

McNair, Harley F. *China in Revolution.* 1968 ed. New York, c. 1930.

[Mao Tse-tung], "Hu-nan tzu-hsiu ta-hsüeh ch'uang-li hsü an-yen (Manifesto regarding the Hunan Self-Study University), *Tung-fang tsa-chih*, XX, no. 6, 126-128 (March 23, 1923).

_____. *Selected Works of Mao Tse-tung.* 5 vols. New York, 1954-1956.

Merwin, Wallace C. *Adventure in Unity: The Church of Christ in China.* Grand Rapids, MI, 1974.

Min-kuo jih-pao (Republic daily). Shanghai, 1922-1925.

Min to (People's tocsin). Shanghai, 1922-1926.

Mok Poon-kan. "The History and Development of the Teaching of English in China." Diss., Columbia University, 1951.

Monroe, Paul. *China, A Nation in Evolution.* New York, 1928.

Morrison, Eliza A. *Memoirs of the Life and Labors of Robert Morrison.* 2 vols. London, 1839.

Morse, Hosea B. *The Trade and Administration of the Chinese Empire.* Taipei, 1966 reprint.

Nairn, Tom. *The Break-up of Britain. Crisis and Neo-Nationalism.* London, 1977.

Nance, W.B. *Soochow University.* New York, 1956.

Nanking, University of. *Report of the President.* 1918-1919, 1924-1925 (UB).

Nathan, Andrew J. *Peking Politics, 1918-1923, Factionalism and the Failure of Constitutionalism.* Berkeley, 1976.

National Christian Council of China. *A Five Years' Review, 1922-1927.* Shanghai, 1927.

New China. Pub. by Chinese Students in America. New York, May, 1927.

The New Mandarin. Pub. by the Student Body of the Yenching School of Chinese Studies. Peking, 1926 (Andover).

New York Times. New York, May 15-July 15, 1925.

North China Daily News. Shanghai, 1927.

North China Herald. Shanghai, 1921-1928.

Ogden, Suzanne P., "The Sage in the Inkpot: Bertrand Russell and China's Social Reconstruction in the 1920s," *Modern Asian Studies* 16.4:529-600 (1982).

Oksenberg, Michel and Robert Oxnam, eds. *Dragon and Eagle: United States-China Relations, Past and Future.* New York, 1978.

Olenik, John K., "Left Wing Radicalism in the Kuomintang. Teng Yen-ta and the Genesis of the Third Party Movement in China, 1924-1931." Diss., Cornell University, 1973.

Palumbo, Michael and William O. Shanahan, eds. *Nationalism: Essays in Honor of Louis L. Snyder.* Westport, CT, 1981.

Pao Tsun-p'eng. *Chung-kuo chin-tai ch'ing-nien yun-tung shih* (A history of China's modern youth movement). Taipei, 1953.

Peake, Cyrus H. *Nationalism and Education in Modern China.* New York, 1932.

Peking Leader Press. *Documents on the Shanghai Case.* Peking, 1925. (Wason Collection of Cornell University Library)

Pepper, Suzanne, "The Student Movement and the Chinese Civil War, 1945-1949," *The China Quarterly,* 48:698-735 (Oct.-Dec. 1971).

Pickowicz, Paul G. *Marxist Literary Thought in China. The Influence of Ch'ü Ch'iu-pai.* Berkeley, 1981.

Planchet, Jean M., ed. *Les Missions de Chine et du Japon*. Peking, 1925-1929.

Pott, F.L. Hawks. *History. St. John's University, 1879-1929.* Shanghai, 1929.

Pringsheim, Klaus H., "The Functions of the Chinese Communist Youth Leagues (1920-1949)," *China Quarterly* 12:75-91 (Oct.-Dec., 1962).

Rabe, Valentin H. *The Home Base of American China Missions, 1880-1920*. Cambridge, MA, 1978.

Reed, James. *The Missionary Mind and American East Asia Policy, 1911-1915*. Cambridge, MA, 1983.

Reformed Church in America. China Mission, Correspondence, 1920-1933. (New Brunswick Theological Seminary Library)

Revue d'histoire des Missions. Paris, 1924-1929.

Rigby, Richard W. *The May 30 Movement. Events and Themes*. Canberra, 1980.

Russell, Bertrand. *The Problem of China*. New York, 1922.

St. John's University, 1879-1929. Shanghai, 1929.

Sanford, D.S., "China's Mission Students." Mimeo. paper, Sept. 10, 1926 (Yale in China archives).

Scalapino, Robert A. and George T. Yu. *The Chinese Anarchist Movement*. Berkeley, 1961.

Schaller, Michael. *The United States and China in the Twentieth Century*. New York, 1979.

Schneider, Laurence A. *Ku Chieh-kang and China's New History: Nationalism and the Quest for Alternative Traditions*. Berkeley, 1971.

School and Society. New York, 1921, 1925-1930.

Schram, Stuart. *Mao Tse-tung*. Rev. ed. Baltimore, 1967.

_____. *The Political Thought of Mao Tse-tung*. Rev. ed. New York, 1969.

_____. "From the 'Great Union of the Popular Masses' to the 'Great Alliance'," *The China Quarterly*, 49:88-105 (Jan.-Mar. 1972).

_____. *Mao Zedong, A Preliminary Reassessment*. Hong Kong, 1983.

Schwartz, Benjamin I., ed. *Reflections on the May Fourth Movement: A Symposium*. Cambridge, MA, 1972.

Scott, Roderick. *Fukien Christian University: A Historical Sketch.* New York, 1954.

Shaffer, Lynda. *Mao and the Workers. THe Hunan Labor Movement, 1920-1923.* Armonk, NY, 1982.

Shang-hai Kuang-tung Chung-hua Chi-tu-chiao hui yueh-pao ("Cantonese Union Church Bulletin of Shanghai"). Shanghai, 1922-1924.

Shao-nien Chung-kuo (Young China). Shanghai, 1920-1923.

Sheng-ming yueh-k'an (Life monthly). Peking, 1922-1925.

Sheridan, James E. *Chinese Warlord: The Career of Feng Yü-hsiang.* Stanford, 1966.

Shieh, Milton J.T. *The Kuomintang: Selected Historical Documents, 1894-1969.* Jamaica, NY, 1970.

Shu Hsin-ch'eng. *Shou-hui chiao-yü ch'üan yun-tung* (The movement to restore education rights). Shanghai, 1927.

_____. ed. *Chin-tai Chung-kuo chiao-yü shih-liao* (Historical materials on modern Chinese education). 4 vols. Shanghai, 1923-1928.

Skocpol, Theda. *States and Social Revolutions. A Comparative Analysis of France, Russia, and China.* Cambridge, 1979.

Smith, Anthony D. *Theories of Nationalism.* London, 1971.

Snow, Edgar. *Red Star over China.* New York, 1944.

Solomon, Richard H., "From Commitment to Cant: The Evolving Functions of Ideology in the Revolutionary Process," in Chalmers Johnson, ed. *Ideology and Politics in Contemporary China.* Seattle, 1973.

Sovik, Arne, "Church and State in Republican China: A Survey History of the Relations between the Christian Churches and the Chinese Government, 1911-1945." Diss., Yale University, 1952.

Speer, Robert E. and Hugh T. Kerr. *Report on Japan and China of the Deputation sent by the Board of Foreign Missions of the Presbyterian Church in the U.S. to attend Evaluation Conferences in China in 1926.* New York, 1927.

Stauffer, Milton T., ed. *The Christian Occupation of China.* Shanghai, 1922.

_____., ed. *China, Her Own Interpreter.* New York, 1927.

Swisher, Earl. *Canton in Revolution. The Collected Papers of Earl*

Swisher, 1925-1928. Ed. by Kenneth W. Rea. Boulder, CO, 1977.

Takami Fujii, "The Chinese Northern Expedition and Moscow," in *Symposium on the History of the Republic of China,* vol. III. Taipei, 1981.

T'ang Liang-li. *China in Revolt. How a Civilization Became a Nation.* London, 1927.

Tao Chia-lin Pao, "Peter Parker and the Cushing Mission to China," reprint from *Thought and Word Magazine,* VIII, 153-158 (Sept., 1970).

Taylor, Joseph. *History of West China Union University, 1910-1935.* Chengtu, 1936.

Thomson, James C., Jr., et. al. *Sentimental Imperialists. The American Experience in East Asia.* New York, 1981.

Thurston, Matilda and Ruth M. Chester. *Ginling College.* New York, 1955.

Ting Chih-p'in. *Chung-kuo chin ch'i-shih-nien-lai chiao-yü chi-shih* (A chronological record of Chinese education during the last seventy years). Shanghai, 1935.

Ting Lee-hsia Hsu. *Government Control of the Press in Modern China, 1900-1949.* Cambridge, MA, 1974.

Treadgold, Donald W. *The West in Russia and China. Religious and Secular Thought in Modern Times.* Vol. 2, *China, 1582-1949.* Cambridge, 1973.

Tsang Chiu-sam. *Nationalism in School Education in China since the Opening of the Twentieth Century.* Hong Kong, 1933.

Tso, S.K. Sheldon. *The Labor Movement in China.* Shanghai, 1928.

Tung-fang tsa-chih ("Eastern Miscellany"). Shanghai, 1916-1928.

Tung, William L. (Tung Lin). *Revolutionary China, A Personal Account, 1926-1949.* New York, 1973.

Tyau Min-ch'ien (M.T.Z.Tyau). *China Awakened.* New York, 1922.

United Board for Christian Higher Education in Asia. China Records Project, Yale Divinity Library.

United Presbyterian Church in the U.S.A. Presbyterian Board of Foreign Missions. Files on Hangchow Christian College. New York.

U.S. Department of State. Archives. Decimal Files on China (893.00, 893.404, 393.116), 1922, 1925.

Van Slyke, Lyman P. *Enemies and Friends. The United Front in Chinese Communist History.* Stanford, 1967.

Varg, Paul A. *Missionaries, Chinese, and Diplomats: The American Protestant Missionary Movement in China, 1890-1952.* Princeton, 1958.

———. *The Making of a Myth: The U.S. and China, 1897-1912.* Lansing, MI, 1968.

Wang Chih-hsin. *Chung-kuo Chi-tu-chiao shih-kang* (An outline history of Christianity in China). Rev. ed. Hong Kong, 1959.

Wang Fan-hsi. *Chinese Revolutionary. Memoirs 1919-1949.* Trans. by Gregor Benton. Oxford, 1980.

Wang Nien-k'un. *Wo kuo hsueh-sheng yun-tung shih-hua* (Comments on the history of our country's student movement). Hankow, 1954.

Wang Tsi-chang. *The Youth Movement in China.* New York, 1927.

Wang, Y.C. *Chinese Intellectuals and the West, 1872-1949.* Chapel Hill, 1966.

Weber, Hans-Ruedi. *Asia and the Ecumenical Movement, 1895-1961.* London, 1966.

West, Philip. *Yenching University and Sino-Western Relations, 1916-1952.* Cambridge, MA, 1976.

Whitehead, James D., Yu-ming Shaw, and N.J. Girardot, eds. *China and Christianity, Historical and Future Encounters.* Notre Dame, IN, 1979.

Whiting, Allen. *Soviet Policies in China, 1917-1924.* New York, 1954.

Wieger, Léon, ed. and tr. *Chine Moderne.* 10 vols. Hsien-hsien, 1920-1932.

Wilbur, C. Martin and Julie Lien-ying How. *Documents on Communism, Nationalism, and Soviet Advisers in China, 1918-1927.* New York, 1956.

———., "Military Separatism and the Process of Reunification under the Nationalist Regime, 1922-1937," in Ho Ping-ti and Tsou Tang, eds. *China in Crisis.* Bk 1, vol. 1. Chicago, 1968.

———., "The Influence of the Past. How the Early Years Helped to Shape the Future of the Chinese Communist Party," in John W. Lewis, ed., *Party Leadership and Revolutionary Power in China.* Cambridge, 1970.

_____., "The Second National Congress of the Kuomintang," in *Symposium on the History of the Republic of China*. Vol. III. Taipei, 1981.

Wu Chao-kwang. *The International Aspect of the Missionary Movement in China*. Baltimore, 1930.

Wu Lei-ch'uan. *Chi-tu-chiao yü Chung-kuo wen-hua* (Christianity and Chinese Culture). Shanghai, 1936.

Wu-ssu shih-ch'i ch'i-k'an chieh-shao (An introduction to the periodicals of the May Fourth period). 3 vols. Peking, 1958-1959.

Wu Tien-wei, "Chiang Kai-shek's March Twentieth Coup d'Etat of 1926," *Journal of Asian Studies*. XXVII, 585-602 (1968).

Yale-in-China files. Day Missions Library, Divinity School, Yale University.

The Yali Quarterly. New Haven, 1922, 1924-1927.

Yamamoto, Tatsuro and Sumiko, "The Anti-Christian Movement in China, 1922-1927," *Far Eastern Quarterly* XII, 133-147 (1953).

Yang Chia-min. *Min-kuo shih-wu-nien Chung-kuo hsueh-sheng yun-tung kai-k'uang* (A general view of the Chinese student movement in 1926). Shanghai, 1927.

Yip Ka-che. *Religion, Nationalism and Chinese Students. The Anti-Christian Movement of 1922-1927*. Bellingham, WA, 1980.

Young, Ernest P. *The Presidency of Yuan Shih-k'ai*. Ann Arbor, 1977.

Yü Chia-chü. *Hsueh-hsiao feng-ch'ao ti yen-chiu* (An investigation of school storms). Shanghai, 1925.

Zen, Sophia H. Chen (Chen Heng-che), ed. *Symposium on Chinese Culture*. Shanghai, 1931.

GLOSSARY

Chang Chi (Chang P'u-chuan)	Zhang Ji (Zhang Puquan)	張繼 (張溥泉)
Chang Ch'in-shih (Neander C. S. Chang)	Zhang Qinshi	張欽士
Chang Ch'iu-jen	Zhang Qiuren	張秋人
Chang Chou	Zhang Zhou	張宙
Chang Chun-mai (Carsun Chang) (Chang Chia-sen)	Zhang Junmai (Zhang Jiasen)	張君勱 張嘉敖
Chang I-ching	Zhang Yijing	張亦鏡
Chang Kuo-hua	Zhang Guohua	張國華
Chang Kuo-t'ao	Zhang Guotao	張國燾
Chang Ming	Zhang Ming	章明
Chang Ping-lin	Zhang Binglin	章炳麟
Chang Po-ling	Zhang Boling	張伯苓
Chang Shou-yung	Zhang Shouyung	張壽鏞
Chang Sung-nien	Zhang Songnian	張松年
Chang T'ai-lei	Zhang Tailei	張太雷
Chang T'ai-yen (See Chang Ping-lin)	Zhang Taiyen	張太炎
Chang Tung-sun	Zhang Dongsun	張東蓀
Ch'ang Nai-te	Chang Naide	常乃德
Ch'ang Tao-chih	Chang Daozhi	常導之
Chao Kuan-ch'ing	Zhao Guanqing	趙冠青
Chao Tzu-ch'en	Zhao Zichen	趙紫宸
Che-hsueh	*Zhexue*	哲學
Chen-kuang tsa-chih	*Zhenguang zazhi*	真光雜誌
Chen-li chou-k'an	*Zhenli Zhoukan*	真理週刊
Chen-li yü sheng-ming	*Zhenli yu shengming*	真理與生命

Chen-tan ta-hsueh	Zhendan daxue	震旦大學
Chen Yü	Zhen Yu	振宇
Ch'en Ch'i-t'ien	Chen Qitian	陳啟天
Ch'en Chih-wen	Chen Zhiwen	陳志文
Ch'en Hsi-hsiang	Chen Xixiang	陳錫襄
Ch'en Hsieh-hsun	Chen Xiexun	陳燮勛
Ch'en Huan-chang	Chen Huanzhang	陳煥章
Ch'en I-lin	Chen Yilin	陳翌林
Ch'en Kung-po	Chen Gongbo	陳公博
Ch'en Kuo-fu	Chen Guofu	陳果夫
Ch'en Li-t'ing	Chen Liting	陳立廷
Ch'en pao	*Chen bao*	辰報
Ch'en Shao-yü (Wang Ming)	Chen Shaoyu (Wang Ming)	陳紹禹
Ch'en Tu-hsiu	Chen Duxiu	陳獨秀
Ch'en Wang-tao	Chen Wangdao	陳望道
Ch'en Yu-jen (Eugene Ch'en)	Chen Youren	陳友仁
Ch'en Yun	Chen Yun	陳雲
Cheng Ch'ao-lin	Zheng Chaolin	鄭超麟
Cheng-chih chou-pao	*Zhengzhi zhoubao*	政治週報
Cheng Hou-lan	Zheng Houlan	鄭侯闌
Ch'eng Ch'ien	Cheng Qian	程潛
Ch'eng Ching-i	Cheng Jingyi	誠靜怡
Ch'eng Hsiang-fan	Cheng Xiangfan	程湘帆
Chi-tu-chiao hsueh-sheng shih-yeh hui	Jidujiao xuesheng shiye hui	基督教學生事業會
Chi-tu-chiao yü Chung-kuo wen-hua	*Jidujiao yu Zhongguo wenhua*	基督教與中國文化
Ch'i-lu ta-hsueh (Cheeloo University)	Qilu daxue	齊魯大學
Chia-yin chou-k'an	*Jiayin zhoukan*	甲寅週刊
Chiang Hsien-yun	Jiang Xianyun	蔣先雲

Glossary

Chiang Kai-shek	Jiang Jieshi	蔣介石
Chiang Meng-lin (Chiang Monlin)	Jiang Menglin	蔣夢麟
Chiang Shu-ko	Jiang Shuge	姜書閣
Chiang Wen-han (Kiang Wen-han)	Jiang Wenhan	江文漢
Chiao-yü chou-pao	*Jiaoyu zhoubao*	教育週報
Chiao-yü chu-ch'üan wei-chih hui	Jiaoyu zhuquan weichi hui	教育主權維持會
Chiao-yü tsa-chih	*Jiaoyu zazhi*	教育雜誌
Chiao-yü tu-li yun-tung	Jiaoyu duli yundong	教育獨立運動
Chien-she tsa-chih	*Jianshe zazhi*	建設雜誌
Chien Yu-wen (Timothy Jen)	Jien Youwen	簡又文
Ch'ien-feng yueh-k'an	*Qianfeng yuekan*	前鋒月刊
Ch'ien Hsuan-t'ung	Qian Xuantong	錢玄同
Chih-chiang ta-hsueh (Hang Cho University)	Zhijiang daxue	之江大學
Ch'ih Kuang	Chi Guang	赤光
Chin Chia-feng	Jin Jiafeng	金家鳳
Chin-ling nü-tzu ta-hsueh (Ginling College)	Jinling nuzi daxue	金陵女子大學
Chin-ling ta-hsueh (University of Nanking)	Jinling daxue	金陵大學
Chin-pu tang	Jinbu dang	進步黨
Chin-tai Chung-kuo Chiao-yü shih liao	*Jindai Zhongguo jiaoyu shiliao*	近代中國教育史料
Ching feng	*Jing feng*	景風
Ch'ing-nien chin-pu	*Qingnian jinbu*	青年進步
Ch'ing-nien chin-pu hsueh hui	Qingnian jinbu xuehui	青年進步學會
Ch'ing-nien chou-k'an	*Qingnian zhoukan*	青年週刊
Chou En-lai (Wu Hao)	Zhou Enlai	周恩來 (伍豪)
Chou Fo-hai	Zhou Fohai	周佛海

Chou T'ai-hsuan	Zhou Taixuan	周太玄
Chou Tso-jen	Zhou Zuoren	周作人
Chu Chih-hsin	Zhu Zhixin	朱執信
Chu Ching-nung	Zhu Jingnong	朱經農
Chu Teh	Zhu De	朱德
Chu Wu-p'ing	Zhu Wuping	朱務平
Chu Yu-yu (Y.Y. Tsu)	Zhu Youyu	朱友漁
Ch'u Ch'iu-pai	Qu Qiubai	瞿秋白
Ch'uan-chiao-shih yu chin-tai Chung-kuo	*Chuanjiaoshi yu jindai Zhongguo*	傳教士與近代中國
Ch'uan-kuo chiao-yu hui pao kao	*Quanguo jiaoyu huiyi baogao*	全國教育會議報告
Ch'uan-kuo chiao-yu hui lien-ho-hui	Quanguo jiaoyu hui lianhe hui	全國教育會聯合會
Ch'uan-kuo chiao-yu tu-li yun-tung hui	Quanguo jiaoyu duli yundong hui	全國教育獨立運動會
Ch'uan-kuo chi-yeh hsueh-hsiao lien-ho-hui	Quanquo zhiye xue-xiao lianhe hui	全國職業學校聯合會
Ch'uan-kuo hsueh-sheng lien-ho-hui (See Chung-jua min-kuo hsueh-sheng lien-ho-hui)	Quanguo xuesheng lianhe hui	
Ch'uan-kuo k-chieh chiu-kuo hui	Quanguo gejie jiu-guo hui	全國各界救國會
Ch'uan-kuo ko-tsung-chiao hsin-t'u kuo-min hui	Quanguo gezongjiao xintu guomin hui	全國各宗教信徒國民會
Ch'uan-kuo kung-hui lien-ho-hui	Quanguo gonghui lian-he jui	全國工會聯合會
Chueh-wu	*Juewu*	覺悟
Ch'un-pao	*Qunbao*	群報
Chung-hua Chi-tu-chiao chiao-yu chi-k'an	*Zhonghua Jidujiao jiaoyu jikan*	中華基督教教育季刊
Chung-hua Chi-tu-chiao hui	Zhonghua Jidujiao hui	中華基督教會
Chung-hua Chi-tu-chiao hui nien-chien	*Zhonghua Jidujiao hui nianjian*	中華基督教會年鑑

Chung-hua chiao-yü chieh	Zhonghua jiaoyu jie	中華教育界
Chung-hua chiao-yü kai-chin she	Zhonghua jiaoyu gaijin she	中華教育改進社
Chung-hua chih-yeh chiao-yü she	Zhonghua zhiye jiaoyu she	中華職業教育社
Chung-hua kuei-chu	Zhonghua gui zhu	中華歸主
Chung-hua min-kuo hsueh-sheng lien-ho-hui	Zhonghua minguo xuesheng lianhe hui	中華民國學生聯合會
Chung-kuo Chi-tu-chiao shih-kang	Zhongguo Jidujiao shigang	中國基督教史綱
Chung-kuo chin ch'i-shih-nien-lai chiao-yü chi-shih	Zhongguo jin qishinian lai jiaoyu jishi	中國近七十年來教育紀事
Chung-kuo chin-tai chiao-yü chih-tu	Zhongguo jindai jiaoyu zhidu	中國近代教育制度
Chung-kuo chin-tai ch'ing-nien yun-tung shih	Zhongguo jindai qingnian yundong shi	中國近代青年運動史
Chung-kuo ch'ing-nien she	Zhongguo qingnian she	中國青年社
Chung-kuo ch'ing-nien tang	Zhongguo qingnian dang	中國青年黨
Chung-kuo ch'ing-nien tang shih tzu-liao	Zhongguo qingnian dang shi ziliao	中國青年黨史資料
Chung-kuo fu-nü tsa-chih	Zhongguo funu zazhi	中國婦女雜誌
Chung-kuo kuan shen fan chiao ti yuan-yin	Zhongguo guan shen fan jiaodi yuanyin	中國官紳反教的原因
Chung-kuo kung-ch'an-chu-i ch'ing-nien t'uan	Zhongguo gongchan zhuyi qingnian tuan	中國共產主義青年團
Chung-kuo kuo-chia-chu-i ch'ing-nien t'uan	Zhongguo guojian zhuyi qingnian tuan	中國國家主義青年團
Chung-kuo kuo-min-tang chou-k'an	Zhongguo guomindang zhoukan	中國國民黨週刊
Chung-kuo kuo-min-tang chang-yang wei-yuan hui tang-shih shih-liao pien-tsuan wei-yuan hui	Zhongguo guomindang zhongyang weiyuan hui dangshi shiliao bian zuan weiyuan hui	中國國民黨中央委員會黨史史料編纂委員會
Chung-kuo she-hui-chu-i ch'ing-nien t'uan	Zhongguo shehui zhuyi qingnian tuan	中國社會主義青年團

Chung Wan-hua	Zhong Wanhua	鍾婉華
Fan Chi-tu-chiao chou-k'an	*Fan Jidujiao zhoukan*	反基督教週刊
Fan ti-kuo-chu-i ta t'ung-meng	Fan diguo zhuyi da tongmeng	反帝國主義大同盟
Fan-tui Chi-tu-chiao yun-tung	Fandui Jidujiao yundong	反對基督教運動
Fan Tzu-mei (T.M. Van)	Fan Zimei	范子美
Fan wen-hua ch'in-lueh ta t'ung-meng	Fan wenhua qinlue da tongmeng	反文化侵略大同盟
Fan Yuan-lien	Fan Yuanlian	范源濂
Fei Chi-tu-chiao hsueh-sheng t'ung-meng	Fei Jidujiao xuesheng tongmeng	非基督教學生同盟
Fei Chi-tu-chiao hsun-k'an	*Fei Jidujiao xunkan*	非基督教旬刊
Fei Chi-tu-chiao t'e-k'an	*Fei Jidujiao tekan*	非基督教特刊
Fei Chi-tu-chiao yun-tung	Fei Jidujiao yun-dong	非基督教運動
Fei tsung-chiao ta t'ung-meng	Fei zongjiao da tongmeng	非宗教大同盟
Feng-t'ien tung-pao	*Fengtian dongbao*	奉天東報
Feng Yü-hsiang	Feng Yu-xiang	馮玉祥
Fu-chin hsieh-ho ta-hsueh	Fujian xiehe daxue	福建協和大學
Fu-nü chou-pao	*Funu zhoubao*	婦女週報
Fu-tan ta-hsueh	Fudan daxue	復旦大學
Fu T'ung (Fu P'ei-ch'ing)	Fu Tong (Fu Peiqing)	傅銅 (傅佩青)
Ho Hung-chien	He Hungjian	何鴻堅
Ho Meng-hsiung	He Mengxiung	何孟雄
Hsia Hsi	Xia Xi	夏曦
Hsia Ming-han	Xia Minghan	夏明翰
Hsiang-tao chou-pao	*Xiangdao zhoubao*	嚮導週報
Hsiao Ch'u-nü	Xiao Chunu	蕭楚女

Hsiao Tzu-sheng	Xiao Zisheng	蕭子昇
Hsieh Fu-ya (N.Z. Zia)	Xie Fuya	謝扶雅
Hsieh Hsun-ch'u	Xie Xunchu	謝循初
Hsieh Sung-kao (Z.K. Zia)	Xie Songgao	謝頌羔
Hsien-ch'ü	*Xianqu*	先驅
Hsin-ch'ao	*Xinchao*	新潮
Hsin chiao-yü	*Xin jiaoyu*	新教育
Hsin chiao-yü kung-chin she	Xin jiaoyu gongjin she	新教育共進社
Hsin ch'ing-nien (*La Jeunesse*)	*Xin qingnian*	新青年
Hsin hsueh-sheng hui	Xin xuesheng hui	新學生會
Hsin-hsueh shu-yuan	Xinxue shuyuan	新學書院
Hsin-min hsueh-hui	Xinmin xuehui	新民學會
Hsin tsung-chiao kuan	*Xin zongjiao guan*	新宗教觀
Hsing-ch'i p'ing-lun	*Xingpi pinglun*	星期評論
Hsing-shih chou-pao	*Xingshi zhoubao*	醒獅週報
Hsu Ch'ien	Xu Qian	徐謙
Hsu Heng-yao	Xu Hengyao	徐恆耀
Hsu Pao-ch'ien	Xu Baoqian	徐寶謙
Hsu Ping-ch'ang	Xu Bingchang	徐炳昶
Hsu Shih-ch'ang	Xu Shichang	徐世昌
Hsu T'e-li	Xu Teli	徐特立
Hsueh-ch'ao	Xuechao	學潮
Hsueh-heng	*Xueheng*	學衡
Hsueh-hsiao feng-ch'ao ti yen-chiu	*Xuexiao fengchaodi yanjiu*	學校風潮的研究
Hsueh-sheng chiu-kuo hui	Xuesheng jiuguo hui	學生救國會
Hsueh-sheng tsa-chih	*Xuesheng zazhi*	學生雜誌
Hu-chiang ta-hsueh (University of Shanghai)	Hujiang daxue	滬江大學
Hu Han-min	Hu Hanmin	胡漢民

Hu Hsueh-ch'eng (Samuel H.C. Hu)	Hu Xuecheng	胡學誠
Hu I-ku (Y.K. Woo)	Hu Yigu	胡貽穀
Hu Nan-hu (Hu O-kung)	Hu Nanhu	胡南湖
Hu Shih	Hu Shi	胡適
Hua-chung ta-hsueh (Hua-chung College)	Huazhong daxue	華中大學
Hua-Fa chiao-yü hui	Hua Fa jiaoyu hui	華法教育會
Hua-hsi hsieh-ho ta-hsueh (West China Union University)	Huaxi xiehe daxue	華西協和大學
Hua-nan nü-tzu wen-li hsueh-yuan (Hwa Nan College)	Huanan nuzi wenli xueyuan	華南女子文理學院
Huang Jih-k'uei	Huang Rikui	黃日葵
Hung Yeh (William Hung)	Hong Ye	洪業
I-shih pao	*Yishi bao*	益世報
Je-hsieh jih-pao	*Rexie ribao*	熱血日報
Jen-ko chiu kuo	Renge jiu guo	人格救國
Jen-min jih-pao	*Renmin ribao*	人民日報
Jen Pi-shih	Ren Bishi	任弼時
Kan Nai-kuang	Gan Naiguang	甘乃光
K'ang Pai-ch'ing (K'ang Hung-chang)	Kang Baiqing (Kang Hongzhang)	康白情 (康洪章)
K'ang Yu-wei	Kang Youwei	康有為
Kao Er-po	Gao Erbo	高爾柏
Kao I-han	Gao Yihan	高一涵
K'o Po-nien see	Li Ch'un-fan	
Ku Ch'ang-sheng	Gu Changsheng	顧長聲
Ku Meng-yü	Gu Mengyu	顧孟餘
Ku Tzu-jen (T.Z. Koo)	Gu Ziren	顧子仁
Kuang-hua ta-hsueh	Guanghua daxue	光華大學

Glossary

Kung-shang-hsueh lien-ho-hui	Gongshangxue lianhe hui	工商學聯合會
K'ung chiao hui	Kong jiao hui	孔教會
Kuo-chia chu-i chiang-yen-chi	*Guojia zhuyi jiangyan ji*	國家主義講演集
Kuo-li Pei-ching kao-teng shih-fan huseh hsiao	Guoli Beijing gaodeng shifan xuexiao	國立北京高等師範學校
Kuo-nei chin-shih-nien-lai chih tsung-chiao ssu-ch'ao	*Guonei jin shinian lai zhi zongjiao sichao*	國內近十年來之宗教思潮
Kuo Ping-wen	Guo Bingwen	郭秉文
Kuo-ts'ui	Guocui	國粹
Lei Yin	Lei Yin	雷殷
Li Ch'un-fan (K'o Po-nien)	Li Chunfan (Ke Bonian)	李春蕃 (柯柏年)
Li Fu-ch'un	Li Fuchun	李富春
Li Hao-wu see	Yang Hsien-chiang	
Li Huang	Li Huang	李璜
Li Ju-mien	Li Rumian	李儒勉
Li Jung-fang	Li Rongfang	李榮芳
Li Li-san	Li Lisan	李立三
Li Ping-hsiang	Li Bingxiang	李炳祥
Li Shih-tseng	Li Shizeng	李石曾
Li Ta	Li Da	李達
Li Ta-chao	Li Dazhao	李大釗
Li Teng-hui (T.H. Lee)	Li Denghui	李登輝
Li Yuan-hung	Li Huanhong	黎元洪
Liang Ch'i-ch'ao	Liang Qichao	梁啟超
Liang Chün-mo	Liang Junmo	梁均默
Liang Shu-ming	Liang Shuming	梁漱溟
Liao Ch'eng-chih	Liao Chengzhi	廖承志
Liao Chung-k'ai	Liao Zhongkai	廖仲愷

Lin Po-ch'ü (Lin Tsu-han)	Lin Boqu	林伯渠
Ling-nan ta-hsueh (Canton Christian College)	Lingnan daxue	嶺南大學
Liu Chan-en (Herman C.E. Liu)	Liu Zhanen	劉湛恩
Liu Ch'ing-yang	Liu Qingyang	劉清揚
Liu-Fa chien-hsueh hui	Liu-Fa jian xue hui	留法儉學會
Liu-Fa ch'in-kung chien-hsieh hui	Liu-Fa qingong jian xue hui	留法勤工儉學會
Liu Fu	Liu Fu	劉復
Liu Hsiang	Liu Xiang	劉湘
Liu I-cheng	Liu Yizheng	柳詒徵
Liu Po-ch'eng	Liu Bocheng	劉伯承
Liu Po-ming	Liu Boming	劉伯明
Liu Shao-ch'i	Liu Shaoqi	劉少奇
Liu T'ing-fang (Timothy Ting-fang Lew)	Liu Tingfang	劉廷芳
Lo Ch'i-yuan	Luo Qiyuan	羅綺園
Lo Lung-chi	Luo Longji	羅隆基
Lo-su yueh-k'an	*Luosu Yuekan*	羅素月刊
Lu Chih-wei	Lu Zhiwei	陸志韋
Lü Shih-ch'iang	Lu Shiqiang	呂實強
Lu Shu	Lu Shu	盧淑
Ma Liang	Ma Liang	馬良
Ma Sung-wu	Ma Songwu	馬頌五
Mao Tse-tung	Mao Zedong	毛澤東
Mei-chou p'ing-lun	*Mei zhou pinglun*	每週評論
Mei Kung-pin (Mei Tien-lung)	Mei Gongbin (Mei Dianlong)	梅龔彬
Mei Tien-lung see	Mei Kung-pin	梅電龍
Mi T'ien-lun	Mi Tianlun	米天倫

Glossary

Miao Po-ying (Liao Po-ying)	Miao Boying	繆伯英
Min-kuo jih-pao	Minguo ribao	民國日報
Min-kuo shih-wu-nien Chung-kuo hsueh-sheng yun-tung kai-k'uang	Minguo shiwunian Zhongguo xuesheng yundong gaikuang	民國十五年中國學生運動概況
Min-to tsa-shih	Minduo zazhi	民鐸雜誌
Pao Hui-seng	Bao-Huiseng	包惠僧
Pao Kuang-lin	Bao Guanglin	寶廣林
Pao Tsun-p'eng	Bao Zunpeng	包遵彭
Pei-ching Chi-tu-chiao hsueh-chaio shih-yeh lien-ho	Beijing Jidujiao xuejiao shiye lianhe	北京基督教學教事業聯合
P'eng Chin-chang	Peng Jinzhang	彭錦章
P'eng Shu-chih (P'eng Shu-tse)	Peng Shuzhi (Peng Shuze)	彭述之
Pi-hsieh chi-shih	Bixie jishi	避邪紀實
P'ing-min chiao-yu she	Pingmin jiaoyu she	平民教育社
Po Ch'en-kuang	Bo Chenguang	博晨光
Sa Meng-wu	Sa Mengwu	薩孟武
Shang-hai Kuang-tung Chung-hua Chi-tu-chiao hui yueh-pao	Shanghai Guangdong Zhonghua Jidujiao hui yuebao	上海廣東中華基督教會月報
Shang-hai kung-t'uan lien-ho-hui	Shanghai gongtuan lianhe hui	上海工團聯合會
Shang-hai p'ing-min nü-hsiao	Shanghai pingmin nuxiao	上海平民女校
Shao Chi-ang	Shao Jiang	邵季昂
Shao Li-tzu	Shao Lizi	邵力子
Shao-nien Chung-kuo	Shaonian Zhongguo	少年中國
Shao-nien Chung-kuo hsueh-hui	Shaonian Zhongguo xuehui	少年中國學會
She-hui ch'ing-nien t'uan	Shehui qingnian tuan	社會青年團

Shen Ssu-liang (William Z.L. Sung)	Shen Siliang	沈嗣良
Shen Ting-i (Shen Hsuan-lu)	Shen Dingyi	沈定一
Shen Yen-ping (Mao Tun)	Shen Yanbing	沈雁冰
Sheng-hsin chung-hsueh	Shengxin zhongxue	聖心中學
Sheng-ming yueh-k'an	*Shengming yuekan*	生命月刊
Sheng san-i hsueh-yuan (Holy Trinity College)	Sheng sanyi xueyuan	聖三一學院
Sheng Yueh-han ta-hsueh (St. John's University)	Sheng Yuehan daxue	聖約翰大學
Shih Fu-liang	Shi Fuliang	施復亮
Shih Ts'un-t'ung	Shi Cuntong	施存統
Shou-hui chiao-yü-ch'üan yun-tung	Shouhui jiaoyuquan yundong	收回教育權運動
Shou Shih	Shou Shih	瘦石
Shu Hsin-ch'eng	Shu Xincheng	舒新城
Shun-t'ien shih-pao	*Shuntian shibao*	順天時報
Su Chao-cheng	Su Zhaozheng	蘇兆徵
Sun Ch'uan-fang	Sun Chuanfang	孫傳芳
Sun Fo (Sun K'e)	Sun Fo (Sun Ke)	孫科
Ta-hsia ta-hsueh	Daxia daxue	大夏大學
Tai Chi-t'ao	Dai Jitao	戴季陶
T'an Chih-t'ang	Tan Zhitang	譚植棠
T'an P'ing-shan	Tan Pingshan	譚平山
T'ang Kung-hsien	Tang Gongxian	唐公藏
T'ang Sheng-chih	Tang Shengzhi	唐生智
T'ao Hsing-chih	Tao Xingzhi	陶行知
T'ao Meng-ho (L.K. Tao)	Tao Menghe	陶孟和
Teng Chung-hsia	Deng Zhongxia	鄧中夏
Teng Hsi-hou	Deng Xihou	鄧錫候
Teng Yen-ta	Deng Yenda	鄧演達

Glossary

T'ien Han	Tian Han	田漢
Ting Chih-p'in	Ding Zhipin	丁致聘
Ting Wen-chiang (V.K. Ting)	Ding Wenjiang	丁文江
Ts'ai Ho-sen	Cai Hesen	蔡和森
Ts'ai Yuan-p'ei	Cai Yuanpei	蔡元培
Ts'ao Yun-hsiang (Y.S. Tsao)	Cao Yunxiang	曹雲祥
Tseng Ch'i	Zeng Qi	曾琦
Tso Shun-sheng	Zuo Shunsheng	左舜生
Tsou Lu	Zou Lu	鄒魯
Tsu Y.Y. see	Chu Yu-yu	
Tsui-chin san-shih-nien Chung-kuo chiao-yü shi	*Zuijin sanshinian Zhongguo jiaoyu shi*	最近三十年 中國教育史
T'u Hsiao-shih	Tu Xiaoshi	屠孝實
Tuan Ch'i-jui	Duan Qirui	段祺瑞
T'ui-hsueh lien-ho hui	Tuixue lianhe hui	退學聯合會
Tung-fang tsa-chih ("Eastern Miscellany")	*Dongfang zazhi*	東方雜誌
Tung I-hsiang	Dong Yixiang	董亦湘
Tung Lin (William L. Tung)	Dong Lin	董霖
Tung-wu ta-hsueh (Soochow University)	Dongwu daxue	東吳大學
tzu-chih, tzu-chueh, tzu-chueh	zizhi, zijue, zijue	自治,自決,自覺
Wai-chiao hou-yuan wei-yuan hui	Waijiao houyuan weiyuan hui	外交後援委員會
Wang Chao-ming see	Wang Ching-wei	
Wang Chia-hsiang	Wang Jiaxiang	王家祥
Wang Chih-hsin	Wang Zhixin	王治心
Wang Ching-wei (Wang Chao-ming)	Wang Jingwei (Wang Zhaoming)	汪精衛
Wang Hsing-kung (Wang Fu-chou)	Wang Xinggong	王星拱

Wang Ming (see Ch'en Shao-yü)	Wang Ming	王明
Wang Ming-tao	Wang Mingdao	王明道
Wang Nien-k'un	Wang Niankun	王念昆
Wei Cho-ming (Francis C.M. Wei)	Wei Zhuoming	韋卓明
Wei Chueh (Sidney Kok Wei)	Wei Jue	韋慤
Wo-kuo hsueh-sheng yun-tung shih-hua	*Woguo xuesheng yundong shihua*	我國學生運動史話
Wu Chih-hui	Wu Zhihui	吳稚輝
Wu Hsiao-t'ien	Wu Xiaotian	吳曉天
Wu Lei-ch'uan	Wu Leichuan	吳雷川
Wu Liang-p'ing	Wu Liangping	吳亮平
Wu P'ei-fu	Wu Peifu	吳佩孚
Wu Shih-ch'ung	Wu Shichong	吳士崇
Wu-ssu shih-ch'i ch'i-k'an chieh-shao	*Wusi shiqi qikan jieshao*	五四時期期刊介紹
Wu Yao-tsung	Wu Yaozong	吳耀宗
Wu Yü	Wu Yu	吳虞
Wu Yü-chang	Wu Yuzhang	吳玉章
Ya-li hsueh-t'ang ta-hsueh	Yali xuetang daxue	雅禮學堂大學
Yang Chia-ming	Yang Jiaming	楊家銘
Yang Hsiao-ch'un	Yang Xiaochun	楊效春
Yang Hsien-chiang (Li Hao-wu)	Yang Xianjiang	楊賢江
Yang Pei-ch'en	Yang Beichen	楊悲塵
Yang Sen	Yang Sen	楊森
Yang Yu-chiung	Yang Youjiong	楊幼炯
Yang Yung-ch'ing	Yang Yongqing	楊永清
Yeh Ch'u-ts'ang	Ye Chucang	葉楚傖

Yeh Ming-chao	Ye Mingzhao	葉明照
Yen-ching ta-hsueh	Yanjing daxue	燕京大學
Yen Fu	Yan Fu	嚴復
Yü Chia-chü	Yu Jiaju	余家菊
Yü Jih-chang (David Z.T. Yui)	Yu Rizhang	余日章
Yü Pin (Paul Yupin)	Yu Bin	于斌
Yü Yu-jen	Yu Youren	于右任
Yuan Chen-ying	Yuan Zhenying	袁振英
Yuan Shih-k'ai	Yuan Shikai	袁世凱
Yun Chen	Yun Zhen	惲震
Yun Tai-ying	Yun Daiying	惲代英
Zia, N.Z. see	Hsieh Fu-ya	

INDEX

Abend, Hallett, 238

American Board of Commissioners for Foreign Missions (ABCFM), 236,239

Amoy, 178,181,214-216, 261,271-272,274,335

Anarchism, 3,35,57,60,64,70,85,113,114,154,308

Anti-Christian Federation (Fei Chi-tu-chiao t'ung-ment), 19,41,48, 55-56,59,62,64-67,74,101,103,104,114,127,128,130,131,133,134,135, 137,138,143,146,147,153,161,167,172,173,188,189,190,195,197,200, 222,282,322,323,325,339-340

Anti-Christian tradition, 1-2,4,12-27,73,141,214,216,288,307

Asia, 89,238,242-243

Association Progress, see Ch'ing-nien chin-pu

Aurora University (Chen-tan ta-hsueh), 30,91-92,123,172,314

Awakening Lion Society, see Hsing-shih she

Baldwin, Stanley, 183

Barnett, Eugene E., 310

Barbusse, Henri, 38,242

Baxter, Alexander, 178-179

Bolshevik Revolution, 10,71,107,225,315; Bolsheviks, 147,154,174, 183-184,195,237,244

Borah, W. E., 182

Borg, Dorothy, 242-243

Borodin, Mikhail, 154,199-201,205,231,247-248,251,340

Bouglé, Celestin, 38

Boxer: Indemnity, 95-96,134,188,242,277; Protocol, 131,324; Uprising, 2,12,26,35,64,66,68,133,145,192,234,241,329

Boycotts, 4,51-52,92,112,164,165,171,185,205,227,243,270,306

Bridgman, Elijah, 21-22

Browder, Earl, 225,344,347

Buck, J. Lossing, 349

Buck, Pearl, 14,235,238-239

Buddhism, Buddhists, 15,30,33,44,82,197,225

Burgess, John S., 54

Burton, Ernest, 122, 330

Callery, J. M., 21

Canton, 52,57,62-63,65,69,77,92,98,104,106,112,123,126,127,131,138, 139,147,162-165,197,201,205,243,249,261,262,265-266,307,317,324, 349,351; General Labor Union, 199,200,202,205,253; Government, 97-98,192,193,201,211,213,214,216,221,230,281; Strike Committee, 199-200,202,308

Canton Christian College, see Lingnan University

"Cantonese Union Church Bulletin," see *Shang-hai Kuang-tung Chung-hua Chi-tu-chiao hui yueh-pao*

Capitalism, anti-captialism, 7,55-61,68,70,76,81,95,97,98,100,127, 132,133,153,254,265,285,315

Chang Chi (Chang P'u-chuan), 39,308

Chang Ch'in-shih (Neander C. S. Chang), 76,79,303,311,313,354-355

Chang Ch'iu-jen, 128

Chang Chun-mai (Carsun Chang), 111

Chang Chung-chang, 232

Changchow, Fukien, 215,274

Chang I-ching, 78-79

Chang Kuo-t'ao, 18-19,55-56,99-100,164,262,296,345

Chang Sung-nien, 137

Chang T'ai-lei, 316

Chang Tso-lin, 232,271

Chang Tung-sun, 303

Changsha, 86,97,101,104,112,123,131,140-141,145,163,221-223,225-228, 230,249,252,255,275,325

Ch'ang Tao-chih, 328

Chao Kuan-ch'ing, 320

Chao Tzu-ch'en, 75,79,82,84,286,287,310,312,337

Che-hsueh ("Philosophia"), 38,62

Cheeloo University (Shantung Christian University), 177,271-272,275, 300

Chen-kuang tsa-chih (True Light Review), 77-78,153

Chen-li chou-k'an (Truth Weekly), 153,313

Chen-li she (Truth Society), 47,88,328,333

Chen-li yü sheng-meng (Truth and Life), 337

Chen-tan ta-hsueh, see Aurora University

Chen Yü, 105,315,318

Ch'en Ch'i-t'ien, 64,70,114-116,141,148,151,152,188,189,194,304,306, 308,320,328,339,350

Ch'en Chih-wen, 324

Ch'en Hsi-hsiang, 217-218

Ch'en Hsieh-hsun, 332

Ch'en Huan-chang, 28-29

Ch'en I-lin, 320,322

Ch'en Kung-po, 63

Ch'en Kuo-fu, 269

Ch'en-pao (Morning Post), 61

Ch'en Tu-hsiu, 11,31-32,56,59,62,65,78,100,104,106,108,117,118,123, 127,163,245,247,261,294,298,304,305,307,308,316,317,320,321,323

Ch'en Yu-jen (Eugene Ch'en), 216,230-231,240-241,251,259

Cheng Ch'ao-lin, 327

Cheng-ch'ih chou-pao (Political Weekly), 117

Chengtu, 163,205,206,341; Higher Normal Institute, 205

Ch'eng Ch'ien, 248

Ch'eng Ching-yi, 30,79,83,303,350

Ch'eng Hsiang-fan, 153,154,328,329

Chi-tu-chiao chiu-kuo chu-i (Christian National Salvation Association), 53

Chi-tu-chiao hsueh-sheng shih-yeh hui ("Christian Scholars United Association"), 47

Chi-tu-chiao yü Chung-kuo wen-hua (Christianity and Chinese Culture), 311

Ch'i-lu ta-hsueh, see Cheeloo University

Chiang Hsien-yun, 262

Chiang Kai-shek, 10,200,201,206,210-213,221,228,230,232,234,240,241, 243-249,255-261,263,268,273,277,340,349,352-353

Chiang Meng-lin (Chiang Monlin), 108,315

Chiao-yü chu-ch'üan wei-chih hui (Society to Regain a Monopoly over Education), 143,144

Chiao-yü tsa-chih (Educational Review), 63,110,151

Chiao-yü tu-li yun-tung (Educational Autonomy Movement), 110,318

Chien-she tsa-chih (Reconstruction Review), 19

Chien Yu-wen (Jen Yu-wen, Timothy Jen), 78-80,88,173,311-313,333

Ch'ien-feng yueh-k'an (Vanguard Monthly), 105

Ch'ien Hsuan-t'ung, 32,298,307

Ch'ien she (Reconstruction), 19

Chih-chiang ta-hsueh, see Hangchow University

Ch'ih Kuang (pseudonym for Shih Ts'un-t'ung?), 56

Chin Chia-feng, 56,60,305

Chin-ling nü-tzu ta-hsueh, see Ginling College

Chin-ling ta-hsueh, see University of Nanking

Chin-pu tang (Progressive Party), 28

China Christian Educational Association, 121,150,153,156-159,174,175, 263,267,329

China Inland Mission, 237

China Mission Year Book, 45,76

China Weekly Review, 66

Chinese Catholic Youth Association, 155, 181

Chinese Communist Party, 3-5,7,10-11,62,67,69,70,86-87,93-107,112,114, 123,128-133,137,147,154,160-169,187,192,195,199-202,204-207,209-214,228-230,245-248,251,254-259,262,264,266,275,281-284,299,315, 317,340

Index

The Chinese Recorder, 45,74,75,76,237-239

Chinese Students' Alliance in the U.S., 168,241,337

Chinese Students' Christian Association, U.S.A., 240

Ch'ing dynasty, 7,22,26

Ch'ing-nien chin-pu ("Association Progress"), 47-48,77,185

Ch'ing-nien chin-pu hsueh hui (Young Progressive Student Society), 81

Chou En-lai (Wu Hao), 64,132-133,137,198-200,202

Chou Fo-hai, 136

Chou Shu-jen (Lu Hsun), 32

Chou T'ai-hsuan, 122,299,328,329

Chou Tso-jen, 37,299,303,307

Chow Tse-tsung, 317

Christian Education in China, 121-122,150,157

Christian Occupation of China, 42,64

Christians, Chinese, 8,33,40,42-54,73,77-89,93,114,120-122,133-145, 153-159,161,171-206,212-213,216-232,234,239-240,249-252,254,263, 268,273,274,277,286,287,290,300,303,332,334-336,354

Chu Chih-hsin, 19-20,296,307,324

Chu Ching-nung, 154,328,329

Chu Teh, 205

Chu Tzu-ch'ing, 18,296

Chu Wu-p'ing, 125,126,323

Cn'ü Ch'iu-pai, 3,52,59,105,163,207,261,316

Ch'üan-kuo chiao-yü hui-i pao-kao (Report of the National Educational Conference), 351

Ch'üan-kuo chiao-yü hui lien-ho-hui (National Federation of Educational Associations), 110, 148-149,189,326

Ch'üan-kuo chiao-yü tu-li yun-tung hui (National Association for Educational Independence), 71

Ch'üan-kuo ko-tsung-chiao hsin-tu kuo-min hui (National Association of Believers of All Religions), 154

Ch'üan-kuo kung-hui lien-ho-hui (General Labor Union), 163,165

Chueh-wu (Awakening), 38,62,73,103,105,123,128,131,132,135,136,138, 144,324

Ch'un-pao (The Masses), 63

Chung-hua Chi-tu-chiao chiao-yü chi-k'an (China Christian Education Quarterly), 153,156,329

Chung-hua Chi-tu-chiao hui ("Church of Christ in China"), 83,180,182, 186,263

Chung-hua chiao-yü chieh (Chinese Educational Circles), 110,114,149

Chung-hua chiao-yü kai-chin she (National Association for the Advancement of Education), 71,116,127,148,153-154,187,188,189,279, 319

Chung-hua chih-yeh chiao-yü she (Chinese Vocational Educational Association), 110, 318-319

Chung-hua kuei-chu (China for Christ), 78,83

Chung-hua kuei-chu (China for Christ), 47-49

Chung-hua min-kuo hsueh-sheng lien-ho-hui, see Student Union, national

Chung-kuo Chi-tu-chiao shih kang (Outline History of Christianity in China), 73

Chung-kuo ch'ing-nien (China Youth), 35,103,104,118,123,126,132,138, 167,192,299

Chung-kuo ch'ing-nien she (China Youth Society), 131,138,319

Chung-kuo ch'ing-nien tang, see Young China Party

Chung-kuo kung-ch'an-chu-i ch'ing-nien t'uan, see Communist Youth Corps

Chung-kuo kuo-chia-chu-i ch'ing-nien t'uan (Chinese Nationalist Youth Corps), 113

Chung-kuo she-hui-chu-i ch'ing-nien t'uan, see Socialist Youth Corps

Chung Wan-hua, 318

Chungking, 68,138,140,158,165,205,206,258,308

"Church of Christ in China," see Chung-hua Chi-tu-chiao hui

Clifford, Nicholas R., 207

Committee for Diplomatic Support (Wai-chiao hou-yuan wei-yuan hui), 102,140,143,199

Index 395

Communist International (Comintern), 96,100,129,154,169,245,248,344

Communist Youth Corps (Chung-kuo kung-ch'an-chu-i ch'ing-nien t'uan), 161,165,192,201,220,249,250,254,259,262,266,327,348

Confucianism, anti-Confucianism, 3-4,9,11-16,20-21,25,27-33,39,44,49, 53,58,70,82,85,107,108,109,114,118,154,277,283,284,286-288,297

Congress of Toilers of the Far East, 97,99

Constantine, Celso, 155,181

Cushing, Caleb, 21-22

Davis, Elmer, 242-243

Death Blow to Corrupt Doctrines, see *Pi-hsieh chi-shi*

Denominationalism, 12,40,42,79,81-84,90

Dewey, John, 93,110,115

Drop-out Federation (T'ui-hsueh lien-ho-hui), 144,146,173,176,190, 220

Eddy, G. Sherwood, 29,87,301-302,303

Education: imperial China, 9,24-25,108-109,119; Republican China, 9, 24-25,108-109,119; Republican China, 9,25,28,40,43,46,71-72,87-88, 109-114,119,147,213,227,265-269,277,279-280,284,318,323,351

Educational Review, 75,77,153,156

Educational Rights Association, 127,130,135,141,151,161,216,217,282

England, see Great Britain

Examination system, 119; abolition of, 6,9,43,107

Extraterritoriality, 13,22-25,85,87,97,98,119,157,169,181,182,185,237, 271,278,294,332

Fan Chi-tu-chiao chou-k'an (Anti-Christian Weekly), 131,132,135-138, 147,323,324

Fan ti-kuo-chu-i ta t'ung-meng (Great Anti-imperialist League), 103, 128,131,143,324

Fan tui Chi-tu-chiao yun-tung (The Anti-Christian Movement), 131-132, 322,324

Fan Tzu-mei (T. M. Van), 79,311

Fan Wan-hui, 83,311,312

Fan wen-hua ch'in-lueh ta t'ung-meng (Great Alliance against Cultural Aggression), 217,222,226-227,344

Fan Yu-jung, 83

Fan Yuan-lien, 154,188,329

Fei Chi-tu-chiao hsun-k'an (Anti-Christian Bi-weekly), 173,194,195, 323

Fei Chi-tu-chiao t'e-k'an (Anti-Christian Special), 103, 128,131,132, 136,323

Fei Chi-tu-chiao ta t'ung-meng, see Anti-Christian Federation

Fei tsung-chiao ta t'ung-meng (Great Anti-religion Federation), 35, 60,62,64,66,71

Feng-t'ien tung-pao (Fengtien Eastern Press), 117

Feng Yü-hsiang, 173,333

Fengtien, 116-118, 127

Fitch, Robert F., 273-274

Foochow, 127,147,163,196,215-217,232,249,252

France, 10,21-24,33,35,38,39.65,86,87,89,96,106,123,124,150,240

Froelick, L. D., 242

Fu-chin hsieh-ho ta-hsueh, see Fukien Christian University

Fu Jen University, 300

Fu-nü chou-pao (Women's Weekly), 123

Fu-tan ta-hsueh, 30,92,123,131,261,325

Fu T'ung (Fu P'ei-ch'ing), 306

Fukien, 92-93,147-148,196,209,214-219,221,255,274

Fukien Christian University, 172-174,215-218,274-275,327

Fundamentalism, 40-41,44-45,89,237,302

Furth, Charlotte, 4

Gamble, Sidney, 54

George, Lloyd, 244

Germany, 3,24

Ginling College (Chin-ling nü-tzu ta-hsueh), 171,233

Gowdy, John, 215, 217, 327, 333

Granet, Marcel, 38

Great Alliance against Cultural Aggression, see Fan wen-hua ch'in-lueh ta t'ung-meng

Great Anti-imperialist League, see Fan ti-kuo-chu-i ta t'ung-meng

Great Britain (England), 7,9-10,21,23-24,52,89,91,96-98,103,105,124, 137,140,160,162,164,166,169,172-173,178-179,182,185,200,201,205, 206,227,228,231-233,240-245,247,254,255,288,324,341,345

Great Proletarian Cultural Revolution, 5,284,287

Gutzlaff, Karl, 21

Haeckel, Ernest, 20

Hangchow, 127,133,139,233,249,252

Hangchow (Christian) University, 250,260,273-274,353

Hankow, see Wuhan

Henry, James M., 203-205

Ho Hsiung-ning (Mrs. Liao Chung-k'ai), 219

Holy Trinity College (Sheng san-i hsueh-yuan), Canton, 91,93,122,124, 126,127,322

Hong Kong, 164,179,199,211,216,243,261,352

Hroch, Miroslav, 94

Hsia Hsi, 140

Hsi Ming-han, 140

Hsiang-tao chou-pao (Guide Weekly), 95-96,98,105,117,123,125,126, 127,131,133,138,146,192,245,317,324

Hsiang-Ya Medical College, 221,226

Hsiao Ch'u-nü, 103,126,323

Hsiao Tzu-sheng, 60,65,308,309

Hsiao Yuan-ch'ung, 200

Hsieh Fu-ya (N. Z. Zia), 299

Hsieh Hsun-ch'u, 116

Hsieh Yin-chang, 117

Hsien-ch'ü (Pioneer), 56,62,64,78,305

Hsin-ch'ao (New Tide), 38

Hsin chiao-yü (New Education), 110,115,122,188

Hsin chiao-yü kung-chin she (Society for the Promotion of New Education), 110

Hsin ch'ing-nien ("La Jeunesse"), 31-32,35,38,62,73,74,108,317

Hsin hsueh-sheng (New Student), 105,123,138

Hsin hsueh-sheng hui (New Student Society), 98,102,127,200

Hsin-hsueh shu-yuan (New Learning School), 177-178

Hsin-min hsueh-hui (New People's Study Society), 60,102

Hsin tsung-chiao kuan (The New Religious View), 78

Hsing-ch'i p'ing-lun (Weekly Review), 38,39

Hsing-shih chou-pao (Awakening Lion Weekly), 114,123,194,260,319-320,334,343,350

Hsing-shih she (Awakening Lion Society), 147,194

Hsu Ch'ien, 30,45,53,137-138,223,298,302

Hsu Ch'ing-yü, 77,80,84,310,311

Hsu Heng-yao, 128

Hsu Pao-ch'ien, 46,78,80,286,301,302,311,337

Hsu Shih-ch'ang, 66

Hsueh-ch'ao, see "student storms"

Hsueh-heng ("The Critical Review"), 38,75

Hsueh-sheng chiu-kuo hui (Student National Salvation Association), 171,282

Hsueh-sheng tsa-chih (Students' Magazine), 62

Hu-chiang ta-hsueh, see Shanghai Baptist College

Hu Ch'iu-yuan, 262

Hu Han-min, 123,201,268

Hu Hsüeh-ch'eng, 76,311

Hu I-ku (Y. K. Woo), 78

Hu Shih, 5,32,71,108,112,168,279,286,287,298,303

Hua Chung University, 171,223,250,251,260

Hua-Fa chiao-yü hui ("Franco-Chinese Education Society"), 60
Hua-hsi hsieh-ho ta-hsueh, see West China Union University
Hua-nan nü-tzu wen-li hsueh-yuan, see Hwa Nan College
Huang, Jih-k'uei, 202
Hume, Edward H., 141-145,177
Humiliation Days, 18,131,133,271,315,352
Hunan, 17,19-20,86,102,104-105,120,123,125,139-146,151,186,197, 218,220-229,248,251,252,255,258,266,326
Hunan First Normal College, 64,96,140-141
Hupei, 186,193,197,218,220,232,255,258
Huping College (Lakeside), Hunan, 226
Hwa Nan College (Hua-nan nü-tzu wen-li hsueh-yuan), 217,218
I Fang Girls' School, Hunan, 227-228
I-shih pao (Social Welfare Newspaper), 43
Imperialism, anti-imperialism, 4-11,17-19,21-27,39,51,55-61,68,69, 76,79,87,90,94-113,124,127,132-133,138,144-146,160-207,210-215, 220-234,247-255,258,259,270-279,285,295,315,337,345,353
Israel, John, 262,269
Japan, Japanese, 3-5,9-10,24,52,57,60,68,70,92,96,97,104,105,112,116-118,125,140,144,160,164,165,166,169,240,247,260,269-273,275,277, 284,287,288,306,352,353
Je-hsieh jih-pao (Bloodshed Daily), 163
Jen-ko chiu-kuo ("Individual character to save China"), 54
Jen Pi-shih, 254,316
Joffe, A. A., 66,97
Kaifeng, 140,326
Kan Nai-kuang, 219
K'ang Yu-wei, 28-29
Kao Er-po, 104,128,213
Kao I-han, 303
Karakhan, Leo M., 97,131,154,169,315
Kiangsu, 19

Kiukang, 228,231,244,246

K'o Po-nien, see Li Ch'un-fan

Kuang-hua ta-hsueh, 176,251,329

Kulp, Daniel H., 54

Kung-ch'an-chu-i ch'ing-nien t'uan, see Communist Youth Corps

Kung-shang-hsueh lien-ho-hui (United Society of Workers, Merchants, and Students), 101,163

K'ung-chiao hui (Confucian Society), 28

K'ung Fu-cho (Fong F. Sec), 321

Kuo-chia-chu-i yen-chi (Collection of Lectures on Nationalism), 194

Kuo Mo-jo, 257

Kuo Ping-wen, 108, 183

Kuo-ts'ui (national essence), 108-109

Kuomintang, 4-5,7,10,19,29,39,60,62,67,93-107,113,125,128,129,133, 136-137,140,160-166,172,187,192-195,197-207,209-215,226,227,230- 232,236,238,240,244-259,264-269,272-277,279-281,283-287,317,338, 340

Kwangtung, 131,146,147,171,193,196,197-198,204,214,255

Kwangtung University (Chung Shan University), 131,136-137,192,200, 323,340,342,345

Lenin, Leninism, 10,18,55-59,94-95,98-99,107,112,195,225,282,285,287

Li Ch'un-fan (K'o Po-nien), 103,123-124,127-128,131,132,138,322,324, 326

Li Fu-ch'un, 202,299

Li Hao-wu, see Yang Hsien-chiang

Li Huang, 123,189,194,195,260,299,319,320,328

Li Ju-mien, 148,328

Li Li-san, 86-87,101,163,231

Li Shih-tseng, 34-35,60,62,65,263,300,307,308

Li Ta, 299,316

Li Ta-chao, 60,61,108,247

Li Teng-hui (T. H. Lee), 328

Li Yuan-hung, 66

Liang Ch'i-ch'ao, 28,62,75,306

Liang Chün-mo, 78-79

Liang Shu-ming, 286

Liao Ch'eng-chih, 139

Liao Chung-k'ai, 132,136,139,198,200-201

Lin Po-ch'ü (Lin Tsu-han), 202,236,346

Lingnan University (Canton Christian College), 4,91,137-139,178-180,202-205,212,213,250,252-254,261,265,266,308,342,355

Liu Chan-en (Herman C. E. Liu), 93, 314

Liu Ch'ing-yang, 137

Liu-Fa ch'in-kung chien-hsueh hui (Society for Frugal Study by Means of Manual Labor in France), 35, 39, 65

Liu Fu, 32

Liu Hsiang, 206,258

Liu I-cheng, 151,328

Liu K'ang-hou, 123

Liu Po-ch'eng, 205

Liu Po-ming, 37,75,299,306

Liu Shao-ch'i, 140,163,231,287

Liu T'ing-fang (Timothy Ting-fang Lew), 46,137-138,174,302,311,328, 333

Lo Ch'i-yuan, 56

Lo Wen-kan, 168

Lo-su yueh-k'an (Russell Monthly), 299

Lu Chih-wei, 79,299

Lu Shu, 56,305

Lü Shih-ch'iang, 294

Ma Ch'ao-hui, 164

Ma Liang, 30,80,91-92,298

MacMurray, J. V. A., 182

Manchuria, 4,116,144,277,284,352

Mao Tse-tung, 60,86,96,102,105,140,190,201,202,210,230,247,283,287, 288,318,321

March 20, 1926 Coup, 201-202,214,245,340,349

Martin, W. A. P., 22

Marx, Marxism, 3,11,18-20,27,35,39,55-59,67-72,93-95,100,102,107,112, 122,132-133,192,202,225,247,257,263,287

Mass Education Association, see P'ing-min chiao-yü she

May Fourth Movement, 2-11,27,39,47,51-53,58-59,66-67,80-81,92,94,95, 98,104,108,112,160,192,207-208,219,264,271,280-283

May Thirtieth Movement, 5,7-8,18,67,72,89,108,116,118,129,130,135,139, 140,148,152,158,159,160-208,219,234,235,241-243,281-283,287,290, 330,342

Mei Kung-pin (Mei Tien-lung, Mei Yuan-lung), 301,324

Mi-Shih Chinese Christian Church, 78

Miao Po-ying (Liao Po-ying), 60

Min-kuo jih-pao (Republic Daily), 38,62,105,117,123,128,131,146,153

Min-to tsa-chih ("People's Tocsin"), 38

Militarists, 98,102,112-114,127,129,133,140,144,151,162,164-167,189, 192-197,207-211,250,254-260,270,271,315

Mission societies, 40-44,83,84,119,121,157,161,238-240,273-274,286, 289,300,336

Monroe, Paul, 110,115,150

Mott, John R., 75,185

Nairn, Tom, 285-286

Nanchang, 230,246,262

Nanchiang Middle School, Swatow, 198

Nanking, 61,126,163,165,170,172,248,252,271; government, 229,230, 246,255-259,263-267,271,272,274-276,279; Incident of 1927, 232-245, 249,252,255,259,263,345,347

National Association for the Advancement of Education, see Chung-hua chiao-yü kai-chin she

National Christian Conference of 1922, 81,330

National Christian Council, 83-85,153,157,185,223,236-237,312,336, 344,346

National Federation of Educational Associations, see Ch'üan-kuo chiao-yü hui lien-ho-hui

National Revolutionary Army, 160,197-198,202,209-217,219,221,223, 233-236,244-246,255,257,270-272,275

National Southeastern University (National Central University), Nanking, 61,75,183,196

National Wuhan University (Wuchang Normal University), 115,131,319

Nationalism, 1-19,25-27,33-43,47-51,55-61,69,70,76-94,109,112,129, 148-160,165-169,173-178,181,186,188,194,207,210,231-238,255-256, 269-275,279-290,295,339,350

New Culture Movement, 3-7,12,27-28,32,36-40,46-50,58-60,62-63,65,67, 70,72-74,77,82,92-93,111,152,189,281,286

New York Times, 238

New Youth, 3,5-7,11,27-28,30-34,48,53,56,67-68,82,85,93,100,101,104, 125,126,167,174,207,272,273,281,283,293

Ningpo, 135,139,249

Ningpo Methodist College, 250,251

North China Daily News, 237,241

North China Herald, 73,183,236,306,307

Northern Expedition, 10,88,129,160,186,187,196,197,199,201-202,205, 207,209-246,255,257,260,269,270,281,290,349

Opium Wars, 21,68,289

Pai hua, 5,286

Pao Hui-seng, 200

Pao Kuang-lin, 310,330

Pao Tsun-p'eng, 318

Papacy, 16,21,41,87,132,166,181,263

Parker, Peter, 21-22

Peasant associations, 186,190,193,202,221,222,227,230,232,248,282, 344,349

Pei-ching Chi-tu-chiao hsueh-chiao shih-yeh lien-ho ("Peking Christian Scholars United Association"), 47

P'ei-hsin Middle School, Hsuchow, 124-125

Peking, 4,6,21-22,29,38,43,46,47,52,56,60-61,104,110,113,131,163,166, 169,170,173,180,184,185,188,195,196,217,236,248,262,271,280,317, 340; government, 66,77,78,86,89,97,107,129-130,145,151,165,169,173, 174,187-188,197,227,272,274,280

Peking *Leader*, 238,332

Peking National University (Peita), 6,32,34-35,37,53,60-61,65,87,137, 166,169,172,181,267,271,280,309,315,337

Peking Normal University, 61,188,329

Peking-Tientsin Times, 236

Peking Union Medical College, 137,180,300

P'eng Shu-chih, 254,349

Pi-hsieh chi-shih ("Death Blow to Corrupt Doctrines"), 19-20,296

P'ing-min chiao-yü she (Mass educational Association), 86-87,102, 110

Pott, F. L. Hawks, 157,175-177

Princeton-in-Peking, 54

Radek, Karl, 101

Rawlinson, Frank, 45,76,237,302

Revolution of 1911, 27-28,58,95,107

Richard, Timothy, 13

Rolland, Romain, 38,299

Roman Catholicism, 1-2,9-10,15-16,20-24,29-30,40-43,45,82,121,154,155, 171,181,193,198,214,216,225,232-233,238,239,263,297-298,312,321, 330,343,351

Russell, Bertrand, 34,36-37,137,299,307

St. James (Ya-ko) Senior High School, Wuhu, Anhwei, 103,326

St. John's University, 52-53,66,136,157,175-177,191,194,196,237,250, 251-252,261,268,277,339

San-min chu-i (Three Principles of the People), 129,165,187,198,209, 215,224,228,245,250,256,265,267,269,277,279

Satow, Sir Ernest, 23

Schram, Stuart, 96

Schurman, Jacob, 139

Sectarianism, see denominationalism

Shaffer, Lynda, 87

Shakee, see Shameen

Shameen, 164,165,171,178-180,191,200,234,241,243,332

Shang-hai Kuang-tung Chung-hua Chi-ti-chiao hui yueh-pao ("Cantonese Union Church Bulletin"), 74,77,78

Shang-hai kung-t'uan lien-ho-hui (Federation of Labor Unions), 163

Shang-hai p'ing-min nü-hsiao (Shanghai Girls' School for the Masses, 104,317

Shanghai, 4,6-7,47,52-61,65,74,77,78,85,87,91,103,104,106,123,125,128, 131,135,137,138,153,160-168,170,176,184-185,194,230-235,241,244, 246-252,255-257,259-264,266,268,270,271; Coup of April 12, 1927, 255-259; General Labor Union, 163,165; International Settlement, 160,168,184,211,244,261-262,278; Municipal Council, 85,160,162, 165,166,168,184,185,236,243,247

Shanghai Baptist College (later University of Shanghai), 54, 170, 199,250,252,254,261-262,299,305,314,329

Shanghai University, 35,103-104,126,131,133,137,162,165,299,316-317,326

Shantung, 3,24,57,68,97,125,134,180,197,270,275

Shantung Christian University, see Cheeloo University

Shao Chi-ang, 324

Shao Li-tzu, 105,123,124,316,323

Shao-nien Chung-kuo (Young China), 33-38,60,62,64,73,74,111

Shao-nien Chung-kuo hsueh-hui (Young China Association), 33-38,44,59, 64,70,73,112,113

She-hui ch'ing-nien t'uan, see Socialist Youth Corps

Shen Ssu-liang (William Z. L. Sung), 329

Shen Yen-ping (Mao Tun), 62,65,299

Sheng-ming she (Life Fellowship), 47-51,78,87,302,328

Sheng-ming yueh-k'an (Life Monthly), 48,50,74,77,153,174,302-303, 311,335

Sheng san-i hsueh-yuan, see Holy Trinity College

Sheng Yueh-han ta-hsueh, see St. John's University

Shih-shih hsin-pao ("China Times"), 147

Shih Ts'un-t'ung, 103,137,323

Shu Hsin-ch'eng, 141,320,328

Shun-t'ien shih-pao (Shun-t'ien Times), 62

Sinification, 8,45,48,78-80,82-86,88,123,137,150,153,154,156-157, 191,218,222,254,263,272,277,286,288,290,337,351,354

Smith, A. H., 309

Social Gospel, 44-54,67,78-86,121,122,128,153,301-302,342

Socialist Youth Corps (She-hui ch'ing-nien t'uan), 35,55-56,59-61, 63-64,67,69,76,102,106,126,137,140,147,308,327

Soochow University, 178,335

Soong Ch'ing-ling (Mme. Sun Yat-sen), 223,344

Soong Tzu-wen (T. V. Soong), 138

Soviet Union, 66,96,97,101,106,113,127,169,200-202,212,229,241,243, 245,246,264,315

Stuart, John Leighton, 239

Student sub-culture, 2-7,47,59-61,68-71,107,115,154,163,174,207,224, 280,283

"Student storms" (hsueh-ch'ao), 4,65,91-93,122,124-126,139-147,151, 154,162-169,175-177,199,202-206,211-228,249-255,269-276,283,326, 334

Student Union: national, 52-53,59,67,102,105,106,127,130,137,161-163,166,167,170,173,177,186,189-195,219,222,259,265,268,270,273, 277,280,281,283,315,338; branches, 53,92,93,102,105,126,133,140, 142-144,146-148,163,167,170,173,176,184,196,199,200,202-204,222, 225-227,230,250,254-260,265,266,268,271,272,280,333,348

Study abroad, 9,109,120,175; "returned students," 9,34,62,142,147,232

Su Chao-cheng, 231

Sun Ch'uan-fang, 196,232

Sun Fo (Sun K'e), 137,204,212-213

Sun Yat-sen, 19,39,63,94,96,97,100,101,105,112,129-130,137-138,147, 164,200,215,225,245,258,263,264,277,279,317,324,325

Swatow, 197-199,200,261
Szechwan, 197,199,205-206,258,308,341
Ta-Hsia ta-hsueh, 131, 165,194,196
Tai Chi-t'ao, 39,56,103,213,260,270,273
Taipings, 16-17,192
Talmage College, Amoy, 272,274
T'an Chih-t'ang, 63
T'an P'ing-shan, 63
T'ang Kung-hsien, 128
T'ang Sheng-chih, 229
T'ao Meng-ho (L. K. Tao), 71,279
Taoism, Taoists, 15,30
Teng Chung-hsia, 316
Teng Hsi-hou, 206
Teng Yen-ta, 342
Thurston, Matilda, 171
T'ien Han, 33-34, 298
Tientsin, 66,137,172,177
Tientsin Massacre, 24
Ting Chih-p'in, 314
Ting Wen-chiang (V. K. Ting), 71,168,279
Ting Wen-fen, 219
Tokyo, 4,6,35,57
Toynbee, Arnold J., 244
Ts'ai Ho-sen, 95-96,103,123,133,140,163,254,314,324,348,349
Ts'ai Yuan-p'ei, 32,62,65,71,108,217,263-264,267,269,298,307,308,309
Tseng Ch'i, 123,189,194,260,319,320,339
Tseng Kuo-fan, 24,228
Tsinan, 269-273,275,352
Tsing Hua University, 18,47,55,65,67,111,172,337

Tso Shun-sheng, 115,123,319
Tsou Lu, 136
Tu Hsiu-ching, 251
T'u Hsiao-shih, 34,36,299
Tuan Ch'i-jui, 101,167,197
T'ui-hsueh lien-ho hui, see Drop-out Federation
Tung-fang tsa-chih ("Eastern Miscellany"), 62
Tung I-hsiang, 103
Tung Lin (William L. Tung), 260-261
Tung-wu ta-hsueh, see Soochow University
T'ung-te College of Medicine, Shanghai, 165
Turkey, 106,124,144,202
Tzu-hsiu ta-hsueh (Self Study University), 102
Unequal treaties, 1-2,5,10,18-22,87,88,94,97,98,105-106,120,151,
    155,160,164,166,167,169,170,180,181,183,185,186,200,213,224,236,
    241-244,277-278,288,290,332
Union Baptist Church for Cantonese in Shanghai, 78
United Front, 10,72,93-95,98-106,114,123,129,161,165,187,192,195,196,
    199-202,204,207,210,212,220,233,234,245-250,254,255,259,262,264,
    281,282,287,299,349
U.S.A., 4,9-10,21-22,40-41,52,66,68,89,92,95,104-106,110,115,120,137,
    139,140,144-145,150,164,168,176,181-183,186,206,212,233,238,240-
    243,263,278,288-290
University of Nanking (Chin-ling ta-hsueh), 76,92,153,233,237,240
Versailles Peace Treaty, 2-3,50,52,57,67,71,97
Wai-chiao hou-yuan wei-yuan, see Committeefor Diplomatic Support
Walsh, James A., 238
Wang Chao-ming, see Wang Ching-wei
Wang Chia-hsiang, 103
Wang Chih-hsin, 73,184
Wang Ching-wei (Wang Chao-ming), 62-63,78,201,202,247,261,264,269,307
Wang Fan-hsi, 262

Wang Hsing-kung (Wang Fu-chou), 34-35, 62

Wang Tsu-chen, 154

Wanhsien, 205,234,241

Warlords, see militarists

Washington Conference of 1922, 61,68,97,144,183,289,306

Wei Cho-ming (Francis C. M. Wei), 260

Wei Chueh (Sidney Kok Wei), 204,213,342,351

Wesleyan Boarding School for Boys, Hunan, 227

West China Union University (Hua-hsi hsieh-ho ta-hsueh), 202,206, 259,274,300

Western Hills faction, 187,200-201,257

Whampoa Military Academy, 103,126,129,136,137,139,198,200,209,262, 343

Whiting, Allen, 317

Williams, John, 235,240

Williams, S. Wells, 22

World War I, 10, 40-41,57,71,88,95,116

World's Student Christian Federation, 47-51,53-55,62,64-68,74-76,79, 87,302-303

Wuchang, see Wuhan

Wuchow, 203

Wuhan, 131,163,165,171-173,182-183,191,192,213,220-225,228,229, 231-232,242,244,249,254,255,262,265,343,349; government, 230, 240,245-248,251,254-256,259-261,264

Wu Chih-hui, 123,127-128,137,213,263

Wu Hsiao-t'ien, 324

Wu Lei-chuan, 79,81,84,88,121,180,286,301,311,322,329,330,335,337

Wu P'ei-fu, 260

Wu Shih-ch'ung, 116

Wu-ssu shih-ch'i ch'i-k'an chieh-shao (An Introduction to the Periodicals of the May Fourth Period), 55, 323

Wu Yao-tsung, 74,76,78,121,304,309,310,311,312

Wu Yü, 31,298

Wu Yü-chang, 205

Yale-in-China (Ya-li hsueh-t'ang ta-hsueh), 96,141-146,172,177,183 226-229,266,295,314,326-327,344-345,353

Yang Chia-ming, 338

Yang Hsiao-ch'un, 320,328

Yang Hsien-chiang (Li Hao-wu), 132,324

Yang Sen, 205

Yang Yu-chiung, 123,124,323

Yeh Ch'u-ts'ang, 123,268,316

Yeh Ming-chao, 303,311

Yenching University, 37,46,88,137,170,171,180,239,271,311,352

Yen Fu, 28

Yen, James Hang-ch'u, 86

Yip Ka-che, 305

Young China Party (Chung-kuo ch'ing-nien tang), 100,113-118,122,123, 128,140,141,148-152,187,189,194,195,219,259-260,299,319

Young Men's Christian Association (YMCA), 46-52,55,63,65,68,74,76-81, 85-87,92,93,96,104,131,133,139,141,144,164,166,180,185-186,190, 191,196,199,216,222-223,226,228,252,266,300,322,348,353

Young Women's Christian Association (YWCA), 85-86,180,185,252,322

Yü Chia-chü, 71,73,115,116,122,141,148,151,194,268,303,306-309,319, 320,321,322,328,339

Yü Jih-chang (David Z. T. Yui), 79,83,164,185,304,329

Yü Yu-jen, 316

Yuan Shih-k'ai, 29-31

Yun Tai-ying, 32,34,36,49,103,118,146,164,192,254,295,298,299,303, 308,323,327,331,338,349